# CRIES FROM THE WALLS

# ALSO BY VAN HAWKINS

*Hampton and Newport News*
A look at two historic Virginia towns, 1975

*Dorothy and the Shipbuilders of Newport News*
The story of an iconic American shipyard, 1976

*The Historic Triangle*
How Jamestown, Williamsburg and Yorktown, Virginia,
made American history, 1980

*Plowing New Ground*
The Southern Tenant Farmers Union
and its place in Delta History, 2007

*Duty Bound*
The Hyatt brothers and Confederates
of the Third Arkansas Infantry Regiment, 2011

*Horizons*
A novel about growing up in a small southern town
in the 1950s and 1960s, 2012

*Smoke Up the River*
Steamboats and the Arkansas Delta, *2016*

*Moaning Low: From Slavery to Peonage*
Involuntary Servitude in the Arkansas Delta, 2019

*A New Deal in Dyess*
The Depression Era Agricultural Resettlement Colony in Arkansas,
Expanded Version, 2020 (First printing, 2015)

*The Colonel's Clay*
A novel about a boy who apprentices with a legendary Mississippi River boat
gambler, 2020

*Unbearable Things*
Fictional account of violent extremists who block advancement of black
American citizens, 2021

# CRIES FROM THE WALLS

## HELL IN ARKANSAS PRISONS

**VAN HAWKINS, EDITOR**

# CRIES FROM THE WALLS

## HELL IN ARKANSAS PRISONS

Copyright © 2024 by Van Hawkins

*All rights reserved. No part of this publication may be reproduced, distributed, or transmitted in any form or by any means, including photocopying, recording, or other electronic or mechanical methods, without prior written permission, except in the case of brief quotations embodied in certain critical reviews and certain other noncommercial uses permitted by copyright laws.*

Printed in the United States of America
ISBN: 978-0-9863992-6-8
Library of Congress Control Number: 2024901330

Writers Bloc
Jonesboro, Arkansas

*For Those Who Never Came Back*

# Table of Contents

| | |
|---|---|
| Preface | 1 |
| Introduction | 5 |
| PART I. *Story of the Arkansas Penitentiary* By William N. Hill | 15 |
| PART II. *Ruled by the Whip* By Dale Woodcock | 81 |
| PART III. Report of the Arkansas State Police Criminal Investigation Division (CID) | 194 |
|     CID Report Photos | 236 |
|     CID Report Aftermath | 261 |
| PART IV. *Holt v. Sarver II*, 309 F. Supp. 362 (E.D. Ark. 1970) Judge J. Smith Henley Rules Arkansas Prisons Unconstitutional | 264 |
| PART V. *Finney v. Mabry*, 534 F. Supp. 1026 (E.D. Ark. 1982) Judge Thomas Eisele Curtails Prison Intervention | 298 |
| Epilogue | 326 |
| Selected Bibliography | 327 |
| Acknowledgments | 330 |

# PREFACE

This is an anthology of shocking materials about people who experienced massive cruelty and exploitation in Arkansas' penitentiary system. Imprisoned people -- men, women, black, and white -- endured hellish conditions. Convicts experienced psychological abuse, impossible workloads, starvation, beatings and sometimes murder. This occurred at "The Walls," an informal name given to the state prison in Little Rock. Mistreatment also existed at Cummins Prison Farm, established in 1902 for black convicts, and Tucker Prison Farm, opened in 1916 for white prisoners. Trustees[1] who ran these facilities, also criminals, did so with merciless brutality. Two former prisoners wrote important and rare books about their experiences at The Walls and in prison work camps. Both books are included here and anchor the story in ways no other literature can.

William N. Hill's 1912 memoir[2] is a terrifying exposé of systemic convict torture around 1900. His account describes sadistic practices that are sometimes beyond understanding. A 1900 census listed him in The Walls for burglary and grand larceny. His wife, Tina McKennon, and their children resided with her parents in Yell County. Apparently out of prison a year later, the June 8, 1901, issue of the *Daily Arkansas Democrat* reported that Dan Mangrum, a public school employee, had been acquitted after shooting Hill in self defense. Hill was partially blinded by this injury. It was not long, however, before he once again went to prison, this time for claiming to be a doctor and performing an abortion. On August 10, 1904 the *Democrat* reported: "Blind Man Goes To Penitentiary" to serve his one-year sentence.

After getting out of prison the second time, Hill and his first wife divorced, and he married Mary Jane McLain during April 1909 in Yell County. The 1910 U.S. Census listed him as a farmer in Hunt. The following year Governor George W. Donaghey pardoned him.[3] Less than ten years later his story took

---

[1] This word is spelled several different ways throughout the text.
[2] William N. Hill, *Story of the Arkansas Penitentiary* (Little Rock, AR: Democrat Printing & Lithographing Co., 1912). Research uncovered only two copies of this book in public institutions in the United States. One is in the New York Public Library System, the other at Arkansas State Archives.
[3] *Arkansas Democrat.* Little Rock, Arkansas, June 12, 1911. George W. Donaghey served as Arkansas' governor from 1909 to 1913. His autobiography fills in much of his history. (George W. Donaghey, *Autobiography of George W. Donaghey, Governor of Arkansas 1909-1913.* L. B. White Printing Company, Benton, AR, 1939.). Though born in Louisiana, Donaghey and his family moved to a farm in Arkansas. He earned money by running errands for migrants in wagons headed for Texas. Donaghey eventually went to Texas and worked on a ranch near Marshall.

an even more bizarre turn. On February 18, 1922, a *Daily Arkansas Gazette* issue announced that Mrs. Izzie Pettigrew had been indicted for first-degree murder of Hill. The *Gazette* referred to Hill as "a blind chicken peddler" who insulted her. On the morning of his killing, "Mrs. Pettigrew said that Hill asked her if her husband was at home, and when she told him he was not," Hill made insulting remarks. According to her version, when Hill tried to draw a pistol she fired a shotgun at close range and killed him.

The August 8, 1922, issue of the *Democrat* offered an alternative, and perhaps more plausible, explanation for Hill's death. According to this article, prosecutors contended that Ned Pettigrew, husband of the killer, had been indicted for production of illegal liquor. Supposedly Ned accused Hill of "talking too much" and being responsible for Ned's arrest. The state charged that the couple plotted Hill's murder. However, without witnesses, Mrs. Pettigrew gained an acquittal. Various stories about Hill create an abundance of unanswered questions. But his book's descriptions of prison atrocities were verified by others, and that is his legacy.

Dale Woodcock, the second author, describes his gruesome experiences in convict work camps during the 1950s.[4] Born Charles Dale Woodcock on March 21, 1925, in Rogers, he served with the U. S. Marines during World War II. After Woodcock's discharge in 1946 he married Blanche McCord the following year. An August 7, 1947, *Northwest Arkansas Times* article announcing their engagement indicated that both had graduated from Rogers High School. She worked at a local telephone exchange, and Woodcock planned to enter Oklahoma A. and M. College that fall. By 1952, however, while pursuing a medical education, authorities charged him with stealing a microscope from Washington County Hospital. After fleeing the area, police in Troy, Ohio, arrested him on a concealed weapons charge, and Washington County officials had him extradited back to Arkansas to stand trial. Though Woodcock claimed to be innocent, a June 18, 1952, *Times* report casts some doubt on his claim.

According to this article, police in Ohio located several microscopes in his possession. One had the same serial number as the microscope taken from Washington County Hospital. Troy police also found receipts for sale of two additional microscopes, including one possibly stolen from Fayetteville City

---

After other adventures and various jobs he attended the University of Arkansas. Donaghey became financially well-to-do while a railroad contractor. In 1908 he ran for governor successfully and won a second term in 1910. Donaghey lost his third race to Joe T. Robinson, but prior to leaving office Donaghey began to pardon inmates and accelerate an end to the corrupt convict leasing system. Donaghey died in 1937.
[4] Dale Woodcock, *Ruled by the Whip. Hell Behind Bars in America's Devil's Island--The Arkansas State Penitentiary* (New York: Exposition Press, 1958).

# Preface

Hospital the same day as the County Hospital robbery. After being returned to Arkansas, Woodcock bonded out of jail until his trial for grand larceny. He failed to appear, however, and police in Portland, Oregon, seized him with an arrest warrant.

Woodcock said that an Arkansas judge sentenced him to two years in prison.[5] Newspaper reports about his behavior revealed significant differences between their story and his version. Denial of the microscope theft lost validity after discovery of microscopes seized in Ohio. Woodcock died January 26, 1991. Despite his personal flaws, Woodcock used prison experiences to vividly describe a vicious and corrupt system. He called about 40 percent of prison inmates "depraved, evil, insane monsters,"[6] and his book is a stunning revelation about inhumanity in Arkansas.

Decades of brutality, corruption and perversity described by Hill and Woodcock passed unabated. An official response held that complaining convicts could not be trusted. And after all, most refused to go on the public record with their accusations. However, this political smokescreen was dispelled by an Arkansas State Police Criminal Investigation Division (CID) report. Through numerous interviews and seized evidence, the appalling truth came out. Several documents included herein tell this story directly: the Hill and Woodcock books verbatim; a complete copy of this appalling CID report including photographs; Judge Henley's legal decision declaring prisoner treatment unconstitutionally cruel and unusual punishment, leading to judicial oversight of the prison system; Judge Thomas Eisele's opinion that ruled the system largely in compliance, given improvements made and promises of more changes to come. Altogether, these primary sources reveal a hellish prison system in Arkansas that is difficult to believe, but true.

---

[5] Ibid., 19.
[6] Ibid., 49.

# INTRODUCTION

Abuse of post-Civil War convicts was not a long time in coming. Confederate states faced financial ruin after the war, and the greatest suffering fell on black freedmen and poor people convicted of criminal activities, many framed by authorities. They experienced cruelty inside The Walls and outside in work camps, treatment which robbed them of hope, health and often their lives. Soon after the war, penitentiaries no longer held mostly white convicts; black men made up the vast majority. Most had been convicted of minor crimes. But prisons couldn't hold them all, so within 15 years after Lee's surrender several former Confederate states began leasing convicts to businessmen and landowners, and the practice grew like kudzu. Vagrancy arrests peaked among southern black men when cotton picking began each fall. Many states, including Arkansas, offered prisoners to private businesses for work, both inside and outside The Walls to make penitentiary systems self-supporting and possibly profitable. When prisons were financially successful, inmates often paid for any profits by being starved and sometimes worked to death.

Arkansas' first prison didn't open until the 1840s, and a contract system of prison management began in about 1853. Contractors came and went until 1863, when federal authorities converted the facility into a military prison. Union troops found it empty upon their arrival. When prominent southern Republican Asa Hodges leased it after the war, he offered an ominous opinion to the governor. Hodges claimed that no man is "suitable for a prison superintendent but one that has a heart as cold as an icicle, and as deaf to human appeals as the Czar of Russia."[7] Unfortunately, many future wardens, though not Romanovs, had the cold hearts that Hodges mentioned and proved deaf to cries of tortured inmates.

In 1875, Zeb Ward took over the prison, and on November 15, 1882, the *Arkansas Gazette*[8] reported that he had accumulated a handsome fortune. When freedmen became convicts after rigged trials, some courts became little more than employment agencies for businessmen. Death rates among leased prisoners ranged from 20 to 50 percent. Those assigned to chain gangs suffered as well. Whipping bosses carried leather straps, and a chain gang survivor recalled that if the gang didn't work like fighting fire a supervisor walked down the line striking indiscriminately.

---

[7] Garland E. Bayliss, "The Arkansas State Penitentiary Under Democratic Control. 1874-1896," *Arkansas Historical Quarterly* 34:3 (Autumn 1975), 197.
[8] Newspaper and magazine articles are identified at their point of use and therefore not footnoted.

Convict rolls grew from about 200 in 1874 to 600 in 1882. This may be attributed in part to changes in the state's larceny law in 1875. A new statute established incarceration as punishment for petit larceny and similar offenses. Black men made up the majority of new inmate increases. Some Arkansas legislators expressed alarm at mortality among convicts in 1880 when about 20 percent of the inmates died. Some politicians called the contract system "cruel, barbarous and inhumane and totally at variance with the civilization of the age." But given the "embarrassed financial condition of the state," they would make no recommendation about it. So a cruel, barbarous and inhumane system continued.[9]

The *Arkansas Weekly Mansion*, a black newspaper in Little Rock, reported on July 14, 1883, the results of convict camp inspections by commissioners and Governor James Berry. During these inspections the governor found many serious violations, including inadequate sanitation in stockades, filthy beds, a practice of mixing sick convicts with healthy ones, and violent deaths without inquests. Commissioners sent a severe assessment to prison contractor Arkansas Industrial Company about one of its subcontractors in Jefferson County. A penitentiary physician found six convicts there in wretched physical condition. Many prisoners lacked clothing and shoes, and guards used a heavy leather strap to punish them. Drinking water came from a stock pond, and the contractor forced sick men to work. Commissioners called this treatment a breach of the state's contract and ordered the company to rectify conditions or its contract would be cancelled.

The legislature passed a new prison law in 1883 that required improvements in convict treatment---at least on paper. It created a commission made up of the governor, secretary of state and attorney general to manage penitentiary affairs. It also established regulations for facility management. The act restricted labor to ten hours per day and required that inmates receive wholesome food. It directed a physician to visit the penitentiary daily to monitor prisoner health and sanitary conditions. Each inmate should have a separate cell, and men and women convicts were to be segregated at all times. Lessors, it seems, usually ignored most, if not all, of these requirements. In a letter from Governor Berry to legislators in January 1885 he wrote that persons in charge of prison conditions attempted to comply with regulations and treat inmates humanely. However, wide dispersal of convicts outside The Walls made it impossible for commissioners to properly supervise wardens. According to a January 14, 1885, *Arkansas Gazette* article, Berry believed that despite financial benefits to the state, "the system of working convicts outside the walls of the penitentiary" is wrong and uncivilized, "and that the evils

---

[9] "Democratic Control," 202.

inflicted upon the state by that system are in no way compensated by the additional remuneration it produces."

There were several types of prison labor arrangements: A contract system kept penitentiaries under state control, but outside contractors supervised production and marketed their products. In a per-piece price system, contractors furnished materials, the state supervised production, and contractors handled marketing. Under public account plans, penitentiaries became little more than state-run factories. Authorities provided materials, supervised production and marketed products to other state institutions. And there was the controversial convict lease system. In 1886, of approximately 64,349 prisoners in the nation, 9,699 worked in lease systems.[10] To meet demand for workers, authorities sometimes forced men to admit to crimes they didn't commit. Southern law enforcement evolved in part from pre-Civil War slave patrols, so brutality started in police stations. Sheriffs, deputies and marshals sometimes used torture in their interrogations to gain confessions.

Historian Alex Lichtenstein says the idea that African Americans would only work effectively when threatened with violence dated back to antebellum days, and it served as an ideological basis for work gangs. He lists common features of the system, similar to what Hill and Woodcock describe. Convicts labored under the gun from sun-up to sundown and ate bug-infested and rotten food. They rested, if you can call it that, on filthy bedding in cages. Punishment included blows from rifle butts and clubs, whippings with a leather strap, confinement in a sweat box under the scalding southern sun and hanging from stocks or bars. Road gangs became a tool for control of rural blacks. They served as an example of what could happen to men who refused to accept jobs, no matter how unreasonable the pay or cruel the working conditions.[11]

Though northern prisons contracted prison labor to private businesses, "only in the South did the state entirely give up its control of the convict population to the contractor."[12] Arkansas legislators allowed convict leasing due to financial considerations, or so they said. But horrors at Coal Hill camp in Johnson County revealed in a March 24, 1888, *Gazette* article created a public relations nightmare. Quita Coal Company operated a mine there, and rumors of abuse led to an inspection by Governor Simon P. Hughes and penitentiary commissioners accompanied by a *Gazette* reporter. Including the journalist proved to be a serious mistake. His story about what they found began in the March 24, 1888, *Gazette* under the headline: "Hell in Arkansas." It accused the current warden's three predecessors of killing several men by beating them

---

[10] 1887 U. S. Bureau of Labor report.
[11] Alex Lichtenstein, *Twice the Work of Free Labor. The Political Economy of Convict Labor in the New South* (New York: Verso, 1996), 183.
[12] *Ibid*, 3.

"into eternity." One victim received more than 400 lashes before he died. Most convicts there suffered from some form of physical abuse, insufficient food and inadequate clothing. About 140 men, including many ill prisoners, lived in a bunkhouse 90 feet long, 18 feet wide and 12 feet high. They slept in work clothes on straw amid a miasma of stinking sweat and excrement. Prisoners told the governor privately that they did not report illness to a physician because guards would whip them. Proof of the consequences existed in a nearby graveyard that held between 60 and 70 bodies.

The *Gazette* did not condemn Quita because the company claimed it only bought coal mined there and denied responsibility for worker mistreatment. Commissioners claimed no prior knowledge of these horrendous conditions, though ultimately they had responsibility. Several follow-up *Gazette* articles during March 1888 described gruesome atrocities. Press reports increased pressure for changes in management of convict labor, and legislators introduced a few improvements. Commissioners appointed an inspector to observe inmate treatment inside and outside The Walls and report to a board every two months. Inspections apparently produced some positive results. In 1891 a prison physician reported death rate declines. Still, commissioners demanded in the name of humanity that the existing system be modified to eliminate cruelty. They called any system objectionable that allowed a convict to be controlled exclusively by a beneficiary of his labor. "In a struggle between self-interest and humanity, self-interest is generally the winner. The lease system satisfies those who make money out of it, but no one else." [13]

When labor organizations, politicians and Arkansas citizens increased pressure for abolition of convict leasing the legislature passed a new penitentiary law in 1893. A prison board would continue to control facilities and cancel lease contracts when appropriate. Legislators would fund purchases of land, buildings and operational assets so that the largest number of convicts that could be accommodated might be confined there. Governor James P. Eagle in 1893 supported implementation of what was called a state account plan, so as many inmates as possible would work inside prison walls. They and convicts outside The Walls would be supervised by a prison board that could not pass control of convicts to private interests. A state supervisor would oversee management, and a physician could excuse any sick or disabled prisoner from labor. An authorizing act allowed convicts to work at state-owned coal mines and timber operations with profits going to the state. However, legislative funding proved insufficient for upkeep of inmates and manufacturing costs, and that trumped everything else.

---

[13] Arkansas Board of Penitentiary Commissioners, Biennial Report, 1891, 42-43.

# INTRODUCTION

Consequently, this board allowed convicts outside The Walls to work on farms operating under the state account system. Additionally, authorities leased prisoners to planters and coal mine companies. However, the board ended some mining contracts after reports of dreadful conditions in camps. According to a prison physician, better management of this penal system improved convict treatment somewhat, but deplorable practices remained. The simple fact is that prisoners cultivated thousands of acres for private landlords while enduring severe conditions. Railroad contractors leased convicts without assurances of fair treatment -- and treatment was rarely fair.

The Journal of the 1901 Arkansas House of Representatives declared that prison officials and wardens were involved in illegal business dealings. It concluded that "in our opinion the provisions of the statute relating to the management of the affairs of the Penitentiary have not been properly regarded." The report goes on for 324 pages.[14] Deficiencies include the following:

- Failure of the Superintendent and Financial officer to file timely required reports.
- Superintendent and Financial agent by and with the approval of the Board executed a contract for the supply of wood by the Penitentiary with Hall C. McConnell, a minor, and the son of Superintendent E. T. McConnell.
- The Superintendent and Financial Agent contracted for the hire of convicts to do railroad work in Washington County without demanding a bond.
- Board did not demand employment termination of and Superintendent did not discharge a warden who stole for personal use state-owned cotton.
- Board purchased the new penitentiary site at a "large price" without inquiring as to the market price of local real estate.
- Superintendent allowed convicts to be hired out as domestic servants in violation of state law.
- Superintendent and Financial Agent in compliance with the Board executed a contract with an Arkansas brick company for materials used in new penitentiary construction without advertising for competitive bids.
- Superintendent offered a bribe to a charitable institutions purchasing agent if the agent would secure for the superintendent a contract to supply coal to the institutions.

---

[14] "Report of the Penitentiary Joint Committee of Arkansas; Penitentiary Committee Report 1901," Leopold Classic Library. Violations that follow begin on page 3 and end on page 6.

- Horses belonging to outside parties and state officers were kept and cared for at state expense.

Members of the House Committee preparing the report offered this summary. "In our opinion there are other affairs of less consequence pertaining to the management that have not been conducted in [a] business-like manner." Personal testimony in the report confirmed their conclusion.

In January 1903, Governor Jeff Davis pledged to clean up the system.[15] He claimed that "there is a crowd of leeches and bloodsuckers that are trying to build up a penitentiary dynasty and political penitentiary ring, the object and purpose of which is to control the politics of Arkansas, and incidentally loot the state treasury while doing it."[16]

He recommended the state acquire property near Little Rock and employ convicts there. However, the penitentiary board purchased 10,000 acres for Cummins in Lincoln County over the governor's objection. At that time a majority of state convicts labored outside The Walls, working on farms, railroads, in mines and for manufacturers. Workplace conditions varied significantly. Investigators learned that prisoner treatment depended on the competency of wardens. One Arkansas convict farm clearly revealed a warden's incompetence. A physician told investigators that prisoners there lacked proper clothing. The supply of winter clothes consisted of 105 suits for more than 200 men. They had only one blanket for every two men. The House penitentiary committee recommended that after expiration of existing contracts these convicts should work on the state account. It made no economic sense to lease convicts to contractors for $1 per day when contractors

---

[15] Raymond O. Arsenault, *The Wild Ass of the Ozarks: Jeff Davis and the Social Bases of Southern Politics* (Philadelphia, PA: Temple University Press, 1984). Born in 1862, Jeff Davis' public service included three terms as Arkansas governor and one as a U. S. senator. Prison issues created controversy throughout his tenure as governor. One occurred in 1899 when the prison was torn down in order to construct a new statehouse on that site. Several hundred prisoners lacked a holding facility so the prison board leased about one-third of them on a ten-year contract, which violated state policy. Davis and many Arkansas legislators had different opinions about prison matters. Conflict between the two sides became prominent in politics. After Davis won control of the legislature during his third term, he reorganized penitentiary system management. Davis died in 1913 during his first U. S. Senate term.

[16] *Arkansas House Journal*. (1903), 35-39, 40-55. Cited in Jane Zimmerman, "The Convict Lease System in Arkansas and the Fight for Abolition." *Arkansas Historical Quarterly* 8:3 (Autumn 1949), 179.

leased them to companies for $1.50 to $1.75 per day. If the state hired out convicts it should pocket any profits, commissioners concluded.[17]

Much horrible treatment fell on men held for only 30 days. Convicts sentenced to several years would be better taken care of since their bodies were more valuable in the long run. Wardens sometimes worked men serving 30 days with such cruelty that they died before release. Managers then asked authorities for replacements with longer sentences. An Arkansas House subcommittee in 1907 made several recommendations: that the lease system be abolished; black convicts be worked on state farms and whites inside The Walls; a superintendent monitor treatment of hired convicts; no subletting of convicts on state account; prisoners be worked no more than ten hours per day and black men not guard white inmates.[18]

On December 6, 1908, the *Arkansas Democrat* reported that during 1906-1908 the black-white ratio ran about 70 to 30. This edition recorded 21 females, 214 escapes, 276 pardons and 95 deaths during that period. Governor George W. Donaghey proposed lease terminations, which meant that a large portion of these prisoners would serve inside The Walls or on state farms. Others would assist counties in building roads, and the remaining men would work for the state on road improvements and construction. His plan failed in the legislature, but Donaghey continued to press for abolition of convict leasing. Allowing convicts to choose between serving out their sentence on chain gangs or working for businessmen who paid their fines may explain the brutality of chain gang guards. Their actions and reputations often led convicted men to make any choice but that one. Many black men arrested in Memphis avoided chain gangs by laboring in Arkansas cotton fields. An October 1, 1910, *Gazette* article explained how accused men fared when harvest time arrived: A judge announced that black persons charged with vagrancy would be freed if they accepted job offers. He added that policemen intended to renew their efforts to clear the city of all vagrants and loiterers.

An *American Magazine* article by famed journalist Ray Stannard Baker described the case of a judge turning a man into a leased prisoner. Baker observed the accused in court after being charged with stealing cotton:

---

[17] *Arkansas House Journal* (1905), 828. Cited in Zimmerman, "Convict Lease System," 180.
[18] *Arkansas House Journal* (1907), 478. Cited in Zimmerman, "Convict Lease System," 180.

"Does anybody know this Negro?" the judge asked.

Two white men stepped up and both said they did.

The judge fined the Negro $20 and costs, and there was a real contest between the two white men as to who should pay it---and get the Negro. They argued for some minutes, but finally the judge said to the prisoner: "Who do you want to work for George?" According to Baker, the man chose his employer and agreed to work four months [generally the length of a cotton harvest season] to pay off his $20 fine and costs.

Both Democratic and Republican political parties condemned convict leasing of this sort, but legislators dithered. Donaghey did not. In December 1912 he pardoned 360 convicts carefully screened for eligibility. The governor took this action after attending a governors' conference in Richmond, Virginia, focusing on prison reform. Governor Cole Blease of South Carolina described at the conference his rationale for making mass pardons, which caught Donaghey's attention. Arkansas critics accused the governor of playing politics with the issue, but many people supported his decision. In a 1913 national academic periodical Donaghey revealed many factors and abuses that contributed to his decision to end convict leasing after legislators refused to stop it.[19] He gathered information about crimes, ages, race, sex, confinement terms and conviction dates of prisoners. The governor described many abuse cases discovered during his investigation, including these:

- Two black men in Phillips County forged nine orders for quarts of whiskey. One man received an 18-year sentence, and the other drew 36 years.
- A young boy with a high fever working near Malvern for a railroad contractor died after laboring in the hot sun. The Malvern *Times Journal* reported that men in the camp had mostly sour pork and beans to eat and slept in crowded box cars amid filth and vermin. Those who complained got a whipping.
- Supervisors shot a boy sentenced for a minor offense who worked for a railroad contractor. While lying on a train station platform waiting for a train to take him to a hospital the boy's blood ran down the platform. When he cried out to people for help the warden refused to allow it. A local newspaper described the warden's cruelty. The young white man lay in this condition for more than an hour. About time for the train to arrive the warden ordered him to get up and walk

---

[19] George W. Donaghey, "Why I Could Not Pardon the Contract System," *The Annals of the American Academy of Political and Social Science* 46 (March 1913), 22.

to the other end of the depot. The boy attempted to but couldn't stand. "I can't walk," he said. "You have one good leg, get down here," the warden ordered. They dragged him to the other end of the platform and put him on a train. The boy died the next day.

- A Chicot County man convicted of a minor offence went to the county farm and worked for a contractor. A judge fined him an additional $250 and added six months to his sentence. Several citizens sent the governor a petition for pardon. They pointed out that the convict's flesh had rotted from around his ankles because of the shackles he was forced to wear.

During Donaghey's efforts to end convict leasing, he mentioned several cases when justices of the peace handed out excessive penalties, many to black men:

- In Jefferson County, three men were sent to a convict farm for petty larceny. One received 1,244 days, another, 319 days and the third, 1,481 days.
- A man in Mississippi County drew 180 days for disturbing the peace.
- In Miller County a man got three years for stealing clothes from a clothesline. He served more than a year before receiving a pardon.

Donaghey called these cases typical. According to him, state farms yielded more revenue and less barbarity. They experienced fewer escape attempts and therefore needed fewer guards. The governor believed that about one-half of state convicts, managed properly, could work on prison farms or public roads without guards.[20] He said that when a state was the only party to satisfy, there should arise no reason for convicts to be treated badly. Despite his assertion, convict treatment inside The Walls remained brutal, and Hill's experiences contradicted the governor's naïve belief. Donaghey outlined criteria used to select convicts for pardon. He set free those with minor offenses and short sentences. People convicted of graver crimes with longer sentences had to serve at least half their time. Good behavior increased a convict's chances for release. Positive recommendations from judges and concerned citizens helped also.

The governor admitted that none of the current penitentiary board members had time to fulfill their duties, so he proposed that a board consisting of three men appointed by the governor be put in charge of penitentiary management. He confirmed that though eligible prisoners deserved pardons, his principal reason for discharging a large number was to end convict leasing. Donaghey supported confinement commensurate with crimes, but selling "their flesh and blood to contractors" was a different matter. He called this system "a crime against humanity, and if continued, will cause a forfeiture of that respect which a state should maintain. In a commitment which accompanies a convict to the

---

[20] Ibid., 23-24, 26.

penitentiary there is an implied judicial guarantee" that though deprived of his liberty, he still has the right to be cared for with "good judgment and mercy."[21] Governor Joe T. Robinson ended the lease system in December 1913, but it sometimes continued surreptitiously.

[21] Ibid., 7-29.

# PART I. STORY OF THE ARKANSAS PENITENTIARY

## BY WILLIAM N. HILL
## (UNABRIDGED MEMOIR)

### INTRODUCTION

You, my dear readers, will find many strange things between the covers of this little book, things which will probably shock your modesty and disgust you altogether.

But, if you find merely the reading of the facts disgusting, think how much more disgusting is the real, and how essential it is that some one should portray the evil of this institution to the public in a manner impressive and not to be misunderstood.

I have numerous reasons for undertaking this work; chief among them, however, being because I have for many months felt it to be a duty to my God as well as my fellow-man, and my duty to my God embraces my whole duty to my fellow-man and any help or warning that I may be able to give.

I will speak out boldly and plainly the truth and reveal the darkest deeds of Arkansas history; many will doubtless object to this book on account of the plainness of the language and the divulging of many of the most atrocious crimes of the age, but, my friends, I have endeavored to speak the truth, and to do so on this subject does not admit the use of delicate language. A mild hint at such inhuman treatment would only serve to give a vague impression and would fall far short of the mission that I wish this book to accomplish.

I wish to open the eyes of the people of the "Grand Old State of Arkansas" to the horrible punishment that has so long been hidden; nor do I attempt to write upon a subject of which I am ignorant, and if this little book should in any degree be useful in the accomplishment of this purpose, I shall feel that I am more than repaid for the effort, and shall willingly and gladly endure all harsh criticisms and condemnations which I know its writing will bring upon me.

Much has been said about the horrors of the Arkansas penitentiary by some of the most honored and trustworthy men of our country, and what has been said has not all been said in vain.

Now, it is not my purpose to personate [sic] any one, neither will I attempt to argue to the public the guilt or innocence of any man or woman, not even of myself.

Now, dear readers, believe as you will, and say what you please, but God alone will know the truth, if no one else will.

In conclusion, I will say that there are persons today serving out terms for crimes some one else has done; also, there are men serving sentences for crimes that never were committed. In all such cases, all you can do is to pray to God for freedom from this curse, and I thank God that I have been made free from my bondage, and will forever praise His Holy name.

PART I. STORY OF THE ARKANSAS PENITENTIARY, WILLIAM N. HILL

## CHAPTER 1
## MY ARRIVAL AT THE PENITENTIARY

It was late one night in April when we arrived at the Arkansas penitentiary---myself and three others---we were conducted by the transportation agent.

At the gate we were halted, and for a few moments stood in front of the great iron thing called a gate that opens into one of the worst and most unmerciful places that could be found.

"Hello," came a voice from the office building, addressing the officer in charge of us. "I see you have lots of fat game."

"Yes," was the reply. "Make ready for a feast." In a moment we were surrounded by five of the roughest looking devils that I ever met. We were handcuffed together, my companions and myself standing in front of the other two.

One of the five parties above mentioned addressed me in a very rough manner, saying: "Hello, fellow; you are too purty to come to the penitentiary." "That is my opinion, sir," said I, "but the judge didn't think so." "Well," said he, "it doesn't matter; we will change your looks as well as your mind before we let you go." "Good," said I. "Perhaps, when you change my mind, I will have a better opinion of you." "Then your opinion of me will be good pretty damned soon, for it is a known fact that we will change your mind and looks also." "Does a man get ugly very fast?" I asked. "Awful damned fast," was the reply. "And the longer you stay the worse you look." "Then you have been here a long time," I said, intimating that he was a convict. Then his companions all gave him the horse laugh, and he gave me a cursing and walked away. This man was deputy warden, and a heartless man he was. Just then the gong taps the signal for the guard on duty inside the wall, the big iron gate swings back, and we pass through, again the door is closed and the big lock turned on.

Now, the shackles are removed, and we begin to realize our awful condition as we were marched to the cell building and locked in our cells for the night.

I asked the guard how many men they had there, and he told me they had something over three hundred inside the building and six hundred on the farm and other places, making a total of nine hundred persons.

Just then the light is turned off, and all was dark and still as death, not a sound to be heard except the heavy footfalls of the guard on duty as he made his rounds to see that all is safe and well.

Now I am left all alone in my cell to cry and pray and to think of my loved ones left at home.

I spent that night and many more in this manner. At 5 o'clock in the morning I heard the guard ascend the stairs to the third floor; then he began to rap on the cell doors and yell at the top of his voice to "Rise and shine." At first I didn't know just what he meant by this kind of talk, but I soon found out, and caught on to what he meant. I was feeling [badly], almost unable to rise, and I was sure I could not shine a bit, though I was not long in getting off my bunk and dressing.

When all was ready, we were turned out of our cells for breakfast. We were ordered down to the first floor, and it was there that I saw the most pitiful sight that I have ever seen---more than three hundred persons all dressed in striped suits. They were the poorest and sickliest number of men that I ever saw. It was all that some of them could do to get downstairs; there was no color of blood in their faces; some were very old and feeble; some badly crippled. It was only a few of the white men that seemed to be nearer alive than dead. The negroes were more able than the whites.

The guard, on looking through the cells to see that all were out, found one man still in his cell. This man told the guard that he was sick; the guard reported this to the warden, the warden told the guard to go back and tell him to come down. Again, the man said he was sick and could not come down. The guard reported back to this same warden again.

The warden told two big rough negroes to go up and bring him down. This is fun for the negroes as they are always anxious to see a white man whipped.

They soon returned, bringing this poor sick man down with them; I shall never forget how pitiful this poor, sick man looked, and how he plead for mercy, but all in vain. His pleadings were not heard, but this same warden ordered these two negroes to strip his clothes down, then told one of them to sit on his head and the other on his feet while he (warden) applied the lash. He at once began to whip this poor fellow, and every lick he struck would bring the blood, and he whipped him until he was satisfied. I do not know how many licks he gave this poor man, but I know that when he quit he was bloody to his shoes.

## Part I. Story of the Arkansas Penitentiary, William N. Hill

The leather that is used in whipping is made of the thickest of harness leather, the strap is at least two and one-half feet long and two and one-half inches wide. The strap is securely fastened to a staff of wood about sixteen inches long.

Now, reader, how would you like for a man of two hundred pounds weight to whip you on the naked hide with that strap, and do you wonder at the fellow looking bad. This is a very small thing compared to some things that I will mention later on.

## CHAPTER II

Now we are lined up, two together, and marched to breakfast. In the dining room were two tables, one for the whites and the other for the negroes; these tables were about one hundred feet long. The seats were made of heavy timbers, and no linen or napkins were there, but each man was furnished with a rusty tin plate and a tin cup, then the waiter would pass up and down along the table, and give each of us a piece of cold bread, one piece of the fattest meat that could be bought; this was cold also. Then we got a cup of stuff they called coffee, but it looked more like soup. This is just what we got for our breakfast every morning, and the same for dinner [lunch] and likewise our supper. I did not eat but little, but was hungry, as I had not had supper the night before. No one was allowed to speak a word while at the table, but I put in my time watching the other men eat. They ate like they were starved, but some of them were unable to eat anything, although the warden said they were able to work, or that they did work as long as they could stand on their feet; I have known as many as three men to die there in one day. I was told by the clerk that the death list ran as high as thirty-seven in one month.

Breakfast is over, and the men march down to begin their daily toils. Myself and the three men who accompanied me to the penitentiary were left on the yard. I was standing, leaning against a telephone post, watching the sick and starved convicts drag themselves away to their daily labor. Among the men that had failed to eat any breakfast was one old man about sixty-five years old, and two others, perhaps forty-five years of age. These three men were about forty feet to the rear of the rest of the squad when they reached the place of work. Just then the warden stepped out into the yard with his whip strap in his hand, and called to one of these men to get down his pants. And the old man, without asking for a word of pity or mercy, with trembling hands removed his clothing, then laid down upon the ground face downward, and then the warden called out two negroes to hold him while he beat him to his heart's content. The other two were whipped in the same manner, every lick bringing blood and hide. This punishment is so severe that it is impossible for a man to lie down and take the whipping without some one to hold him in the proper position. My three companions had joined me at the telephone post, all crying but one, and the the oldest man of the four says to me, "What would you do to that man if you had a gun?" I told him that I would make a good man out of him, and he said, "I wish you had a gun, for I would admire him much more if he was good." He also said that he would like to have the honor of kissing the man that made him good. I told him it would be more painful to grant him the honor that he spoke of than it would be to make the warden good. One of my party said that he had rather be shot down than to be beaten that way. I told him that I thought the chances favorable for him to get something that he considered worse than death, and it turned out that he got several whippings and then died.

## CHAPTER III

When the warden had gotten through with his brutal treatment of these three men he returned to where my companion and myself were standing, and said to us: "You damned fellows follow me, and I will shape you up for business." We followed him, and he led us up to the second floor of the dining room. This was called the tailor shop, and then we were ordered to take off our clothing, and a complete description was taken. I stood five feet five and one-half inches barefooted. I weighed one hundred and eighty pounds, and the warden declared that I gave the best measurement of any man that he ever put the tape to, and he said that he wanted one hundred men just like me for the farm.

After completing our measurement, then we put on the striped clothes, and next we were taken to the barber's department, where we got our hair cut to the skin and a very close shave. One old man of my party had a long, black beard, and this old man disliked to part with it, but the warden told him they had to come, and so they did. The old man looked odd after giving up his long beard and all his head of pretty hair.

We were now ready for work, and were marched down to the works; they were then laying the foundation for the new State Capitol. There was lots of work going on, shoveling dirt, crushing rock, wheeling rocks, and many other things to do. The warden put me and my friends to crushing rock and we crushed all we could get our hands on, and it was a lucky thing, indeed, that we could not get our hands on the warden at this time, for we were now in an attitude to do crushing work.

The warden whipped a man just in a few moments after we began work. This man was not more than five feet away from where I was working. Everything looked bad to me, as the blood spattered on me, and me knowing all this time that the poor fellow was so sick that he could hardly stand. He was unable to work as fast as others, and this was the reason he was whipped.

This was my first day, and this was the fourth man I had seen whipped this morning.

The old man that had lost the long black beard became so excited that he made a wild blow with his hammer and bursted [sic] his thumb. The warden looked at him a minute, then said, "Damn you, pick up that hammer and get to work, or I will ruin your back with this leather."

The old man obeyed at once, and he worked with all the power he had until the whistle blew for the noon hour.

As the whistle blew, we were all lined up and marched back to the dining hall. There we sat down and tried to eat, those of us that were able, and again, in a very short time, the whistle blew the work-time signal, and we all went at once. Everything went very well until two sick men got unable to work longer, then the warden whipped them and put them to work again. They tried to work, but were unable scarcely being able to stand. They were then picked up and carried to the hospital, and one of them never was able to return.

Now, friends, what do you think of that kind of punishment? And this is not the worst treatment that convicts get, and dear reader, what do you think of the new State Capitol? The great enormous sum of money it has cost the grand old State of Arkansas, and this vast sum does not equal anything like what the cost of human lives of convicts are. And nothing of this great question ever reaches the public. Do you, my dear reader, know the reason why? Do not take my word for this, but see other men and talk this matter over with them, and after you have carefully read this little book, go and talk this matter over with your Honorable Governor [Donaghey], and see if he does not verify my statement. This thing, in my opinion, has been for a long time a damnable curse to our grand old State, as well as to humanity.

Governor Donaghey or any one else, never has, nor never can, say too much against this State Capitol. What say you, Mr. Senators and Mr. Representatives, while you stand in the great magnificent building called the Capitol of Arkansas—the one great building that has cost the taxpayers hundreds of thousands of dollars, even millions, as well as the lives of many of your countrymen? Do you ever stop to think out and make any estimate of the cost when you have assembled yourselves together for the purpose of deliberating and making laws by which the great State of Arkansas shall be ruled? Do you ever think that the grand old State is disgraced, and that the new Capitol building stands out boldly as a monument to the graves of the convicts who were whipped, cuffed and beaten until nearly dead on the scene of this spot, and then transferred to the hospital there to die all alone with no one to even speak a consoling word, and say you have done a great part in erecting this monument, which has cost scores of men their lives? Do you think that a convict does not have some estimate on his life? Do you, my readers, think that the people of this grand old State should tolerate such treatment? Do you not think that your convicts should be treated more like humans?

Or, will you allow these demons to predominate? Or will you, in the name of our blessed Redeemer, and for the sake of so many precious souls, and for the sake of your own souls, do something for the poor unfortunate ones.

It is in your power. Act wisely and quickly. We want and must have a penitentiary, but we do not, in my opinion, need or want an institution controlled by a set of wardens who are criminals, and whose every actions are calculated to make a man even worse than when he was sentenced.

Give the unfortunate and fallen man a chance by placing him in the hands of men who will have some thought of his future and whose life will show up to the convict as one worthy of imitation, one who is capable of leading men to a higher plane of living and a higher standard of morality.

Do you, kind reader, think that your association with such men as I have described already would elevate your mind or would it make you a worse man?

I say again, give the down-fallen man a chance; and better treatment, even to the convicts, will make better men of them just as well as bad treatment will make bad men worse, and good treatment will make bad men good.

Now, dear reader, stay with me on this proposition. If you oppose on this question, you are a murderer to that extent that you do not care what becomes of the State convicts. Reader, this is true as gospel, and I will not take anything back that I have said in this little book, for no man in the State of Arkansas knows better than I do what would happen if I should write a lie.

## CHAPTER IV

Now, back to the rock pile and crusher: Night has come, supper is over and I'm hungry, laying on my bunk, thinking of my loved ones at home and wondering if I ever will be permitted to see them again. Oh! How bitter the thought is!

While in this sad state, or mood, sleep steals gently over me, and I dream of loved ones at home, friends whom I have not seen for many months, when suddenly my slumbers are disturbed by calls and rapping on my cell door, and a voice calling, "Arise and shine." "I will rise and do my best to shine," I answered.

I feel so bad this morning; my head aches, my eyes are red, and I am hungry.

"Time's up for breakfast," came the command. I see the warden on the yard, his tie unfastened, and his hat is turned crosswise on his head.

A man behind me pinched my arm, and said to me, "That old warden is going to whip some one inside of an hour." I asked him how he could tell, and he said, "By the way he wore his hat." And, sure enough, he did whip three before we left the dining room.

Now, reader, I don't know just how the devil looks, though I'm perfectly certain that they favor a great deal. He doesn't smell just like a negro, neither does he smell like a polecat. I guess he smells just like the devil. Tim Kaleane [several different spellings are used] said he did, and I believe he knows. Well, breakfast is over and I am still hungry.

The warden whipped three men in the dining room; I don't know the cause. The whistle blows the hour for work. "Get on those rocks," was the order, "and beat hell out of them." I was already there, dealing terrific blows; I was almost equal to a steam crusher. I could make little gravel out of any kind of big rocks. The old man that mashed his thumb yesterday has got the worst looking thumb I ever saw. He has it bundled up in a way that makes it look like a big rag doll, but the old man is pounding rock just the same. A man gets whipped this morning. This man had dropsy in a bad form. The warden whipped him, and in less than one hour, he was carried to the hospital by two negros and afterward died.

As we go to dinner on our way to the dining room, we meet three negroes, trusties, [also spelled trustees] carrying some old dirty planks they had picked up in the yard. Some one asked what they were going to do with those planks. They said they were going to make some boxes to bury some dead men in. "How many are dead?" some one asked. "Jus three," was the reply. "Several more nearly dead, and dat ain't de wus yet; de Colonel's old dog is dead, too, and de Colonel had rudder lose all his men dan to lose dat dog." In a short while, they had made three old muddy boxes. The dead men were placed in them and hauled off to be buried. The old dog was thrown up on top of the three corpses, and hauled away with them. That is the kind of respect shown the dead by the officers of the Arkansas penitentiary.

## CHAPTER V

Thousands of men repose in this lonely spot, long forgotten, and shall be until the day of judgment, when the graves shall give up their dead.

Then those poor unfortunate ones shall rise and shine, as they have so often been commanded to do, and I trust and believe that scores of them will stand among the righteous with bright stars in their glittering crowns of gold. "Shine on, shine on, bright stars, forever." Then, where shall those officers stand? Amid the flames of a burning hell, fighting fire instead of sick men and booze.

Again, supper is over and I am still hungry. The gong sounds the signal that visitors are coming. Here they come, the officials and some of their friends. They are drinking heavily. Old man John Wilson---Hominy John, as we called him---is an old sore-legged white convict, and there are not many men living that I think can beat him playing the violin. Tim Kaline [also spelled Kaleane] was a young Irishman, full of wit and music, and also a fine singer. Old John and Tim were called out to entertain the officials and their guests. Tim sings while John plays the violin, and they make some fine music. After several pieces of music had been executed, they then called out Jim Scroy.

Jim was a fine young fellow, about twenty-eight years of age, good-looking and a fine dancer. He could do all the latest dancing; he had spent some years of his life on the stage in this way. Most of the visitors were entertained. The visitors most always gave the boys a few dimes; this was greatly appreciated by them. The dance is over, the visitors are gone, the lights turned off; all is dark, and still I lay on my bunk, tired, hungry, and sleepy, yet there is no sleep for me. I am thinking of the dear ones at home, and I wonder if God will spare my life, and permit me to return to all that is dear to me. In this way each night was spent, until I would fall asleep, to awake in the morning with a sad and heavy heart with no one to cheer me---not one word of comfort do I hear---all is sad. A rap on my cell door; again I hear that melodious voice calling up, to "Rise and shine!" The gong taps the signal, more convicts have arrived, the big iron gate swings back, a wagon passes through loaded with twelve sick convicts.

Most of these men were unable to work, and were carried from the wagon to the hospital. This was on Saturday, and on Sunday two of the twelve died.

These sick men were brought from the brick yard. They had been making brick for the great Capitol building; they had worked as long as they could stand on their feet, and when they could no longer stand, they were picked up, thrown into a wagon, and hauled off to die.

Again the gong taps, more convicts to arrive, this time only three.

These three fellows had tried to make their escape and all were shot down; two of them died the third day after entering the hospital. One of the boys that was killed only lacked a few days having his time served out.

I talked with these boys Sunday before they died, on Wednesday. I asked the one that had his time so near served out why he tried to escape. He said his health was failing him so fast he didn't think he could make it. He also stated that he had been sick for several days, and had been whipped several times, each time when he was doing his best. He said he was whipped the day before he was shot. He said, "I had but little hopes of getting away when I started, but I had rather be shot and killed as to be sick, starved and beaten to death."

Then I asked him if he thought he would get well. "No, it's impossible," was the reply. I was sure he would never get well, but wanted to see what he had to say about dying. Then I asked him if he had hopes after this life. He smiled and said, "All hopes," then the tears rolled down his pale face, and he said to me: "I have only a few things to regret; one is, that I have to die here and be buried like a dog, and no one ever know my resting place." He further stated that he had been there nearly one year, had worked hard all this time with little to eat. "Now, I give my life to right the wrong I did. I got drunk," he said, "and done wrong, but I feel that all my sins have been forgiven." I started to go, but he took my hand and said, "If I am living, see me in the morning; if not, be good until we meet again." Next morning I returned to see my friend; the end had almost come. He knew me, for he took my hand whispered, "Goodbye." Then, pointing to the bunks where the other two were lying, he tried to say something, though I could not understand. I think he wanted me to talk with them as I had with him. I stood by his bunk for a few moments, then he was dead.

## CHAPTER VI

I talked with the other two boys, and in a few hours, one of them was dead. The other one recovered, and I hope is living this day.

These three fellows were bright young men from eighteen to twenty-two years of age. They were also brick-makers, for that great Capitol, and it cost them their lives. Wake up, reader, to what is going on.

Now, back to Saturday. On this day one of the trusties goes around and sees all the convicts, and those that happen to have a little money can give him an order for anything they want to eat. You can also buy your own underwear; otherwise, you do not have any, summer nor winter. I am going to have something to eat for supper. I gave an order for fifty cents worth of steak and onions. I had half of my steak cooked for supper, the other half for breakfast. The steak was sure good. I ate more for supper than I had eaten in the last three days all put together. If all the convicts could have had what I had for supper, I would have enjoyed it much more, although there was not more than one-fourth of them that had money to buy with. Supper over, and the night spent in the usual way until that melodious voice calls for risers and shiners. It being Sunday, we will get to rest today. I can't think of anything but that steak that I will have for breakfast. Now we go for breakfast. I have two big onions in my pocket that I brought from my cell. Just to my left about six feet sat an old man seventy years of age. The old man was thin and haggard. The old grey-headed fellow had nothing to eat but the common fare, he having no money to buy with, and his fare was a piece of fat meat and bread. The waiter comes along with a cup of coffee. The poor old fellow held out his cup for coffee; the negro waiter just passed on by, and didn't give him any. Again the waiter passed along [and] the old man raised his trembling hand for coffee. The waiter just frowned and passed on, and the old man sat his cup down on the table. I could see the tears roll down his cheeks. I had not eaten anything yet. I was watching what was going on. This treatment of the old man was more than I could stand. I got up from my seat, took my plate, also my coffee, walked over to the old man and offered it to him. He looked up at me and shook his head and the tears rolled down his cheeks. I reached and picked up his plate and sat mine down in its place, walked back and sat down. The old man ate my steak and onions and cried all the time he was eating, and I cried, too, though I enjoyed that meal more than any I ever ate. Soon the waiter come in again and I held up my cup, but was not caring for coffee—I just wanted him to refuse me, for I had much rather he had refused me than the old man.

Well, as today is Sunday, we expect visitors. We are always glad to see them, for they are kind to us, and give us a look of sympathy. I hear the gong—visitors have arrived—gentlemen and ladies. The warden shows them all around, then calls out the negro quartette. Then we have lots of good and funny songs. While the visitors were here some of the boys slipped into the cook room and begged the cook for something [to] eat. There were eight of them in number. There were some of them that had no money to buy with. They were starving for something to eat. A negro happened to see them and reported to the warden. It is a negro's delight to see a white man get whipped. After the visitors had gone the warden called them and the two cooks who had fed them out, ten in number, and after eight of them had been whipped he called out the cooks. One of the fellows that had been whipped already stepped out and said, "Captain, I will take their whippings, sir, if you please, as I am the first man that called for something to eat. I was hungry and they fed me. It was the love of God that caused them to do it, and I will willingly take their punishment." "You go to hell," was the warden's reply. "Damn you, I will beat the life out of you if you fool with me just a little." The convict said no more, but turned and walked away. The warden turned and cursed one of the cooks and told him to get his clothes off damn quick. He did so and then laid down and took his whipping; the other one did likewise.

Reader, what do you think, what do you say on this question? Do you think it is right for men to be treated like that? The bell rings for supper; I will turn in and get an onion as that is almost all that I will have to eat. Supper is over, the gong taps nine, the lights are out, all is off until morning again. I lay on my bunk, my mind returns back to those that I so dearly love. I think of the happy days gone by and of the many pleasures and joys of life, and wonder if they shall ever be mine again. Then hope comes to me, and I pray to God for life and liberty. After allowing my thoughts to dwell upon these things for some time I fall asleep.

Now it is Monday morning; that same old racket appears at my cell door; just as he raps on my door I run my hand through between the iron bars; it being dark in my cell he could not see me, and when I thrust my hand between the bars he became badly frightened, jumped back and said, "What in the hell are you doing?" I told him I was just trying to shine a little. From that time on that guard looked down on me, though he would not look at me at all when he could help it, and he never reported me to the warden, either. The laugh would all have been on him. From that time on he never called on me to rise and shine. He would pass my cell door and never say a word. Out we go to breakfast. I have two big onions in my pocket. The whistle calls for work, and we have to move. Five men get whipped today and three are carried to the hospital. Nothing else out of the ordinary happened today.

Another night passes in the same old way. After breakfast the whistle sounds the hour for work, and ten minutes later the music of two hundred hammers can be heard pounding the rocks, picks and shovels keeping time with the music. A negro causes a white man to be whipped, then the white man knocks the negro down with his hammer and the negro is carried to the hospital. The white man gets whipped again, and is carried to the hospital nearly beaten to death.

Five more men are brought in from the brick yard, and one of them died within six hours after he arrived. Another life given to the State Capitol.

Now comes a line-up for the brick yard. More sick men from the railroad camp. Worked, beaten and starved to death, one of these men showed me where he had been whipped. He had sores on him as large as my hand. He said that there were several in the same shape. At that time the State leased the convicts to the railroad companies at 50 cents per day, and the State furnished the rations for them and also furnished the guards. Although it don't take much to feed them and one convict will do more work than two free men, here is the difference: A free man will work only as he can stand it, the poor convict works as long as he can stand it, then he has to lay down and die.

There is a railroad boss always on hand cursing the convicts and calling them all kinds of names and the warden is there ready to whip them. In this way the work is carried on. They work in rain and mud, then lay down at night with their wet clothes on and try to sleep. Often in the winter time when the weather was cold I have known them to lay down at night with their clothes frozen stiff with ice. They wore all the clothes they had and were compelled to sleep in them. I have seen men that were unable to sit down, and when they were not standing were compelled to lay flat on their back; they were beaten so badly and were so sore they could not sit, though they were able to do two men's work every day as long as they could go, and were whipped when they could go no longer. Now, friends, this may seem strange to all of you who know nothing about the penitentiary and there is no one who knows anything about it except those who have served time there and those dirty, cowardly curs that manage this institution. All of these officials will put on a long, sad face and tell you this is not the truth. Just any time they deny it they lie, although that would be easy for them to do, as there is nothing too bad for some of them to do. Well, I hear the gong tap. More sick convicts from the railroad camp, all unable to work.

## CHAPTER VII
## A NEGRO'S SAD STORY

He said he had been whipped nine times in five days. He said he was whipped three times the day before he was brought to the hospital. He said he had the chills and when his fever was high he would go crazy. Then they would whip him. He said one day while he was crazy after he had been whipped they chained him to a post and he lay there all the evening in the hot sun without any water. He told of other similar incidents. He said when a convict dies they dig a hole, roll him into it and that is the last of him. I asked the negro the cause of so many men being whipped. He said that in most cases the railroad man was always grumbling and cursing the convicts. Then the guard would report to the warden and have them whipped. But when the warden was present himself and heard the grumbling he just begun to whip when every man was doing his best. The railroad man didn't care how many men that he had beaten to death. Neither does he care how soon they die. The State is to furnish him so many men by contract, and the sooner he has a crew beaten to death the sooner he will get a fresh one.

Then I asked a negro if the convicts ever caused any trouble. "Yes, sometimes," he answered. He stated that now and then a negro would tell a lie on some white man and cause him to be whipped. "What kind of a lie would they generally tell?" I asked. "Well, he would tell the warden that some white man was laying some plan to get away. Then the warden would whip the white man when there hadn't been a word said or anything done to that effect." Now, reader, that is a point I want you to see. The one that is always telling the warden a lot of lies gets the least punishment. The negroes should be worked to themselves; and if ever the penitentiary is conducted by a set of thoroughbred white Americans that is the way it will be managed. Work the whites and blacks in separate gangs. What do you think of a warden that will place a double-barrel shotgun in the hands of a black negro to guard a crew of white men? And it is often done. Any warden that is guilty of this is just as sorry as any kind of a negro, and most all the wardens prior to 1904 are guilty. After Mr. Pitcock, of Van Buren, was appointed superintendent of the penitentiary I think he took off all the negro guards and placed them back in the ranks; then took some of the white men and placed them on guard. That is the way to do business. Mr. Pitcock is a fine gentleman and has good principles, and has some love and respect for fallen humanity.

One Friday night it was reported among the convicts that there was to be a big line-up made for the farm. This was sad news for the convicts, as the farm was the most dreaded place of all the works. It is not like working on the farm at home. All is very different.

Again it is Saturday morning. We hear a melodious voice calling for us to rise and shine and make ready for the farm. Breakfast over, "Line up, every damn one of you," came the command from the warden. Then he stepped out with his leather and said, "I don't want a grunt out of any of you damned fellows, for I am going to send the last damned one of you to the farm." Then the warden and physician marched up and down the line. This was done before the doctor had made his morning visit to the hospital, and the warden had gone in there and run out a lot of his sick men and had them lined up with the balance of the crew. When the doctor discovered what had been done he took them all back to the hospital. There was not a well man in the crew, but they had to go to the farm. After the doctor had gone back to the hospital with his men the warden from the farm picked out one hundred men to take with him. He handcuffed us altogether and marched us down to the boat. Now we are on board the boat ready to go up the river to the different convict farms. At that time the farms were managed by three big devils. This was before the State purchased a convict farm. On we go up the river, many sad hearts among the white men, many of them felt sure that they would spend the rest of their days on the convict farm. They were sure that in a few weeks their health would entirely give way. They were sure they could not undergo the brutal treatment that would be imposed upon them. The whipping, starving and overwork is more than they can stand. Then we could fully realize that it was only a matter of time when many of our number would have to lie down and die; then to be hauled away to the lonely convict graveyard, there to be buried, the whites and negroes all together. Then you are lost from all the world; no friend nor loved ones will ever know your resting place.

It was late Saturday afternoon when the boat landed and we were marched up to the stockades. There we met a lot more convicts. These men looked as if they had just been dug up out of the ground, they were so dirty, thin and pale. Then we were halted in the yard.

The warden had been absent from the farm for two days. "Well," said he to one of the guards, "have you got anything for me to do? I would like to pitch that leather awhile; I don't want to get out of practice." The guard quickly spoke up and said, "Yes; that man there can give you a job," pointing to one of the convicts that had been left with the guard. Without making any investigation, the warden called out to the convict and said, "Get out here, God dern you, and I will put new life in you; you look too damned druggy to suit me," said the warden. The poor convict marched out and said to the warden, "What are you going to whip me for—what have I done?" "I don't know what you have done, and I don't give a damn. Get them clothes down damned quick or I will knock you down." The convict did as he was commanded to do without asking any more mercies.

## PART I. STORY OF THE ARKANSAS PENITENTIARY, WILLIAM N. HILL

I am sure that this man had not done anything. The warden just wanted to play tough, as we were new men and he kept this whipping going on every day. When we were marched in for supper there we found a long dirty table. This is what we had to eat: One piece of cornbread, one big spoonful of cowpeas and one cup of water, all being cold. The corn that the bread was made of was chopped. I have found whole grains of corn in my bread. This bread didn't have any salt in it. It was made up with cold water and nothing more. The peas were cooked in water and nothing else. There was plenty of salt in a tin bucket on the table. The water that we drank may have been secondhand; I could not tell by the taste. For breakfast we had meat instead of peas and sometimes coffee instead of water. All that is used on the farm in the way of seasoning for the cook is plenty of dirt in everything that you eat. You had to eat it. Supper is now over, and we are locked in the bunk house for the night. This is a long building. Whites and blacks all sleep in the same building. Lights are kept burning all night. There is always a guard on duty at night. Reader, I wish you could see what we had to sleep on. Our bunks were made of straw, dirt and chinch bugs. More dirt and chinches than straw. We could not sleep but little. Well, it is Sunday. Rise and shine this beautiful Sabbath morning. "We will give you this day and tomorrow we will give you hell." Friends, how would you like to hear something like that on the Sabbath morning? Would it in any manner help you to keep the Sabbath holy? Breakfast being over, we are locked up in that dirty bunk house for the day, and today I get acquainted with all the convicts. I listen to many sad stories from them. They all told me that the farm was the worst place in the penitentiary. They are away off in the bottom where no one seldom came around that they might find out what was going on. They told me how they had seen men shot down and beaten to death. One man was whipped three times one morning and then died while the rest of the crew were eating dinner [lunch]. This man had been sick for several days, though he worked every day. On the last day he fell down, unable to rise. For a while the warden whipped him and told him that he was trying to get out of work. The poor fellow tried to convince the warden that he was not. When he was again able to stand on his feet he tried to work. Again he fell to the ground. The warden whipped him again. Still he could not get up for some time. He lay there unable to get up. The warden returned once more and hit him three times. That was the third and last time forever, and in less than two hours this poor man was a corpse. We hope that he found comfort and rest. This man was some woman's son and some one's brother. How would you like for your father, son, brother or husband to be treated like that? Would you not feel like killing some one? Sure you would, although if you killed one of those dirty scoundrels then you would have to serve a term for killing a dog, if you did not hang. There is only one way to stop this murderous gang, and that is to put them out of business. There is plenty of men and good men that can and will run this institution, though instead of getting at this business as it should be gotten at, this is what they do: Some time while the Legislature is in session there will be a committee appointed by this body to inspect each convict camp and make a thorough investigation as to how the convicts are treated. Here is the way they do it: After this committee has been appointed most all the newspaper men of Little Rock will furnish a full account of the appointing of this committee, also stating just about the time the committee will make this investigation. Then what is next? All the camps will be cleaned up and made ready for this committee, and here is what the poor fools will do: They will go from camp to camp; everything seems to be in very good condition. They will then look at the crop, and the crop looks fine. All this time the warden is trying to look innocent and is trying to do something that would make a favorable impression on the committee, and in most cases that is easy to do. Then this committee will ask some trusty how he is treated. Sure he will always tell them that he is treated good. And it is true he is, compared with those in the ranks. Then they will [ask] some one who is in the ranks how he is treated. He will tell them that he is treated all right. He would be afraid to say anything else. The warden would kill him if he was to tell the truth. Though I will state just here that after all the blunders in making these investigations there have been some reports that were not so favorable for the officials of the penitentiary, though there has never been a committee that has been able to make anything like a correct report, as they don't seem to understand how to get at this matter, though it is easy to get the truth if you will get at it in the proper way. Don't ever ask a convict to tell anything publicly. First, assure him that it will be a private matter, then assure him that his statement will have to corroborate with the statements of others in order that you may believe him. In this way you can get the truth. Then put each man on private examination, about twelve white men from each camp. Don't never ask a guard anything about the treatment of convicts. They will always tell you a lie. Any man that can hold a job guarding convicts for sixty days that man is a dirty, low down cur. He will steal, he will lie, he will murder you for two dollars if he could catch you asleep. It is impossible for a good man to hold a job as a guard. They don't want a man that will treat the convicts as they should be. Readers, did you ever see a convict guard? They can't look at you in the face. They always look as if they had stolen something, and if they haven't it is because they haven't had a chance.

Now, old guards, this is true, isn't it? Though it will make you hot for me to tell you of these things, I wish I had you all together face to face with me. I would like to talk to you. I wouldn't have any hopes of doing you any good, though I would like to tell you more about what you are, things that I would not say here, and I would like to whip all of you; but the man will have to be more fleet of foot than I am to do that, because the man that whips one of you will have to run you down. I don't know of but one man that I think that I can whip within five miles of where I live. Though I believe I can whip any man that ever guarded convicts as long as sixty days and didn't get fired, and if there is any law that will make a man pay for running I will make you run and then I will pay your fine for you if you will give me the chance. Now, old nothing, if you think this is hot air let me hear from you. I will always respond to your call. The guards and wardens that I have reference to were those in charge prior to 1905. And those of you that are living, I don't care anything about you, and if you are dead I know exactly where you are, and that is just where you ought to be.

## CHAPTER VIII

Back to Sunday afternoon. I had by this time gotten acquainted with all the convicts. They were free to talk, and I listened with great attention to those sad and pitiful stories. I was so interested in their stories as they related them to me. My heart was heavy and I was forced to weep. I had attracted the attention of some of those old men who had been there for several years. Those poor old men with feeble and tottering steps gathered around me, and each of them had sad stories to tell. Their faces were pale, their eyes were dim and sunken. Their heavy head and shattered form told the story of many bitter griefs and sorrows.

They told me how they had entered the penitentiary from five to twenty years before stout and healthy. They told me how they had been driven through rain and snow. They also told how they had been starved and beaten until health had failed them. They told how they had seen men fall and die in the field from overwork and starvation. They told me they had seen men try to escape and be shot down then the bloodhounds would rush upon the fallen man and tear his flesh and clothes while warden and guards would laugh and hiss their dogs. They said for a time after they were convicted they had hopes, though after their health had failed their hopes were gone. They told how they had gotten into trouble while drinking and had killed some one while in a drunken row. That is what whiskey will do. Many times did they speak of their families and friends; then they would break down and cry as little children.

One of these men had a life-time sentence. He said his friends would write to him at the beginning and then they quit and now he is dead to the world. "I am forsaken by all except my blessed Redeemer, and if I could have the assurance that I could once more look at my old home and see those that are left I would be happy, and would pray to die. That one hope is all that I live for," he said; may "God grant this favor." While the old man told his story to me the tears were rolling down his pale and furrowed cheeks. This old man told me that there were only a few men that could tell the story of a twenty-year prison life. This is found to be true. Some smart people will say, "Well, they ought to have kept out of trouble." That is true when it can be avoided. And everybody ought to go to heaven, too, though the Bible says there are only a few that will enter therein.

If men and women were today placed on trial for doing just what God has commanded us to do how many of us would be convicted? Or, in other words, how many would be found guilty? Be careful, my dear reader, of what you say and what you do. I hope you will never have to go to the penitentiary, though if you do not perhaps you are no better than many who have gone. If everybody that committed a penitentiary offense was convicted at once we would have a time; there would be no one left to do business.

Now, friends, I do not say that we are all bad, though at some time in our lives we have made mistakes. Suppose we all quit drinking whiskey, we will soon put the penitentiary on a bum. That is just as true as it can be. And at the close of this Sabbath day I find myself in possession of many sad and pitiful stories, some that I will mention later.

It is Monday morning. Again we hear that familiar voice calling, "Arise and shine, and don't forget what we are going to give you." We all remembered that he had on this day promised to give us hell. There wasn't any one that seemed to doubt it. We were turned out for breakfast and nothing to eat that a man can eat unless he is starved to it. Outside came the command from the warden. We marched out on the yard. "Squad up," shouted the warden, "and don't look so damned druggy," he added.

Now, we began to squad up, about twenty men to the squad. It had rained nearly all night and was still raining. It was too wet to do any work on the farm so we were armed with axes. And off to the forest we go to clear more land. Each guard in command of his squad conducted us to the place of work which was about two miles away. We marched two together. We were ordered to move at a lively pace. This trip was a painful one to the sick men and to those that were afflicted with rheumatism or dropsy, and all the men that had been there for any length of time were afflicted with one or the other. Some of those poor fellows were compelled to trot to keep up with their squad, and it was sure that they had to keep up. When we reached the place of work some of those poor fellows were almost out of breath and they panted like a fox hound after a long day's chase. We reached the forest and were all placed in one squad. We began to work, some chopping and some piling brush; some sawing and some piling logs, and the warden was pitching the leather. He was giving those sick and broken down men just what the guard had promised them. I do not know just how many men was whipped that day, but it was awful to see how they were treated. How would you like to see some poor old man whose hair is white from old age, and whose health had long since failed him, buckled down and whipped? And how would you like to see an old man who is an invalid for life lie down upon the ground with all his clothes stripped down and then some big, heartless man beat him just because he was not able to work? I have seen this done many times.

Well, it is still raining. We are all wet through. That doesn't matter; we are still working. Think of one hundred men clearing land together and each man doing two men's work. It looked like business to me. Our dinner was brought to where we were working. A negro drove up with a barrel of water, a tub of cowpeas, a dirty cotton sack filled with cornbread, and a lot of fat meat so near rotten a dog would almost gag to smell it. He then took his arm full of tin plates, threw them down on the ground in a row in the mud, then took a big tin bucket, dipped it down into the tub of peas just as you would dip up a bucket of slop from a barrel. Then with a big spoon in his hand he walked down the row of tin plates. He would run the big spoon into the bucket, draw out a heaping spoonful of peas and threw them on the plate, never making any halt until the last plate was filled. This negro had become an expert at this business. He seldom ever missed a plate. Next, he would get his bucket of meat, then take a big, long fork and pitch each man a piece of meat. The negro said one day that he ought to have a pair of gloves to handle the meat with as it was too nasty to handle without them. Then he would get his sack of bread, walk down the line and throw each man a piece. Next, he would throw each man a tin cup, then pass around the water, then dinner was over. The warden would yell out, "Get to work, and do it damned quick."

Young men and girls, think well of what I tell you, and keep out of trouble, if possible. See that your companions are first-class, and, if you drink, stop it today. It is not often that a wise man will get into trouble that he can not get out of if he is sober. I think at least 75 per cent of the crimes that are committed are done by persons while under the influence of whiskey. Perhaps some one will not agree with me on this question, though you must remember, my dear reader, there is always a smart set ready to dispute the truth, and this smart set that I have reference to are those that never do anything wrong, and never see any one else do anything that is right and they always know it all; perhaps they do, but they so seldom tell the truth. They are not worth anything to civilization.

Well, our day's toil is over. Sick, tired, worn out and with sad and heavy hearts, we return to the stockade only to lay down and weep and wait for the coming of another day. Then we are made to wonder who will be the next to pass away to quit the walks of man.

Now, the rain is over and the ground is dry enough to plow and hoe, some of us to plow and the rest of us to hoe, and today the leather was used more than I had ever seen it in one day. I do not know how many men were whipped, though not less than twenty-five. We made corn and cotton to let. We tended one thousand acres of cotton, and I do not know just how much corn, but lots of it, and the warden seemed to think a great deal of his stuff, and if you happen to make a mislick [sic] and cut down a stalk of cotton or corn that should have been left you would get a whipping if the warden found it out. At dinner the hoe hands all eat in the field. We were fed in the same manner as we were while we were clearing land. Three men in the hoe gang, after having been whipped, fell down completely exhausted and for some time were unable to stand on their feet. They were sick and very weak, caused from overwork, starvation and whipping. Another day's work is done. We are marching home as we deem it for the present. Many of us are almost unable to travel. Many times I have seen both old and young men when returning to the stockade at night as weak as if they were only a little child. They were suffering much pain, caused from overwork, rheumatism and dropsy and wounds inflicted upon them by whipping them unmercifully.

Their condition being so critical, all hopes have vanished. A poor, hungry man gets whipped for eating a piece of corn bread. One day at dinner I failed to eat as I often did. A man that sat near me picked up the bread that was on my plate and eat it, this being against the rules. Though this poor starving man didn't think that any one would report him, a negro happened to see him get the bread. He then went to the warden and reported it. The warden then called him out and beat him unmercifully. The poor fellow plead for mercy. He told the warden that he would not eat any more bread as long as he was a convict if he would not whip him. It was a sad thing to hear this poor man pleading and he had offered to do all that he could do; had even offered to quit eating bread for the remaining part of his term, which was nearly one year, though all of his pleading was in vain and his clothes were stripped down and two negroes held him. The warden then whipped him to his own satisfaction.

## CHAPTER IX

### A Crazy Convict is Drowned

This man had been crazy for about ten days and was getting worse all the time. The warden whipped him every day. He was a horrible looking sight where [he] had been whipped. One day he became so crazy that he didn't know anything. The warden claimed that the fellow was playing off, but after whipping him twice one morning he carried him to the stockade and locked him up. The next morning when the negro was turned out he ran; the guards fired two shots at him, but failed to hit him. The man ran about six hundred yards and jumped into a slough and was drowned. The blood hounds were upon him by the time he reached the slough and they may have helped to drown him. After the warden let the dogs chew him for a while the dead man was carried back to the stockade and was thrown down upon the ground and lay there in the hot sun until noon. Then two negroes made a box and placed him in it and hauled him out to the convict graveyard and buried him there, and then all was over with this poor man. His punishment was great while here on earth and I trust that he found rest among the angels.

### An Old Negro was Made to Pray While He was Being Whipped

We were hoeing cotton. The warden rode up to where we were and asked the guard if he could give him something to do. The guard replied that he could, and the warden jumped off his horse with the leather in his hand. The guard pointed out an old negro who happened to be nearest the warden. "Come out here, you old G--- d--- black devil; I am bloodthirsty." This old negro was seventy years old and a very small man, and so feeble. The old man laid his hoe down and said to the warden, "Boss, I'se done all de work dat I can do; I'se sick, and you know, Boss, I'se done you lots of work, and now I'se not got but a few mo' days to live, am seventy years old, and, Boss, tell me what you'se going to whip me for, what is I done? Ask any of dese here men, Boss, if I don't work all de time and I don't ebber bother nobody. If all dese here men don't tell you dat I will not say any more. Boss," he said "you done wrong when you let dat guard cause you to whip dese poor men like you'se beat dem ebery day. I'se praying for you, Boss, and I ask God to forgive you and I prays for all dese men." Then the warden said to him, "Get your pants down, God damn you. I will have you to pray again." Then the tottering old man pushed down his clothes and laid down upon the ground. The warden then made two negroes hold him while he beat him. When all was ready the warden hit him with all the power he had and said, "Now, pray, damn you." The old negro prayed with all his might. He prayed for the warden, the guards and all the convicts, white and black. He prayed for his wife and children. At every lick the blood would fly, and the warden would curse him and say, "Pray."

However, he prayed as long as he could and when the warden had quit whipping him the old negro was completely exhausted, and he lay on the ground for a moment, then reached out his hand to one of the negroes who had held him and the negro helped him to his feet; the blood ran down to his shoes and dripped off to the ground. This was a sad affair. There were no dry eyes among those that witnessed it except the wardens and the guards. This old negro was the most harmless man that I ever saw. While the old man was talking to the warden before he was whipped I looked for the warden to knock him in the head, though for some reason he was prevented. I think that God gave this old negro the power of his talk. His words were true when he told the warden he didn't have long to live, and when the poor old slave had breathed his last I trust that God will give him a home around the throne of mercy where wardens never go.

### The Warden is Bloodthirsty

Whipped nine men in succession. We were hoeing more cotton when the warden rode up. The first thing that he said was, "I am bloodthirsty; what can I get here?" "Plenty," the guards replied. The warden jumped off his horse and said, "Show me one damned quick." The guard pointed to a while boy about eighteen years old. The poor boy was almost scared to death. He hadn't done a thing in the world. He had no idea what he was to be whipped for. The warden called out to him and said, "Get out here, Johnnie; by God I will not be as easy as your damned old dad. Get your clothes down." This poor boy was trembling from head to foot, trying to talk, but could not say anything. The warden then ordered two negroes to hold him and then he began to whip him. When he was done whipping him he was the bloodiest man I ever saw and he would rub his wounds and then his eyes and then rub all over, and I thought the boy was going to have fits. Then the warden whipped eight more in the same manner. This white boy had got on a big drunk, got into trouble and was serving a one-year term, and Johnnie told me he was done with whiskey. May God help and bless and help you to keep your promise wherever you may be. Just think of nine men being whipped in succession, and it just took that to satisfy the warden. He had taken a few drinks and wanted to do something. However, he does something every day like that.

Five men fall in the field, caused from overwork and starvation, and they are carried to the stockade; then the sick men are carried back to the walls to be treated, and they are so near dead that they are unable to work. As long as a man can work he must work, and it don't matter with the warden if you do die, and the hot summer days now come and we sicken and die, some dropping out most every day on account of the heat and sickness or death, and it is bad to hear the cries and moans of these poor starving, sick and dying men. However, the work goes on and the whipping is never complete, and with a few exceptions you are never safe from the death-dealing blows of a warden until the chilly waves of death have carried you over the mighty deep and landed you on the shores of the great celestial. No matter what your deportment may have been, it is then and only then that a poor convict can find safety and rest; and this consolation will bring comfort and rest to every poor soul that believes and in time he will give you rest.

### Three Men Hope for Liberty

Today we are back in the forest clearing more land and the weather is warm. Most all the men are sick and weak, but the work goes on. Several men are whipped before noon and three young men had planned to make their escape at the first opportunity. One of these was to act as leader and it was understood that they were always to work close together as possible and when the leader made his leap the other two were to follow. They were bright young men, one of them serving a five-year sentence and the other two were serving three years each. It happened that while they were drinking they had gotten into trouble. They had been in the penitentiary a little more than one year, and after having worked so hard with so little to eat and had been whipped so often, their health was failing them. They didn't think they could live to serve out their sentence, and, if so, they were sure that their health would be so impaired that they would never regain it, and just a few days before they made their escape one of them told me that he could not live if he had to serve out his sentence. He said that he had done wrong and was sorry for it, and he also said that he felt that he had humbly paid for his wrong and that he had no hopes for a pardon, as he had no relatives and no money, and that he was alone in the world; had no one to care for and no one to care for him; and, when these last words were spoken, tears were in his eyes; "and this is my conclusion," he added: "I am going to quit this camp at the first favorable opportunity. Two other fellows are going with me," he said. "I am to act as leader." And then he told me who was to go with him. He said they had all agreed to tell me of their intentions and no one else. And then "if we are killed and you ever chance to meet a friend of ours you can tell this story." And then he gave me the names of his friends—two young men and one young lady. "And now will you do all this for me?" he asked. And I assured him that I would, and then I gave him my best ideas of how to make their escape, and then I gave him a word of advice as to how to conduct himself if he was so lucky as to gain his freedom. My first advice was not to drink any more whiskey. After I had finished my advice to him he took me by the hand and said, "Your advice is good; I will accept it all, and I will never forget you," he added. "Keep still until we are gone." Then after saying goodnight to me, he walked over to his bunk and laid down for the night, and he never mentioned this matter to me again until noon of the day that they made their escape, and when dinner was called we sat down on the ground, these three men sat near me, and the leader said to me in a whisper, "We will try to leave you this evening." "I wish you good luck," and then we slipped our hands together and I said to them, "God be with you all, and don't you forget to pray, and I feel sure that you will make it." These last words finished, the tears were streaming down his cheeks, and we never spoke to each other again. And now dinner is over and it is work time and we are beginning to work. Some were chopping and sawing while the rest were piling brush and logs and I was keeping my eyes on these three men as much as I could, not knowing just when they would make their break. While I didn't think they would make the run until late in the evening as night would soon be on, and that they would have a better chance to make their escape, and everything went on smoothly and no one was whipped that afternoon and guards were placed on all sides of the works some thirty or forty yards from where we were working when it was only a few minutes of the time to quit; the guards that stood just a few steps back in the brush had stepped out in the open where we had cleared, and then the order was given to line up to march in and then every one was in motion and I kept a watch for these three men, who were keeping close together, and then the leader glanced at me; then he gave a keen yell and at the same time he sprang into the woods and the other two men in quick succession yelled at the top of their voices and sprang after him; every one was taken unawares, guards and convicts also, and the guards were all jumping up and down and running about. They didn't seem to know what had happened. At last one of them fired both barrels of his gun in the direction of the three men who were then out of sight; then several shots were fired in the same direction, but neither shot took effect and the dog man was on the scene and he cut all his dogs loose and they picked up the trail at once. Now for a lively race, and for a few moments the hounds made a straight run and then they began to circle and they were in a large bottom of timber, and the boys must have been five or six hundred yards ahead of the dogs. The dogs made a short turn to the right for about two hundred yards and then they halted for a moment and then opened up on the track again.

At the time the boys had made their run the warden was absent about a mile away, and on hearing the shooting and the hounds he made haste back to where he had left us as fast as his horse would bring him. He ran up and brawled out, "What in the hell is the matter?" The guards all began to talk at once, and at last the warden found out what had happened, and if you ever saw a man mad this man was mad, as he wanted to know of the guards if they were all asleep, and one of them told the warden that he thought the three men that ran off were wide awake, as they didn't move like men that were asleep, though if they were asleep he said he thought that each of them was having a nightmare as they started to run. This talk only served to make the warden more mad, and he cursed all the guards and everything he could think of. Now the dogs are playing a lively tune. If dogs have any music about them those dogs must have been musicians, as they carried all the parts of music. There was an old brindle dog in the pack and they called him "Sig." One old negro convict declared that old Sig had the best alto voice he had ever heard except his sweetheart's voice, and that their voices were very much alike.

Well, it is now sunset. Two of the guards and the dog man had followed on after the hounds, leaving three with us, and we are on march for the stockade. The warden, two guards and the dog man are in pursuit of the three men who have escaped; and now we hear the hounds running all over the bottom and they seemed to be somewhat confused and are on back trail most of time. The boys have given them the dodge. And after we arrive at the stockade the other three guards join in the chase. They were out most all night and the dogs running in all directions, though I think they were after rabbits, and I think the boys have made good their escape. I was certainly glad to know it, but I didn't tell the warden so, for he was mad at everything in camp, and two of the guards were fired and the three convicts are free once more—good luck to each of them wherever they may be.

While everything is in an uproar at the camp the warden whips men every day and men are dying every day—some sick, others dying worked, starved and beaten to death, and you can hear those sick and starving men wishing for something to eat; and on the farm is not like being at the walls. There you can send out and buy something to eat if you have the money. On the farm it is different. The warden and guards have plenty to eat but these starving men will slip around to where they can watch them while eating. I have seen them cry as if their hearts were broken, though they would not dare to call for anything to eat. No matter how much was left on the table, the warden would never offer them anything, not even to those sick men. They would give it to their dogs first.

## CHAPTER X

### A Man Gets a Pardon

Today at noon when the warden returned from the post office he brought with him a pardon for one of the men in our camp. The warden called out the man that had been pardoned, told him to get down his pants and this poor man, without asking any questions, removed his clothing, then laid down and took his beating. After the warden had whipped him as long as he wished he then took the pardon from his pocket and handed it to the poor man, who was sobbing and trembling from head to foot. The poor fellow took the big envelope in his trembling hands, then dried away the tears and opened the letter, and when he saw what he had he sank to the ground and wept; then lifting his pale thin face towards heaven cried out, "I thank thee, oh Lord, my blessed Savior; bless the Governor, I pray thee; bless all these poor, dying convicts; forgive those who are so heartless and cruel." And then he looked the warden in the eyes, and when the warden could no longer stand the gaze of his brilliant eyes that were fixed upon him, he turned away and brawled out, "Time's up, all you d—s—of b—, and that means all of you." And as we started off to work the man that had just been whipped waived us a last farewell; and I shall never forget the pure and simple words of gratitude offered by this convict. He spoke from the depths of his heart, and back to his home he returned. His loved ones will welcome him, and I trust the dear Savior will do so when he shall knock at the golden gates.

### Scenes on the Farm

Now, the weather is warm and the men are starving, sick and dying; however, the work goes on and whipping is often and terrible. As I have stated before, each convict is furnished with two pairs of pants and two shirts. You are only allowed to keep one of these suits of clothes in your possession.

Each Sunday morning we change clothes, and when you are compelled to work in the rain and mud your clothing becomes very dirty and filthy, especially those who are whipped several times during the week, as their flesh is so badly beaten up and their clothing becomes so bloody and filthy. I have known the flies to blow their wounds, and I remember two poor fellows who were in this condition and maggots had gotten into their wounds where the hide had been whipped off of them, as they had no opportunity to take a bath except on Sunday morning. These men had been in this condition for about three days before they found out that they had flyblows[22] in them, and then they reported to the warden and he cursed them for everything he could

---

[22] Infested with eggs or young larvae of a blowfly.

think of. They do not have any doctor on the farm, but they keep a little outfit of drugs. Some one of the convicts issues the medicine to those in need of it. The warden told the medicine man to pour carbolic acid on those men to kill the worms, and they were held by two Negroes while the man poured the medicine on. They were doctored just as you would doctor a cow for worms, such as are commonly called screwworms, and after he had suffered all this torture the warden told him that if that failed then he would knock them out with the leather. Now, reader, this was not a case of filthiness on the convict's part; it was unavoidable to them, as they do their best, and men in their condition are entitled to all your sympathy. Don't you think so? Now, after these men had been doctored for these worms they were driven off to work. What do you think of that kind of treatment? Do you think the people of Arkansas should allow this to be carried on? We have plenty of honest men in the State; why not use them? Come on, all you good people, and we will do something that God will bless us for.

### Picking Cotton on the Farm

The convicts are divided into three squads and then each man is given a task of so many hundred pounds to pick, and all of the most able-bodied men are in squad No. 1, and the next most able men are in squad No. 2, and squad No. 3 is composed of men who are sick, crippled and old. These men have only a few weeks, or months at best, to live, and each man in squad No. 3 must pick 200 pounds or get a whipping, and if you pick 199 pounds you get your whipping just the same; and squad No. 2 is also composed of sick men, although they are more able than No. 3. The task for No. 2 is 300 pounds. Now comes No. 1. Their task runs from four to five hundred pounds, and each man must get the amount that is assigned to them or they will be whipped just as often as they fall short of the amount assigned. To miss your amount only one pound will not save you. There is plenty of men that can pick four or five hundred pounds of cotton in one day if they are well, although to pick it now and then is not like having to pick it every day, and when a free man is picking his four or five hundred pounds per day he has something to eat, but the poor convict does not have anything to eat that a free man could or would eat.

### What the Convicts Eat

Now, I will tell you of a few things that the convicts eat. In the fall of the year there are lots of black birds, robins, quail and other birds. Also there are plenty of rabbits. On Sundays the guards and the trusties will go out hunting. They often kill birds and rabbits that they fail to find. Then it is a common thing for a convict to find a dead rabbit or bird that had been killed by some of the hunters and many times the rabbits or the birds had been killed four or five days prior to the time that they were picked up by the convicts, and these starving men would pick up the rabbit or bird and take it to the stockade at night and then they would dress their game and have it cooked for supper. I have had men to tell me they had eaten rabbits and birds after they had been dead so long the insects had eaten their eyes out and the flies had blown them. It has never been my misfortune to have to eat anything like that, although I know plenty of men that were so near starved that they have eaten just what I have mentioned and they were glad to get it. These poor men would be more pleased to find one of these dead rabbits or birds that was half rotten than you would be to find a ten-dollar gold piece. I have had men tell me they had eaten rats. Many times the trusties would catch the rats at the barn and trade them to the convicts for tobacco. One old man told me that he and three other men ate a big tom cat and he said it was fine. Now, reader, all this may seem strange to you, and it may be hard for you to understand why men will be so cruel as to treat men in this manner, and it is embarrassing to me to tell just what the poor convicts were compelled to eat and are compelled to put up with, although I will speak the truth if it costs me my life. There are hundreds of men today that will testify in any court to all that I am saying, and the people of Arkansas have been ignorant of what is going on in the Arkansas penitentiary. Now, reader, you have often heard the facts in this case and can learn more of them if you will only try. Will you keep still or will you be an honest man and come to the relief of those poor souls who are sick and dying every day, caused from unmerciful beating, starvation and overwork. Now, all you good men, come to the front, and all you dirty cowards, sneak off somewhere. That is all you will do and all you could do; and you people that keep still may sneak off with them, as you are not worth anything to your country or to your fellow man; you are no good.

### More About the Farm

The weather never gets too cold to pick cotton. On the convict farm they pick when there is ice all over the cotton and when everything is frozen over with ice, although the poor men work with only one pair of thin cotton pants on and a shirt of the same material, a pair of old shoes and most all of them without socks, and many times their fingers and toes would freeze. I have known their toe nails and finger nails to come off and most of the flesh on the toes, as they have no clothing and nothing to eat; consequently, their blood is very thin and they die with pneumonia by the dozen, and often when a man dies he is just reported as an escaped convict. This is often done in order to keep down any investigation as to how the man lost his life, and then if they beat one to death the record will show that he escaped. In this way they cover up many dirty crimes. The female convicts are all sent to the farm, and are all kept in one squad to themselves, no men with them except the guards. The women do all work that men do except plough. They have to work hard and are whipped just like the men on the naked hide. Governor Davis would not let a white woman stay in the pen; he would pardon them all, and I think the Governor was right. I will say no more about the women, as there are so many things that are too bad to speak of.

### Three Men Try to Make Their Escape

Men were being whipped every day because they were unable to pick the amount of cotton required of them. Three men were so badly whipped that they became sick and had to lay up for a few days, and while they were unable to work they laid their plans to get away if the warden didn't treat them better. These three men were all white men and they were almost worked to death. They were sick and very weak and had worked hard all day, and when the last [sack] was weighed up they fell short of the amount that they had to have. They knew that they would get a whipping, so they made a break to get away. One of them had run only a few yards when he was shot down and died in a very few minutes. Then one of the other two was shot down, although he recovered from his wounds; and the other one had run about one-half mile and got into a boggy swamp and was so weak he could not get out. His strength had failed him and was brought back to camp and was beaten almost to death; and several others who had fallen short of their parts were also whipped.

## CHAPTER XI

### Convict Captures Guard

This guard had been having men whipped every day and having them whipped for nothing, and there was one man in the crew that the guard would trust more than any of the rest. He would have this man to bring him water now and then. This man made up his mind that he would spring on to the guard and take his gun off of him the next time he carried water to him, and so he did. The guard told this man to bring him a drink about 3 o'clock in the afternoon, and the convict did as he was ordered to do, and when the guard raised the cup to his mouth the convict sprang upon him, grabbing the guard around the waist and then he got hold of the pistol that was in the scabbard, told the guard to drop his shotgun, and the guard dropped the gun like it was hot. Then the convict picked it up, then ordered the guard to pull off his belt and the guard did so at once. Then the convict buckled it on. By this time some of the other convicts were making preparations to run, but the convict that had the gun told them to be seated for a while. He had not told any of the convicts that he was going to capture the guards, as this was all his trick, and after he had made all the convicts sit down he told them that they would all go together, and said that he would kill the first man that disobeyed his orders. They obeyed him and he said to the guard, "Pull off your clothes, old chap, I am going to swap you a suit of clothes that you ought to have had long ago." The guard told him this was all the good suit of clothes he had, and the convict said that his suit of stripes were all that he had and that was the reason that he was going to swap them off. "Get off the clothes, and do it quick," came from the convict. "I am going to be warden, guard and Governor, also," and the guard began to pull off his clothes, and then the convict stepped back a few feet and began to undress himself. The convict didn't have on any underwear. The convict piled all his clothes that he had pulled off, shoes, hat and all together, then told the guard to pull off his underwear, shoes, hat and everything. Then the convict told the guard to change places with him, and then the guard walked over to the pile of convict clothes. While the convict pulled on the guard's clothes the guard was about four inches taller than the convict, and when the guard had dressed himself in the stripes he found his pants about two inches above his shoe tops, and the shoes were too large for him, as the convict has taken his socks. Then the guard picked up the old flopped hat and stood holding it in his hand and was nearly ready to cry. The convict told him to put on the hat and the guard put it on and it dropped down over his ears. Most of the crown was gone and his hair would stick up through the hole, and then the convict told him that he was dressed up to his notion, and when the convict was done dressing in the guard's clothing he was looking good. All this time the rest of the convicts were having some sport laughing at the guard. The convict happened to run his hand into his pockets, found the guard's pocketbook with a few dollars in it and then he found a watch in the pocket. It was a cheap watch. The convict threw the pocketbook and watch over to the guard. This was a surprise to him, as he expected the convict to keep his money and watch, but he would not keep a penny, and when the guard put his money in his pocket he found that the bottoms were out of both pockets, and he had to carry his money and watch in his hand. Now they are ready to start, and the convict stands up and tells the boys to line up, and they do so at once, and until now the guard had not thought of having to go with them, and when the man with the gun told him to line up he became excited. The gun man told him to line up and keep quiet if he didn't want some trouble, and the guard lined up at once. It was only a short distance to the timber. They struck out and were soon in the bottoms, traveling at a rapid pace. They traveled this way until dark and then they were several miles from the convict farm. Then the man that carried the gun warned them that there was no one living near where they were. This guard had been awful mean to this crew of convicts, but the man that carried the gun would not allow any of them to abuse him, and after they had stopped the gun man told one of the convicts to go and get him a good hickory, and when he returned with it the warden, as he then called himself, asked the guard if he didn't think that he ought to give him a good whipping, and the guard said, "I don't know." Then the new warden asked him how he could tell when some one else needed a whipping. Again he said he didn't know. "Well," the new warden said to the guard, "I am going to whip you, not because I wish to but because I just want to teach you a lesson that you will never forget." And the guard began to beg and tell how badly he hated that he had caused them to be whipped. "Well, we hear all that you say, but you won't know how to sympathize with us until after I have whipped you. I have a good cause for whipping you," he said, "and you never had any cause for having any of these men whipped." The guard said, "I had to do that to please the warden. If I didn't have some one whipped I would lose my job." "Well, don't you think you have lost your job?" "Well, I guess I have," said he. "I am going to fix you so that you will not want to guard any more convicts. Get your clothes down." Then he began to beg the new warden not to whip him. He offered him all his money, watch and both his guns. "No, no; I don't want your money, watch or guns; I just want to make a man of you. It is all for your good. Get down your pants, and, remember, that you have had me to pull down them same old pants; come on, get down with them pants. Get hold of him, two of you, and get him in shape." Then two negroes took his pants down and held him in proper style while the new warden whipped him. They then let him up. Then the gun man acted as Governor. He told all the convicts that he would grant them all a pardon except the man that he had just whipped. There were twenty of them. He told them to scatter out and travel all they could and stay in the woods. Then he and two other men took the guard and traveled all night, also the next day, through the mountains. Awhile after dark he told him that he would take the pistol and cartridges and would give him the gun. The guard then made the convict a present of the pistol. Then taking his shotgun, started back to the farm that was several miles away. These three men were never recaptured, but some of the rest were and I hope that was a good lesson to the guard, as they treated him much nicer than they had been treated. When the guard had returned to the farm he found everything in great confusion; the blood hounds had lost the trail of the missing convicts, and when the guard arrived with his suit of stripes on the warden and other guards had some fun out of him. He told his story and they listened with great interest. He told the warden that he was through guarding convicts. He said that he had learned a good lesson. All guards and wardens ought to have the same lesson.

### In the Water All Day

When the water is over the farms the convicts are driven into the water and kept there all day long floating logs, and when the weather is a little cool they almost freeze. Sick men are driven in the same as the well men. An old man told me one day that thirty men had been floating logs all day. Some of these men were sick. These were called out of the water and whipped with the leather during the day and that night one of them died; the other two died the next day. Sometimes this kind of work is continued for five or six days, and in such cases several men die afterwards, but the warden does not care how many men die, neither does he care what camp he dies out of. It almost breaks the warden's heart to see a man get a pardon. I think the warden had rather see the men die than be set free.

### Too Good for a Damned Convict

One Sunday afternoon a trusty [sic] had gone to fish for trout awhile. He had fine luck and caught three trout, one of them weighing five pounds and the other two one pound each. He sold the large one to three of the convicts for fifty cents, and just then the warden stepped up and asked, "Let me see that fish. Who does it belong to?" And the trusty told the warden that he had sold it to three of the convicts for fifty cents and that it was all the money they had, and the warden then said, "I guess I will eat this fish. It is too good for a damned convict," and the trusty gave the fifty cents back to the three men who had bought the fish, but the warden didn't pay the trusty anything for the fish and the three convicts that had bought it were disappointed; they would have given three dollars for the fish if they had had the money. Two of these poor men were so hungry and hated to give up so bad that they sat down and cried. Then the trusty that had caught the fish gave the two little ones to the three men that had first bought the big one and they paid him twenty-five cents for them, but they were so disappointed for having lost the big fish that the trusty said that he would run back to the river and set out his hook and try to catch a cat fish. He had more good luck, caught a fine fish, dressed it and cooked it and he and the other boys ate it before the warden knew anything about it. Reader, what is your opinion of that warden that took the fish? Here is my opinion: He will lie, he will steal anything that he can get his hands on when there is no bravery required. He will do anything that is dirty and cowardly.

### One Man Gets One Hundred Licks

This man was whipped several days in succession and today the warden hits him one hundred licks. One of the negroes that helps to hold him counted the licks (the warden told him to count and that he was going to give him all that he could stand), and so he did. This man was not able to stand up for some time after the warden got through with him. This man was very slow and could not do quite as much work as some of the rest of the crew. For that reason he was whipped often and unmercifully. Several more men are whipped because they are sick. The man that received one hundred licks gets a pardon just in a few days after he was whipped.

### Convicts Eat Cow's Head

The warden had the trusties kill a beef cow one day, although the convicts did not get any beef, and the next day after a convict asked where the cow's head was the trusty told him that it was in the lot where the cow had been butchered, and the convict asked the trusty if he would bring it to him and the trusty said that he would if he could. The trusty brought it to him, and this starving man and two or three others cut the hide off the head and then salted it and baked it on an old heating stove and after it was cooked the best that they could cook it they picked every morsel of meat from that head and ate it and said it was good, but they didn't have any bread to eat with it, and when they were through with that old head there was nothing left except the horns, teeth and bones. Reader, do you think that these men were hungry? I have known the convicts to buy corn from the trusties and make hominy at night and on Sundays they would make the hominy in a tin bucket. They would pay a trusty ten cents for one-half gallon of shelled corn, and one day a negro reported to the warden that some of the boys had been cooking corn and the warden then whipped all concerned in it. That night after supper when they were locked in the bunk house one of the boys that had been whipped knocked the negro down with a stick of wood and came near killing him, and while this man was clubbing the negro another negro ran up to interfere and then another white man landed on him with a zinc bucket about half full of water, knocking the negro down and cutting his face badly. The white man kicked the negro several times. Both negroes were gloriously whipped. I have no objections to that kind of whipping. While the fight was in progress the guards were running around yelling like they were scared half to death. Some of the convicts were scared badly. Some of the sick and crippled men were run over and trampled down. One poor old sick cripple was lying on his bunk and was not able to get off.

## Part I. Story of the Arkansas Penitentiary, William N. Hill

Several men had run over him and had stepped on him several times. The old man raised up on his elbow and said he would kill the next man that run over him and all that heard the old man had to laugh a little. Then the old man said, "Laugh if you want to. If you don't believe that I will kill you just run over me if you dare," and the old man's will power was good, but he could not stand on his feet ten seconds if it would have saved his life. Then the fight was over for the night and the next morning the guard reported to the warden and the four men that were in the fight were called out and the warden whipped the two white men but didn't whip the negroes, and that night when all was locked in the bunk house again the two white men got hold of a stick of wood and got in after the negroes and they chased them over the house several times. Finally one of the white men threw his stick of wood at one of the negroes and knocked him down, then jumped on him and beat him as long as he wanted to, and the other white man stands by to keep any one from interfering, and when they were through with this negro they both got after the other one and were not long in tumbling him up; then the other white man got his money's worth as these negroes were not able to work for several days. While the fight was going on the guard had sent for the warden, but the fight was over when the warden arrived. He cursed and blowed about what he would do and told the white men that he would beat them to death if they jumped on the negroes any more, and one of the convicts said to him, "Do your worst, sir, when you like it, as you have the power, and can take the authority to kill us the same as you do to kill other convicts, and if you whip us for what we have done I will kill both of them negroes." "You will not," said the other white convict, "for I will kill one of them myself," and the other said, "If you whip us for this, don't lock us in this house with those two negroes. I don't want to kill a convict, but those negroes have treated us bad and ought to be killed. I don't want to kill any one, but if you whip us we will kill the negroes if you do not keep them away from us. I was hungry when I cooked the cow and I am hungry now. We are all hungry," he added. "If you would feed us this trouble would not have occurred and you are to blame for it all. Now, Mr Warden, I will tell you just a little more. If I had eight more men like my partner I would turn this entire camp loose and I would take you and all your guards with me and I believe that I could find that many good men in this camp if I could convince them that it could be done." By this time the warden was getting hot. He was cursing the convict, calling him all kinds of a s—of a b—, and the poor convict hated to hear the warden curse him in that way but he had no way of helping himself. Then the warden leaves the stockade for the night, and next morning when he returned to the stockade he didn't say anything about whipping the two men, although he whipped them several times in the next few days, never telling them what he was whipping them for, though he acted prudent and sent the two negroes to another camp, which was only a few miles away, and swapped them for two more negroes. The two white men were good, straight men, and they got into some trouble with some negroes while drinking and killed a pair of saucy negroes and were serving a three-years' sentence.

A message came to the warden: "Bring in all the men that you can spare. We want them for the railroad and brick yard." This message came from the walls and when we arrived at the walls we found the hospital and the yard full of sick men. Sick men from every camp. They had many sad stories to tell. The boys were glad to meet each other, and on making inquiry for those we did not see they found that many of them had died. It was there that I saw more sick men and starving men than I had ever seen before, and all of them that had as much as five cents were looking for a trusty to send out for something to eat. I have seen men sell the shoes off their feet for one-fourth their value to get money to buy a little something to eat. I have also seen them sell the last hat they had and all the underwear that they had just for anything that they could get for them, and then send it out for something to eat, and then after they had eaten they were then without money, shoes, hat or clothes, but when a man is starving he will give all that he can get for a little something to eat. The work still moves on at the Statehouse and the State gives more money, and the poor convicts give their lives.

Every bunk in the hospital is full and more sick men on the yard than there are in the hospital. They are just laying down wherever they can get a chance, and now and then a man will have to be picked up from the yard and carried into the building. Men are dying fast. Supper-time has come; I am sure hungry. We have corn bread, fat meat and sorghum molasses, and that is a fine supper to what they have on the farm and railroad. Supper is over; some one is whipped; I don't know what he had done; I guess he had a little more fever than the warden wanted him to have. Now the gong taps nine and our light is turned off. For a while I lay on my bunk, listening to the moans of the sick men in the hospital. A negro is dying and he is happy. He shouts praises to his blessed Savior and says that he can see his Savior and hear Him calling for him. Now, the negro says he will soon be gone. He said that he was going to heaven. Just then the night guard stepped up to the dying negro's bunk and asked him where it was that he was going. The poor negro told the guard that he was going to heaven. The guard says, "No; you are going to hell," and the man then said that he could see Jesus. "No; that is the devil you see," said the guard. "Stop that damned racket, or I will let you see the warden." The negro said, "I have seen—I have seen the warden for the last time. The warden has done all for me that he can do. He has worked, starved and beat me to death, and now I will soon be gone. Over there I will find rest." Then he began to shout, though his voice was very weak. All this time the guard was cursing him and trying to make him hush, but the dying man did not listen to the guard. He shouted and sang as long as he could speak. In less than three hours the negro was dead. I hope that he found rest and I am sure that he did. I wish all persons that don't believe that a negro has a soul could have heard the dying words of this poor negro. Reader, I don't mean to say that I wish all the disbelievers had been convicts and had been in the penitentiary at that time. I just mean to say that I wish these people could have the same evidence that I have that the negro has a soul. Well, reader, what do you think of that guard? Do you think that he has a soul? Here is what I think of him: I am sure that he once had a soul, but that he had lost it, as he always looked just like he had lost something and looked just like he wanted to steal something. One day a friend of his says to him, "You look like you would like to have a drink of whiskey." "I am sure that I do, for I never deceive my looks." Now, if that is true that man will steal just as certain as you live, because he always looked just like he wanted to steal, although all convict guards look that way. Well, this is Saturday. We will send out for something to eat today. Breakfast is over. Jim Scroy said the warden whipped him just for luck. There were several more men whipped during the day. Well, I send for twenty-five cents worth of steak, twenty-five cents worth of pork chops and twenty-five cents worth of onions. I am going to fill up.

Once more the gong taps and more convicts arrive sick—men from the railroad. One wounded man. This man had tried to escape and was shot down and died in a few days. He told me that he had worked all that he could and that the warden whipped him almost every day. Then he lost his health, but said that he worked every day. He said that he could see that he didn't have but a short time to live, if he had to stay there and be treated as he was. He said that men were dying fast for the lack of food and were beaten to death: When a man dies they just dig a hole and roll him in it, then cover him up; they do not place him in a box. That is the way the convict is treated on the railroad. Now, what do you think of it, reader? Don't you think it your duty and the duty of all good men to do something that will bring relief to these poor, suffering souls? I trust that this book will prompt you to action. Investigate this matter; see that I am telling you the truth. Hundreds of men will testify to what I have said. Follow the advice that I will offer before I close and your minds will be satisfied that I have spoken the truth. You will also find that the half has never yet been told. Many things you will find to be worse than I tell you in this book. Think well of all that I have here said, and follow the bidding of our blessed Redeemer, and we will adjust this matter. We can for it is easy. All that are not willing to assist in this good work should leave the State to never return.

## CHAPTER XII

A man from Logan County, Arkansas, was convicted for murder and was sent to the penitentiary. I do not remember the length of his sentence. I think that this man had served about one year of his time. He was a young man, in perfect health when he entered the pen, but his health soon gave way on account of hard work, and being whipped so often and with so little to eat. He was also exposed to all kinds of bad weather. It never gets too hot nor too cold to work in the penitentiary. On account of exposure this man had taken pneumonia. While he was sick his wife came to see him and this lady also brought with her a strong petition to the Governor asking him to pardon her husband. For some reason the Governor refused to grant him pardon at that time, but I think that he promised to pardon him in the near future. When this lady arrived in the city of Little Rock she came to the penitentiary to see her husband. Poor lady. Her heart was almost broken when she saw the pale, thin face of her husband. The sick man was almost overjoyed to meet his wife, and he tried to be cheerful. After his wife had spent a few moments with him she then called to see the Governor, feeling sure that she would return to her husband in a short time with a pardon for him, but in this she was disappointed, as the poor sick man was also disappointed, for when she returned to her husband she was almost heartbroken, but tried to be cheerful. She tried to comfort him by telling him that the Governor had promised to pardon him soon. After spending an hour or more with her husband she then had to leave. This was hard to do, she said, to leave her sick husband, and no one to speak a comforting word to him. He was left to suffer and die all alone. They wept and then they said goodbye to each other, hoping to see each other again soon. As she walked down the isle to the door his eyes followed after her until she had passed from the building. Then the poor dying man turned himself over and wept. They never met again. Poor man, he died with a broken heart. Some time after his wife had gone I talked with him and he told me that he did not think that he would get well. I tried to cheer him all that I could, and the next day I talked with him again, and I could see that he was growing weaker. Poor fellow, he talked a great deal about his wife and family, and didn't have any hopes of ever seeing them any more. It was this thought that grieved him so. He continued to get worse, and in a few days he died.

I hope this poor man was prepared to die, and I trust that some day he will be reunited with his loved ones in a better world where all is peace and love, and this thought should be a comforting one to us all, and should our pathway in this life be a rugged one and should we, from any cause, have to depart from those we so dearly love, we should live in a manner that we will all be reunited around that bountiful throne of God, there to dwell in peace and love forever.

PART I. STORY OF THE ARKANSAS PENITENTIARY, WILLIAM N. HILL

## A Sad Story of Three Convicts

These three men had been brought in from the railroad. They were sick and starved and told me how they had to work in the rain and snow with only one suit of thin cotton stripes on and no underwear at all, with their shoes so badly worn they could hardly keep them on their feet. They told me that often their clothes would be wet and would freeze stiff on them and they would have to lay down at night with these wet frozen clothes on with but little bedding and would have to lay all night shivering and freeze and many of them sick also, and then in the morning, when they would be turned out for breakfast they would get a piece of frozen bread and meat and sometimes a cup of black coffee, the cheapest that could be bought, and then when breakfast was over they were driven off to work, and many times, on account of the feebleness of some of the crew, they would be thrown down and whipped before they had left camp, and they had known men to die in less than twenty-four hours after they had been taken off of the works. They would have no medical attention except a few drugs that the warden would have. He would then appoint some one of the trusties to prescribe for the dying man and then the trusty would take a gun and guard them until they had died. Then they would dig a hole, throw them in and cover them up; and then when the crew had run down so low that the warden would have to have more men, he would go back to Little Rock after them to kill, and if some of his crew were so near dead that they were unable to work the warden would take them to the hospital. This he was supposed to do with all sick men, although this law is violated just as all the rest of the laws are that govern the State penitentiary. While I was in conversation with these three men I asked them if they had any money. They told me that they had not, and had not had any for several months. Then I asked if they had any people, and each of them said that they had, but they said they could not hear from them. While they were on the railroad they had written home for money, but had failed to get it, and they said if their people could get their letters they knew that they would have sent them some money. Then I asked if they had written since they had been back at the walls and they said that was the first thing they did after they had got money to buy postage. One of them had swapped hats with another man and got ten cents in the trade, although there was one dollar and fifty cents deserving. They said that they were so near starved that they could eat most anything, and I told them that I would send out and get something for supper for them. For this little act of kindness they were so overjoyed that they clasped their hands together, thanking me and crying, all of them. I found a trusty and gave him one dollar and told him to bring me fifty cents worth of round steak and fifty cents worth of onions. I had half the steak cooked for supper and the other half for breakfast. Two of these men could have eaten the fifty cents worth of steak for supper, but I didn't want them to overeat themselves, as they were already sick. I gave each of them two large onions for their supper. These men ate faster than I ever saw any one eat and they told me that they enjoyed that meal better than any that they had ever had. Next morning I gave them two more onions for breakfast and then we ate the balance of our steak. After this meal was over one of them told me that he did not sleep but little the night before. He said he was thinking of the steak that he would have for breakfast. After breakfast was over I took the onion that was left and gave each of them an equal portion with myself. Under ordinary circumstances each of us would have had plenty of onions to last us a week, but those starving men would eat their onions as if they were apples, and they told me that they would pay back to me all that I was out for them just as soon as they could get some money from home. Several days had passed before they got any hearing from home. At last each of them had gotten a letter from home, also each one of them had gotten some money and each one paid me his part that I had spent for him, and after I had fed those fellows for supper and breakfast they told me that they felt better and had more life in them than they had had for several months. They also told me their troubles and how they came to get into trouble, and like thousands of others they had gotten into trouble while drunk. That is the time to find it, my dear reader. Get drunk and you can find trouble most anywhere. Keep sober, dear friends, and help me to say something and to do something that will help the many suffering and dying souls that have wrecked and ruined their lives and lost their honor, all on account of this damnable whiskey.

Arkansas is getting a big and grand State building, and this thing has cost many men their lives and will cost many more the same before it will or can be completed. Every day men are beaten unmercifully just because they are sick and not able to work. Five men are taken to the hospital after two of these are whipped. One of these died. This poor fellow told me that he had been beaten so often that it had caused him to get sick, and he said that he had two more years to serve and it would be impossible for him to live and be treated as he had been. He showed me where he had been whipped. There were pieces of skin bursted [sic] loose on him two inches wide and three or four inches long. The skin was nearly ready to fall off, and this place looked as if it had been burned with a hot iron and was inflamed and badly swollen. After a few days of suffering the poor man passed away, and before he died he told me that he had a mother, one brother and three sisters, but none of them knew where he was, and he refused to tell me his real name. He said that he did not want his people to know where he was. He said that it would grieve them more to see him die in the penitentiary than it would to never know where he was. He told me how he had been starved and whipped, and this was the cause of his death—worked, starved to death while working on the Statehouse.

## CHAPTER XIII

Well, this is Sunday. I hear the gong tap, and visitors are coming. We are always glad to see them come. These are young men and women, and they have a basket of apples and oranges. One of the young men carried a basket and two of the ladies handed them to the convicts. They are very kind to us, and after the apples and oranges have been distributed among the boys the warden calls out the musician and entertained them for a while. Then they leave us. More convicts arrive from the brick yard—all of them sick and unable to work. Three of them die in a few days after they are brought to the hospital, and these men have been making brick for the Statehouse and they told me how they had been treated. Told me that the hide was whipped off of them. They took sick and began to fail. The warden would whip and curse them, and as long as they would be able to stand they would have to work and then when they could no longer stand they would be brought back to the hospital [to] die. One of these men told me that he was prepared to die. He said that he was not guilty of what he was sentenced for. He said that it was hard to have to serve a term in the penitentiary for something that you are not guilty of, and be starved and whipped to death, but it will all soon be over, he said. "I am going home to my mother in heaven. I promised that I would meet her in heaven and I am going to do so. All the time that he was talking he was happy, and the next day the poor fellow passed from the penitentiary to heaven to join his dear old mother. Two of the other men that were brought to the hospital at the same time this one was died also, although I did not get to talk with them any.

### Big Line-Up for the Railroad

Several more men are now on their way to meet their doom. Poor fellows, if they could fully realize just what was in store for them they would have revolted. Many of them were sure that they would never return, and it was clear to the minds of many that the grave would soon be their home somewhere along the Rock Island road. These poor fellows do not mind the work, although each man has to do at least two men's work, but the whipping and starving is what kills them; also exposure to all kinds of weather, as they often have to sleep with their wet and muddy and frozen clothes on all through the winter.

### A Man is Whipped and Then Dies

This man had been sick for several days and had been whipped several times one day, and when he was no longer able to go he fell down on the ground and then the warden called to him, telling the poor fellow to come out and he would put new life in him. The sick man was unable to walk. He tried to work but sank back to the ground and then the warden walked up to him, cursing and telling him to get down his clothes. The poor man was not able to do this, and then the warden hit him on the head with the leather and then called on a negro to come and take down the sick man's clothes. Then when the sick man's clothes had been removed the negro held the dying man in position for the warden to whip him. The poor fellow could not have gotten up from the ground had the negro not been holding him. After the warden had beaten him almost to death, he told him to get up. The poor man tried to raise up but was too weak. This poor man was never whipped any more. He was carried to the hospital and in a few days died.

### White Convict Kills a Negro Convict

As I have before stated, some of the negroes caused many of the white men to be whipped, but this does not excuse the warden, for I am sure he does not believe but little that is told him by these lying negroes, but he will whip the man that is reported. Now, with reference to the killing, as mentioned, this man was working on the railroad. The white man was an experienced hand at track work. The negro that was killed was also familiar with this kind of work and the warden had appointed this negro to boss over the balance of the crew, and his job made a fool of him, and it cost him his life. The white man knew more about railroad work than the negro and for that reason the negro was afraid the white man would get his job. The negro began to make trouble for the white man. He would curse and order him around as if the white man was a negro and he the warden. The negro wanted to get the white man whipped, and that was easy for him to do. After he had accomplished this purpose he still continued to curse the white man and the white man put up with this abuse for some time, telling the negro to let him alone. The negro did not care for that kind of talk, and again giving orders to the white man, cursing and calling him a s—of a b—, the white man was in a few feet of the negro and had a spade in his hand, and with one blow split the negro's head with the spade, killing him instantly. That is the fruits of working white men and negroes together. Although the negro got just what he needed, the warden was to blame for this. The white man that did the killing was an old, gray-headed man. After killing the negro the old man lost his health and had to be brought to the hospital. There I talked with him several times, and he told me of several sad and horrible things that had happened in the convict works on the railroad.

### Death of Carl Sanders

Carl was convicted at Van Buren. He was a jolly good fellow, and was worked hard, whipped often and starved all the time, and after having this kind of treatment for some time he lost his health, which is always the case with all men. Carl was brought to the hospital. For several days he laid there and it was there that I first met him. He was in a bad condition, although after a time he began to improve slowly. I talked with him every day as long as he was in the hospital, and although he was discharged from there long before he should have been, for a few days after he had been discharged he lingered on the yard with several others that were convalescent, although they should have been in the hospital. One day Carl told me that if he was carried out on any of the works in the condition that he was in he would be sure to die. At that time a big line-up for the farm was expected every day and in a few days the warden from the farm was up after some men to kill. Poor Carl, he was lined up with many more to be taken to the farm, there to spend the rest of his days. This was late in the afternoon, and when the warden had selected his men to take to the farm they were not to start to the farm until the next day. Carl came in to see me. He told me that he would have to go to the farm the next day, and said that he would not live long and that it would be impossible for him to work, he was so weak. He was not more than able to stand, as his fever was not yet broken up. He said if he could have remained in the hospital a few days longer he would have some hopes, though as it is, he said that he had no hopes of living but a few days, and yet he tried to be cheerful, yet it was clear to my mind that all his hopes of ever returning to his home and friends had gone. He told me of many things that he would like for his friends to know and he told me things to tell them if I should ever meet them. He had one special friend that he was interested in and told me many things to tell her if I should ever meet her, but I have never been able to meet any of his friends that he spoke of. Next day, just before they were to start, Carl came in to see me to bid me goodbye. He took my hand and then said: "This will be our last farewell. There are only a few more days for me; then all will be over. Don't forget me. Think of what I have told you. Deliver my message if you have a chance." I assured him that I would do all this for him if it ever was in my power to do so, and then we said goodbye to each other, and with feeble steps he walked away, and in a few days he was reported dead. I was only acquainted with this man a short time. He told me a portion of his past life. He said that he had done many things that he should not have done, and said that he was sorry for all the bad that he had done. He told me that he had drank whiskey and while drinking got into trouble. Think, dear reader, what whiskey has done for this poor man. It sent him to the penitentiary, there to be worked, starved and beaten to death. There no friends are gathered 'round you to comfort you in your dying hours, and no one there to weep for you. You are left alone to die. Think of all this, boys, and, if you drink, cut it out now, for whiskey often makes criminals of good men. Take my advice and let it alone.

### A Convict Refuses to be Whipped

This man had been whipped several times, and each time for nothing. His crew was on the railroad and the warden had appointed a negro as straw boss and the negro wanted to be like all mean negroes. Wanted to curse some white man and cause some white man to be whipped. This white man was a good fellow. Did all the work that he could possibly do, but the negro would lie to the warden and then he would whip the white man. The white man had been whipped several times, and the guard, not knowing the cause, made some inquiry, he being a new man on the job, as to what the man was being whipped for. The warden told the guard that it was because the man was not working. The guard told the warden that he had not seen the man playing off at any time, and that afternoon the negro reported to the warden again, and the warden cursed the white man, telling him to come out and get down his pants damned quick, "I am going to beat the hell out of you." The white man told the warden that he would not take any more whippings, that the negro had been lying, and that he had done all the work that he could do, and said that he would not be whipped any more for nothing. He told the warden that he could kill him, but could not whip him. The warden told two negroes to bring him out. The man drew his spade and told them that he would kill the first one of them that got in reach of him. The warden then drew his pistol, told the man to drop his spade. The man said that he would not do it. Just then the guard threw his gun on the negroes and told them to stop or he would kill them. He also told the warden that he could not whip the man, as he had whipped him several times for nothing, and could not do so any more. The guard told the warden that the negro had been lying to him and that he did not intend for the man to be whipped any more. This made the warden a little hot, but he was up against the real thing, and the guard said that he didn't want any trouble, but said that he would shoot the first man that touched the white convict. This guard was a gentleman, and he lost his job as a good man could not hold a job as guard under any of the old wardens prior to 1904. This poor white man would have been killed had it not been for this guard, as he had made up his mind to die rather than be whipped any more on account of that negro's lying on him. Although this poor man was badly treated after this occurrence, the last time that I heard of him his health had given away. He had been beaten and starved until he was almost gone. He was a good man and only had a short sentence, though I fear that he didn't live out his sentence.

### Drummer Gives Lecture to Convicts

It was Sunday afternoon, a bright Sabbath day. It was a day of rest for the poor slaves. We were lounging here and there on the penitentiary yards. Some seemed to be in deep meditation; some were planning for the future, discussing among themselves what course they would pursue, while many others that were so near dead and hopes all gone, sat with their faces buried in their hands. They were more dead than alive—no hopes for the future; their fate was sure. We were informed by the building tender that some one would deliver a lecture to us in the afternoon. This was a treat to us. Then the gong sounded and the warden and a gentleman of middle age, very handsome and neatly dressed, passed through the entrance and walked up to the dining room where arrangements had been made for the lecture. The warden accompanied this gentleman to the dining room where we were anxiously awaiting the stranger to come. Then the warden, without offering any introduction of any kind, left the stranger in the midst of this assemblage, passed into an adjoining room, closing the door after him, then seated himself upon an easy chair to listen to what was said, although he felt himself too grand to remain in the same room with the convicts, although if he had remained with us he could not have heard this talk without turning his back to the speaker. He could not have held his head up. After the warden had left the stranger in our midst for a moment he glanced about the room, then he looked into the faces of more than three hundred men and all eyes were fixed upon the speaker. Every mark of sympathy and love and every mark of honesty and intelligence was plain to be seen on his countenance, and his preliminaries were lengthy though pleasant. Every expression was one of sympathy and regret. He then introduced himself in a pleasant manner, also stated his purpose in visiting us. Then prayer, and then a song; title of the song; "What a Friend We Have in Jesus." All were invited to sing. The music was grand. I think more than two hundred voices could be heard singing that good old song. Some voices rang out loud and clear, while others were weak and trembling, though all in perfect unison, and no discord to be heard. Never before or since have I heard that song executed with greater spirit than it was on that day. We listened to one of the most pleasant talks that I ever heard. This man was a Christian. All of his advice was good. "Don't forget to pray," he said. "Prison walls were never built so strong that the earnest, fervent prayer of the poor convict could not penetrate, and God will hear your pleadings for mercy." Every one listened with great attention. Before closing his remarks he invited all to join him in singing "Nearer My God to Thee." Then he said, "while we sing this good song, all that love God and will trust in Him, come give me your hand." Then while all parts of the grand old song was being executed every man in the building shook the hand of this Christian man. Myself and two companions led the way, then all followed. Not many dry eyes could be found among that line-up, and I have seen many line-ups for the farm, railroad, brickyard and other places, but that is the first time that I ever saw the whole trick lined up for one piece of work; no guards, no warden were used in this work; all that was needed for this line-up was a kind-hearted gentleman. That is the kind of men we want to run the penitentiary. The lecture was grand. This man was a traveling salesman for some wholesale grocery house; I do not remember his name. When the lecture was over he then bid us all goodbye, with best wishes, and he and the warden left us. The warden seemed to be looking for something on the ground, but he will never find what he was looking for, as he was looking for a clear conscience, and I am sure he will never have it.

## A Sick Man Surprised

A man by the name of Adcock, who had only been in the penitentiary a few weeks, got a pardon on Christmas. There were several pardons granted at the same time. This was one of Governor Davis' Christmas treats. The Governor could not have done anything that would have been more honorable, unless he had granted more pardons. This man Adcock was working at the rock crusher and by some means his pardon had been misplaced. I had gotten acquainted with this man on his arrival at the penitentiary. I gave this man a little advice as to what to do and what to expect. This advice I often gave to new men when I could see that they were so badly in need of it. A few days after Christmas Mr. Adcock was taken very sick and was brought to the hospital. The next day, while I was passing through the hospital, he called to me and I stopped by his bunk and talked with him. At first I did not recognize him. Then he called my attention to the advice which I had given him and which he found to be good. This old man had worked hard with nothing to eat. He was badly out of heart. I happened to think of the list of Christmas pardons and remembered that Adcock was one of the number that had been pardoned. I called his attention to it, for he had not seen the list of those that were pardoned. I told him that his name was among those that were pardoned. He could not understand why he had not been released. Of course I was not able to tell him the reason why he had not been. Then he seemed to think that I was mistaken about his name being on the list, and I told him that I could cite him, as I had a list of all those pardoned, and I have got them today, and then I went to my cell and got the list, took it and showed it to him; then he began to get a little better. He wanted to know how he could find out about this matter; I told him that I would find out for him. I took the list of pardons, went to the warden and showed him the list of names and then I asked him why Mr. Adcock had not been released. "I suppose he has been," said he. Then I told him to go with me and I would show Mr. Adcock to him. We walked into the hospital and I pointed him out and the warden talked with him for a few moments and then got up, left the hospital and did not give any explanation as to what he thought of it. After a few minutes the warden returned to the hospital with the pardon. This poor old man was one of the happiest men that I ever saw. The warden told him that the pardon had been lost. The next day this old man left for home, although he was very sick. I had a letter from him one month after he had returned home, and he had just recovered from his illness. Had it not been for me this poor man might have died in the penitentiary, and if not, he would have been kept to serve out his time.

## A Man Gets Killed Trying to Get Away

This man was on the railroad. He jumped from a hand-car and was shot in the back and died in a few days. This was a boy eighteen or nineteen years of age. I talked with this boy and he told me how he had been treated.

## PART I. STORY OF THE ARKANSAS PENITENTIARY, WILLIAM N. HILL

He said that he was worked as long as he could stand up and whipped nearly every day, and was starving for something to eat. It had been only a short time since he was in the hospital and he was sick when he was taken to the railroad, and when his health was failing him the second time he said he had no hopes of recovering, as the treatment was so terrible, and he said it would be impossible for him to live. For that reason he tried to make his escape and was killed. He was too weak to run very fast. This dying boy told me that he had seen men whipped one day and buried the next. After this boy was shot and brought to the hospital I heard him say to one of the hospital stewards that he was going to die. He said that he was starving for something to eat. I had heard the doctor say that it was sure that the boy could not get well, and when I heard him beg for something to eat I fed him the best that I could get, but very little at a time. Poor boy; I will never forget him, and how much pleased he was when I would feed him. He only lived a few days after he was shot. Now, reader, do you think that I should remain silent on this matter any longer? No; I am sure that you do not. This work should have been done many years ago. Line up, good people. Say that justice shall be meted out to all, for this is God's will. See that the convicts are fed. See that they are worked in the bounds of reason, and see that they are whipped only as they need it, and then as the law of our country provides. See that they are treated kindly, and then the whip will not be in demand, and men will repent and return to their homes in good health and with a resolution to be good citizens. [As the] matter is conducted at present, a man is lucky to come out alive. In most cases his health is so impaired he doesn't often regain it; he is generally an invalid for life.

### A White Girl Gets a Pardon

This girl was eighteen years of age, serving a term of one year in the penitentiary. In the penitentiary all women are carried to the farm shortly after their arrival. While they are kept at the walls they are kept locked in their cells until there is a line-up for the farm. This girl had been in the penitentiary some three or four weeks and all this time kept at the walls, as there had been no line-up for the farm; and while she was there this girl was kept locked in a cell just a few feet from the hospital. It is a strict violation of the rules for a man to speak to any woman prisoner. There are two men appointed to wait on the sick. One of them is on duty during the day and the other at night. The one that was on duty at night at that time was a young man who was just finishing a three-year sentence, and he became deeply in love with this girl, and she loved him, and they began to correspond on the sly, and now and then they would have a little chat and were not long in coming to a conclusion and they agreed to marry as soon as they were free. This young man only lacked about one month having his time served out, and she was just beginning on a one-year sentence, and the agreement was that he would meet her at Little Rock at the expiration of her sentence. He told me of their agreement, my cell being next door to the cell that the girl occupied. One day I asked her if any one was trying to get a pardon for her, and she said that she didn't have any one to help her, as she was the only child of a widowed mother and that her mother was old and very poor. Then I asked her why she didn't write the Governor a letter, asking him to pardon her, and she said that she could not compose a letter of that kind. I told her that Governor Davis was a good man and that he would consider all honest appeals made to him by any one. And then she asked me if I would write a letter to the Governor for her. I told her that if she would state all the facts in the case, and make an honest statement, then I would write a letter to the Governor. The poor girl made a confession to me, stating all the circumstances in the case. While making this statement to me she wept freely. She was young, very beautiful and intelligent. After asking her many questions relative to the charge for which she was convicted, I became familiar with the case, and that night I made an honest confession to the Governor, stating all the facts just as she had stated them to me, and then after a solemn promise that she had made to me that day as to what her future progress would be, I then appealed to the man of mercy for a pardon for this poor girl. The Governor quickly responded to this appeal, and the next morning I handed this letter to the girl and she read it and was pleased. She signed her name to the letter and sent it that day to the Governor, and on the following day the Governor pardoned her, and the pardon was brought to her on the same day that it was granted. This, I think, will add another diamond to the Governor's crown, and I hope that he has never found cause to regret this good act. I am glad to confess that I feel good for playing the little part that I played in helping this poor girl to get a pardon. The girl was free, her lover having one more month to serve in the penitentiary. She told him that she would return to Little Rock on the day that he would be discharged, and she made her promise good, and on the day that her lover was set free she stood at the big iron gate that had at one time shut out all the world to her, and on that day the same old gate would open unto her more than two such worlds as to her opinion; for they met and were married, and I am told that they are happy and highly respected. This is only a bit of the many good things that Governor Davis did for the poor convicts while he was Governor of the State of Arkansas.

### More Sick Men from the Brickyard

Five men were brought to the hospital and three of them died. These men had been making brick for the new State Capitol and had been in the penitentiary only a few weeks and when they came they were stout men and were in good health. They were sent out to the brickyard, and in a few weeks they had been worked, starved and whipped until they had lost their health, and were brought to the hospital to die. I talked to these men and they told me they had been kept out in the yard at the works as long as they could stand. They were whipped because they could not stand, and these were all young men, perhaps from twenty to thirty years of age, and one that died had a family, and he was aware that he was going to die. He spoke of his wife and little ones. He was very much grieved to know that he would never see his loved ones again. He said if he could only see them once more to tell them a few things that he would like for them to know, then he would be more willing to die. He said if the world could know just how the convicts were treated, surely something would be done to save men from being murdered as he and hundreds of others had been. He said that there would not be so many little orphans left in the world without home or friends. This poor man was heartbroken. He said that he was prepared to die, and hoped to meet his wife and babies in a better world. Two days after this conversation the poor man died. I hope this man may meet his wife and children that he so dearly loves, and dwell in love and peace forever. The other two men only lived a few days, then all of them were laid to rest in the lonely convict's grave, there to await the calling of the roll up yonder. Then all will rise and the righteous ones will shine, dressed in their robes of white, with palm leaves in their hands. Where shall the warden stand with the whip in his hand? —perhaps in the flames of a burning hell, forever.

## Men Work in Snow Until Their Feet are Frozen

Sick men from the railroad and rock crusher are brought to the hospital. These men had been driven out to work in the snow when their shoes were so bad they could hardly keep them on their feet. It was only a few of them that had hose to wear. They would stand all day in the snow and their feet would freeze, and often their hands also. I have seen them so lame with frozen feet they were almost unable to walk to their work, but they never got too lame to work, and then they are sure to be whipped because they are not able to go more. On account of the exposure, men are dying with pneumonia. I have seen men brought in from the farm, railroad and other places, with frozen hands and feet and with hide whipped off of them, with a bad case of pneumonia and starved almost to death. It is needless to say that when once in that condition they seldom, if ever, recover. Then when it is impossible for them to work they are carried to the hospital to spend the remaining few days of their life in the greatest suffering, and when their time on earth is ended and the death angels call them home they are then thrown into a crude box and laid to rest in a convict's graveyard, and that is the last tribute of respect shown the dead in the Arkansas penitentiary. Reader, can you see where any improvements are needed in this institution? If so, let us hear from you.

## A Story of an Ex-Convict

This man had served more than twenty years in the Arkansas penitentiary. He had gotten into trouble. I do not know the particulars of the case, but he killed a man and then gave himself up to the authorities and pleaded guilty to the charge, and was sentenced to the State penitentiary for life. He was then a young man, large and strong. This man had the reputation of being an honest man before and after his conviction. He was liked by all who were associated with him. This man was an old farmer and a renter. He had no money, and it is a well known fact that a man in this condition is looked upon as if he were a worthless article, and in most cases persons in that condition have but little show in the court, although the court officials are not to blame for this. Now, reader, I do not wish to impress upon your mind that I have any defense to offer for the old man under consideration. I only wish to say that I think the old man's sentence was too great, and if the old man had been able to employ sufficient counsel, the judge might have seen fit to impose only a short sentence instead of a lifetime sentence. I think this man was convicted about the year '79, and in the year 1900, the Governor who has done so much for the State, and the Governor that did so much for the poor suffering and starving convicts of Arkansas, it was he who granted a full and complete pardon for this old man after he had served so faithful for more than twenty years. For several years prior to his release from the penitentiary, his health and strength had failed him, and at the time that Governor Davis freed the poor man from this awful place of torture he was almost unable to work, although he had at one time been an awful strong man, and there is not one man in a hundred that can live twenty years in the Arkansas penitentiary. From one to three years in most all cases is sufficient to kill most any man. This man, when he was convicted, had a family, but while he was toiling his life away he lost his wife and children and he was then all alone in the world, although I am sure that he can find friends who will care for him the few years that he may have in this world. This old man was an object of pity. Several months after this old man had been set free he was permitted to give a lecture to the convicts on Sunday afternoon. I will never forget this old man, or the many sad stories that he related to us. He told how he conducted himself as a prisoner. "Love God," he said, "and trust His Holy Word, and he will carry you through." He told us to pray night and day and do no harm, and "He will set you free." He said after his family were gone, and his health had failed, he then prayed to God that he might be set free before he had to die, in order that he might tell his story to the outside world as to what the poor convicts had to put up with. Also he said that when the good Lord saw fit to call him from this old world, he wanted to be handed down to his grave by tender hands. When this old man was serving a lifetime sentence he said that God had impressed upon his mind that he would some day get his freedom, "and now," he said, "my prayers have been answered, and I will spend the rest of my life for Him who saved the world." While this poor man related the many sad recollections of his prison life, several times he was overcome by emotion and was forced to weep, and many others wept with him. He told how he had been whipped when he was sick and was doing all that he could. He told how he had been starved and what he was compelled to eat. The old man's story was heard with great appreciation, and each story related was perfectly true and familiar to all except those that had recently come to the penitentiary. He tried to comfort us by saying that we would get better treatment. He said that Governor Davis would do something for the convicts, and this was true, for Governor Davis did more for the convicts of the State than any Governor had done for them prior to his election as Governor, and if Governor Davis had been in possession of one-half the corruptness [sic] of the penitentiary it is my opinion that he would have pardoned every man in the penitentiary, if nothing short of that would have brought relief to these poor suffering convicts, though all that was done for them fell far short of what should have been done, and if Governor Davis could have had the proper assistance, and if he could have known one-half what I knew concerning the Arkansas penitentiary, he would have done much more. As I have said so much with reference to the many good things that Governor Davis did for the State and for the convicts, doubtless you, readers, will think that he did me some special favor, but that is not the case. Governor Davis never granted any pardon to me. I wrote the Governor a letter asking him to pardon me, but never heard anything from him. Sometimes a strong petition and a good lot of letters from friends to the Governor will fail to get a pardon. In such cases the Governor just fails to understand the facts just as they were, and I feel sure that the reason why Governor Davis failed to pardon me, although be it as it may, I am glad to tell the public that I am yet a friend to him because of the many things that he has done for the grand old State of Arkansas. All the officials of the penitentiary, I am sure, would have given half their wealth if they could have had Governor Davis under their control for a few days. The Governor would not have had anything to set on when they let him go, for they were all bitter against the Governor, although the officials at the penitentiary, at the time of his administration would not attempt to whip any one unless they had two of their negroes to hold him, and they might have whipped the Governor if they could have gotten some one to hold him for them. That is the only way that they will fight. Just so they can have some one to hold for them, then they will knock the tail off of anything. I feel sure that these officials had much rather see a convict die than to see one of them get a pardon. Governor Donaghey is also a good man, and I think he is one of the best governors that Arkansas has ever had. I think he has fought a good fight for the people's interest and the welfare of the country. He has also been merciful to the convicts of Arkansas. He has pardoned lots of men, and I feel sure that he would have pardoned as many more if he only knew how they were treated; and what Governor Donaghey has said with reference to the State Capitol sounds good to me. There are not many of the penitentiary authorities that are very deeply in love with him, although I have never heard of any of them whipping him as yet. Perhaps they can't get any one to hold him.

## CHAPTER XIV

### Story of an Old Man

This man, at the time he was convicted, was just in the prime of life. He became involved in a row, killed his man, was convicted and sentenced to twenty-one years in the penitentiary, and shortly after his arrival he was carried to the farm, where he was whipped, starved and driven through all kinds of weather, as it is never too hot or too cold on the farm, and every man is compelled to do all that is possible for him to do. This man was kept on the farm, worked and treated in the manner described, until his health had completely given away, and then he was carried back to the walls, placed in the hospital where he remained for several days, and after a long and serious illness he began to recover, and as soon as he was able to hobble about in the yard, he was again carried back to the farm and was treated in the same manner as before, and soon his health failed again, and the second time he was taken to the hospital. This was repeated from time to time until he at last become a physical wreck. His story was a sad and pitiful one. He told me that he had seen men suffer and die, caused by the brutal treatment that they received from the officials of the penitentiary. He told me that he had worked and seen others work when they were almost unable to stand, and then were whipped because they were not able to do more. He said that he had seen men so near starved they would beg for something to eat, and at the same time be so near dead they could scarcely talk, and in this condition they are compelled to suffer and die, as no loved ones are there to feed them. Fathers and mothers, do you think that this kind of treatment is right? Do you think that God intends for us to treat each other in that way? Think of your own children and of your own self, for you do not know how soon that you may have to take the place of some of these dying men or women. There are many ways to get into the penitentiary, and just a few chances to get out alive.

### More About the Farm

In the fall of the year each man is given a task of so many pounds of cotton to pick, and if you fall short only one pound of the task assigned to you, you will be whipped, and it is always a sure thing your task will be as much as it is possible for you to get. Readers, how would you like for some big, dirty scoundrel to whip you and beat the hide off you after you had picked every pound you could pick?

Three men capture the weigh boss. One of them is killed and one of them is shot down by a guard. They were going to get away, but failed. They had been whipped so often they had become desperate and were not careful in laying their plans.

# PART I. STORY OF THE ARKANSAS PENITENTIARY, WILLIAM N. HILL

### This is What They Do at the Rock Crusher

The work is heavy and dirty; their hands and feet are sore from cuts and bruises; their lungs are filled with dust; they eat dust; sleep in the dust; and when they sit down to eat, a dusty negro brings the grub to you in a dusty tin plate. All the flunkies are negroes, and they always feed the negroes first. The whites have to sit there and wait until the negroes have been fed. The work is hard, the whippings are awful, and often the grub is not fit for a dog to eat. It is not fit for anything to eat, except the warden and guards, and they will not eat it. It never gets too cold in the winter time for the poor old convicts to handle those rocks. I have known them to get sick and come to the hospital half naked and almost barefooted in the coldest time of winter. Three men are brought in from the rock crusher to the hospital. One of them dies before morning, after having worked all day; and that is what I call putting in all your time. We hope that he found rest where all is love.

### Negro Convict Kills a Guard

I think it was in the year of 1901 a crew of convicts were working on the Rock Island road, near Danville, Yell County, Arkansas. A message was received at the penitentiary asking the officials to send this negro, Bud Wilson, to the railroad to do a special job of work, as he was an experienced railroad man. Wilson was a bad negro, and most all the officials and convicts were afraid of him, and when the warden told one of the guards that he would have to take him to the railroad, the guard refused to go, and at his refusal another spoke up and said that he would take him, and boasted of not being afraid of Wilson. He also said that maybe he would get a chance to kill Wilson. This conversation between the warden and the guard took place while the convicts were eating breakfast, and Wilson heard all that was said. The warden informed the guard that he could have the pleasure of taking Wilson to the railroad. Wilson had nothing to say in this conversation, although he may have been thinking the matter over. When breakfast was over Wilson was told to get ready for the railroad, as they would leave some time in the afternoon. Most of the convicts have a small wooden box that they use to keep their clothes in. Wilson gathered up all of his earthly treasures, placed them in his box and was ready for the journey. Before leaving the walls he bid most of the colored boys goodbye, telling them that he hoped to see them again. Some time in the afternoon Wilson and the guard took the train for Danville, Ark. Little did they think that, as the train pulled out of the city of Little Rock, neither of them would ever see their homes and friends again. It was early in the night when they arrived at Danville, and there they got off the train, and the convict camp being about one mile east of town, the guard and Wilson started down the railroad, intending to walk to the camp. They had not gone far when Wilson complained of the box that he was carrying being heavy. He found a piece of iron near the track and asked the guard if he could get the iron to swing the box on in order that he could place the iron across his shoulder. He hung the box on one end of the iron, this making it more convenient for him to carry. They guard gave him permission to pick up the iron, and after fixing the box on his shoulder as before mentioned, again they walked on down the track. They had not gone far when Wilson quickly raised his hand, the box slipped off the iron and as quick as thought Wilson struck the guard, knocking him down and springing upon him killed him, and then he dragged his body a few steps from the tracks, took his revolver, stripped him and threw his body behind a log, and dressing himself in the guard's clothing, walked back to Danville, and after looking about for a short time he found the residence of a colored man. He stopped with this man and got something to eat. He didn't have on any shirt, except an undershirt. He asked this man if he would go up town and buy him a shirt, telling him that he would just remain there until he returned, claiming that he was very tired. The man with whom Wilson had stopped took the money and went up town to get the shirt, although he had become suspicious that something was wrong, and while up town he saw the town marshal, one Mr. McCarroll, told him of his visitor, and they accompanied him back to his home, and after these two men had talked with Wilson for a while they were sure that something was shaking, and at this conclusion they arrested Wilson and placed him in jail, and the next morning the body of the guard was found where it had been placed by Wilson. He and Wilson were both identified by the convict crew. Then Wilson confessed to the killing. He was tried, convicted, and then hanged by Sheriff Cole, of Yell County, at Danville, Arkansas.

    As stated in the beginning of this chapter, Wilson was a bad negro. He often caused trouble with the convicts. He was a big, black, burly fellow, and could easily handle two common men, and he was then serving an eight-year term. His physical ability and his dirty disposition made a bad man of him. Perhaps the hanging of this man was several years later than it should have been. I was personally acquainted with the guard and with Wilson, also, and it is my honest opinion that negro Wilson was better than the guard, morally, and while it is true that this guard held the position as convict guard for several years, and it is said that he had killed several convicts, I have heard among those that knew him, that it seemed to be great sport for him to shoot and kill the poor convicts who were so cruelly treated; that they would take all kinds of desperate chances to free themselves from the wrath of such men as this guard and some other officials of the Arkansas penitentiary. While if these unfortunate men who have been so unmercifully treated by beating them and by starving them, if these men had been humanely treated as God would direct them to be, or if they had been treated as the laws of our country direct, men would not become so desperate that they would risk their lives before the fire of these dirty guards who are not worth the room that they will occupy after the day of judgment.Treat a man right and he will give you good service. Treat him kindly and you will reform him. The bad negro, Wilson, didn't forget the conversation between the warden and the guard. Oh, how different it all turned out compared with what the guard wished it to be. God works in many mysterious ways his wonders to perform.

### Guard Kills a Warden

I do not know the particulars of this affair, more than it is said that this warden was an awful mean man, and treated the convicts so badly that the guard would not put up with his cussedness; and it is said that on this day that the warden had whipped several men and one or more of them he had whipped more than once that day, and some of them were sick. Again he got bloodthirsty, and got his whip to use on a sick man that he had whipped two or three times that same day, and the guard forbid his whipping this man. The warden became enraged at this, cursing the guard and the convict. He then started to carry out his aim, and the guard again forbid him, telling him that he would kill him if he struck the convict. The warden did not heed, and the guard shot him down. That guard was a good man. He ought to have been placed on the pension list and been permitted to have drawn fifty dollars per month the balance of his life, and then when his time on earth is over, a costly monument should be erected at the head of his grave, bearing this inscription:

*Behind this rock in sweet repose,*
*Beneath this mound of clay,*
*Now sleeps a pure and noble heart,*
*To await the judgment day.*
*We hope that he on that great day,*
*With righteous ones shall stand,*
*With a harp of gold and a glittering crown,*
*To join the happy band.*

This man was tried for murder and was convicted. I do not remember the length of his sentence. He was sent to the penitentiary for doing just what he ought to have done under the circumstances. If all convict guards would do their duty as this man did, the penitentiary would soon be controlled by an honest set of men and all the rotten ones would soon be killed out. Although the truth is that any time prior to 1904 an honest man could not hold a job as guard longer than thirty or sixty days, and when you meet a man that has guarded convicts in the State of Arkansas longer than sixty days and didn't lose his job, you can safely say that he is a dirty cur, and when you look into the face of one of those guards who has served several months or years, it is then that you look into the face of a dirty murderer and one of the blackest type, one who has caused the life to be crushed and beaten out of men. Readers, those of you who have a father, brother, relative or friend who are now serving time in the penitentiary, think of these awful conditions. These old pie-mouthed hypocrites will sneak around and tell you that there is nothing to this statement. It is sure that we do not expect them to confess to these dirty crimes that they have so long kept hidden from the world, and it is also sure that any man who is dirty enough to commit the crimes they have so long committed in the Arkansas penitentiary will not only tell a lie, but they will swear to it, if necessary.

### The Officials have a Big Spree

Some of the officials' friends visit them, and on occasions like that they always try to do something smart, though they have not sense enough to know just how or what to do, and they always make a mess of anything they undertake in the way of entertainments. Old Sam calls these entertainments "blow-outs," and I am of the opinion that Sam has a correct idea of the matter, as he has been present on several occasions. Sometimes they get so badly stuck they have to get some of the convicts to come out and entertain their guests. They call out the negro quartette, and the music would put new life into all of them. Then they would turn on the beer freely, and after the negroes would sing a few songs all would seem to get new life in them. The negroes would be ordered back to their cells. Sometimes they seem to be a little embarrassed, saying that some of the officials would act so silly that it was embarrassing to them. At one of these blow-outs, while Governor Davis was making a second race for that office, the officials and several of their friends congregated at the office building of the penitentiary to have a spree and to curse him. There was only one Davis man in that party, and he a little fellow from Malvern, Arkansas. They all got full and all got mad and squalled and shot their pistols. One of this party said that any one who would vote for Davis was a damned s— of a b—. Now, what do you think of a man that would talk like that? Don't you think that he is a liar? I know that he is. I am sure there never was a man on earth that was hated more than Governor Davis was by the officials of the penitentiary. They also had the same feelings for Donaghey. Reader, do you know why these two gentlemen are so much disliked by this gang that have so long been starving and murdering the poor convicts of Arkansas? Here is the reason why: Davis and Donaghey are honest men, and they have great love and respect for suffering humanity. Not only that, they have proven that they honor and love the grand old State of Arkansas and everything pertaining to the welfare of our country and her worthy citizenship, and that is why these distinguished gentlemen are so much disliked by the gang referred to. All is so different to the desire of their own ears it has caused them great pain, and it is a perfect shame and an outrage to a civilized world for an institution to be controlled in the way and manner that the Arkansas penitentiary has been managed in the past many years, and I trust that what I have said in this book will open the eyes of the public and especially those who have a controlling power to enforce the laws governing the rules and regulations of the penitentiary, for we, as a civilized people, should not tolerate the evil-doing that has so long been permitted in the Arkansas penitentiary. The authorities who have the power to adjust these things are not wholly to blame, for I am sure that they are ignorant of the many horrible things that have so long been practiced in the State penitentiary. And as I have before stated, I do not ask any one to take my word alone for what I have said in this book. Talk with others and see if they do not corroborate my statements. As to the laws governing the penitentiary, I have no complaint to make; enforce the laws as the State statutes provide. See then if the death rates are not much lower each year than they stand today, and those who are lucky enough to serve out their sentence, see if they are not more reformed than most of the men will be after they have been so cruelly treated, for in most cases where a man has served one or more years his health is so impaired that he is unfit for manual labor for several months, and in many cases for the remaining part of his life to be an invalid and to live in sorrow and sadness, and then die a pauper; when, if they had been treated as God intended for men to be treated, these same men could return to their homes, full of hope and joy, ready to begin life anew, resolved to make good and honest citizens. There has been lots of good men sent to the penitentiary, there to toil and starve and be beaten unmercifully. Then often the chilly hand of death will hand them down to their grave in sorrow and shame; and many of these have a pure and noble heart. It is easy for a good man to get into the penitentiary, unless we know each other's hearts. It is true that we have lots of mean men in the world, and some of these are in the penitentiary, and some are free. When a man is convicted and sent to the penitentiary he should be treated as his deportment merits. If a man is obedient and works all that he is able, he should be fed and furnished sufficient clothing, and he should not be whipped and beaten and starved to death, which is so often the case in the Arkansas penitentiary. When a man is disobedient, lazy and trifling in every particular, then the leather should be applied, though always judiciously, just as the statutes provide. All the tough characters should be kept in a squad to themselves, not allowing them to cause the good men to be punished; and then as a man becomes submissive to what is right, place him in ranks with the good men. To handle men in that way they would do just like the fellow said his sweetheart would do after she had given him the bounce. It would only be a matter of time when they would all come to their milk [conform], although in the Arkansas penitentiary they are treated in this way: They are all worked out of reason and starved, most always beaten unmercifully and not sufficient clothing for winter. Reader, if you have a friend or relative in the penitentiary, see after them, furnish them a little money each month, as they will have to board themselves if they get anything to eat. Just here I will mention one more little skin game that has been going on for a long time. When a man goes to the penitentiary with a few dollars in his pocket the officials will take charge of his money, except a little change something like a dollar, and when you spend that dollar you can draw one more at a time if you happen to be at the walls; and if you happen to be on the farm, railroad or any camp, they will keep your money for you—and if you get sick and die, they will still keep it for you. If you should happen to live out your sentence and should have two or three dollars on deposit with them, and then when you are discharged if you happen to be down on the farm or the railroad perhaps one hundred miles from the city of Little Rock, they will keep your money for you until you call for it, and if your deposit has not all been drawn out perhaps they will give you your money, though if it cost you three or four dollars to collect half that amount you are apt to just pass it by. I am certain that they would not care if you did. All these little deposits after a while will make a nice little jackpot for some one. I do not know who the winner will be, though it looks to me somehow—well, readers, you can see for yourselves just how it looks.

### One of Tim's Large Stories

Tim Kaline was a young Irishman, full of wit, good looking and a fine singer, and was a good entertainer. One Sunday afternoon a young man and three young ladies visited the penitentiary. Tim was the building tender. It was also one of his duties to see the visitors and show them through the building. At that time there were three large brick buildings inside of the penitentiary walls; then there were three more smaller buildings and at the entrance stands the office building. This is used by the officials. After the visitors had been shown through the cell buildings and the dining room they stopped on the yard. Tim felt it his duty to make all necessary explanations on matters they might be anxious to know about. He then pointed to the big brick building that stood a few rods away, telling them that this building was the hospital, and one of the ladies said that the white men that she had seen in the penitentiary looked to her just like they ought to be in the hospital. Next Tim pointed to the bath house, the light plant and the wash house. Then one of the ladies pointed to the office building that stands just on the outside of the walls and asked what that building was used for. Tim got his Irish wits in operation and decided that he would have a little fun. He told the lady that it was the office building, though it was used principally for keeping the lunatics in.

"Oh, have you some crazy men here?" she asked.

"Sure," said Tim. "We are never without them."

"How many insane men are here?"

"Only three or four at present; sometimes there are more."

"What do they do?" she asked.

"Fight the other convicts," Tim answered.

"Do they hurt any one?"

"Sure they always bring blood," answered Tim.

"Why don't you keep them locked up?" she asked.

"That would be hard to do," was Tim's reply, "besides, they need the exercise, and we let them out on the yard every day and it is then that they jump on the convicts," and then the lady began to look a little frightened and another one of the ladies asked if any of these men were on the yard at that time.

"No, ma'am," Tim replied, "though I am expecting them to come soon." One of the ladies said that she was ready to go. The rest of the party agreed that they were also ready to go, though Tim was not yet through with the joke. He insisted that they should let him show them through the hospital, and to this they agreed, and after spending some time in the hospital looking and talking with the sick men they returned to the yard, and as they walked along through the yard the gong tapped and all eyes were fixed upon the big iron door to see who was coming in. Then the big door swings back and three men stepped into the yard and the gentleman in front was the State physician and the others were officials.

"Who are these men?" asked one of the ladies.

"That gentleman in front is our doctor, and the other two men are two of our crazy men. The doctor is taking them out for a little exercise."

Then the three ladies stepped up close to Tim and their companion and whispered to Tim, "Do you think that they will try to hurt us?"

"No ma'am," answered Tim. "If you will not have anything to say to them. If they speak to you, ladies, don't say a word and they will pass on by."

Soon the doctor and the two officers passed near where the visitors and Tim were standing, when they lifted their hats and spoke to the ladies, though neither of the ladies spoke a word. When the doctor and those two officials had walked a few feet away the two officers looked back over their shoulders at the visitors. They wore everything else on their faces except a pleasant look. After they had passed on the gentleman who was with the ladies said, "These men seem to be in good health."

"Yes, their health is excellent," said Tim, "and they wear good clothes," he added.

"How long have they been crazy?"

"I am not sure how long; for several years, I think."

"Do you think that they will ever recover?" asked the visitor.

"No; I am afraid not," said Tim.

One of the ladies shook her head and said, "Perhaps they will recover some time, though it is easy to tell by the look of their eyes and by their general appearance that they are in bad shape at the present."

"Sure, it is easy to see that, though if you could see their eyes when they take one of their spells I think that you would feel sure that they would never be any better."

"Why do these crazy men not wear stripes like the rest of the convicts?"

"Well it is this way," said Tim. "Their people visit them often and it would grieve them more to see them in stripes."

"Yes, yes; that is true. Who is the doctor?" asked one of the ladies.

"Doctor Witt," said Tim.

"He is a fine looking fellow," she said.

"He looks good out of his eyes," said one of them.

"He is not crazy, either," said Tim. "He is a good fellow and a fine physician."

"I'll bet he is," said one of the ladies.

"And what is your name?" said one.

"Kaline is my name."

## Part I. Story of the Arkansas Penitentiary, William N. Hill

"And your given name?" she asked.

"Tim," was the answer, and then stepping a little closer to her he asked, "How do I look out of my eyes?"

"You look good," she said, though somewhat embarrassed, and the other ladies laughed at her. By this time the ladies had gotten over their fright of the crazy men, and had walked over all the yard and seemed to enjoy their acquaintance with Tim very much. And he, too, was having a barrel of fun at the officers' expense. They had spent more than an hour with Tim and this little time was pleasantly whiled away, as they had seen and heard some things that they never knew before. After each of them assuring Tim of their appreciation of having met him, also expressing much gratitude for the hospitalities that he had shown them, Tim was also pleased over this little meeting and it was easy for him to show signs of his appreciation for all their flattering remarks that they had made to him. They moved on slowly to the big door that would soon separate them and perhaps forever, though Tim was not yet through with his joke, and just before reaching the big door mentioned, Tim stopped them and said, "Now, there is two more crazy men in the office, and as you will have to pass through the building you are apt to meet them." This again alarmed the ladies, though Tim told them he would tell them how to do [ it] and if they would follow his instructions they would get through without any trouble. They assured him that they would follow his instructions.

"These men are very fond of tobacco," said he. Then he took from his pocket a piece of tobacco and cut off four small pieces, gave one to each of the ladies and one to the gentleman. "And now," said Tim, "if these men are in the room don't say a word to them, but walk up to them and hand each one of them the bit of tobacco and then pass on." Tim expected some of the officials to be in the office, but they were all out and no one was in the building except the old guard who was gatekeeper. After they had entered the room they looked for some one, but there was no one to give the tobacco to but the old guard and he was a hard-looking old fellow. One of the ladies looked at him after she had passed by where he stood at the door and when she glanced back at him he happened to be looking at her. She threw her piece of tobacco to him and then ran out the office. These ladies were beautiful and very intelligent and no more excited than any other lady would have been under the same circumstances, though this was only one of Tim's large stories.

To all the honest citizens and the law-makers of Arkansas, and to those who have the power to enforce the law, I wish to call the attention of all with reference to what I have said in this book. I have endeavored to speak the truth, and now I appeal to you all to help to adjust to the facts that you now have before you.

And now, kind friends, I sincerely hope and trust that all the good citizenship of Arkansas will do something to bring relief to those poor sufferers, and that we can soon write a book commenting upon the reformation of the Arkansas penitentiary officials as well as to the convicts, and I feel in my heart that this little book will be a great help in the matter of reformation so much needed, and if this should reach the hands and hearts of these officials I shall be more than pleased.

Respectfully,<br>THE AUTHOR

# PART II. *RULED BY THE WHIP*

## BY DALE WOODCOCK
## (UNABRIDGED MEMOIR)

### CHAPTER ONE

A young, stockily built deputy sheriff was standing beside the Ohio sheriff as I was led down the stairway from the second-floor cell block. A five-pointed star flashed on his ill-fitting shirt pocket. He wore a sport shirt, slacks, and a big hat, but was unarmed. His complexion was like a fish's belly.

"Is this the fellow we want?" he drawled in soft Southern tones, as he glanced at the sheriff.

"That's your boy," the sheriff replied.

"Woodcock," the deputy grinned, "it's been a tough extradition fight, but we won."

"Your car is in the garage, and your clothes are at City Police Headquarters," the sheriff interrupted. "What do you want to do about them?"

"I'll return to get them as soon as I make bond," I answered.

One of the sheriff's deputies opened a safe sitting in a corner of the room and pulled out a manila envelope which contained my personal property--a wrist watch, two rings, wallet, a fountain pen, and several hundred dollars. He gave it to the deputy who stuck it under his left arm, shook hands with the sheriff, opened the front door, and told me to walk to the car parked at the curb. The deputy's wife, a pretty young blonde with a delicate skin, sat waiting in the front seat. She was thumbing through a movie fan magazine. As I climbed into the back seat she turned and scrutinized me with shrewd eyes as if I had been a new horse brought home from the fair. Her face was as cold as a clean bedsheet.

The deputy slid under the steering wheel and pressed the starter button.

"Good luck, Doc," the sheriff said, as he stuck his arm through the open car window to shake my hand. "When you get out of this mess, son, get yourself straightened out."

As we turned the corner at the end of the block the dark brown, ancient stone jail was obliterated from view. The deputy settled back in the seat, turned to his wife, and said, "This is the character that stole the microscope from the County Hospital."

She laughed and it was a good thing to hear, sort of cracked and giggly and smooth all at the same time, the way real woman laughter is, not a production, not a controlled thing full of do-re-mi and G-clefs and birdsong. I had been waiting six months for the Arkansas officials to come to Ohio to get me, and this was the first pleasant laughter I had heard since I had been locked in a cell. I had become accustomed to the coarse, raucous language of my fellow prisoners.

In a matter of only a few minutes we reached the city limits of the Ohio town, and the deputy began questioning me about conditions in the jail, then quickly switched to asking questions concerning the microscope theft. I told him I had been treated and fed well, but parried the questions concerning the theft as well as I could.

"Well," he drawled, "I guess they feed better than we do. But we feed better than they do at the Arkansas State Penitentiary. That's where you're goin', too; you know that, don't you?"

"I believe that will be for the jury to decide," I answered.

"You're gonna git smart, huh, Woodcock? We've got a jail full of wise guys like you."

I remained silent after that statement. I had no desire to have the deputy give a bad report to the sheriff and judge when I was returned to face the larceny charge that was filed against me. I was hoping I would receive probation, as I had never knowingly committed a misdemeanor or felony.

It was growing dark and a thick fog drifted like a blanket across the road when we stopped at a drive-in restaurant in Indiana for supper. The deputy reached into the glove compartment and pulled out a pair of handcuffs. He opened the door, stepped out, bent over, and pulled a pair of shackles from under the car seat. Then he walked around the front end of the car, opened the rear door, and ordered me to get out. He ignored his wife, who was forced to open her own door. She stepped from the car, her hazel eyes bright with anger; the rustle of her vaporous blue dress was raised from a whisper to a cry by the vigor of her movements as she violently slammed the door and walked toward the restaurant.

## Part II. *Ruled by the Whip*, Dale Woodcock

The deputy snapped the shackles tightly around my ankles. He placed the handcuffs on my wrists and said, "Now then, let's see how far you go if you decide to run."

I shuffled through the door of the crowded restaurant and the patrons stopped eating to stare at me. Due to my height of over six feet I was accustomed to taking long strides, so the twelve-inch chain connecting the shackles made each step short and hazardous. Each time I stepped forward with one foot it would jerk the chain and almost pull the other leg from under me. The shackles indicated that I was in the position of one accused of the worst of crimes.

"You can have what you want to eat, the taxpayers are paying for it," the deputy guffawed.

A young, attractive waitress placed a menu before me. She was very polite and seemingly tried to ignore the fact that I was a prisoner. Throughout the meal she made special trips to our booth to refill my coffee cup. This special attention made the situation worse by focusing attention on me.

The stares of the people in the booths around us and the embarrassment of being shackled caused me to lose my appetite. I felt weak and dizzy. Blood was racing through my head and my stomach was tied in knots. I ordered a sandwich. The deputy and his wife, ordered steak, French fries, salad, and apple pie.

A gloomy, thick fog covered the world when we stopped at Vandalia, Illinois, to spend the night. I was lodged in a jail located in an old, two-story dwelling at the edge of town. When we stopped in front of the jail the deputy told me to get out and walk inside. He walked behind me as I entered the front door.

"You got a prisoner there?" a policeman sitting at a desk asked me as we entered.

"He's the prisoner," the deputy growled, pointing a crooked finger at me.

"Oh! I'm sorry," the policeman said, and a smile spread across his face. He grabbed a ring of huge keys hanging on the wall and motioned for me to follow him. He led the way to an empty cell block which was without lights. It was chilly so I slipped my topcoat on and sat down on a bench pushed against the outside bars. I stuck a cigarette in my mouth, lit it, inhaled deeply, and was shaking out the match flame when I heard a feminine voice say, "Where are you from fellow?"

Startled, I jumped from the bench and stared around me in the darkness.

"I'm up here, right over you, on the second tier," the woman said.

I leaned against the bars to talk to her. We spent the remainder of the night discussing subjects ranging from the Illinois State Fair to the books of Bertrand Russell.[23] I never knew how old the woman was; what her name was; what she looked like; what her offense was or how long she must stay in jail, but I'll never forget her friendly, pleasant voice echoing in that dark, cold jail.

We arrived at the County Jail in Fayetteville, Arkansas, shortly after three o'clock the following afternoon. The deputy hurriedly wrote my name, age, address, etc., on a card in the empty office then led the way to the bullpen.

There were only three prisoners in the jail, a young schoolteacher who had forged a check, a short-change artist serving a jail sentence, and a man who had recently been released from the Arkansas Penitentiary and was awaiting trial on a burglary charge.

"I was a trustee guard," the ex-convict said with pride. "Even if the Hoot Owl sends me back, I'll have a gun and be a guard within a month."

I walked inside a gloomy steel cage, containing twenty-four bunks, which sat in the middle of the large room, shook the dust and dirt from a tattered blanket and stretched out on a dirty mattress. I had lain on the bunk only a few minutes when the door was opened by the sheriff. He held the screen-covered door open with one hand and his other hand was braced against the doorsill as if he expected someone would try to run past him. He was a huge man with a round face and large round eyes from which he had received the nickname "Hoot Owl." He chewed viciously on a jawful [sic] of tobacco.

---

[23]Bertrand Russell is a tony author to have been discussed by two Arkansas jail inmates. The British intellectual was born in 1872 and died in1970. His books on philosophy and mathematics made Russell influential in Europe, and he lectured at several of America's premiere universities. *The New Columbia Encyclopedia*, 2376.

"I just came back to see what you look like, Woodcock," he said, as he spat tobacco juice on the floor.

I rose from the bunk, walked to the door of the cage, and asked, "May I call my mother to let her know I'm here?"

"Where does she live?" he inquired.

"Nineteen miles from here."

"No. We're not paying for any long-distance calls."

"I'll pay for it."

"Well, maybe, in a day or two. Not now."

The sheriff slammed the door and walked away. I returned to the bunk and sat on the edge. I had been sitting there only a few minutes when the deputy who had returned me from Ohio unlocked the door, stuck his head inside, and said, "Someone here to see you, Woodcock."

I walked into the room which connected the bull pen and the front office. My mother was standing in the doorway. There were tears streaming down her face. Tears of disillusion, of blasted hope. There was a hurt look in her eyes. The wish for success, respectability, and happiness which she hoped, as mothers do for their children, would be mine was gone. I had failed her.

"This is something, isn't it?" she said bitterly. "Is this what you went to college for?"

I tried to explain to her I hadn't stolen the microscope. "It was stolen on December twenty-sixth. That was the day of Dad's funeral. You know I was home all that day and night. The only time I was out of the house was for the funeral services."

"Why didn't you tell them?" she asked.

"I've been telling them for six months." I proceeded to tell her how I had agreed to sell used equipment to the members of my profession on a commission basis for a medical equipment salesman, who took the equipment on new sales he made. "The day I got your telegram I told him I had to come home. He drove behind me. We split up at in Rogers. He said he was going to Hot Springs. He probably stole that microscope when he came back through here, because he brought it to my office when I returned."

The sheriff walked in at that moment, and my mother pleaded with him to free me on bond.

"Naw," he replied, "some people from the hospital want to look at him first. Maybe tomorrow."

My mother left but returned within a few minutes with a sack of fruit, cookies, candy, and sandwiches. She promised to return the next morning. Immediately after she left the second time the short-changer was called to the sheriff's living quarters on the second floor of the jail. He returned carrying four pans of cold, white beans and a pot of black coffee. I offered to share the food my mother had brought. The three prisoners eagerly accepted and threw the beans into the commode.

Next morning we were given a tin bowl of oatmeal for breakfast. After breakfast the deputy took the schoolteacher and me to the Courthouse which was a block away. The courtroom was vacant except for the judge, prosecutor, court clerk, and the schoolteacher's wife, who held a baby in her arms.

The judge talked first to the schoolteacher, who kept pleading for probation. The judge told him he would consider it. He gazed at a piece of paper for a moment, then looked at me.

"You're charged with taking a microscope from the County Hospital," he said. "Anything you want to say?"

"Not guilty," I responded.

"You'll need a lawyer to enter a plea. Do you have money for bond?"

"Yes sir," I answered cheerfully, "The sheriff has it."

"Bond will be a thousand dollars."

The sheriff returned with me to the jail where he took the bond money from the manila envelope and handed the remainder to me. I hurried to the bus station to catch a bus home.

I returned to Fayetteville the next morning and asked the judge for permission to return to Ohio to get my clothes and car.

"You can go," he said, "but make sure you're back here Monday with a lawyer."

I went by plane to Ohio. My car had been placed in a private garage and had accumulated an outlandish storage fee. The moths had enjoyed a prolonged banquet on my clothes. Nothing had been confiscated except two one-dollar bills enclosed inside Christmas cards, which a nun and a priest had given me for presents while I was working at a Catholic hospital, and a bank containing forty dollars in quarters.

I returned home on Sunday evening, hired a lawyer to represent me at the hearing scheduled the next day, and spent most of the night talking to my mother.

Early next morning the lawyer from my home town and I were at the judge's private chambers. I sat on a bench in the hallway while the lawyer went inside to talk to the judge. He returned in approximately five minutes and said my trial had been set for November tenth.

I spent two more days with my mother. I had a great fear of being sentenced to the Arkansas Prison. Since childhood I had heard sadistic and brutal stories concerning it. On the third day I decided I would rather forfeit the bond money than to take the chance of being sentenced there. I left home at noon, intending never to return to Arkansas.

I was gone almost four months. Most of that time I stayed in Los Angeles, but during the early part of February I decided to go to Western Canada or Alaska and open an office. I was arrested in Portland, Oregon, after stopping there to spend one night. A man I thought was my friend called the police and told them I was a fugitive from justice.

The same deputy who came to Ohio to get me came to Portland. He was accompanied by a fellow deputy. They intended to have no more trouble with me, especially on the return trip, so they thoroughly shackled and handcuffed me for the return. We returned in three days, stopping only one night in Grand Junction, Colorado, for sleep.

There were twelve prisoners in jail when I was returned. I was taken to the Courthouse immediately after our arrival. My mother had heard on the radio that I had been rearrested and was being returned. She had hired another lawyer to defend me and he was waiting on the Courthouse steps.

"You're back, are you, Woodcock?" the judge bellowed in a voice loud enough to be heard throughout the Courthouse, as I was led into the courtroom. His face was livid with anger, and I noticed the top of his bald head was also tinged.

"Your honor," my lawyer began.

"No. I don't want to hear anything about this boy," the judge bellowed again, waving his arms in the air, his form tremulous with rage.

"But, Your Honor," my lawyer interrupted.

"No," the judge roared, "this boy lied to me. I gave him permission to go to Ohio to get his car. I also gave him orders to be back here on the next Monday, with a lawyer, and this is the first time I've seen him since that day."

"I did come back," I interrupted, and named the lawyer from my home town who had represented me when the trial date had been set.

"Take him on back to jail," the judge roared. "There'll be no bond set this time."

I was returned to the County Jail, where I remained until the day of my trial the following June. While I was awaiting trial several of the prisoners became sick on the jail food. We were fed twice a day; a bowl of oatmeal anytime between sunrise and noon and a bowl of beans anytime between noon and midnight. One of the youngest inmates had grown so weak on the inadequate died the suffered from fainting spells. He told me he needed to get out to see a doctor and asked me to loan him enough money to pay his fine. He promised to return with the money the next day. I loaned him fifty-five dollars but didn't see him again until four days later when he returned, intoxicated, and brought me a hamburger and an *Esquire* magazine. I paid the fine of another prisoner, who also faithfully promised to repay the money as soon as he could find his brother. He was tossed back in jail that night in a state of drunken stupor. He failed to being even a magazine. My faith in mankind began to falter.

Life in the jail was extremely dull and monotonous. The only diversion was provided by the activities in a National Guard armory Building located next to the jail, where dances were held every Saturday night which helped to relieve the monotony. We could listen to the music and watch the couples come and go. Occasionally a drunk man, or woman, would stagger to a window of the jail which had a large hole in the heavy screen covering it and pour whisky into the prisoners' cups.

The sheriff and his wife also inadvertently provided entertainment. In April the sheriff's shapely young wife began wearing tight-fitting shorts. Each time her footsteps were heard on the stairway leading from the living quarters above the jail the prisoners made a mad rush to the door, where they watched her wiggle across the room that led to the front office. She would always turn to look at them, occasionally smiling, and staring at them at other times with a dead-pan face as if they were a roomful of freaks. The sheriff would occasionally open the heavy, barred and screened door, then walk away leaving it unlocked, acting as if he had forgotten to lock it. We knew he was waiting in his office for someone to walk out. After a period of time someone would yell and tell him to lock the door. He would peek around the corner, then sheepishly come and lock it, after first spitting tobacco juice on the floor and gritting his teeth at us.

A few days after I had been returned from Oregon my lawyer came to discuss his fee. First, he said, he needed a little money for a retainer. I had paid he county expenses for returning me from both Ohio and Oregon and had also bought the hospital a new microscope to replace the one that I had been charged with stealing. I had thirty-four hundred dollars remaining in an envelope in the sheriff's office and told him to take some of it. He left and a few minutes later the sheriff came to the bull pen and I asked him much money I had.

"Doc," he grinned, "you don't have anything left. That lawyer didn't even leave the envelope that money was in!"

On a hot, humid morning in mid-June the deputy who had made two trips to return me to Arkansas opened the cell door and told me to be ready for court in fifteen minutes. My mother had brought a brown suit, white shirt, and a yellow-checked tie for the trial. Because of the heat I decided not to wear the coat. As we were waiting in the front office another prisoner who had continuously tried to break out and given the deputies a great deal of trouble began throwing glasses and cups in the bull pen. The sheriff and both deputies dragged him into the front office where they twisted his arms and beat him into docile submission. I leaned against the wall to avoid being splattered by blood.

After the carnage was over one of the deputies led me outside. I was momentarily blinded by the bright sunshine, but in a moment or two was able to distinguish objects around me. As we walked up the sidewalk toward the

Courthouse I noticed a group of men standing on the Courthouse steps. Some were dressed in overalls, blue work shirts, and wore big straw hats.

"Hey," one of the men yelled, "here comes that ol' boy we're gonna send to the penitentiary!"

"Yeah," another yelled, "look at him, he's all dressed up!"

"That jury looks and sounds rough, Woodcock," the deputy smiled. "You'd better plead guilty."

Court began with the selection of twelve jurors from the group. Each prospective juror stated he knew nothing about the case except what had been written in the newspapers and what he had heard on the radio. The prosecutor, a sallow-complexioned, hatchet-faced man, sat across the table from me, my lawyer, and my lawyer's assistant. My lawyer provoked the prosecutor before the trial began by making derogatory remarks about his appearance.

"Woodcock," the prosecutor said a few minutes after the trial began, as he sat toying with a pencil with a hair-shrouded hand, "if you'll plead guilty and stop the trial, we'll give you six years."

I looked at my lawyer, hoping he would advise me. "It's up to you," he stated dolefully.

I looked at the jury.

"I believe the jury will give me less than that, if I'm convicted," I told the prosecutor.

"I'll see if I can't get you twenty-one years," he retorted. "I believe I can, too."

He begged the jury to give me twenty-one years. He had a fascinating voice—sonorous, musical, flexible. He spoke with magnetic fervor. He accused me of being a nationwide microscope thief and a slinking snake, which palpably impressed the jury. They found me guilty without a reasonable doubt, but recommended I be sentenced to only two years in the state penitentiary.

"Hell, I don't believe anybody could do much more time than that in the prison Arkansas has," one of the jurors said, as he walked behind me to leave the courtroom.

## Part II. *Ruled by the Whip*, Dale Woodcock

A few days later I was shuttled by State Police to Little Rock, where I spent the night in the County Jail. I was placed in a bull pen with eighteen wetbacks waiting to be returned to Mexico. They spoke very little English and I could speak no Spanish other than buenos and hasta la vista, so we conversed by sign language. There was only one in the group I could understand. He kept asking if I had been to Acapulco as he made obscene signs with his fingers to indicate one of the fascinations of Mexico's famed tourist mecca. I sat on a bench looking out the window most of the night. Across town, on a hilltop, stood three radio towers. The red lights outlining skeletal structures were unblinking. I watched the top lights blinking on and off in offbeat cadence until sunrise.

Near eleven o'clock next morning the jailer opened the bullpen door and told me to get my things, as the "dog wagon" had come for me. I had nothing with me except some underclothes and stamps and envelopes, as I had been told I could take nothing else into the prison. I followed the jailer to the front office where I was released to an official of the Arkansas Penitentiary.

"Come on, boy, follow me," the official said sternly after glancing at me, and led the way outside.

A pickup truck with a cage built of heavy mesh wire on the back was parked in front of the jail. Across the street a man wearing a sport shirt and khaki trousers stood in the middle of the sidewalk. In his hand he held a pistol. He waved the pistol hand, motioning me to get into the cage.

The elderly official, who was wearing a suit, pushed the door of the cage shut as I climbed inside and locked it with a heavy lock. Then he returned to the jail office. The young man wearing the sport shirt walked to the truck to check the lock after the other official had left. I asked him how far it was to the prison.

"Aw, about seventy miles," he scowled. "You in a hurry to git there?"

"Are you an officer there?" I asked.

"Hell, no. I'm a convict jest like you. You tryin' to be funny?"

I thought he was the one trying to be funny. I couldn't understand why a man sentenced to the penitentiary was standing in a street in Little Rock with a gun in his hand, with children playing innocent games around him.

"You ever pick any cotton?" he asked.

"I've never seen any, except in the drugstore."

"Well, you'll have the opportunity to pick some now."

"The Arkansas Penitentiary is a rough place, isn't it?"

"If you're a line bull, it is. This is the third time I've got a life sentence for rape. But the 'Bear' always makes me a trusty and then gits my time cut. I'll be out again before long. This life sentence the court gave me doesn't mean a thing."

He was correct in his conjecture. Eighteen months later his time was cut to eighteen years, which made him eligible for immediate parole.

"Who is the bear?"

The warden. When you go through the gate down there say a prayer, because your ass belongs to him. That man has unlimited power. He can rent you out to some ol' farmer if he wants to, so you may not have to stay at the prison."

The other official returned, so we terminated our conversation. He drove and the convict guard kept strict surveillance, watching through the back glass to see that I made no escape attempts. The driver hit speeds up to eighty-five miles an hour after we left the outskirts of Little Rock, tossing me around the cage as he took every turn. He forced other cars off the highway. There were two or three hazardous truck and bus passings which made me think that would be my last ride. I later learned he had had several wrecks and scared every man he had transported to the prison. His driving ability was a standard joke.

He stopped at the police station in Pine Bluff for a few minutes. It was noon, so he bought me a hamburger and two Milky Way candy bars. People gathered around the truck to stare at me as if I were some rare animal that had been put on exhibit. I could hear several laughing. As we drove out of Pine Bluff people pointed and yelled, "He's got one!"

A short time later we turned off the highway onto a dirt road leading through pastures and fields. Three or four miles' journey on that road brought us to the prison which was a farm. We drove through the entrance gate without stopping, after the trustee stationed there took a cursory glance at the driver. We stopped in front of a cement-block building which served as the

Administration Building. Here all new prisoners were finger-printed and photographed.

The driver unlocked the cage and told me to get out. I followed him into the building. As I walked through the door I saw an inmate I had met in jail. I said "hello" to him.

"Damn it, come on here, boy," the elderly official growled. "If you were at Tucker Farm, you would have been shot already."

I followed him to a desk where a balding young inmate sat at a desk puffing on a cigar and drinking a coke. The clerk ordered me to sit in a chair beside the desk and flung the typewriter carriage back with a clattering smash.

"First," he said, "I'm gonna give you some advice. This is the roughest prison in the country. Never talk back to a warden, rider, or guard. Let them cuss and beat you, there's nothing you can do about it, except get killed. This is a dangerous place. It's the only prison that convicts operate, and every time one of these convict guards kills somebody he gets an indefinite furlough, so they're looking for somebody to kill so they can get out of here. Half of them aren't civilized anyway. Watch yourself and you'll be able to walk out of here instead of being hauled out."

He wanted to know my name, address, aliases, and who they should notify if I was killed. I gave my mother's name and address and he typed it in red. When he completed this he told me to go into another room where I would be fingerprinted and "mugged."

"How much time you got?" the fingerprint man asked, as he smeared a gob of ink on a piece of glass with a rubber roller.

"Two years," I answered.

"Two years in any other prison would be just a vacation. Here, it seems like a lifetime. I've been in Alcatraz and a Jap prisoner-of-war camp. I'd gladly volunteer to go back to either to git out of this place."

He took several sets of my fingerprints, then led the way into a small room. With a number placed across my chest, he photographed me facing the camera and in profile. Then I was led outside. As I stepped out the door I glanced at a seal painted on the side of the truck which had brought me to the prison. ARKANSAS STATE PENITENTIARY, JUSTICE AND MERCY, it read.

## CHAPTER TWO

A convict guard sitting astride a long, lean, spavined mule was waiting for me to come out of the Administration Building. He was, I later learned, the sheriff of Seven Camp. His duties were to take new prisoners to Seven Camp, and to go to the fields to get them if they had out-of-state visitors. Relatives or friends who lived in Arkansas could visit only on visiting day---the second Sunday of each month.

Dilapidated buildings, built on high concrete pillars, with large double doors and small windows, seemed to be grinning ogres as I walked down the dusty road. Flowering cotton fields stretched over the endless miles of pancake-flat land stretching to an empty horizon. Heat waves were performing a shimmy dance above the dark-green leaves. I walked at a rapid pace, but the heavy footfalls of the mule were gaining on me.

"Git a move on," the convict growled, "or I'll run this mule over you." He raked the animal's ribs with his spurs and the mule jumped, knocking me forward. "Short Hair, If you don't git along a little faster Ah'm gonna blow yore ass off."

I began trotting as I heard the ominous click of the rifle bolt opened and slammed shut. My brain was awhirl. So much that was new and exciting had crowded into it within the last few hours that I was incapable of rational thinking.

He took me to the hospital, which was a long, two-story building with a rusty tin roof. It leaned perilously and looked as if a good strong wind would blow it over. A few flowers brightened the small front lawn. Three women inmates from Camp Four stood on the end of the sagging front porch.

Inside the hospital army cots were lined up neatly along two sides of the room. There were nine or ten patients. They looked like zombies. They had worked until they had dropped from exhaustion.

An elderly negro with a soot-black face pushed a button on the wall and told me to go upstairs. I began walking up the stairs which turned left onto a landing, then turned left again. As I reached the landing my passage was blocked by a girl. Her dress was pulled up around her hips, exposing white, round thighs. Her fingers were busily fastening a small white package in the hem of her panties. She glanced up with a startled expression, then continued with her task.

When she completed pinning the envelope, she dropped her dress and smoothed it around the pelvic curves with deft movements of her hands.

She was comparatively plain to look at. She had a bold, angular face. Her nose was long and straight. Her cheekbones were high, but not too prominent. Her lips were full-blown, sensuous, and beautifully shaped. Her figure was something to dream about. She was young, little, and stolid, and the sun had toasted her skin a tawny gold. She wore a yellow-and-black-checked dress. Her head and shoulders were covered with a faded green shawl drawn tightly together under her chin.

"Got a cigarette, honey?" she asked in a husky, feminine voice that makes a man listen with his ears, fingertips, and sex organs.

I pulled a pack of cigarettes from my shirt pocket and gave her one. When I flipped the wheel of my cigarette lighter she stepped closely in front of me. She reached up, grabbed my hand, and expertly held the flame under the end of the cigarette. She glanced up with cool, dreamy green eyes that held a trace of mockery; an all-knowing, wanton look.

"I've got to go, honey," she stated suddenly. "You make trustee and come over to our camp barn, and you and I will have a butchering party."

She stepped around me with a delicate tread and hurried down the stairs. Her body moved like something boneless but sensuous. It moved with the poetry of motion.

I walked on up the stairs and entered a room to which a trustee pointed. A heavy-set, middle-aged man stood at a wash basin washing his genital organs. The room contained a rumbled bed, a pair of scales, and two chairs with chicken-wire bottoms.

"Anything wrong with you?" he asked, as he pointed to one of the chairs.

"Pleurisy bothers me when it gets cold."

"It's hot here all the time." He grinned at his sly joke. "You got any money?"

"Some."

"Did you see that split-tail that just now left here?"

"I met a girl going down the stairway."

"Anytime you have ten dollars let me know. I'll call you over here and you can knock that out."

"What kind of doctor are you?" I asked angrily.

"I'm the con doctor, and she's doing time jest the same as you and me. After you've been here a while you'll look at things with another viewpoint. Right now, you git the hell on out of here."

A mousy-looking inmate was waiting for me to come out of the office. He was hunchbacked, terribly emaciated, and had long, spidery, talon-like fingers. He took me into a room where a blood specimen was taken. He was a tubercular patient and lived in a shack located at one side of the hospital which served to segregate the tuberculosis patients. His voice was low and squeaky. He would cough, grab his chest with both hands, then expectorate a bloody froth into a five-gallon oil can sitting in the middle of the floor which served as a wastebasket.

I felt grateful when he said I could go. I hurried down the stairway and returned to the yard, where the Seven Camp sheriff was waiting for me. He jumped astride the mule, which was contentedly nibbling grass, pointed toward the road, and began beating on the skinny animal with a switch he had picked up on the lawn of the hospital.

I walked back down the road approximately a hundred yards when the sheriff yelled for me to turn left. I turned onto a smooth pathway of gravel which led to the front of a long building which sagged sideways. The paint was chipped and bare in numerous spots, windows were broken out, and the long front porch sagged and looked as if it might fall completely off at any moment. Small guard shacks, resembling outhouses and in similar conditions of disrepair, surrounded the larger building. An aged goat was browsing phlegmatically under a huge tree. He ceased to chew and looked curiously at me with unwinking glassy eyes. Nearby a turkey gobbler drummed among his wives. I stepped onto a creaky porch, and a distinguished-looking man wearing plastic-rimmed glasses opened the screen door and commanded me to enter with an imperative gesture. I stepped into the dingy interior which afforded grateful relief from the glare and sulphurous [sic] heat of the sun.

I was stunned by the sight that greeted my eyes. The building was constructed entirely of wood. I had always pictured a prison as being constructed of fireproof steel and concrete. About four feet from the wall rough oak two-by-fours ran from the floor to the ceiling to form a huge cage. Uneven rows of nail heads in the walls looked as big as hazelnuts. The walls were painted white but had turned yellow with age. The fly-specked ceiling was painted dark brown. Two empty fifty-gallon oil drums served as stoves; one sat near the front of the building and the other sat about seventy-five feet away in the back end. Green army cots were jammed closely together, leaving a small space to form two narrow aisles.

"What's your rap, buddy?" the man with the glasses asked, as he searched me. He found a twenty-dollar bill I had concealed in the watch pocket of my trousers and that was the last I saw of it.

"Grand larceny," I answered.

"What did you steal?"

"A microscope," I gritted through clenched teeth.

"Did you sell it?"

"No."

"Dammit, don't ever steal anything you can't sell!"

He unlocked a door cut into the two-by-four bars and motioned for me to enter the cage.

"Short Hair for you, Stacy," he yelled to someone in the back of the building.

"Come on back here," a man said as he rose from a cot.

I walked around the oil-drum stove and saw a barber chair I had overlooked when I first entered. It was the most beat-up piece of equipment I had ever seen. It was constructed of wood, had originally been painted white, but was now black with dirt and the paint had peeled. The seat was ripped, torn, and in shreds. Tufts of straw protruded through the holes. The seat and cloth covering looked as if it had been attacked by a pack of starving wolves.

"Right up here," the barber said, as he patted the seat of the chair. He began cutting my hair with a pair of dull, rusty scissors. He used no clippers. When he finished there were tears in my eyes caused by tufts of hair being pulled out by the roots.

The only decorations in the building were tacked on the wall of the barbershop. One, a pencil sketch, showed a picture of two inmates engaged in an act of sodomy. The other was a painted sign which read:

*A wise old owl lived in an oak.*
*The more he heard, the less he spoke.*
*The less he spoke, the more he heard.*
*Why can't you be like that old bird?*

It was very quiet in the barracks; a bumblebee blundered from the hollyhocks outside through a broken window and snored loudly at the panes. Overhead could be heard the faint footsteps of the trustee guards and riders who worked nights. When the barber completed cutting my hair he stepped backward a couple of steps and surveyed his handiwork.

"Fine job, fine job," he gloated.

I brushed the hair off my clothes and tried to get it from under my shirt. He had placed no towel around my neck. He had simply grabbed the scissors and began clipping.

I was called back to the front part of the building, which was called the front picket, by the yard man when the haircut was completed. "Off with them clothes," the yard man, who was top trustee at the camp, said, as I approached the bars. In his hand he held a pair of overalls, an army dungaree jacket, and a pith helmet. I took off my shirt and the trousers that completed my suit. He pulled them through the bars, and I never saw them again. "Off with them shoes, too," he snapped.

I slipped the shoes off my feet, and he jerked them through the bars. Next day I saw a shotgun guard wearing them.

When I had stripped to my underclothes the yard man pushed the overalls and jacket through the bars. They were covered with patches, and the jacket was full of holes and ripped open down the seam on one side. The letters PW were painted in white on the back. The pith helmet wouldn't slip through the wooden bars so the yard man kicked it through, bending it out of shape and tearing a piece out of the top. While I put the overalls and jacket on he rummaged through a pile of worn-out shoes. He finally picked out a pair that had no strings, were run over on the side, too large, ripped at the seams, and covered with dried, caked mud and manure.

I was given nothing other than this; no socks, towel, soap, or toothbrush.

"Well, you can work the rest of the day in the vegetable house, come on," the yard man said, as I slipped the shoes on.

I followed with an awkward gait, trying to keep the string-less shoes on my feet, as the yard man led the way down the gravel pathway and across the dirt road to the vegetable house. The patched clothing was several sizes too large, and the pith helmet slipped down around my ears.

"It's about quitting time, isn't it?" I asked.

"Hell, no, it's only three o'clock," he snorted. "There's four more hours of work."

## CHAPTER THREE

The vegetable squad rider stood in an indolent attitude in the vegetable house doorway, his hands shoved deep in his pockets. His baggy, dirty, khaki clothes needed pressing. He possessed a thin, gaunt face, and bushy eyebrows which met in the middle. His black, beady, lustrous eyes had that melted blackness which seemed to focus to a burning glow and were alert and glancing, like those of some small wild animal. His long nose hung down over his mouth like a beak, resulting in his nickname of "Boot Nose." He had been in the Arkansas Penitentiary almost forty years, most of which he had served as a rider. The convict boss of each work gang was called a rider because they rode horses.

The vegetable house was an unpainted building constructed of rough oak boards and a tin roof. It leaned, as all the buildings did, and the boards near the foundation had rotted away. Five or six old men sat on the dirt floor inside the shack shelling peas. They were too old and crippled to work anywhere else. They suffered from cancer, tuberculosis, and general diseases. They never took a bath. They sat in crouched positions, shelling peas into buckets, mumbling to themselves, and scratching their ulcerated, bleeding shins and faces. The peas they shelled each day were taken to the mess hall, dumped into pots, and cooked without being washed. It was their job also to hobble into the fields surrounding the vegetable house to pick the peas and onion tops.

"Put this Short Hair to work the rest of the day, John," the yard man told the vegetable house rider.

John stepped out of the doorway and extracted a hoe from a stack of garden tools leaning against the side of the building. A toad hopped suddenly at the vibration of his feet, and he crushed the small, insolent brown body underneath his foot. He turned and led the way down a turn-row to a ditch where a solitary inmate stood cutting waist-high grass with a hoe.

"Catch in there and help him," John said, as he pointed to the ditch where the prisoner was standing in ankle-deep water.

I jumped into the ditch and began cutting weeds and Bermuda grass clogging the flow of water.

"Watch out for water moccasins," John cautioned, as he turned to leave.

## PART II. *RULED BY THE WHIP*, DALE WOODCOCK

The young man in the ditch stood slamming the hoe listlessly against the ground. Sweat was standing in shining beads on his face.

"Keep busy, Short Hair," he warned. "Boot Nose is watching all the time. He loves to have people whipped."

"What is this Short Hair business?" I asked.

"That's the name given to all new men. You'll get used to it. The main thing here is to keep busy. I know. I was here before. Even if it doesn't make sense, act like you're working."

He told me his name was Ben Sanford. He had been returned the day before from Leavenworth Penitentiary and would be given a trial within a few days for escaping from the Arkansas Penitentiary a few years earlier.

"I escaped from here and the Feds picked me up and tried me on the same charge I had already been convicted on here," he moaned. "Hey, man, I had it made when I was here before. I took care of the Governor's quarters at the Warden's Mansion. I ate good and the Warden had a bunch of women prisoners from Four Camp working for him and they kept my rear end dragging the ground."[24]

Ben was near thirty years old, the soft, boyish lines of youth were fading to show the heavier, final lines of maturity. He was a good-looking boy, with a quick grin, a laugh in his sunny blue eyes, and short straight, brown hair. A small, square jaw and a strong nose saved him from being too handsome.

"If they use the whip on me," he continued, "I might not have a trial. You should see that whip they use on escapees. The Warden has to use both hands to swing it. That thing will mutilate a fellow's ol' rear end."

---

[24] For more on treatment of women at Cummins see *Men or Mules*, "Chapter Eight, The Black Women's Stockade at Cummins," 120. Author Clyde Crosley claims that in 1936 Cummins held about 25 black women. He describes their housing as a delapidated [sic] wooden building. It sported clapboard siding, a tin roof, and short planks of wood nailed across the windows for bars. It was too cold in winter and too hot in summer. A patchwork fence about ten feet high around the stockade kept women convicts in and men convicts out, supposedly. Enterprising people on both sides of the fence sometimes broke the rules.

"I didn't think there was a prison in the world that still used the whip," I replied.

"I don't know about the rest of the world," Ben laughed, "but they sure use plenty of it here."

John ambled down the turn-row at that moment and sat down on the edge of the bank. He asked me numerous questions.

"I sorta like to talk to you," he said, as he rose to leave. "Most of them that come out here ain't got sense enough to tell me their name!"

Ben and I cut weeds the remainder of the afternoon. At six-thirty I noticed two squads of men running and walking across the top of the levee that ran for miles alongside the prison farm to protect the low fields from the Arkansas River. The squads were surrounded by guards walking and riding horses.

"What's that?" I asked Ben.

"That, my boy, is the long line. You and I will probably be in it tomorrow," he answered.

"Make it up," John shouted from the vegetable house doorway.

"That means quitting time," Ben told me. "I was indeed ready to call it a day. My skin was turning bright red. The months I had spent in jail had bleached my skin to milky white.

The old men hobbled out of the vegetable house and we formed a column of twos. There was only one shotgun guard assigned to the vegetable squad. He walked behind us as we headed for the small yard at the side of the barracks. We were the first to arrive on the yard. The long line straggled in a few minutes later. Most of the men in the line were young, with dust-laden hollows under their sun-wearied eyes. They were all dressed in ragged overalls, powdered with dust, jackets covered with patches, with PW painted on the back, and a few were barefooted. They dropped to the ground as soon as they came into the yard. A few fell on their backs on the burned, dry grass, motionless, with arms outstretched. All except new inmates were gaunt, haggard, and wore vacant expressions. A gloomy silence prevailed.

Ben and I sat leaning against a concrete pillar until the yard man yelled, "Make it up!"

The prisoners lying scattered around the yard struggled to their feet and formed a long line in front of the mess hall door.

Tighten that line up," the yard man barked, as we filed into the mess hall. The mess hall was a wooden addition built on the side of the barracks. The rough oak boards were unpainted and there were cracks through which the wind whistled as Death's scythe might whistle if he were mowing down men with a right good will. One oil-drum stove sat in the middle of the floor. A row of wooden tables lined each wall. The prisoners walked down one side until the benches were filled, then filed down the other side. We remained standing, holding the pith helmets, until the yard man yelled, "Sit down!"

The prisoners' faces and hands were covered with dirt and dust. There were no facilities for washing before eating. There was a water bucket filled with black-eyed peas on each table; also a brass bowl half-full of boiled onion tops and a tray of cornbread; a gallon jug filled with water; and tin cans with one end cut out served as cups. This was the type of food that smashed the health of the inmates. The camp was filled with tubercular patients who should have been segregated. The bill of fare never changed except for Christmas, Thanksgiving, and the Fourth of July holidays.

The yard man hadn't finished saying 'sit down" when the men dropped their helmets which clattered and rolled around the floor. They reached for the cornbread stacked on a tray which was covered with green flies. They clawed, scratched, and acted like wild men. The cornbread disappeared as if by magic. I stood and watched with awe.

"It's who gets here fustest with the mostest," Ben said.[25]

I dipped out a spoonful of the peas, but couldn't eat them. They were tasteless, having been dumped into a pot of water and boiled without any seasoning.

"You took 'em, so eat 'em," the yard man said, as he tapped my shoulder. "That is, if you don't want your ass busted the first day."

I forced the peas down, gagging with each swallow. There was an overpowering odor of sweating bodies and feet. The other prisoners ate the bucket of peas and onion tops with gusto. When they emptied the bucket and pan they realized there was nothing else to eat so they turned on the benches

---

[25] This statement sometimes is attributed to Confederate General Nathan Bedford Forrest when the general explained how he won so many battles.

and began pulling their shoes off. A few wore socks; these they shook until the air was filled with dust.

The yard man walked around the mess hall to check the pans. When he saw they had all been emptied he opened the double doors leading into the barracks. As he opened the door trustees poured from the barracks where they had been conducting a shakedown. This ritual was performed each evening. The trustees scattered the belongings of the rank men around the building each time they shook down. They also stole what they wanted. The rank men formed lines as the door was opened and the trustees searched them, doing a thorough job. As we filed into the barracks the yard man and night yard man stood on each side of the door counting. The first rank man through the door called out, number "one," and the men following him counted consecutively. If an inmate failed to hear the number of the man in front of him, the yard man would box his ears.

"Everybody back out here. Can't you idiots count?" the night yard man said in a tone of voice that sounded like the snarl of a cougar, as the last man came through the door, and his lip curled with the snarl.

We returned to the mess hall and filed, counting, through the door again. The door was padlocked after the second count. I stood in the middle of the huge cage, bewildered.

"Go see the floorwalker," Ben told me, "he'll assign you a cot."

I walked to the back of the building where the floorwalker was making and selling coffee for a nickel per cup.

"Where am I to sleep?" I asked.

"Aw, hell," he said, as he slammed a spoon on the table disgustedly. He turned and gazed around the room. "There's no empty bunks, sleep with anybody!"

"You mean I'm supposed to walk up to somebody I've never seen before and ask if I can sleep with them?"

"That's right. There are no empty bunks. Go on. Git out of my face!" he replied without a trace of emotion, so flatly and with so quiet a tone that I was dumfounded and uttered not another syllable. I walked to Ben's cot and told him what the floorwalker had said.

"We've got two beds here," he replied. "There are three of us sleeping here, but if we sleep sideways we can get four in."

The two cots serving as a bed for four were originally painted green, but a coating of dirt had turned them black. Some of the hooks which fastened onto the wire that held the mattresses were missing, permitting the springs to sag. The mattresses were black with dirt and spotted as if someone had urinated on them. There were no pillows or sheets and only one blanket. The whole place was pervaded by a smell of long prevalent squalor. Inadequate little light bulbs swayed and twinkled, barely illuminating the dingy cage. Guards walking outside the cage continually fired blanks in their pistols.

"Git them clothes off," the yard man screamed from the front picket.

The inmates began pulling off their overalls and jackets. Only a few had underclothes which their relatives had brought them. Those who had no underclothes walked around naked. The prison officials never issued underclothing in the summer.

Ben's cot was near the front picket, which was approximately twelve feet wide and stretched the width of the building. As I sat down beside Ben I noticed a short, stocky man stride into the barracks with the pompous air of a field marshal. He had a square, strong face. His shirt sleeves were rolled high, exposing sinewy arm muscles which bulged like steel cables. He wore khaki clothes, a big straw hat, and cowboy boots. A tomblike silence fell over the building as he walked in. He muttered something inaudible to the yard man, who hurried into a small office constructed in one corner of the picket. The yard man emerged carrying a whip. The whip was approximately four feet long, five inches wide; was about one-eighth inch thick near the handle and sloped to a finer degree of thinness near the end. It had a square one-foot handle.

"Bring ol' smilin' boy to me," the man wearing the cowboy boots said.

The floorwalker walked rapidly to the center of the building, where a young man with buck teeth sat on the edge of a cot.

"Git up from there," the floorwalker gritted, as he kicked the young man's shins.

"Who is that?" I asked Ben, as I pointed to the front picket.

"That's the camp warden. Watch your mouth and your finger or they'll have you out there too!"

The floorwalker shoved the young inmate through the door which was relocked. The inmate walked to where the camp warden stood swishing the whip over his head and lay down on the floor on his stomach, his rounded posterior protruding and presenting itself as a target. A convict guard sitting in an opposite corner rose to his feet and pulled the pistol from his holster and held it in his hand.

"What's wrong with you?" the warden asked, as he slung the whip over his shoulder. "Captain, I'm doing the best I can," the prisoner replied.

The warden rose on his toes and brought the whip downward with all the force he could throw into the blow. It landed with a dull thud on the prone man's buttocks. He bounced completely off the floor, but uttered no sound. Three more lashes were administered before he began to moan and threw his hand behind him to shield his buttocks and caught the next blow on his knuckles. Two trustees standing nearby dropped on him. One knelt on his shoulders and held his arms while the other held his ankles. As the tenth blow was administered he was begging the warden to stop. The eighteenth blow ripped open the seat of his overalls and he was screaming. Twenty lashes were administered before the prisoner was permitted to stagger back to his cot, holding his bruised, bleeding buttocks. Throughout the whipping the warden's face was devoid of human passion as the face of a marble angel over a sepulcher.

I noticed another inmate sitting a few cots away holding his head in his hands and sobbing with the deep, hoarse notes of masculine anguish.

"Why is he crying?" I asked Ben. "He didn't get whipped."

"They're brothers," he responded.

I later learned the inmate had been whipped because the long line rider had asked him for a pack of cigarettes and he had refused to buy them. The rider then told the warden the inmate had not been doing enough work. The warden would whip any inmate the convict guards and riders asked him to. No questions were asked. It was his duty to comply with their demands. If he refused the trustees would lose their authority.

The warden stayed in the building approximately thirty minutes talking and joking with his trustees. Inside the cage the gloomy silence prevailed until he left. As he walked out the door to leave the building there was a sudden stir, and a sigh of relief that was distinctly audible.

"Could I borrow a stamp, buddy?" a naked inmate asked me after the warden left. "My little girl is sick and I want to write to my wife."

I gave him a stamp and a smile brightened his face. No stamps, pencils, or stationery were issued. If an inmate had no money, he was forced to beg, borrow, or steal stamps and stationery in order to write to his family. It was a pathetic sight to watch the inmates stroll the aisles each night begging for these articles.

"You got any money, Doc?" Ben asked with a grin as he saw me give my last stamp away.

"They took what I had," I answered, "but I have money at home."

"We can go in together and buy something to eat when you get some money. You can't live on the slop they feed you here. Hogs eat better than we do."

A small commissary was located in a corner of the front picket. It consisted of a small cabinet hung on the wall whose four shelves held tobacco, candy bars, a few canned goods, and toilet articles. A cold drink box sat near the two-by-four bars.

The commissary was operated by the Head Warden's most trusted trustee. He had gained this position by saving the Head Warden's life several years before when a convict tried to kill the Head Warden when he was a camp warden. The commissary trustee was feared by rank men, other trustees, and even the camp wardens. He could do no wrong in the eyes of the Head Warden, who upheld whatever he did. He owned his own horses and saddles, got a furlough to go to Little Rock or Pine Bluff anytime he wished, and was permitted to visit the taverns and dance halls located near the prison. His iron-gray hair, deeply carved features, and cavernous black eyes gave him the air of power that his reputation demanded.

Ben bought two cokes and two candy bars and gave me one of each. I tore the wrapper off, conscious of the stares of the hungry men around me. I glanced up and all the inmates nearby sat stoically, dully, watching me eat the candy. I broke the bar in two parts and gave half to a sixteen-year-old boy sitting across the aisle. I had no desire to eat with two dozen hungry men watching me.

"It's hard, Doc," Ben said, "but in a month or two, you'll be as hardhearted as the Bear."

I slept very little that night. It was the most uncomfortable bed I had ever attempted to sleep in. I was beginning to feel the effects of the sunburn. I turned from side to side in feverish unrest.

We were awakened at three-thirty the next morning by the violent clanging of a dinner bell at the front of the building. Wearily I arose and rubbed my rebellious eyes. I slipped my clothes on and went to the section built onto the rear end of the building which served as a toilet and shower room. It was a small place, approximately eight feet wide and twenty feet long. There were four face bowls, four commodes, and five showers, but only three were in working condition. Over two hundred men were trying to wash in the four face bowls. A few of the inmates didn't bother to wash before breakfast. It was so crowded I couldn't get in. The men were pushing, cursing, and shouting. I found a small piece of soap in a crack of the floor after I managed to squeeze in. Someone turned on the showers, and the inmates gathered around them to wash. I washed my face and hands but had no towel to dry with, so I used toilet paper. The floorwalker saw me unwinding the paper and called me a few choice names, and some I had never heard before.

"You idiots git up yere," the floorwalker said after we were permitted ten minutes to wash. "It's time for ham and eggs."

I was pushed along in the mob that rushed to the door leading to the mess hall. The yard men were standing beside the camp warden as we walked through, counting. Each man walked through the doorway with bowed head, staring at the floor. I looked the warden in the eye as I walked through.

Before we were seated one of the inmates at the next table grabbed the spoon in the oatmeal bowl and held it until the yard man gave orders to be seated. Thus he was first to dip from the bowl. The yard man saw him holding the spoon and told the warden. The warden brought the whip into the mess hall and whipped him while the other inmates went ahead eating, ignoring the screaming, squirming inmate lying on the floor.

When the warden had finished whipping the man, he walked over and tapped my shoulder. I turned to face him.

"Short hair," he drawled, "when you come through that door again don't look at me. I don't want no damned convict looking at me." He glared fiercely at me to see that no insolent response was made.

Breakfast consisted of an enamel pan full of unsweetened, lumpy oatmeal. The pan was chipped, bent, and had holes which had been plugged with greasy rags. There was a gallon jug of black coffee and a bowl of watery gravy which was tasteless. Bread was the only eatable thing on the table. The coffee was gone before the jug was given to me. I gave half my bread to Ben. He advised me to eat and stated it would be a long time until dinner. The other men at the table sat gorging themselves as if they were at a feast. The filth and slime made me feel ill. There were particles of food left on the trays from the previous meal. The spoons were rusty.

"Outside," the yard man roared after he checked to see that the pans had been emptied. Everyone rose and went into the yard. Each man dropped his spoon into a large lard bucket sitting in the middle of the floor as we filed out of the mess hall. Ben told me to follow him, and he sauntered over to join the vegetable squad.

"Captain," the laundry rider said when the squads had been formed, "I need a new washing machine."

"I'll git you one," the warden answered dryly. He walked to the long line and grabbed a young, blond-headed, harelipped inmate by the shoulder, pulled him from the line, and shoved him toward the rider. "Here," he said. "You can have Pretty Boy Floyd."

The clothes were boiled in a large kettle, then scrubbed on washboards.

By dinner time that day I had turned lobster red. I realized that seven more hours of weed cutting that afternoon in the broiling sun would give me a sever sunburn. I stopped working for a few minutes before noon when I noticed John coming down he turn-row carrying a hoe handle across his shoulder. He said nothing as he approached but slid down he bank to where I stood trying to fasten the torn places in the jacket I was wearing.

"I'll learn you to keep working," he said in a soft tone of voice, and struck me on the head with the handle. The blow sent me reeling. I saw red streaks, then a searing white light seemed to explode, blinding my eyes. The sun seemed to dance and dart across the sky, expanding awesomely and contracting almost to nothing. A whirlpool of roaring pain sucked at my mind. I sat up in a dazed way, conscious of a racking pain in the head and of a sickening weakness. I placed my hand on my head. The hair was wet and matted, and the hand, when drawn away, was red. I now suffer short blackout periods caused by that blow.

"I hated to do that because I like you," John said, as I staggered to my feet. "But that's a good lesson. Some of these other damned ol' sorry riders would have had you whipped if they had caught you not working."

Dinner consisted only of a bowl of peas and a tray of cornbread. I still couldn't eat the peas. I nibbled on a piece of bread. The blow on the head had given me a throbbing headache and I felt sick to my stomach. I tossed the bread onto my tray and went to the yard and sat under the shade of a tree which rose like a great, gray, gaunt ghost from a depression in the yard.

By quitting time that evening my hands were burned so badly I couldn't close my fingers because of the swelling. My neck was also burned and swollen so much that I could not turn my head without excruciating pain, and my face was on fire. I expect to carry the scars from those burns to my grave. My head was throbbing and my eyes grated in their sockets. I ate none of the peas and onion tops for supper. I intended to borrow five dollars from the floorwalker to buy food at the commissary. He charged 100 per cent interest on all loans, but I had reached the point where I was willing to pay it.

"How do I know you got money at home? You may be tryin' to beat me," the floorwalker stated when I asked to borrow five dollars.

"You'll have to trust me," I told him. "I'm not trying to beat you out of anything. I'm trying to avoid starving."

"Yeah, yeah, I know," he snarled, "but I learned a long time ago not to trust anybody, especially these convicts."

"If he doesn't pay you, I will," Ben told him.

The floorwalker had known Ben before his escape and agreed to loan me the money.

"Short Hair," he said as he pulled a leather pouch filled with metal disks from his pocket, "I'll be watching for you to git a check. When you do I want my money."

There were at least a hundred dollars in the pouch he pulled from his pocket. The metal disks were called brozine by the inmates, and were substituted for money. When the checks were sent from the front office the commissary trustee issued the disks in exchange for the checks. The disks had Cummings [sic] or Tucker Prison Farm stamped on them and a large number representing their amount. When the disks were received from the commissary trustee, it was necessary to guard them closely. Most of the inmates kept the disks in a tobacco sack pinned inside their overalls. It was necessary to carry them at all times, especially when going to the shower room. One inmate made a practice of crawling on the floor at night stealing money. He would crawl under the cots of the sleeping inmates and search the clothing lying on the floor. What he stole he split with the floor walker, who was his partner in this lucrative enterprise.

I gave Ben fifty cents and he added an equal amount. He then went to the commissary to buy food. The commissary was owned by the Head Warden, and he doubled the price on practically all articles sold, especially the food.

While Ben was gone, a tall, sallow-complexioned, bleary-eyed youth walked to my cot and sat down beside me. "You don't know anything about me," he said in a low tone, "but my time is up tomorrow and I can go home if I can borrow enough money to buy a ticket home. I've already borrowed two and a half dollars, but I need fifty cents more. If you'll loan me that much, I'll send it back when I get home."

When an inmate completed his sentence he had to have his own clothes to wear out and money to buy a bus ticket. If he was indigent and had no clothes, he was held in custody ten extra days, for which he received three dollars and a khaki shirt and trousers.

I contemplated a moment. Fifty cents was an insignificant amount. But it was also a great deal of money in the predicament in which I found myself. I also thought of paying the fines of the prisoners in the County Jail and not getting repaid.

"I'll take a chance on you," I said, and handed him a fifty-cent disk. His eyes sparkled with happiness as he grabbed the disk, jumped to his feet without saying a simple "thanks,' and ran to the front picket where he showed it to the yard man.

Eight days later I received a fifty-cent money order from him.

"Ben returned carrying a small jar of peanut butter, a jar of syrup, and a box of crackers which he had purchased with the dollar. We walked to the back of the building where the floorwalker was busily brewing coffee. Sitting at one end of the hot plate was a gallon can filled with knives, forks, and spoons. We asked to borrow a knife to mix the syrup and peanut butter.

"I'll loan you one if you buy a cup of coffee," the floorwalker stated.

"We were gonna buy some anyway, you cheapskate bastard," Ben retorted. Ben made sandwiches and we sat on the floorwalker's cot and ate several, washing them down with the weak coffee which tasted as if it had been made in a shovel. From that date on I ate little of the prison food. I survived on peanut butter and candy bars. Five dollars was all we were permitted to draw from our account each week, but Ben told me of a way to circumvent this rule. We could purchase anything we wanted on credit from the commissary as long as we had enough money on the books at the front office to cover it. We were then permitted to draw extra checks by putting the commissary trustee's name on them. This procedure met with the Head Warden's approval, as he was making a nice profit from the eight camps scattered over the two farms.

I slept less that night than the night before. I found it impossible to get into a comfortable position. I was repeatedly aroused from an uncomfortable doze by a snoring inmate a few cots away. The sunburn on my neck was swollen so much I could not turn my head without great pain. The bare, rough mattress grated against the burn like sandpaper. My head was lying in one of the large stained spots that looked like it had been caused by urine, so I sat on the edge of the bed most of the night.

Breakfast the next morning consisted of a gallon jug of molasses, bread, and black coffee. I sat next to a crusty, crotchety old man named Page. He was in his seventies and walked about with a hickory club for a cane. He would strike anyone with the cane who bothered or irritated him. He was as withered as a brown apple. There was never enough coffee in the jug for everyone at the table, but Page always poured his cup full to the brim. He would drink about half of it; then say something to attract the attention of the other inmates, and as they looked up he would spit in the remainder so no one would drink it. His feet were gray with crusted dirt. He never took a bath. One night the inmate sleeping next to him asked the floorwalker to make him take a bath. "Man," the disgruntled inmate said, "I can't stand that smell. Make that old codger take a bath, let me move, or do something!"

"Boy," the floorwalker answered, "do you know what you're asking? That old man has been here thirty years and never took a bath. One now would kill him!"

Page had recently been returned from the Girls' Training School near Little Rock where he had worked as a gardener. While there he had written a letter to a newspaper accusing the male superintendent of having sexual relations with the teenage girls entrusted to his supervision. A reporter went to the school to investigate, and Page was called to the superintendent's office where it was expected he would deny sending the letter. Instead he told everything he had seen and heard. The superintendent denied everything Page told.

"Don't call me a liar," Page roared and struck the superintendent with his fist, sending him sprawling on the floor. Page was returned to the prison for this escapade, but he was not whipped, probably because of his age.

I poured some of the molasses from the jug and dipped the bread into it; it tasted good but gritty. Three months later I was able to understand why it had tasted gritty. I had taken four or five bites when I noticed the man sitting directly opposite me picking little round black objects out of the bread and dividing scowling stares between the bread and the cook who was standing in the kitchen door. I ate no more breakfast. "How do you like this place, Short Hair?" Page cackled, as he punched me in the ribs.

"He don't like it worth a damn," Ben answered before I could open my mouth. "But you must like it, you nasty old bastard. They offered to let you out to live with your son and you refused."

Page clamped his jaws tightly together and stared at Ben with a gloomy, evil look on his withered old face. "I'll knock you in the head with this cane, you young punk," he retorted.

"If you ever hit me with that cane," Ben responded, "Ill stomp all the hair off your ass. Your age means nothin' to me."

"If I hear any more noise at this table, I'll have every man sittin' here whipped," the yard man said, as he walked briskly from the table where the camp warden sat in a tired, ungirt [with belt loosened or removed] position, leisurely sipping a cup of coffee. "Sanford," the yard man continued, "there's enough heat on you now. A little more and you'll find yourself in the hot spot."

When we were forming into work squads on the yard a red-headed inmate who had been brought in during the night was placed in the vegetable squad. He was called Society Red by the other trustees. He had served several sentences in the Arkansas Penitentiary where he had served each sentence as a guard. Many of the trustees were sadists and returned o the prison where they could see and have other inmates whipped. Several returned while they were on parole and asked to be readmitted, and several more committed new crimes in order to receive new sentences.

"I wouldn't come back if I knew I wouldn't be a guard," Society Red stated, as he, Ben, and I began cutting knee-high Bermuda grass in a two-acre onion field. He had hair that was wild and red; his complexion was similar. He was tall and bony; his hands flapped loosely from his jacket sleeves. His voice was windy and sneering.

Society Red divulged the details of an escape I had read about in a detective magazine while I was in jail in Ohio. He had been one of the guards who helped capture the escapees and killed an innocent man in the process.

The escape occurred at Tucker Farm. Four inmates killed a yard man and fled. Approximately one hundred trustees were ordered to search for them. The trustees were armed with rifles, shotguns, and pistols, with orders to shoot to kill on sight. They were given authority to stop and search all cars and authority to enter any home. Many of the trustees were classified as "sexually dangerous psychopaths." Yet they had authority to search honest, law-abiding citizens and enter private homes with guns.

The following day, officials at the prison received an anonymous tip that the escapees were hiding at a private residence in Little Rock. The officials promptly loaded armed trustees in cars and sped to the capital city.

The house was surrounded and orders given for the occupants to come out, with hands over their heads. No response was made to the request, so the trustees opened fire on the house. As bullets plowed into the house the front door opened and one elderly man stepped out on the porch. The trustees riddled him with bullets. When identification was made it was found the man was completely deaf. He was the owner of the house and no escapees were hidden there. An innocent man had been murdered by kill-crazy convicts. The murder was ruled an accident and the incident dropped. The citizens of Arkansas have no assurance there will never be another occurrence of this type.

All the escapees were apprehended, after having been shot. I met three of them later when I was transferred to Two Camp. One had been crippled by a bullet and was able to hobble about in the vegetable squad. The other two worked in the long line where they had been since their recapture. One of these inmates was assigned the hardest work possible, and it was common knowledge that the prison officials were trying to work him until he was broken in body and spirit. The escapee who had fired the bullet that killed the yard man was assigned to help the water boy. He had gained his position a year or two after being returned. He realized he would have to serve a long sentence and volunteered to turn informer. He was known as "the Fink," and told the yard man or warden anything that might benefit him.

"There was enough bullets in that old man," Society Red told me, speaking of the slain man, "to hold him up straight and when he fell over and hit the porch it sounded like a lead bar falling."

He laughed as he told me about other details of the manhunt, especially when he described chasing a high school girl to her front door.

Society Red had been returned the night before from the Arizona Penitentiary to complete a sentence he had been paroled on. He was released a few months before I was. Upon his release he committed a federal offense, was sentenced to Leavenworth Penitentiary where a group of prisoners who had known him in Arkansas poured gasoline on him and set him on fire. A witness said he was almost burned to death, but alert guards smothered the flames and he survived. Many trustees were found murdered after they were released.

As we filed into the barracks that evening the yard men issued each inmate a five-cent bag of RJR tobacco. Only one bag was issued.

My hands were sunburned so severely when we quit work at seven that night that they were turning purple and green. The convict doctor came to the barracks after supper to administer to the ills of the inmates. I stepped into the line forming at the front of the building. An elderly man in front of me took several minutes in describing his aches and pains. He rattled on and on with whimpering volubility.

"This man needs a treatment," the doctor said, as he turned to the warden standing on the front picket.

"I got the treatment that makes the blind see and the lame walk," the warden responded.

The elderly man was led onto the picket and given seven lashes with the whip.

"What do you want?" the doctor asked after the inmate had been placed back in the cage, and he turned to me.

"I would like to have something to put on this sunburn," I replied somewhat fearfully.

"Sunburn," he scoffed. "Hell, you ain't been here long enough to git sunburned."

After he and the trustees had laughed at his remark he poured me a handful of salts. He gave salts or laxative pills for practically all ailments.

I went to the bathroom, dumped the salts into a toilet bowl, and flushed it, making sure none of the guards, floorwalker, or yard men were watching. I then removed the dusty overalls and jacket and stepped under a shower. The cool, softly falling water relieved the throbbing and burning of the sunburn, although I could not bear to have a heavy flow of water on it. I stayed in the shower almost an hour, conscious of the curses that the men sitting on the stools were mentally hurling at me. The stools were almost directly under the showers, and anyone sitting on them was drenched when the showers were turned on.

After the shower I stood in the room for a few minutes in order to let the wind blowing through the windows dry me. I was also watching for the laundry workers to bring in clean clothing.

Clean clothing was issued every Saturday night. Ben had told me the laundry squad brought the clothing in and dumped it in the middle of the floor. The floorwalker would yell "clothes," and the prisoners would then jump up from their cots and dash for the clean clothing, snatching and grabbing what they could. There were never enough clothes for everyone. The laundry squad would bring in eighty or ninety pair of overalls and jackets to outfit the entire camp. It was sometimes comical to watch two or more men grab the same overalls or jacket. A tug-of-war would follow. The losers would get no clothes; by the time the tug-of-war was over the pile of clothes would be gone. At other times it wasn't comical because the tugging, cursing inmates would get into a fight. The floorwalker would let them fight until one, or both, was badly beaten, then he would take them to the front picket where the warden would use the whip on the belligerents. A fight usually erupted around the clean clothing pile every Saturday night.

I pulled an old, faded pair of overalls from the pile. They were threadbare. The hooks were torn off so I borrowed a knife from the floorwalker and cut holes in the bib. I then ran the shoulder straps through the holes and tied them on. The overalls were so short they came almost to my knees.

"You're prepared for high water," the floorwalker laughed, as I tied them on.

I was unable to get a clean jacket. By the time I had pulled the overalls from the pile, the jackets had disappeared. I shook the dust from the one I had and prepared to wear it another week.

After the clothes were issued someone sat a gambling table up in the back of the barracks and several inmates gathered around it to play beat-the-dealer. Had the occasion been a clinic, the game a corpse, and the dealer an operating surgeon, the group about the table could not have been more absorbed or more quiet; a cold, deathlike, ominous silence seemed to saturate the very air. The only sounds were the click of the rolling dice, like the chattering of teeth, and the monotones of the players as they placed their bets.

I asked the floorwalker for permission to sleep on one of the wooden benches enclosing the barbershop. He grudgingly consented.

Ben spent an hour at the gambling table and lost two dollars. Afterward we made some sandwiches and sat eating them while the warden whipped four rank men and a trustee, who had been caught committing a crime against nature with a dog while he was on duty as a guard in one of the shacks surrounding the barracks.

Before the lights were turned out, I sat on the bench observing the antics of the prisoners and listening to their vulgar language. They described in flowing terms the newspaper, radio, and television publicity they had received when they had been arrested. Most convicts in their feeble, warped minds picture themselves as glamorous big shots. They described the beautiful women they would make love to when they were released, the banks they would rob, and the Cadillac cars they would drive. I soon formed the opinion that at least 40 per cent of the inmates were depraved, evil, insane monsters.

## CHAPTER FOUR

I slept soundly that night on the wooden bench. I slept as if in a trance; overpowered by leaden slumber. The mental and physical strain had taken its toll.

We were awakened before daybreak the next morning by a screaming inmate who was being whipped on the front picket. The screams sent cold chills stepping up my spine to the base of my brain. Dazed with sleep, I sat up and tried to collect my scattered senses. I was to be awakened many mornings in the future by this type of alarm clock. The inmate being whipped had gotten off his cot during the night to get a drink of water without first getting permission from the floorwalker. It was necessary to say "getting up" in a loud voice when leaving he bed. The floorwalker would then give his permission for the inmate to leave the bunk.

While we were eating breakfast the yard man came into the mess hall carrying two sheets of paper, which was a list of twenty inmates who were to be transferred to Tucker Prison Farm immediately after breakfast. The transfer left a few vacant cots, and I was fortunate enough to get one near the middle of the barracks. As I sat down on the edge of the cot I noticed an inmate on the opposite cot reading a letter and cursing policemen out loud.

"You undoubtedly don't care for policemen," I said to him.

"Cops—kill 'em all, the damn bloody bloodsuckers," he retorted. "That's my motto, and the judges and lawyers too. A damn cop helped send me down here, now he's tryin' to lay my ol' lady. When I get home I'll cut him a new asshole. Law! What's it good for? If they'd put everybody in jail that's out an' everybody out that's in, it wouldn't make any change. Them on the outside is the biggest crooks. They jest ain't been caught. You can be put in jail for adultery. Now then, if they put everybody in jail who's been in bed with somebody they're not married to, how many of them people would have a record? How many of them out there never done anything they could be sent up for?"

I stretched out on the cot and contemplated this bit of philosophy. It had a bit of truth to it, I thought.

We were not permitted to get off our cots on Sunday. Exceptions were to go to the bathroom, buy coffee, or get a drink of water. There were no water fountains. We drank from the face bowls in the shower room. We had no cups or glasses, so in order to get a drink we turned on the water and caught a drink in our cupped hands.

After breakfast the inmates sat on the beds, silent and morose, smoking; each wrapped in his own somber thoughts. The barracks was filled with a blue, hazy smoke. Most of the men smoked all the tobacco they had received the night before. They did this every Sunday and begged cigarettes and tobacco from the inmates who had money the remainder of the week. I bought a pack of cigarettes, and Ben and I spent most of the morning in the back of the barracks smoking and drinking coffee.

At noon there was a tray of cornbread and a pan half-filled with black-eyed peas on the table where I sat. It was visiting Sunday, and the cook probably estimated he could prepare less peas on that day because visitors were permitted to bring food with them, and the inmates could bring boxes of food into the barracks.

The pan of peas was passed down the opposite side of the table where they were all dipped out. The last man on the bench poured the water on them into his tray and dumped his cornbread into it. This left everyone on the side of the table where I sat with nothing to eat except cornbread. The man sitting next to me picked the pan up and held it over his head.

"How about something to eat?" he asked the yard man who strolled over to investigate.

"I tol' you idiots when you drove up there that was all the peas they was," the yard man replied.

"But---we didn't git anything to eat on this side."

"Whether you git anything to eat or not," responded the yard man, as he waved his hands with a consummate expression of indifference, "doesn't bother me. I'm lookin' out only for number one. You idiots even want to eat on Sunday when you don't work."

"Ain't this a damned shame?" the disgusted inmate asked me. They work you until your eyeballs and asshole pooch out and then won't give a fellow anything to eat! I wish to hell somebody would do somethin' about this place."

"Any more lip and I'll do something about you," the yard man snapped. "I'll be sittin' on your head on the front picket while the man is droppin' the leather on your ass."

The inmate became silent. He knew it was useless to argue and the yard man could have him whipped by simply snapping his fingers.

Visitors began arriving at the camp immediately after dinner. They were ordered to park their cars on a lot at the side of the building which was used as a storage space for junked farm implements. Trustees searched each car thoroughly and frisked the car's occupants. When I saw this practice I wrote and told my mother never to visit me. The visitors straggled across the yard, carrying boxes of food, carrying babies in their arms, and dragging reluctant children by the hand. They were forced to congregate in the yard in the hot sun until the yard man permitted them to enter as a group into the mess hall which was used as a visiting room.

Inmates who had visitors lined up barefooted in front of the door leading to the mess hall, where they were searched. After they entered the mess hall they were permitted to put their shoes back on.

Rank men were permitted to have visitors only once a month while the trustees could have visitors anytime. When wives or girl friends visited the trustees, they were permitted to take them to the guard shacks and various buildings scattered around he farm.

Any visitors arriving after two o'clock to visit rank men were turned away. When an inmate walked barefooted through the mess hall door, he was joined by a trustee who sat beside him at the table. The trustee listened to every word the rank man said to the visitors, and if he made any derogatory remarks concerning the institution the trustee reported it to the warden who would administer a whipping.

The trustees expected to receive what they wished to eat from the boxes of food the visitors brought and the addresses of any girls that attracted them. An inmate who did not share his food with the trustee who sat with him at the visiting table was destined to receive a whipping, as the trustee would ask the warden to whip him after visiting hours were over or sometime during the following week.

The most sadistic practice the trustees were involved in was making fun of and ridiculing the rank inmates' visitors, especially the female visitors. One particular case of this practice involved a young inmate from Texarkana, Texas, named Jimmy. Jimmy had a sixteen-year-old sister who always accompanied his mother and father when they drove to the farm on visitors' day.

We were picking butter beans when a shotgun guard walking behind the squad began asking annoying questions about her. "I'm gittin' out of here next month," the guard said in a loud voice so he could be heard by everyone in the field. "Do you think your sister would go for me if I go down to visit her?"

Then the guard began asking thoroughly depraved questions about the girl, while the other guards laughed. Most of the guards had been committed for sex offenses, and that was their favorite topic of conversation throughout each day.

Jimmy continued to pick beans rapidly, pugnaciously, but the guard's remarks finally became so lascivious they enraged Jimmy, who jumped to his feet with clenched fists and advanced toward his tormentor, his eyes ablaze like August lightening, his face seared with his passions as with the torture iron.

"Come on, come on," the guard taunted, as he drew a bead on Jimmy's chest with the shotgun. "Take one more step and the undertaker will be stuffin' cotton in yore ass and tyin' a knot in yore dick."

Jimmy realized the guard was not joking so he halted. The guards could kill anyone they chose to and there would be no investigation. They could drag his body out of the field, tell the warden he had attempted to escape, and that would be the end of the investigation. The camp warden was the only one employed by the state. He drove to the field two or three times a day just to whip several inmates. There were days when he was never seen.

When the warden drove to the field a few minutes after this incident occurred the rider rode out to where he sat in his jeep. A minute or two later the rider climbed on his horse and rode back into the field to where Jimmy sat picking beans and took him to the warden, who gave him sixteen lashes with the whip.

"My time will come," Jimmy said when he returned with tears streaming down his face. "If that low-life scum ever touches my sister I'll kill him."

A similar occurrence took place a few days later, when the same guard began asking lascivious questions about an inmate's mother. This particular inmate, however, didn't jump to his feet and advance toward the guard. He realized the futility of this rash act. He sat as stolid as a boiler, only the steam gauge of his eyes denoting the pressure as the vituperative razzing continued. Finally he responded with the only weapon he had. He called the guard, the guard's family, and ancestors, every foul name he could think of. He was something of a master of insult, and moreover, he dived into his memory to bring forth imprecations. He exhausted his stock of adjectives and epithets. The customary melancholy of his face was supplanted by a gleam of satisfaction. As the guard stalked away he again hurled at him vituperations thick and fast. He, too, received a whipping for "talking back to a guard!"

Ben had visitors that first visiting day. He didn't tell me who they were and I didn't ask, but they brought a box of food and magazines which he shared with me.

"I want all magazines out of the barracks by Wednesday," the floorwalker growled after the visitors had departed. "If I find any under any mattress Thursday mornin', somebody is gonna git his ass slapped."

After supper that evening the inmate whose screams had awakened us that morning as he was being whipped was called to the front picket.

"Drop yore britches, boy," the warden said, as he peered through the bars. "I want to see what kind of a job I did on your rump."

The inmate inflated his nostrils and looked mutinous. He flushed and looked wrathful. He opened his mouth to reply, thought better of his purpose, and smiled somewhat painfully. He turned around, unbuckled his overalls, and let them fall down around his ankles, exposing his bruised, discolored buttocks.

"I did a pretty good job on it," the warden guffawed, and he grew suddenly genial under the mellowing influence of what he considered a joke. Unaccustomed laughter shook him. He even squandered a smile on the hapless inmate standing timidly before him. "I was going to give you another whippin' now, but that looks pretty bad, so I'll let it go for ten or fifteen minutes!"

He whipped the inmate again at nine o'clock that night.

The various camp wardens usually slacked off on their whipping rampages a day or two before visiting day, especially on Saturday. The main reason for this was because an inmate who had been whipped on four consecutive days before visiting day a few months earlier had pulled his overalls off in the mess hall and showed his battered buttocks to his mother and the other visitors assembled there. His mother went to see the Governor about her son being mistreated, so the wardens preferred not to have a similar incident occur.

Monday morning Ben and I stood in the vegetable squad, hoping we could get off the yard before the yard man or warden saw us and put us in the line.

The yard man stood beside the warden, studying the roster sheet he always carried. He glanced at each squad, spotted us, and said, "You two Short Hairs catch the line."

We walked to the long line and fell in on the back end. The yard man, warden, and line rider then counted us.

"Git way!" the yard man said, as the warden completed his count. Until that moment there had been a few whispered conversations, a certain restlessness, and the occasional clarion call of a bloodhound. Those who had been nervously smoking dropped their cigarettes and stepped on them.

We marched in a column of twos to the small yard at the rear of the barracks where tools were stored.

"Git them idiot sticks," the line rider shouted, as we walked around the corner of the barracks.

Everyone broke ranks and scrambled for the hoes stacked against the tool shed. I was knocked sprawling in the rush. The men at the front of the line reached the hoes first so they got the hoes with manufactured handles. This had precipitated the scramble. The inmates at the rear of the line got the hoes with handles made at the prison. I got a hoe with a hickory handle. It was rough, crooked, and weighed about ten pounds. Its length was about seven feet.

"Make it up," the line rider shouted after everyone had acquired a hoe.

We formed a column of fours, so we could be counted by the rider and all the guards before leaving the yard.

"Make that line up," the rider roared, as he counted the second time. "What's the matter with you idiots? No wonder you all got caught!"

"The idiot riding the horse should know how to count, too," a man behind me muttered.

"Take 'em to the field, Chief," the rider yelled, and waved to an inmate at the head of the line.

Chief had spent the biggest part of his adult life in the Arkansas Penitentiary. I never heard him called anything other than Chief. He had escaped a few years earlier and had worked in the line since he was recaptured and returned from Minneapolis, where he had secured employment in a flour mill. He was working at the sorghum mill when he escaped. He stole a rifle, blew the boiler whistle five times, denoting an escape, and headed for the Arkansas River two or three miles away.

"I blew the escape whistle to let them know I was taking a brush parole," he confided to me one day. "They had me surrounded in a corn field once and they were pretty hot because I had run off, but I cooled them off with that 30-30."

The guards fired their rifles and shotguns into the air as we began marching off the yard, and headed down a muddy road. There had been a heavy rain the night before. Before it had rained the red dust in the road had been ankle-deep. The dust was now a quagmire. We slipped, fell, and staggered in the deep mud and water. The guards and rider screamed and cursed until we reached the field.

Several men lost their shoes in the sticky, ankle-deep mud. I had put strings torn from an old blanket into mine, but they broke and the shoes were pulled from my feet. I carried them in my hand and walked barefooted. Most of the inmates were carrying their shoes when we reached the field over three miles from the barracks. We were permitted time to put our shoes back on after the rider again counted us.

"Catch in," the rider yelled after the rifle guards had taken their positions surrounding the field.

The line was divided into three squads. The first squad was called "one spot," the second squad, "two spot," and the third squad "three spot" or "piss leg" squad. Three spot contained the older men, cripples, and weaker inmates who couldn't keep pace with the workers in the other squads.

Ben and I stood on the turn-row waiting to be placed in one of the squads.

"Catch two spot, Sanford," the rider snapped at Ben, "you're gonna work this time."

Ben began working on the last row in Two spot as the rider turned to me. He was middle-aged but his thin face was heavily wrinkled, giving him the appearance of being much older. His hair was jet black with only a few gray hairs appearing at the temples. All his front teeth were missing except the two incisors which gave him the appearance of possessing fangs. He was muscular and tall and quick of movement. His jaw was crooked, as though a blow had knocked it sideways. His nose slanted in the opposite direction from his jaw. He appeared to be blind in one eye. It had a streak across it; thin as a razor blade from one corner to the other.

He was a hard, domineering, sardonic, brutal, snarling driver of men, who cared for nothing in the world except himself. He had served several previous sentences and traveled as a carnival roustabout between sentences where he sold pornographic pictures and booklets. He carried a blacksnake whip which he used on the rank men throughout each day.

"Got any tight-roll cigarettes?" he asked, as he turned to me. I pulled a new package from my pocket, pulled the cellophane band from around the top, and handed them to him.

He pulled one from the package, stuck it in his mouth, lit it, inhaled deeply, and exhaled with his mouth open wide. He pulled six more cigarettes from the pack, stuck them in his shirt pocket, and gave the pack back to me.

"You're a doctor, huh?" he asked.

"I was," I answered.

"You got money, though, ain't ye?"

"Yes," I told him. I was to regret that answer the remainder of the time I was at Seven Camp."

"You're gonna make it all right," he grinned. "Catch in with three spot."

I began hoeing knee-high corn at the end of the line. The corn had been hoed recently and there was no thick, tough Bermuda grass, only a few stalks of Johnson grass. I couldn't distinguish between the corn and Johnson grass, which were similar in appearance. I chopped down as much corn as I did grass.

"Move, move," the rider screamed throughout the morning, as he rode among the squads, snapping the long bull whip.

The shotgun guards walking behind the squads fired repeatedly into the air and even into the squads, barely missing the workers. Every few minutes one of the rifle guards who sat on horses at each corner of the field would also fire at someone.

A guard walking behind me kept pulling his pistol from his holster and firing into the ground around me. Once, when I stooped over to pull a clump of grass too close to a stalk of corn to be cut with the hoe, he fired his shotgun. The buckshot plowed into the ground with a squishy thud, throwing mud into my face.

Bloodhounds bayed and howled mournfully as they were led on practice runs around the turn-rows and through the fields by two trustees. Overhead, large, white birds squealed dismally. A frightfully hot, withering, and powerful wind was abroad. The thermometer stood over a hundred in the shade, and the wind, so far from being a relief, was suffocating.

Water was brought to the line on a cart which held a fifty-gallon barrel. The water boy carried water to the squads every thirty minutes. By the time he reached the squads the bucket would be filled with grass, bugs, and grasshoppers. No one was permitted to stop working until the bucket was set on the ground. But every man kept his eyes on the water boy, and as the bucket touched the ground each would drop his hoe and charge for the bucket. They would bowl each other over trying to be the first to get a cup. Fights which broke out in the fields usually erupted around the water bucket.

I was the fourth to drink from the cup. The old man who handed it to me had a mouthful of tobacco. As he dipped out a drink of water he spat the chew of tobacco onto the ground beside the bucket. He rinsed his mouth a couple of times, drank with feverish eagerness, and spat a mouthful of water out in a glittering spray.

At ten o'clock that morning the water boy came through the field carrying a bucket of coffee. Anyone who had money could buy a cup and stop working long enough to drink it. I bought a cup and paid for another, which the water boy promised to give to Ben when he reached that squad.

While we were drinking coffee the camp warden drove to the field and stopped beside the water cart. The rider had seen him driving down the turn-row and had led four men from the field. The warden pulled the whip from a cloth bag, dragged it through a mud puddle to make tit heavier and more effective. The four inmates lay down in the road and each received fourteen lashes. The warden usually whipped two or three men each time he drove to the fields, in the belief it would make everyone work harder.

At noon a wagon drawn by a team of mules lumbered into the field with our dinner aboard. We formed a column of twos. The rider counted us and said, "Sit down." A large lard can filled with peas boiled in plain water was carried between the lines, and a spoonful put on each tray by the rider. The wagon driver walked behind the rider dragging a wooden box filled with dust-covered cornbread. The cornbread was soggy and smelled sour. It had been made of meal, water, and a dash of salt. The meal was coarsely ground, occasionally almost a whole kernel of corn could be found in the bread. The meal was ground at the prison, cob and all.

"Hell," I heard the camp warden say one day, "horses eat corn, and anything that's good for a horse should be good for a damned convict."

There were several other buckets of food brought on the wagon, but this special food was for the guards and rider. The trustees dined on pork chops, butter beans, sweet potatoes, and fresh tomatoes. There was also plenty of milk and coffee for them.

The wagon driver had also brought the rider a watermelon. The rider pulled a switch-blade knife from his pocket, cut the melon in half, and sent part to a rifle guard. He cut the heart from the half he kept and squashed it into his mouth. Juice ran down his chin and dripped onto his shirt. When he finished eating the heart he picked the remainder of the melon up and tossed it onto the round between the two lines of rank men. The men lying on the ground rose to their elbows and gazed hungrily at the melon, now covered with dirt, then lay down again and stared at the sky. The rider laughed as he saw them staring at it.

We were given a twenty-minute rest period safter dinner.

"Give me another tight-roll, ol' short-haired boy," the rider said to me before we returned to work.

"Quit bummin' cigarettes from that ol' doctor. He's gonna need all his money for his funeral," the guard who had shot at me all morning yelled to the rider, as I pulled the pack from my pocket.

"This boy here is all right---as long as he has tight-rolls," the rider answered.

"Why is that guard riding my back?" I asked Ben. "I've never seen him before."

"That's old Queer Boy," he answered. "He never went to school a day in his life. He heard you were a doctor and here he is holding a gun on you. He's drunk with power."

As we lined up, prepared to return to the field, the wagon driver walked to where I stood and stated he had two turtles for sale. I bought both for fifty cents, and he told me the cook would have them fried when we came in for supper.

We completed hoeing the corn a few minutes after returning to the field and went to the cotton gin, where we lugged heavy sacks of fertilizer from one building to another the remainder of the day.

That evening when we filed into the mess hall the cook brought a tray filled with the fried turtle meat. It was tough but delicious. Ben and I took some and divided the remainder among the other inmates sitting at the table. They grabbed it from the tray and wolfishly ate it. Only one had enough manners to say "thanks."

As we marched barefooted up to the door to be searched, the guard nicknamed "Queer Boy" placed his hands on my shoulders. "Up higher with them hands," he growled.

"I'm sunburned, I can't get them any higher," I answered. I was holding them over my head, but he was still dissatisfied.

"If the captain gives you a little help, you'll get 'em higher."

He looked in my helmet after he saw I was not going to raise my hands higher. He placed his foot in the small of my back and kicked me into the barracks. I staggered, off balance, into the cage, fell against a cot, knocking it over, and fell to the floor. The other guards guffawed as I climbed to my feet.

The count had barely been completed when I heard my name called by the yard man from the front picket. Wearily I rose and walked to where he stood leaning against the bars. The warden stood behind him.

"What's wrong with you and this trustee?" the warden said in a tone of voice that sounded like a seventeenth-century cello, as he folded his arms comfortably on the bars.

"Nothing," I answered, which was followed by a sudden and uneasy pause. The air seemed charged with some subtle electric current. I glanced at the guard. On his face there was a kind of smile, cynical, wicked, deadly. It was evident he expected to hold me down while I was being whipped.

"I'm gonna let you slide this time, Short Hair," the warden drawled, staring at me with icy, steel-blue eyes. "But if you're brought in front of me again, I'll knock your ass up between your shoulders."

I glanced at the guard. His facial expression changed to one of disappointment. I turned and walked away without changing my own puzzled facial expression. I realized then the guard was an ignorant man, and nothing is more dangerous.

I had barely returned to my cot when the yard man dragged a drunk trustee into the barracks and dropped him on the floorwalker's cot. The trustee was so drunk he could not talk coherently or stand by himself. He had been given permission to go to Pine Bluff, where he had become intoxicated in a tavern and created a disturbance. The tavern operator called the police, who in turn called the Assistant Head Warden, who drove to Pine Bluff to return him to the penitentiary.

The drunk trustee went to the field the next day but was not forced to work. The rider permitted him to sit in the shade of the water cart all day. The following week he assisted the water boy. A few days later he was returned to trustee status and volunteered to bring me whisky or narcotics from Pine Bluff--for a fee. He was not punished in any way for his drunken escapade.

"Check signers," the yard man roared after the drunk had been quieted. I went to the picket where a short line had formed and signed my name on a sheet of paper. I had received a letter from my mother with a money order enclosed that day.

Ben strolled to my cot after he had also signed the paper. He had a cigar clenched between his teeth which looked like a relic from a pyramid. It had the odor of a smoldering shoe impregnated with sheep dip.

"Made by a tiny factory that caters to a few cultured men with a taste for real tobacco," he grinned as he reached into his pocket, pulled out another cigar, and tossed it to me.

Ben made several sandwiches while I sat puffing on the cigar. "Chow time, Rooster," he said, as he screwed the lid back on the jar of peanut butter.

The inmate lying on the cot next to mine sat bolt upright and looked around the barracks like an enchanted gopher. He sent up a shout of laughter that even caused a collie dog lying on the front picket to raise his head and look about alertly. "Rooster" had received his nickname because of the snuff he dipped which had a red rooster outlined on the can. He had been sent to the penitentiary from the State Mental Hospital at Little Rock. He had evidently been too much for them to cope with. Rooster never talked to anyone unless something was said to him, but he mumbled incessantly, holding a conversation with someone or other visible only to himself. He would sit at the mess hall table as stoically as a wooden Indian, eating nothing unless it was offered to him. He would shovel the peas into his mouth mechanically, stupidly, after someone handed him the pan.

Rooster slept on a filthy mattress. He always kept a coffee can, which he used for a spittoon, sitting on the mattress instead of the floor. He missed the can as often as he hit it when he spat; consequently it sat in a large, damp brown pot.

With awkward, trembling fingers, Rooster took the sandwich Ben offered him. He scrutinized it with exaggerated interest and atrocious grimaces, then crammed the entire sandwich in his mouth. Peanut butter, syrup, and tobacco juice were mixed in his long, black bristly beard. Rooster never shaved unless he was forced to. It wasn't always a simple matter to force him, so he was permitted to go long periods without shaving or getting a haircut. He was the only inmate at Seven Camp who was never whipped. The last whipping he had received was in the mess hall several months before. The warden had administered only two lashes when Rooster threw off the trustees holding him down, jumped to his feet, grabbed the warden around the neck, jumped on the warden's back, and rode him out the mess hall door into the yard. The warden was yelling for the trustees to pull Rooster off as he went out the door, and they finally managed to subdue him in the yard. After this incident the warden often said there were only two "bulls" at Seven Camp---he and Rooster.

## Part II. *Ruled by the Whip*, Dale Woodcock

Rooster was silent for several moments after he consumed the sandwich. Ben made another one and handed it to him. Rooster took it, but laid it on the dirty mattress. His trembling hands moved about in bewilderment, fumbling over his person as if he had lost something. "You better put every hair back on my head," he yelled, as he suddenly jumped to his feet and glared at the barber who was shaving an inmate. Rooster's stubbly black hair stood out from his head as if bristling defiance toward every point of the compass. His brows stood out like bristles, and the eyes under them were red and fierce like a mad bull's.

"Lay down, you crazy bastard," the barber shouted, and waved his razor at Rooster.

Nonplused, Rooster turned, shook his tightly clenched fist at the yard man who sat in a rocking chair on the front porch picket. "I know ye," he screamed. "You're another one of the ten thousand."

The yard man ceased rocking, bent forward, peered through the bars at Rooster, and resumed rocking.

After this tirade in which he had vented his wrath on the barber and yard man, Rooster sat down, picked up the sandwich he had laid on the mattress, and again crammed it all in his cavernous mouth.

"How do you like sleeping next to Rooster?" Ben asked, and grinned the width of his face.

"Better than the one sleeping beside you," I answered.

The elderly inmate sleeping on the cot next to Ben's worked in the vegetable squad and suffered from syphilis and tuberculosis. He would sit on the edge of the cot and bark like a dog. Occasionally he attempted to bite the legs of the inmates who walked past his cot. At other times he waltzed up and down the aisles and pirouetted around the barracks like a freed butterfly.

A fight between two inmates broke out while we were eating. After this had been quelled and the two men whipped by the warden, Ben and I walked to the commissary to buy two cokes. We had barely returned and sat down when a guard walking outside the cage stopped and said, "Come here, Short Hair."

"What do you want?" I asked, as I walked to the bars.

"The rider needs some smokin'. He said to tell you to bring him a pack of tight-rolls tomorrow."

"Does that man know you have money?" Ben asked, as I returned to my cot.

"I told him today I had some. He saw me sign for a check, too."

"Doc, you've got a long row to hoe with a dull hoe. You'll have to buy things for that rider and the rest of the guards or suffer the consequences."

A cool breeze was blowing gently through the open window, playing over my cheeks, but it didn't help the anger welling up inside me.

"You've got a problem, Doc," Ben said, as he rose to return to his own cot.

I went to the barbershop and got a shave after Ben left. The barber shaved sixty men each night within a two-hour period. He rarely sharpened the razor. The inmates compared his shaving technique to "scraping a hog." Each time he shaved me I left the chair with my face covered with blood.

After the barber had given me a quick shave and I had gone to the shower room to wash the blood off my face, I went to the dice table and played thirty minutes. I won seventy-five cents before I returned to my cot.

I sat smoking and drinking coffee until the floorwalker yelled, "Bedtime." By that time I had spent the seventy-five cents buying stamps and Bull Durham tobacco for several inmates.

The floorwalker brought a ragged blanket after I lay down. It was full of holes, frayed around the edges but clean. It had been sneaked into the building that afternoon by one of the laundry workers.

"Thanks," I said, as he tossed the blanket in my face.

"Anytime you need to borrow money," he responded, "I'll have it."

"I've heard of loan sharks," I retorted sharply, "but you're the first I've heard of that charges 100 per cent interest."

"Aw, that's because I lose a lot of money. Half the guys I loan money to get transferred to Tucker or Two Camp before I git paid. When they git transferred I've kissed it good-by."

Ben returned after the floorwalker left. He brought a new pair of cloth, leather-palmed work gloves and dropped them beside me.

"You'll need those when we get into the cane and the woods," he said, as he turned and walked away.

One of the inmates whom I had bought a sack of tobacco brought me a new pair of shoestrings after Ben left. I put the strings in my shoes and stretched out on the mattress, listening to the doleful call of a whippoorwill and the drowsy notes of night insects. A low, hollow wail of a bloodhound arose in the darkness outside. It mounted to a howl, then died suddenly away, only to rise again, wild, sorrowful, hungry, appalling, and savage. The howl produced a bitter melancholy and a startling sense of weakness. The blood-covered ceiling seemed to be moving down to crush me.

## CHAPTER FIVE

During breakfast the next morning a teenager sitting on the opposite side of the table asked the yard man's permission to go to the hospital to have a tooth pulled. The yard man told him he would ask the warden.

"You don't know what you're doin', do you kid?" the inmate sitting beside him said, "That con over there don't know nothin' about pullin' teeth. He pulled one for me two years ago, and I'm still hurtin'. He breaks more jawbones around here than the wardens."

The youth made no reply because the warden was approaching the table.

"Why do you want to go to the hospital?" the warden asked. "Do you think you'll git out of workin?"

"No, sir," the frightened youth replied humbly. "My tooth is hurtin' me."

"Which tooth?" the warden queried.

"This one here," the young inmate answered, as he opened his mouth and pointed to a front tooth.

"All right, you can go over there," the warden responded with a deadpan face, "but if you come back with that tooth not pulled, I'm gonna knock it out when you git back."

The young inmate looked at the warden incredulously. But he must have convinced the dentist it was hurting; when he returned he wore a big grin and there was a vacant space in his row of straight, white teeth.

The sun was peeping over the levee when we marched off the yard and headed for the fields. It was a round, red ball of quenchless fire when we reached our destination. A light rain squall had worn itself out during the night. The air was close and unbreathable with the steam that rose from the wet ground. There was a blistering breeze that came and went in jerks, and piles of thick white clouds in the southwest indicated thunderstorms later in the day.

I began hoeing in Three Spot. I had gone only a few feet from the turn-row when the rider rode up on his horse and stopped beside me.

"Where's my cigarettes, Short Hair?" he asked.

"I didn't bring any," I answered.

"How come you forgot them?"

"I didn't forget them."

"What do you mean you didn't forget them?" he asked, leaning over in the saddle to leer down at me.

"I decided I wasn't going to buy my way through here."

The rider straightened up in the saddle and stared at me for several seconds. "You get your tail over there in One Spot," he barked, as he viciously spurred his horse which jumped across the rows of beans we were hoeing, trampling vines into the dirt. He jerked the bridle reins until the bit cut the horse's mouth when he reached the last row in One Spot. He ordered Two and Three Spot to move over one row. He pointed toward the ground and said, "Right here, Short Hair, right here."

He turned to the shotgun trustee walking behind the squad and growled, "Watch him, if he gets behind let me know."

The bean field was covered with Bermuda grass. I chopped and dug until I thought I would drop from exhaustion, but the other men in the squad were leaving me behind.

"You're stickin' out here in a dangerous place, Short Hair," the rider jeered when I was about eight feet behind the others. Then he rode out to the turn-row where the water boy was making coffee beside the water cart.

A few minutes later the warden drove to the field. The rider strolled to the jeep, said something to the warden, then climbed on his horse and rode into the field. He called an inmate's name in Two Spot, who stopped working. The face he turned toward the rider bore a curious expression of blended amusement and fear. He dropped his hoe and headed toward where the warden sat. The rider rode up beside me, pointed toward the warden, and said, "You too, Short Hair."

I walked to the turn-row which the other inmate had already reached. The warden crawled from the jeep with the whip in his hand. He gave it a couple of swishes over his head.

"I can't stand much more of that whip, Captain," the inmate working in Two Spot said. "I'm gittin too many whippin's."

"I can't stand for you comin' down here and eatin' all my peas and not doin' any work, either," the warden responded. "Nobody sent for you. Git down there!"

The inmate lay down in the road and received twelve lashes. He didn't scream or beg the warden to stop, he merely grunted as each blow struck him. He jumped to his feet at the command to rise and ran into the field holding his buttocks.

The rider pointed to the ground at the warden's feet and told me to "git down."

I lay down in the dust, and placed my arms under my head. The warden stuck the whip between his knees, lifted off his tight hat, wiped out of his eyes a little shower of perspiration which rolled suddenly down from above, winked at the rider, and said, "I'll bet this ol' boy has a rear end as tender as a chicken's liver!"

I watched as the warden threw the whip over his shoulder, rose on his toes and brought the whip downward with all the force he could. Involuntarily I bounced off the ground as the blow landed with a dull thud. It felt as if someone had set a white-hot chunk of metal on my buttocks, and it was all I could do to refrain from yelling. As he prepared for the second lash I knew I would feel the first one for the remainder of my life. The mental pain was worse than the physical; the humiliation of lying at someone's feet to be whipped and the loss of pride and ego.

As the sixth blow struck me I was groaning but determined the rider would not hear me cry out or beg the warden to stop, so I bit into my shirtsleeve and arm.

"Git away," the warden snapped, as he delivered the fourteenth lash.

I began rising slowly from the ground. When I had risen half-way to my feet the warden struck me again and drawled, "When I say git away I mean for you to move fast!"

I walked back into the field and picked up my hoe.

"Doc," the inmate hoeing on the row next to mine said, as he stepped over on my row and began hoeing, "we thought yesterday you were gonna come in here, act like a big shot, and buy what the rider wanted. But you're gonna be O.K."

"Yep," another said, as he stepped over on my row, "we like a man who can hard-ass that warden. In a week you'll be toughened up and be a high roller. Until then we'll give you a little help."

When we reached the yard late that evening I was so tired I could hardly walk, and sick and shaky from hunger. I dropped onto the yard and stared into a cobalt-blue sky islanded with shining regiments of wonder. An immense blue cloud seemed hung in the center of the blue dome, and I resorted to a childhood fantasy of trying to form figures in the clouds to take my mind off my sordid surroundings. I continued to stare into the fathomless vault with an intolerable homesick pensiveness and a deep vacancy of reproach within me.

Suddenly I felt something wet on my wrist and rolled over to investigate. I stared into the sad, droopy eyes of a yellow and white, shaggy-coated dog. He licked my hand again and I gave him a slap on his shoulder. He lay down with his nose squeezing the grass and replied with a muffled sound, more touching than whine or howl---a sound such as the dumb make in their throat, with closed mouth. He stared at me with wide-open, beautiful brown eyes which had a human, appealing expression. I reached over, pulled loose two cockleburs entangled in his dirty coat of white hair, and patted his head. His tail swatted the ground with a rhythmic thud.

I named him Amigo. He met me as I came into the yard each evening thereafter until he was shot and killed a few weeks later by the guard who had shot at me and tried to have me whipped the first day I worked in the line.

Immediately after supper the warden whipped ten inmates. After he had left and Ben and I had eaten some sandwiches, I went to take a shower. Blood had run down my legs and dried as a result of the whipping. I turned to inspect my buttocks as I stood under the cool, refreshing water pouring down over my head. All the bruises had turned an ugly, dirty yellow, the more severe ones blotched with purple. I ran my hand over a large blister and turned around again. An inmate standing under the adjoining shower grinned and winked. I began laughing and so did he.

I went to the commissary to buy a writing tablet after I left the shower. I stretched out on my cot and began taking notes of everything that had happened since my arrival.

"What are you doing?" Ben asked, as he strolled to my cot carrying two cokes.

"I'm gonna write the great, hairy-chested American epic," I answered, as I took one of the cokes he held out. "I'm gonna tell 'em about the Arkansas Penitentiary."

Ben examined the notes for a few seconds and said, "You've got about as much chance of selling a book as I have of becoming a Chinese navigator. How weak do you think those book publishers are? Even if you could convince one to print it, people wouldn't believe you. They wouldn't believe a place like this exists in America, even if it is a penitentiary, and in Arkansas."

"It's worth trying."

"Go ahead. I like westerns. But the best thing you can do is take that paper and pad the seat of your overalls."

As darkness fell over the barracks a trustee from the Administration Building carried a 16 mm. movie projector and screen into the building and dropped it on the floor. Inmates grabbed the equipment as it was shoved through the door and carried it to a table at one side of the building. As it became a little darker the yard man yelled, "show," and everyone rushed to the side of the building where the movie equipment sat. Five or six men sat on each cot while others huddled on the floor. The gate on the front picket was opened and trustees poured into the cage. They carried benches, chairs, and buckets to sit on. I found a vacant space on the floor in front of the projector and plopped down.

The film was an old one. "The Ghost Goes West" was the title. Robert Donat was cast in the starring role. The movie looked as if it had been in the twenties or thirties. The characters were dressed in the clothing of that era and moved with jerky, unnatural movements.

The inmates seemed to enjoy the movie immensely. It was deathly quiet. The projector broke two or three times, but every man stayed rooted to the spot where he sat, anxiously watching the operator as he toyed with it. An occasional movie was the only diversion in the monotonous, dismal, sapless daily routine. They applauded and cheered loudly as the movie ended and gathered around the operator inquiring when they would get to see another.

And after the movie equipment was taken from the barracks a trustee asked the warden to whip an inmate who had refused to relinquish his seat on a cot to the trustee. The warden complied with eighteen lashes.

I brushed my teeth after the whipping, wrote a letter for an illiterate inmate, and went to bed wondering what the next day held in store.

The workers in One Spot helped me hoe until my soft, flabby muscles hardened and became accustomed to the hard work. At first I was digging the grass. One of the men showed me how to sca-bo, as they called it. This was accomplished by dragging the blade of the hoe over the surface of the ground, cutting the grass from the roots.

In the middle of the week we began hoeing peas. Every man in the line cut down as many of the pea vines as possible without being observed and covered them with dirt.

"If they ain't got 'em to cook, we won't have to eat 'em," Chief yelled, as he began hoeing on the first row in the field.

"Anybody caught cuttin' peas down will be killed," the rider warned, as all the men began hoeing. Nine inmates were whipped, but a fifth of the vines were cut and buried.

"We'll git the rest of them the next time we go through," Chief yelled to the rider, as we finished the field.

Occasionally a rabbit would jump from a clump of grass in the fields. When this happened every man in the line stopped working and gave chase, attempting to catch the rabbit before it crossed a guard line. The inmate fortunate enough to catch the rabbit could send it to the mess hall by the water boy, and the cook would fry it.

The rabbit chases were always dangerous. The inmates would throw hoes, rocks, clubs, or whatever they were working with at the dodging rabbit, and the guards would be shooting at it. Someone was usually injured when a rabbit was flushed. It was especially dangerous in the woods during the winter time where axes and iron wedges were thrown. Very few rabbits escaped the frying pan.

Friday morning an inmate who was a sex degenerate---he had been sentenced to the prison for life for raping a young schoolgirl he had waylaid as she was on her way to school---came to the field while the line was sitting on a turn-row eating dinner.

"I caught a possum and three rabbits," the inmate, aptly nicknamed "Silly" Willy, said, as he walked between the two lines of prostrate men. Willy had a round, beardless face, blood-red eyes as vacant of expression as those of a cow, and a mouth which wore a simple, meaningless smile. "I want two bits each for them. I'll skin them and they'll be ready for supper."

"I want the possum," Chief yelled.

I bought one of the rabbits.

When we were seated at the table that evening, the cook carried a large pan to Chief. It was filled with dark meat covered with sweet potatoes. Then the cook brought a tray of fried meat to me.

I watched Chief devouring the pan of meat and sweet potatoes as I nibbled on a piece of meat. When he had eaten half of it he dipped into the pan with his spoon and pulled out a large, flat piece of meat. He held it up, closely inspected it, and dropped it back into the pan, which he shoved away. He motioned to me and the others who made the purchases from Willy to stop eating.

When we filed into the barracks, Chief walked to the commissary instead of going to his cot, bought a twelve-ounce bottle of soda water, and stood leisurely drinking it. He drained the bottle to the last drop, wrapped his hand around the bottle neck, and walked to where Willy sat on the edge of his cot wearing a look of innocence.

"Willy," Chief said, "I want to know what that was you sold me. It you don't do some fast talkin' I'm gonna tear your head off!"

Willy cast furtive glances around the room, and began talking like a clock gone mad; incoherently babbling self-accusations mixed with pitiful attempts at explanation and palliation of his crime. His babble suddenly ceased, he pondered a moment, then whimpered, "You know that little crippled bulldog that belonged to the captain. Well, that was your possum!"

"What was that you sold for rabbits?"

"Cats," Willy blurted. "I caught them in the barn."

Chief raised the bottle over his head to strike Willy, but the floorwalker, standing nearby, wrestled it from him and led both to the front picket where he explained the nature of the ruckus to the warden.

"You killed my dog!" the warden bellowed. "Bring him out here."

It took four trustees to drag Willy onto the picket. They dumped him unceremoniously on the floor at the warden's feet and two sat on him. The warden gave Willy twenty-one lashes, and he screamed so loud he made the broken windows rattle. When the warden told Willy to "git away," he tried to climb over the door to get back into the cage as the yard man was trying to unlock it.

"I'll bet they heard him in Pine Bluff," Ben said to me.

"How far is it to Pine Bluff?" I asked.

"Thirty-five miles"

Immediately after Willy had been whipped the sheriff led a new inmate through the front door and demanded, 'I want this man whipped right now."

The new inmate was still wearing his own clothes. The sheriff wanted him whipped because he had refused to move out of the center of the road to permit a warden to pass as he was led down the road.

"How many prisons you been in, boy?" the warden asked genially.

"I just got out of one," the new prisoner replied.

"Yeah. You jest got out of one of them Northern prisons where guards scold you and you run to cry on the chaplain's shoulder about it. What do you do on the outside?"

"I'm a ballet dancer."

"You've got a few things to learn, boy, git down there."

The new inmate stood uncomprehending before the warden. The two trustees who had held Willy wrestled him to the floor, and the warden gave him eighteen lashes. "There's a lot of that here for you, boy," the warden said, as he folded the whip neatly and dropped it into a sack.

"I've done time all my life, but I've never seen or heard of anything like this," this inmate said to me a few days later.

Saturday afternoon when we began hoeing, after a lunch of collard greens and cornbread, the rider rode among the squads and stated if we finished the field we were in by three o'clock we could have the remainder of the day off. The guards stopped shooting at us, the rider put his bull whip away, and everyone worked harder. We finished the field at two forty-five.

"Make it up," the rider yelled in a jovial tone, and we began the march to the barracks.

When we reached the barracks the rider rode across the yard and stopped at the latrine ditch. A pipe from the shower and toilet commodes emptied into the ditch approximately thirty feet from the building. The ditch ran through a pasture and emptied into a pond three or four hundred yards away. The rider pointed to the ditch and told us to clean it out.

"Hey, you damned ol' sorry thing," Chief yelled to the rider, "you told us we could have the rest of the day off."

"Yeah," the rider drawled, "but I lied, and look who to. A bunch of ol' sorry, ragged-assed convicts. That was jest an excuse to get more work out of you idiots."

The water in the latrine ditch was black. Waist-high grass and weeds covered the banks. It was infested with turtles and water moccasins. The turtles I had been buying and eating came from this ditch. Working in the ditch dampened my enthusiasm for eating turtles.

The legs of our overalls were covered with filth when the rider let us quit work at five-thirty. I was fortunate enough to get a clean pair that evening. Some of the inmates had to wear theirs two or three more weeks.

Sunday afternoon a preacher came to the camp to conduct church services. Religious services were held once a month, on the Sunday following visiting day. Only Protestant services were conducted; priests and rabbis were not permitted to hold services. The preacher was disliked by most of the inmates, because he disturbed them on their day of rest. He was disliked most by men in the vegetable squad, because he drove there each day to get fresh vegetables.

"That preacher is the biggest bum on the farm," the vegetable house rider complained on numerous occasions. "Every time we start to do somethin' he drives up and wants somethin' picked out in the fields."

We had returned to the cage only a few seconds from Sunday dinner when the yard man rang the dinner bell at the front of the building and yelled, "Church!" The old bell knelled sullenly, with a dead thud in the air after each stroke.

Church attendance was mandatory, so the inmates rose to the sides of their cots and began slipping their shoes on, cursing under their breaths.

"Oh, why should I worship the Pope in far-off Rome, when we have Father Divine right here at home?" Chief said, as I stepped into the line.

We sat at the mess hall tables as mimeographed songs were handed to each inmate. The preacher stood behind a makeshift podium, his face freshly shaven; his kindly blue eyes looked pleasantly on the world and he smiled benignly. He chose a tottering old man sitting near him to lead the singing, and church services got under way. We sang three songs, not because we wanted to, but because the yard man had said we had better sing. With eloquence and with a voice vibrating with emotion the preacher described the place we were destined to spend eternity unless we changed our errant ways. He described an eternity of torment. A tangible searing hell alive with flame and devils, a sea of liquid fire, an ocean of boiling pitch, Satan commanding in the midst, and a myriad of fiends working his tormenting will.

"We're already there!" a husky voice piped up from the rear of the room. A sudden electric thrill ran over the listless rows of faces. The minister made a half-turn like a top on a pivot; he frowned at the unseemly interruption. He concluded the services with a prayer read in a dry, ecclesiastical voice; then gave a vivid description of a vacation trip he had recently taken to Chicago.

"Inspiring, wasn't it Doc?" Ben whispered in my ear, as we rose to return to the cage.

"Well, we're rid of that moocher for another month," another inmate interrupted.

"Man," Chief said, as we walked through the door. "I shore wish that preacher had took me to Chicago with him. I know ten thousand whores there. I could have shown him how to spend a vacation."

After the preacher left the building the yard man had an inmate whipped for turning his back during the services.

"Git up from there," the warden said, as he finished whipping the man, "and the next time we have church I want to hear you singin' louder than anybody."

In August we began picking butter beans. There were several fields of beans scattered over the farm. These were grown to feed the trustees' and the wardens' families. We began in a field three or four miles from the barracks.

"I don't want to see nothin' but assholes and elbows," the rider instructed, as he issued cotton sacks into which we were to throw he beans. "You idiots ask me before you smoke. You better not do any standin' up or sittin' down. The warden wants these beans in the bins in three weeks, and I'm here to see that we git it done. We'll weigh at nine o'clock and you'll bring out ninety pounds. If any man ain't got it, it's his o' rear end. Now, hit them rows, and bring me some beans."

The vines were loaded with dried, weightless bans. They were easy to pick, but the torturous part of this type of work was remaining on bent legs and knees for thirteen hours each day. My legs felt like they were broken by the time of the first weigh-up.

We had been picking beans approximately thirty minutes when the warden drove to the field with a wooden tripod on the back of his jeep. The water boy sat it up on the turn-row and hung a pair of scales from it.

"Well there it is, Bullies," the rider yelled when it was erected.

"What is it?" Chief yelled to the rider. "A scaffold or the ol' rugged cross?"

"There's gonna be some rear ends crucified out there in an hour or two," the rider answered

At nine o'clock the rider rode into the field and yelled, "Tie it up." At this command we rose to our feet and tied a knot in the top of the cotton sacks.

We walked in squads to the turn-row and formed a line in front of the scales. After each man weighed his sack he fell into one of two squads. One squad, which was for the men who had picked the weight they were assigned, formed in the field. The other squad, those that didn't have the weight, formed a line in front of the warden. The squad which formed in front of the warden contained more men than the one waiting to return to the rows.

I was in the line sanding before the warden. He gave me twelve hard lashes before he said, "Git away." I rolled to one side and rose quickly to my feet before he could hit me as I rose from the ground.

I didn't have the weight I was assigned at the noon weigh-up either, but wasn't whipped. " You better start puttin' some beans in that sack, Short Hair," the warden admonished, "or you'll git killed out here."

"Doc, the man on the next row said when we began working after dinner, "you're puttin' nothin' but beans in that sack. Put somethin' in it that will weigh." He grabbed my sack and threw several handfuls of dirt in it. This procedure worked fine until a stump was found in a sack. The rider then proceeded to paint numbers on the sacks and made a list of who they were issued to. Thereafter each sack was closely checked.

The warden issued an edict that any inmate who picked a hundred pounds during the morning or afternoon would receive a steak dinner. Only one man was able to pick that many beans---Chief. When we filed into the mess hall that evening, a table, covered with a red-and-white-checked cloth, sat in the doorway so that each man was forced to walk around it to get into the mess hall. On the table was a big steak, a bowl of butter beans, salad, a cherry pie, and a gallon jug of milk.

"I just got out of the Missouri Penitentiary," an inmate sitting next to me said. "If they pulled off something like this there, those cons would wreck the place."

"The Missouri Penitentiary isn't run like this one, though," I replied.

Chief received a sumptuous meal on three successive evenings. By that time the warden realized Chief was the only man in the line who could pick the hundred pounds of beans so he discontinued the contest.

I was so sore and stiff by the third day I could hardly walk. The muscles in my thighs felt as if they had all been torn loose. The skin had been scraped from my knees and the pain became so great at times it made me sick and I vomited. My body was covered by itching bumps caused by mosquito bites. Mosquitoes swarmed in black clouds over the bean vines each morning.

A few of the inmates were unable to walk to the barracks when we quit work late each evening. Their legs would give away under them when they began walking. The water boy always had to wait to follow the line in during this period. When we began the march to the barracks and someone dropped in the road the line would be halted, the rider would curse and kick the downed man before he was carried to the water cart and thrown on it.

We suffered many troubled, sleepless nights during the bean-picking season. Squatting all day brought on severe attacks of sciatica, cramping muscles, and aching spinal columns. When the bell rang each morning the inmates would rise by grabbing something for support, or by helping each other out of bed. Each man rose with baggy, bloodshot eyes.

On the third day, when I ached the most, an inmate nicknamed "Whisky Red," in order to distinguish him from "Society Red," began crying and beating the ground with his clenched fists. He begged the guard walking behind the squad for permission to stand up and stretch.

"If you've got a hard ass," the guard replied, "go ahead."

Whisky Red didn't stand up, but he sat on the cotton sack and began rubbing his aching thighs. The rider kicked Whisky Red in the back as he walked down the row.

'Oh!" Whisky Red moaned.

"What you doin' sittin' down?" the rider demanded.

"I'm hurtin'," Whisky Red groaned again as he held his back with both hands. "My legs are killin' me."

Your ass is gonna be hurtin' too, soon as the warden gits here. I told you idiots about sittin' down."

The threat of being whipped incensed Whisky Red. He jumped to his feet, his face was livid. He was a giant of a man with pendant jowls and a small forehead. His pouchy cheeks were crisscrossed by a network of bluish blood vessels set against the scarlet of his cheeks. His lips were puffy and slate gray in color. He had dull blue eyes with fat lids hanging over them. The veins of his forehead were markedly distended. He wore a piece of rope tied around his waist, giving him the appearance of a sack of feed tied around the middle.

Although Whisky Red quickly jumped to his feet, he winced with pain as he attempted to stand up straight. The rider hit him alongside the head with a singletree he carried in his hand. Whisky Red dropped to the ground like a floored bull. The rider kicked him in the ribs, chest, and face until he was a bloody, gory mess. Whisky Red tried to rise to his feet, but the rider again beat him to the ground with his fists.

Slowly, painfully, Whisky Red tried to rise again. He struggled to his knees. The rider picked up the singletree he had dropped on the ground and growled, "Come up any higher, Red, I'll scatter your brains all over this row!"

Whisky Red sank to the ground and stared mutely at the rider. The rider turned and walked away. When the warden came to the field Whisky Red was whipped for attacking the rider.

During the second week of bean picking I had a harrowing experience with a rattlesnake. I was crawling along from vine to vine, not watching ahead. I crawled across an empty space where vines had died. When I raised my head I was staring into the cold, glassy, slitted eyes of the gruesome reptile. The snake was approximately five feet in length and several inches thick around the middle of its kaleidoscopic body. The snake was about eight feet away. I froze into a motionless position.

The snake had probably crawled into the field to hunt field mice and sought out the shelter of the vines to escape the searing sun. The rattler coiled, stuck out his vibrating, forked tongue, hissed, and began an incessant rattling.

I remained motionless, watching the snake draw into a tighter coil, while the inmate on the next row, who saw my predicament, threw the cotton sack strap over his head and crawled backward to tell the guard. The guard circled, took careful aim, and smashed the snake into a bloody pulp with buckshot.

One morning during the third week of bean picking, word was passed across the field that no one was to eat dinner. "We're goin' on a hunger strike to see if we can't git somethin' to eat besides soured cornbread and peas," the inmate who told me about it divulged. The rumor traveled fast. It swept like wildfire over a prairie.

"What do you think about that, Doc?" Chief asked when we weighed the sacks at nine o'clock. "These guys have been hungry ever since they got here, but they jest now realized it."

"Hey, idiots," Chief yelled, as he peeped through a mess hall window when we reached the yard that evening, "they're droppin' a feast on us!" He stood first on one foot and then on the other, like a boy at a candy-store window.

When we sat down to eat there was beef stew with plenty of meat and vegetables, sweet potatoes, white bread, chocolate pudding, and coffee on each table. When the pans were emptied two waiters hurried to the kitchen to refill them. Supper went forward with the invariable alkali etiquette, all faces brooding and feeding amid a disheartening silence as of guilt or bereavement that springs from I have never been quite sure what---perhaps reversion to the native animal absorbed in his meat.

While we were eating, the camp warden, Assistant Head Warden, and two wardens from other camps walked into the mess hall. They strolled up and down the mess hall peering over the inmates' shoulders into the pans. Then they walked to a table near the front of the mess hall, sat down, and began drinking coffee which the yard man carried to them in a white pitcher.

"Somethin' is up those wardens' sleeves," Ben said to me. "They don't put up a feed like this for nothing."

"You better enjoy it," Chief interrupted. You're gonna pay for it. I'd bet my front seat in hell there's gonna be a hide line a mile long. There'll be so much singin' and yodelin' on the front picket tonight it will sound like the Grand Ol' Opry!"

Every inmate sat apprehensively on the edge of his cot when we were inside the cage. They sat in a silence which was tense with expectation. The three camp wardens stood staring through the bars at us. Each inmate sat stoically, each one like the legendary bird hypnotized by the snake, incapable of looking away from the hard-eyed stares. The Assistant Head Warden plopped into the yard man's rocking chair and gave a sigh of relief and comfort, heaved from the billowy amplitude of his person. His ample form filled the chair to overflowing, and he draped one leg over an armrest. The chair squeaked and groaned harshly under this weight. Miraculously, the silence which had been so deep and unbroken deepened and intensified still more. The cooing of mourning doves on the roof could be plainly heard.

PART II. *RULED BY THE WHIP*, DALE WOODCOCK

The yard man yelled for the floorwalker who ran to the front picket, bumping into cots and inmates on his way. He conversed briefly with the yard man, then turned, walked down the aisles pointing his finger at various men. "You, up front," he said as he pointed to each inmate.

When he had completed his trip around the barracks he had chosen forty-five men to go to the picket. They stood in a line in front of the gate which opened onto the picket. Every trace of color had left each face. They stood like frightened cattle; in awe, in silence, as men stand around a closing grave.

The floorwalker looked at me and walked on past. He didn't point to any of his better coffee customers. The inmates he had chosen went through the gate one at a time where the wardens took turns whipping them. The Assistant Head Warden sat in the rocking chair encouraging them with such remarks as, "Pour it on that one, he's the sorriest man on the farm" or, "Hit that one a little harder, he's got a tough ass."

When the forty-five inmates had been whipped and put back inside the cage the Assistant Head Warden rose from the rocking chair, took a whip from a camp warden, and said, "Bring me ol' Slick Top."

Slick Top had been at Seven Camp for several years. He worked at various semi-trustee jobs such as water boy, wagon driver, etc. He had cooked a pot of butter beans at the grain bins the day before and carried them over a mile to the barracks, where he brought them into the mess hall and divided them among the inmates. He was being whipped for this act.

"Cap'n," he said as he walked onto the picket, "I shore wish you'd let me slide. You caught me with my drawers off."

The warden was determined to deliver a whipping, and would accept no excuses. "Does that hurt?" he asked each time he struck Slick Top, who screamed like a wounded panther.

"Slick Top ain't got a very tough ass has he?" one of the camp wardens asked.

"Yeah, he has," the Assistant Warden responded. "I raised him. He's been here since he was twelve years old. He's got a hard ass. I believe he's puttin' on a little bit."

"Let me go, Cap'n, and I'll never do it again," Slick Top wailed.

149

"You're lyin'. You know you're lyin', the Warden replied dryly, and delivered a stinging blow.

Slick Top received only six lashes. He was put inside the cage and the warden left.

"I guess you idiots want to go on another hunger strike, huh?" the yard man yelled from the picket

"It would be worth it," the floorwalker muttered, "if we got another meal like that."

"How about some butter beans, Slick Top?" the warden grinned, as we were forming into squads on the yard the next morning.

"Naw, sir," Slick Top responded. "I don't believe I want anymore. Them beans shore did make my ass sore."

PART II. *RULED BY THE WHIP*, DALE WOODCOCK

CHAPTER SIX

We completed picking the butter beans on schedule and returned to the toilsome hoeing. The rider ordered me to lead Three Spot as we arrived at the field. The leader of each spot, or squad, was required to keep ahead of the other men in the squad. If a man in the squad got ahead of him, the leader was whipped; and if the leader got over fifteen feet ahead of anyone in the squad, then the man who was behind was whipped. Thus there was a constant, cursing struggle between the squad leader and the workers in the squad.

The rider screamed, cursed, and lashed the men in my squad throughout the morning, trying to force them ahead of me. He had three of them whipped by the warden, and two dropped from exhaustion and were carried from the field.

When we retuned to work after dinner I told the fourteen men in the squad to form a straight line across the field and to say in an even line. "That rider can't do anything," I told them, "if no one is behind."

That was a mistaken viewpoint I had. We made two trips through the field, and One and Two Spot had gained half a row on us. The rider had every man in the squad whipped, including the leader.

That same night I received another whipping. My buttocks were cut, bruised, and blistered from the whipping I had received earlier in the day, and the second whipping forced me to raise my voice a bit.

A detail of six men were chosen after supper to unload hay from wagons from other camps and stack it in the barn to be used for the winter feeding of livestock. The yard man glanced at his roster sheet and chose me for the detail.

It was hot and stuffy in the loft. My flesh was burning dry, and the stirless air had the baking quality of fire. The twilight provided little respite from the torture of the days, and a sickening stench emanated from the open sewer ditch at the rear of the barracks. The humidity caused us to perspire freely. We had worked only a few minutes when our jackets were drenched with sweat and spotted white with salt. We took the jackets off, but the raspy hay leaves and straw stuck to our moist skin and we were forced to put them back on. After we had worked a few minutes we asked the guard standing at the front of the barn for permission to get a drink of water.

"No," he drawled. "We came out here to unload hay. Not to drink water, and my name is Mr. _____. Not son-of-a-bitch."

An hour later we became so thirsty it became imperative we get water. We again asked the guard if we could have a drink.

"No," he answered adamantly.

"I'm gittin' a drink, Mr. Son-of-a-bitch," an inmate nicknamed Chickenshit Slim called, and began climbing down the ladder. We followed suit and walked to a water trough and drank from the faucet.

The guard ran to the barnyard fence, climbed up, and screamed for the yard man.

"What's wrong out there?" the yard man called through the darkness, as he stood on the end of the dilapidated, dimly lit porch as insects billowed around him like a swirling winter blizzard

"Send the captain out here," the guard answered.

A few minutes later the warden drove down the twisting, dark road that wound around the barracks. The guard opened the gate and he drove onto the barn lot. There were no brakes on the jeep, and only one headlight, but no lights were needed. The dim light, which is not star-given, but seems as if it were the return of radiance stored by day in the sunlit earth, lent to all things the tenderness of indistinct outlines.

"What's so important that I have to come back here after I get home?" the warden inquired.

"They climbed down and quit workin'," the guard sputtered.

The warden strode to his jeep, got his whip, pulled up his trousers, adjusted his hat, and said, "Bring 'em to me!"

It was useless to try to explain our reason for the work stoppage. An effeminate, pink-cheeked inmate named "Rosebud" attempted to but was repulsed by the warden's, "I don't want to hear it, git down there."

The warden must have remembered whipping me earlier in the day because he was lenient and gave me only nine lashes.

"I'm goin' home again, and if I have to come back here again tonight, I'll bring my blackjack," the warden said, as he climbed into the jeep.

He stepped on the accelerator and crashed into the gate the guard had closed when the jeep entered. The warden jumped from the vehicle and bellowed, "You harebrained idiot. I'm gonna beat all the laundry off you. Git down!"

The guard leaned his shotgun against the fence and stretched out on the ground. The warden gave him twelve lashes.

When the warden told him to get up, the guard jumped to his feet, ran to the gate, opened it, and took off his hat which he held over his heart as the warden drove through.

We taunted the guard the few remaining minutes we worked in the loft. We felt brave because we knew he wouldn't call for the warden again that night.

Next morning the warden walked up and down the line looking each man over from head to foot. He reached into the line and grabbed me and five others by the collar, and roughly jerked us out and told us to form a squad.

"What are we goin' to do?" one of the men in the new squad asked me.

I had no idea why we had been pulled from the line, so I shrugged my shoulders.

"They're gonna try the bloodhounds out today," an inmate standing in the line sneered.

After the other squads had left the yard, the yard man wrote our names on a slip of paper, turned, and waved to a fat, bald-headed, red-faced trustee standing in the road in front of the barracks. The fat trustee waved for us to follow him. We walked to the road, two guards stepped from a shack, fell in behind us, and we walked toward a group of buildings a mile from the barracks.

"You guys are goin' to help me thrash ten bins of butter beans," the trustee told us. "Now, not all the trustees are as sorry as they can be. You boys work, and I'll take care of you."

A peanut thrasher sat in the roadway between the two long rows of tin storage bins. A Negro brought a tractor from Eight Camp and we put a belt on the two machines. Next we opened the doors of several of the sealed bins to sweep and spray them. It was torrid inside the bins. We killed several rats and threw them into the road.

"Man," the Negro tractor driver said to the trustee, "can Ah have them rats?"

"What you gonna do with dead rats?" the trustee inquired.

"Man, them's meat on the table."

The tractor driver skinned the rats, dropped them into a bucket of water, and placed the bucket in the shade of one of the bins until quitting time.

Thrashing the beans was easy work, and we enjoyed working for the trustee, a weighty, rubicund, jovial body, with a roll in his gait and in his voice, and a way of puffing his cheeks out and blowing up after each separate sentence, as if his ideas were a fleet of ships which he sent out toward you, and which he then followed up and sped on with a hearty breeze from his own lips. He was always in a jovial mood, never had anyone whipped or raised his voice. He went into the tomato, cantaloupe, and watermelon fields surrounding the bins to get things for us to eat.

Three inmates carried beans from the bins and poured them into the noisy machine. I caught the shelled beans in a bucket as they poured from a spout on one side. I handed the bucket to another inmate, who poured the beans into a sack and weighed them, and the sixth man carried the hundred-pound sacks and stacked them in the empty bins we had swept.

We worked diligently until we suddenly realized we would be returned to the line as soon as we thrashed the remaining two bins. We began conniving, trying to find a means of prolonging the thrashing job.

"How about wrecking the machine?" I said jokingly.

"That's it," a young bank robber from Van Buren, Arkansas, said.

During the next four days the bank robber loosened nuts and bolts in vital spots on the thrasher. A few seconds later the machine would come to a clanking, rattling stop after it had thrown parts in all directions.

The line was scheduled to begin cane cutting to make sorghum molasses and silage the morning we rejoined it; however, it was raining, so the warden told the rider to take us behind the levee to clear land. We checked axes, saws, and hoes from the tool shed, climbed a twisting road which led to the top of the levee where another road had been constructed, and began a long trek to the woods.

The warden had driven off the yard ahead of us, but his jeep had stalled on top of the levee approximately half a mile from the barracks. As we drew near the jeep the rider pointed to eight men and told them to push the vehicle. All of them couldn't find room, at first, to push as they gathered around the jeep. Five were pushing and three were walking along nonchalantly behind.

The warden was watching from the rear view mirror. When he saw three weren't pushing he slammed on the brakes, jumped from the jeep, waved his whip at them, and bellowed, "Every man better git his hands on this car. If you ain't pushin' you better look like you are."

All eight inmates placed their hands and shoulders on the jeep and gave a mighty heave. The jeep fell into a deep rut in the road and the warden lost control of the steering wheel. He slammed on the brakes, and the machine jumped from the rut and skidded toward the bank of the hundred-fifty-foot-high levee.

"Turn loose, turn loose," the warden screamed, as he frantically tried to regain control of the jeep.

By sheer force the eight inmates pushed the wheel-locked, skidding jeep to the very edge of the levee before they relinquished their hold.

"What a bunch of idiots I got at Seven Camp," the white-faced, shaky warden said, as he climbed from the jeep. "Take 'em on to the woods. I'll call the garage."

That morning we sawed and burned dead trees, stacked brush, and pulled stumps. The stumps and trees lay in a shallow depression that was infested with rattlesnakes and water moccasins that had crawled into the decaying wood. We killed twenty by noon. The huge trees were still standing, but leafless and blackened from root to crown. They were the unburied dead which the forest fires had left after one of their wild forays. Each separate tree was an effigy of desolation, uplifting in its charred and rigid limbs as if in mute attestation of its wrongs. The wind could get no more music out of them; the birds forsook their branches; the lowing cattle missed their spicy shade. They could no longer offer either rest, shelter, or concealment to any living creature.

"Watch that one of these snakes don't git you," a middle-aged inmate told me. "Here's where one got me a couple of years ago." He held up his right thumb for me to see. Half of it was missing.

After dinner we moved to higher ground which was to be cleared and used for pasture for the hundreds of cattle the prison owned. It was covered with head-high bushes, which we cut and stacked to be burned later.

I had been assigned to carry brush. I had worked at this an hour when the rider called me to the water cart where he stood eating a sandwich and drinking coffee. He handed a piece of paper to me and told me to read it to him. He was unable to read or write, although he could scrawl his name.

There were three names on the paper. It was a note sent by the warden asking the rider to send the three inmates listed to him for a fishing detail. There were muddy ponds in the low areas which the Arkansas River filled when it overflowed during the heavy spring rains.

I read the names on the list and added my own.

The rider jumped astride his horse, rounded up the three men listed, assigned a shotgun guard to the detail, and we began walking toward the warden's jeep which looked like a red toy in the distance.

The warden had fastened a seine on two hickory poles. His trouser legs were rolled to his knees and he wore his hat slouched over his eyes; the torn rim hung down over one ear. He was in a carefree mood. All his severe dignity, all the excess of responsibility and apparent studied calmness was gone. He didn't question the fact the rider had sent four inmates when he had asked for only three. We removed our shoes, rolled our overall legs high, and stepped into the dark-brown water.

Chief was in the four-man detail. He picked up the seine lying entangled on the ground, stepped into the water behind me, and handed me one of the bark-covered poles as I turned around. We waded into deeper waters of the pond whose bottom was covered with soft, deep mud.

"Watch out for snappin' turtles, ol' Doc," Chief warned, "they'll take a toe or a leg off if you step on them."

"How can I keep from stepping on them if I can't see them?" I asked.

We waded into the water to our waists when I noticed a huge water moccasin swimming straight for me. His ugly head was held high above the water. His thick, short, undulating body formed waves and ripples on the quiet surface of the water.

"Git back in there, Woodcock," the warden bellowed, as he saw me drop the seine pole and come splashing to the bank.

"I'm afraid of snakes," I told him, noting I had been called by my name instead of Short Hair.

"Well," he drawled, "you can git back out there or go down. Which do you want?"

"I'll have to choose the whip, I guess," I answered. "I'd rather face it than that snake."

"Aw, hell, git out there," he said to another inmate standing beside a washtub, which was to be used to hold the fish, if we caught any.

I turned to watch Chief staggering around in the pond. He beat the water with the pole, fending the snake off. Finally he managed to get the end of the pole under the snake. He gave a mighty heave, and the snake sailed through the air, landing several yards away with a great splash. It disappeared under the water.

Several fish were ensnared in the seine. They were dumped into the tub which the warden took to the barracks as we walked back to rejoin the line.

"You didn't help catch those fish, so you don't git any," the warden said, as he walked past me in the mess hall that evening. The cook, who was walking behind him with a pan of the fish, walked past me. When the warden left the mess hall the cook returned with three pieces of the fried fish and dumped it on my tray.

After supper I went to the back of the building to drink coffee and listen to a radio the floorwalker had smuggled into the barracks that evening. The count had been completed, most of the men had taken their showers, and a tranquil peacefulness had settled over the building. The floorwalker had tuned in a program of soft, soothing music of Mantovani's orchestra.[26] The volume was turned low so the yard man or warden, both standing on the front picket, couldn't hear it.

As I sat sipping coffee, listening, an inmate walked to the radio and twisted the knobs until he picked up a barbaric cacophony of hillbilly music on a Little Rock station. A shrill-voiced woman was singing in a strident, nasal voice; telling the heart-rending story of how a man had done her wrong. The twanging guitar music carried to the front picket.

The yard man walked to the bars, stooped, peered through, and roared, "Bring that God-damned radio up here!"

The floorwalker angrily jerked the cord from the wall socket, wound it carefully around the radio, and walked to the front picket, muttering, "You screw-headed, countrified bastard, I'll have your ass knocked out."

He returned from the picket and told the inmate who had tuned in the hillbilly music to follow him. He led the way to the picket and asked the warden to give him ten lashes. The warden administered fifteen without knowing why he was whipping the man.

The warden asked me to pick out ten men to go to Tucker as guards. "Do you want a gun?" the floorwalker asked me when he returned from the picket.

I refused the offer.

---

[26] Annunzio Paolo Mantovani, born during November 1905, in Venice, Italy, became a successful conductor, composer and entertainer until his death in March 1980.

## CHAPTER SEVEN

The weeks turned into periods of time without definite divisions. The days were caricatures of a nightmare. It was a strange, lifeless interval. I seemed to be drifting and dreaming in some sad, remote existence. I felt scarcely alive; a deadness had fall'n upon me, a profound apathy for life. We not only had the tyranny of the wardens and trustees, and the killing work, the filth and cruelty, but there was no restraint put on the brutality of the inmates toward each other: the bullies maltreated the weaker ones, made homosexual attacks upon them, took their money, and made them do more than their share of the work, pounded and beat them, and worried them every way possible.

It was mid-September and the heat of late summer hung on with dogged resistance. There was a profound silence in the mess hall. Dawn cracked the sky to the east, and a strange gray light crept through to herald the sunrise. This was the morning we were to begin the cane-cutting season, which the imprisoned men disliked more than any other job. The warden walked through the door as we sat sipping the weak, black coffee. Rooster turned on the bench as the warden walked behind him and said, "Git yore gloves and catch the line."

"Damn you. You're not talkin' to a convict," the warden roared, and slapped Rooster with his open hand. Rooster was knocked off the bench and landed on the floor on his back. "I'll beat on yore head 'till you won't have any ears left," the warden growled, as he towered over Rooster.

"Well, let's git on with it then," Rooster said, as he jumped to his feet and performed a little jig dance. The warden walked away and Rooster climbed back on the bench. His face suddenly crumpled. He sobbed and began nervously crumbling his bread with a large wasteful hand. He spit and cursed after the warden with viperish resentment.

"Git 'em outside and let's start cuttin' cane," the warden said to the yard man.

We began working in a cane field that had been cut into blocks to afford the guards a clear view of each other standing at each corner of the block. First, we went through each block stripping the leaves from the stalks. It was stifling. No breeze could be felt in the thick cane.

We were allowed to work in pairs during the stripping. Ben and I worked on the same row. He stripped the bottom part of the stalks, as I was the tallest and could easily reach the tops.

The rider rode constantly up and down the cane rows, screaming at the top of his voice and lashing the men with his whip. We worked at superhuman speed, but he was dissatisfied with our progress. The warden sat on the turn-row in his jeep, and the rider took eighteen men to him to be whipped on the first day. We never had enough cane stripped and cut to load the wagons of the plow squad when they came to the field. At noon the lines of Three and Eight Camps came to help us. They stripped the leaves while we followed them cutting and stacking the cane.

Cutting the cane was more toilsome than stripping it. Again we worked in pairs. Three or four large stalks grew in each hill. One man would grab the stalks in one hand, while his partner attempted to cut them with a dull hoe. The crooked hoe handles made it difficult because they would twist and glance off the stalks. We were going through the field at a trot, and the men with the hoes tried to cut the stalks with one swing in order not to fall behind.

I caught the cane with one hand, trying to avoid being struck by hoes glancing off stalks. It was dangerous when several men were working close together. Several inmates were severely cut by glancing hoes that afternoon. The cane was stacked every few feet. When the handful of stalks were cut I would quickly switch them to my left arm and drag the armload along the row so it became necessary to run across the field with the load of cane, quickly drop it, then return to the row at a trot in order to keep from falling behind.

The stalks mutilated hands. The ripe tassels shattered and showered us. The seeds and lint from the tassels dropped down our collars and stuck to our sweaty bodies to itch and burn.

Two water boys constantly carried water to the squads. It was full of cane seed, leaves, and bugs, but this no longer bothered me. I was always one of the first to rush for the water bucket when it was set on the ground now. It was necessary to be one of the first, as the bucket was usually knocked over by the milling, cursing inmates.

"Six weeks ought to knock this cane out, Bullies," the rider said, as we were walking to the barracks that evening. "That is, if you idiots start workin' and quit foolin' around."

Two inmates began a friendly scuffle before we began work the next morning. One of the inmates was from Ohio and was given that nickname. The other, Wayne, was from southern Arkansas. They had become good friends, worked together, and bought and shared food. They were working together on the same row, and the Arkansas inmate told a joke with Ohio's name woven into the tale to make it more spicy.

Ohio responded with a caustic joke with Wayne's name involved, which brought a round of laughter from the assembled inmates. Ohio gave Wayne a friendly shove as he completed telling the joke. Wayne's heel caught against a cane stalk and he stumbled and fell. Ohio helped him to his feet, brushed the dirt from Wayne's jacket, and they began cutting cane.

The rider, standing near the water cart drinking coffee, witnessed the incident. He sat the coffee glass on the cart, jumped on his horse, and rode across the field.

"You idiots want to fight, then fight," he said, as he jerked the horse to a skidding halt.

"Man," Wayne told him, "we were just playin'. This ol' thing and me are buddies."

"I said fight," the rider screamed, and began lashing both men with his whip. They staggered under the blows, throwing up their hands and arms to protect themselves.

"Fight," I said," the rider roared. He spurred his horse, which jumped against Ohio sending him sprawling.

Ohio jumped to his feet, moved quickly around Wayne, raining blows from all sides. Wayne batted his eyes like a bullfrog in a hailstorm and stared at his erstwhile friend with a confused, perplexed expression. Wayne was gentle, easygoing, and softspoken, but he became a maniac when riled. He was like an overcharged bottle of soda water. Into the fusillade of blows he stopped. One caught him on the mouth and the blood streamed. He stood like an immense gorilla about to spring and snarled between oaths. He grabbed for Ohio, but missed. He was stockily built and moved with the grace of a pregnant elephant. He grabbed again, his teeth grinding, his tongue licking the blood from his battered lip. He caught Ohio by the collar and his heavy fist smashed with horrible precision into Ohio's face. The head went backward as if pulled suddenly with a rope. As Ohio fell unconscious Wayne kicked him in the ribs.

As Ohio crumpled to the ground his loosely fitting jacket fell over his head. Still enraged, Wayne dropped to the ground on one knee and smashed his fist into Ohio's covered face, which sent a convulsive shudder through the motionless form. Wayne drove another blow from over his head into Ohio's face, jumped to his feet, and grabbed a hoe and raised it over his head to strike the unconscious man lying on the ground.

The rider leaned back in the saddle, his arms folded across his chest and a smile on his face. But as he saw Wayne grab the hoe he again spurred his horse, which jumped against Wayne, knocking him off balance. Wayne was restrained by four inmates standing nearby. His temporary state of madness soon vanished, and he walked to where Ohio lay and helped lift him from the ground. There were tears streaming down his cheeks and his body shook with convulsive sobs.

Ohio was carried to the water cart, his face cleansed, and he was permitted to rest until midmorning. Wayne and Ohio were on friendly terms again within a day or two, but never close friends again. The fight wasn't reported to the warden. "I ain't gonna have nobody whipped for puttin' knots on a Yankee's head," the rider stated.

A short time after this incident the rider rode up beside an inmate who had been buying him cigarettes and said he needed some tight-rolls. The inmate he addressed was nicknamed "Handsome," which rhymed with his name. Handsome had been released a year or two earlier from the Federal Mental Hospital at Springfield, Missouri, and came to Arkansas, committed a crime for which he had been sentenced to the prison. Handsome received a monthly disability check from the Veterans' Administration, which the trustees, and particularly the line rider, got a huge share of. Handsome had an obnoxious habit of singing over and over the first line of a hillbilly song entitled "Always Late with Yore Little Kisses."

Handsome told the rider he didn't have any cigarettes, so the rider ordered him to follow as he rode toward an old gray stump in the middle of the field. Handsome dropped his hoe and meekly followed. When they reached the stump the rider told Handsome to climb up and stand on it.

"Handsome, you got a head like a dick, like a dick, like a dick," the rider taunted. "Sing, damn you, sing."

Handsome began singing the first line of the monotonous song in a halting voice, then suddenly stopped. His big, sun-browned, sweaty face was twisted with embarrassment. His fingers trembled as he fumbled in childish resolution at the buttons on his jacket. He passed his hand over his brow in a troubled sort of way, then looked at it curiously. He stood moodily gazing into space, His thick lips swelled out, his shifty eyes opening and shutting sulkily. Rivulets of perspiration ran down over his nose, his temples, and around his ears.

The rider crawled from the saddle, hit Handsome twice with the whip, and repeated, "Sing, Handsome, sing that beautiful song, God-damn you, anyway."

Handsome stood on the stump two hours singing the same line over and over. When the warden came to the field the rider had him whipped, but Handsome achieved a small amount of dubious revenge near quitting time.

The rider had trained his horse to swing his head when he rode up behind an unsuspecting inmate. I had been bowled over once by a vicious swing of the brute's head.

Near quitting time the rider swung from the saddle in the middle of the thick cane and began walking up and down the rows in an attempt to catch someone not working. The horse made too much noise for this purpose. I was working two rows from Handsome when I noticed the riderless horse wandering down the row toward me with bridle reins dragging the ground.

Handsome also saw the horse and stepped over on my row as the animal drew near. He swung his hoe in a vicious arc and struck the horse a brutal blow on the nose. The horse squealed, reeled backward, and fell to its hindlegs, its nose bleeding profusely.

"Git up, you head-swingin' bastard," Handsome laughed gleefully. "I got one harder than that for you."

The dazed horse struggled to its feet and began running across the field, tearing down cane in its wake. Handsome delivered another blow to the horse's flank as it began to run.

The horse ran all the way to the barracks, four miles away. The rider was forced to walk along beside us when we quit work, although he threatened to ride the backs of two or three inmates.

A dark suspicion lurked in the rider's mind that someone had struck his horse, and as we approached a field in back of the hospital that was covered with waist-high weeds he ordered us to "jump in and knock it out" before we could go to the barracks. "If I find out somebody bothered my horse," he threatened, "I'll run him across a guard line."

As for Handsome, he looked like a child thrilled with scared triumph at getting its own way, one who rejoices even in the midst of correction at its own assertion of freedom.

Next morning the rider led me and five others into another field and told us to cut the heads off stacks of cane that had been cut the day before. Four men went ahead and straightened the stacks and pulled the heads even. The fifth man and I followed, cutting the heads off and stacking them. The seed heads were to be saved for the next season's planting. When the wagons of the plow squad came to the field we stopped this work long enough to load them. This was easy work, and the rider was in another field with the main body of the line so we enjoyed a bit more freedom.

It was midmorning when the heavy, rickety farm wagons of the plow squad, drawn by lathering, dust-covered mules, rumbled into the field for the third time. We saw them waiting, but the rider hadn't told us to load them. He finally rode up and pointed to two men working on the stacks and said, "You and you."

"Do you want me too?" the inmate helping me cut off the heads asked.

The rider leered evilly at him, smiled, and said, "Yeah, you can come too."

Instead of taking them to load the wagons the rider led the way to the warden's jeep and had them whipped. As I heard the whip popping and the men screaming there came the plaintive voice of Handsome singing "Always Late with Yore Little Kisses."

The rider rode behind the three men as he brought them back to the field. As they reached the spot where they had stopped working the man who was helping me stopped, grabbed his hoe, and delivered a roundhouse swing with the instrument at the rider's head. The rider ducked quickly under the blow, which probably saved his life, but the corner of the blade grazed the top of his head. His hat sailed through the air and a trickle of blood ran down his face as he spurred his horse. The guard astride a horse behind us leveled his rifle on the rank man and ordered him to drop the hoe. The rider escaped into the next field. He rode to tell the warden what had happened. The camp warden in turn went to the Administration Building to tell the Assistant Head Warden. They both returned to the field, severely beat the man who had attacked the rider, and transferred him to Two Camp.

There were weevils and worms in the peas the wagon brought to us that day. Most of the inmates skimmed the watery surface with their spoons and continued to eat, as I sat munching candy bars. One of the inmates disgustedly threw his tray on the ground. In retaliation the rider picked ten men, including me, to be whipped.

"Bullies," the rider said, as we were marching to the barracks that evening, "I've been good to you boys, but you've let me down. The man is all over my back, because we're not cuttin' enough cane. I guess tomorrow Ah'm gonna have him start usin' the leather." The rider was already having an average of twelve men whipped each day.

I was fortunate. I only had to work in the cane fields three days. On the fourth morning I was sent to the silage pit, and Ben was sent to the sorghum mill. As we were walking to the pit in the early twilight an inmate from South Dakota told me the silage pit was worse than working in the fields. "I've been in that pit a week, and already lost ten pounds," he stated.

The silage pit was about ten feet deep at one end, and sloped to a depth of four feet at the shallow end. It was approximately fifteen feet wide and a hundred feet in length. A silage cutter sat on the brink of the pit and a long pipe blew the silage into the pit like a Gatling gun.

Silage – green corn stalks and cane – was hauled to the pit on wagons and trucks. Eight men carried armloads of stalks to the machine. They were forced to run in order to keep the man feeding the machine busy. If he stood idly waiting for stalks, the eight men were whipped.

The pit rider told me to jump into the pit and walk on the silage to pack it down.

"This stuff is fed to cows, isn't it," I asked, as I slid into the deep end of the pit.

"Cows, hell," the rider laughed. "That's for the convicts. You'll be eatin' that for breakfast this winter."

"If the State could afford a little milk and sugar, I'd rather eat it than that greasy gravy," the inmate standing beside me said.

The rider assigned four of us to work in the pit. We walked in a continuous circle packing the silage down. The silage cutter was cranked, and the pipe blowing it into the pit was placed over our heads. The large chunks of cane and corn were blown into the pit with terrific force. It felt like being pelted with stones. Some of the chunks were two or three inches in length and almost knocked us down. We pulled the pith helmets down around our ears and borrowed extra jackets for protection in spite of the 118-degree heat. To make it more unbearable a garden hose was stretched to an irrigation ditch, and the rider stood on the edge of the pit spraying us with water. There was not a cloud in the sky and no shade, except for the warden, who lay asleep on a blanket under a nearby Chinaberry tree.

Walking on the soft, spongy silage put great strain on the muscles of our legs. By two o'clock three of us suffered from muscular spasms and were unable to walk any longer. The rider stopped the machine and we were dragged from the pit. We were allowed to rest for a few minutes, then exchanged jobs with three inmates who had been carrying stalks to feed the machine.

When the rider stopped the machine it awakened the warden. He grabbed the whip lying beside him and ran to find out why the machine had been stopped. He called us sissies and girls, but didn't whip us.

"What's the matter, Doc," he asked me, "you having your menstrual period?"

Next morning as we stood in the yard the warden walked to the squad, grabbed my arm, and pointed to the squad of men working at the sorghum mill.

"This job isn't too bad," Ben said, as we walked off the yard. "There's plenty of heat on the place, though. There's so many wardens hanging around they have to wear badges to keep from whippin' each other!"

Four men, including Ben and I, carried armloads of cane from where it was stacked head-high on the ground at one side of the mill. There were only two mills so we were able to keep ahead, which gave us a few moments to loaf occasionally.

The cane being hauled from the fields was covered with dirt and mud. The juice was piped to a large tub inside the cooking room, where it was dipped out and poured into the vats without being strained. As the juice reached a boiling point dirt was plainly visible. A muddy froth covered the surface. The dirt mixed with the juice gave the molasses a gritty taste.

I had worked at the sorghum mill three days when an incident occurred that I believe contributed to Ben's untimely death. I was standing approximately thirty feet from him when it happened. He had stooped to grab an armload of cane when a car with a young woman driving came down the road, turned the corner in front of the sorghum mill, and disappeared down the road in a cloud of dust.

"Hey, Doc," Ben called to me, "did you see that little minx driving that car?"

"Yeah, man," I answered. "Do you think that cat could purr?"

"Purr!" Ben shouted. "I'll bet she could cut more tricks on a six-inch dick than a monkey could on a hundred-foot grapevine!"

A trustee from another camp standing nearby but unobserved by Ben bellowed, "Why, you son-of-a-bitch, that's a warden's daughter."

He struck Ben with a club he carried. Ben staggered backward and fell on his back. The club wielder kicked him in the ribs and stomped on his abdomen.

Ben staggered to his feet after the beating. Blood was running from his mouth and he held his abdomen with both hands.

"Doc," he said, "I think something tore loose. It's burnin' and feels like I'm bleedin' inside."

Ben vomited continuously thereafter. He began losing weight and was unable to eat the coarse cornbread and peas. Milk was the only food he could hold on his stomach. He wasn't permitted to go to the hospital and was transferred to Two Camp a few weeks later.

I tried to keep in contact with him through a wagon driver from that camp. He informed me Ben was working in the line and had become so weak and emaciated he had begun fainting. When he fainted the trustees would dump a bucket of water in his face, then make him work more.

Late one night the wagon driver walked into the barracks. I hurried to the front picket to check on Ben's condition. "You don't have to ask about ol' Ben any more," he said, as I approached the bars.

"Why not?" I asked, fearing the answer he would give.

"He kicked the bucket this mornin'," he drawled, as if he were giving an unimportant baseball score and plopped into the yard man's rocking chair.

Thus ended the life of my best friend, in the full flush and prime of his youth. A young man of gentle, inoffensive thoughts and manners; with a personality as frank as a pup's tail and to whom bachelorhood had always seemed the most delightful state in the world.

Ben was the closest friend I ever had. A criminal conviction and incarceration disclose a man's true friends.

Handsome was transferred to the sorghum mill during the third day I worked there. Another inmate named Crane played a humorous but cruel trick on him the next day.

I stood pulling an armload of cane from the stack the first time I talked to Crane. He was an ignorant, uncouth individual, who had been returned to the prison recently for parole violation. He had violated the parole by beating his elderly mother- and father-in-law with a baseball bat.

He asked for a cigarette as he strolled to where I stood. I pulled a pack from my pocket and gave him one, and he stuck it behind his ear. He pulled a photograph from his pocket and handed it to me.

"That's my wife's picture. It was taken a week before we were married." He used the most base, scurrilous language possible in his description of her. "She came from one of them square-John families. You know, that go to church and all that bunk. They didn't want her to marry me, but she did anyway."

"Why didn't you marry someone your own age?" I asked.

"Naw, man," Crane replied, "who wants to marry an ol' wore-out nag? Any woman over thirty is a trollop."

I glanced at the snapshot. It was a photograph of a girl of about sixteen, with a sweet, rounded face; upon it was the expression of dreamy innocence. Her brown eyes were wistful and a little sad, but they expressed the shy hopes, the romantic fancies, the beautiful, eternal dreams of girlhood. As I gazed at the photograph my mind filled with a sudden amused pity for Crane's rawness and ignorance.

"I made a fine thief out of that little girl," he continued. "I trained her for three months. She would walk with a pillow between her legs. We never paid for anything we ate or wore. She stole me a truckful of clothes."

"Perhaps that's why her folks didn't want her to marry you."

"Naw, they jest didn't like me. They didn't know I had trained her to steal and sell pussy. Man, I shore worked their heads over with that ball bat."

Crane asked for a match, lit the cigarette I had given him, and grinned. "I'm gonna have some fun out of Handsome."

Through curiosity I followed him inside the room where Handsome stood over a vat, stirring vigorously and singing "Always Late with Yore Little Kisses."

"Handsome," Crane said, as he nudged Handsome with his elbow and displayed an amused, superior smile, "do you know you make better molasses than anybody here?"

"That's right," Handsome smiled. "That's what the warden says too, and this vat I'm cookin' now will be the best ever made on this farm."

"I'll tell you what," Crane said, "my folks are comin' down Sunday, so you put some of the molasses from that vat into a jar and I'll have them take it home and enter it in the County Fair. You'll win a blue ribbon."

"You really think so?" Handsome asked, and his big face brightened.

"The way you make molasses, you're a cinch to win. The Governor will come down here to pin the ribbon on you. They'll take your picture and it'll be in all the newspapers."

Handsome complied good-humoredly, with the nonchalance of a big boy condescending to be taught the rules of some childish game. He paid the water boy four packs of cigarettes to go to the commissary to get a pound of margarine. While the water boy was gone he ran to the cannery a few yards away and washed two quart jars.

"They'll probably give you a furlough when you win that blue ribbon," Crane told him when he returned.

"Boy, oh, boy," Handsome exclaimed, "I can go home to see my mother. I got a good ol' mother. She's gittin' ol' and this might be my last chance to see her."

Handsome pulled the sticks of margarine from the box and dropped two in each jar. He poured hot molasses over the margarine, stirred it, and stuffed toilet paper in the top of the jars to seal them. He gave one to Crane and kept one for himself.

Crane told him he would send the jar to the barracks, but when Handsome wasn't looking he tossed the jar into a ditch behind the mill.

The preacher drove to the side of the mill a few minutes later. With a great, puffing effort he climbed from his car and walked inside. "I want some molasses," he told the rider, as he walked through the door.

"We ain't got nothin' but molasses," the rider responded.

The preacher spotted the jar Handsome had set in the window, walked over, held it in the air inspecting it, and asked, "How about this one?"

"Shore," the rider told him. "Take it."

"I'll be damned," Handsome wailed, as the preacher walked out with the jar in his hand. "Them was my molasses."

"What's the difference?" the rider asked angrily. "There's four more vats full."

"Yeah, but they ain't half-margarine," Handsome wailed.

Four days after the next visiting day Crane told Handsome his parents had broken the jar on the way home.

"There goes the chance I had to see my mother," Handsome whined, as he stood wiping tears from his eyes with the back of his hand like a disappointed child.

"Aw, you crazy bastard, you wouldn't have won anything if I had sent it."

Handsome realized then that a crude joke had been played on him. He grabbed a paddle used to stir the cooking molasses and dipped it into a boiling vat of juice. He swung the paddle in a half-circle, spattering Crane and the other men working inside. They ran from the vat room, screaming and rubbing where the hot juice had spattered them.

## PART II. *RULED BY THE WHIP*, DALE WOODCOCK

They refused to return to work unless Handsome came outside. After a long delay Handsome was persuaded to work in the boiler room. The vats of molasses were scorched when the others returned to work, but they were canned anyway. One morning the following winter we were served scorched molasses for breakfast, and I thought of this incident and silently laughed as the inmates sitting around me were complaining.

We finished making molasses in the middle of October. We ground the last stack of cane near eleven o'clock. Handsome and another man stayed behind to scrub and lock up. The rest of us went to the mess hall to eat dinner and rejoin the line which was digging sweet potatoes.

When we filed out of the mess hall after dinner the warden saw an inmate carry a handful of cornbread out to the yard and toss it to the pack of dogs lying under the barracks. He gave the inmate a whipping.

"What you tryin' to do, boy?" the warden asked, as the man rose from the ground. "You'll kill these dogs with that bread. It'll give 'em ulcers."

When the squads had been formed and counted the warden turned to the yard man and said, "I want somethin' done about these dogs."

We followed the plow squad down the long rows of sweet potatoes, picking them up and dropping them into crates. When the wagons came to the field I was one of six designated to load the crates onto them. Two men climbed onto the wagon and we set the heavy crates onto the wagon bed. After an hour of this we were exhausted. We could hardly lift the crates off the ground, especially after they reached the second and third tier on the wagon.

"How about lettin' us change jobs for a while?" one inmate asked the rider.

"I'll let you change as soon as the man gits here," the rider leered.

He had all six of us whipped when the warden drove to the field.

A group of extra trustees followed the warden to the potato field and began killing the dogs which were romping in the freshly turned earth.

"There'll be meat on the table tonight," Chief yelled.

I saw a trustee take aim and fire at Amigo. The dog howled as the buckshot hit him and he tumbled into the dirt. He managed to get to his feet and staggered toward me. He painted his blood across the plowed ground, painted it bright. He fell a few feet away, looked at me with a haunting pair of eyes, whined mournfully, and died.

Amigo's body was thrown on a cart and hauled behind the levee. Next day there was a black, swirling mass of buzzards flying over the spot where the dogs were dumped.

When I reached the barracks that night there was an empty space in the dust where Amigo usually lay. There was no mass of wiry, warm hair to smooth.

PART II. *RULED BY THE WHIP*, DALE WOODCOCK

## CHAPTER EIGHT

November, the brown month, skeletal, bleak, austere. The work days had grown shorter, and a smoky haze was banked up against the horizon each sunset. The blazing, broiling, almost unbearable days had ended.

We had been told as we were awakened we would begin picking cotton that morning. Cotton was the prison's main money crop, and each man had a quota to pick each day. All camp lines picked cotton, including the female prisoners, and the wardens whipped mercilessly until the cotton was picked.[27]

We lined up in front of the door leading to the mess hall. Chief stepped into the breakfast line behind me, laughing. He was going home after breakfast.

We were given three pancakes and a pat of butter for breakfast. Chief reached and took a dozen more pancakes when the tray was replenished.

"Did you git enough pancakes, Chief?" the yard man asked, as he walked to the table and looked down at the stack on Chief's tray.

"Oh, these aren't for me," Chief responded. "I'm gonna take these to your ol' greasy, peg-legged maw. I know she's hungry."

"You're a sorry son-of-a-bitch," the yard man, who wasn't accustomed to back talk, gritted between clenched teeth, and he bristled visibly.

"Yeah, I know," Chief replied, "that's what your maw used to tell me when I let her git up off the bed."

---

[27] For treatment of female prisoners in Arkansas check Ryan Anthony Smith's article "Laura Conner and the Limits of Prison Reform in 1920s Arkansas," *Arkansas Historical Quarterly*. 77:1 (Spring 2018) 52-63. Governor Thomas McRae in 1921 appointed Conner, a committed reformer, to the Arkansas Honorary Prison Commission. She became an outspoken critic of the other commissioners and prison management. Conner chose press coverage to expose sadistic practices, many of them illegal, used to dominate and punish convicts. She also revealed deep-rooted corruption tolerated by the system. Conner advocated with limited success less onerous punishment for breaking prison rules. Also, Smith's "Gendered Confines: Women's Prison Reform in 1920s and 1930s Arkansas," (Master's Thesis, Arkansas State University, 2017) For more on the subject: Report of the Arkansas Penitentiary Study Commission, January 1, 1968, 3.18.

The yard man turned on his heel and walked away.

"Tonight I can go in and sit down to a fine feed," Chief remarked, wistfully, "an' sleep with a woman in clean sheets that ain't lousy. An' pat the little wife on the butt in the mornin' an' she'll git up an' cook some ham an' eggs."

"What do you plan to do after tonight?" I inquired.

"I don't know for sure," he answered. "I've been worked, fed, and beat like a mule for a long time, and tomorrow I may start collectin.' I may git a jug of sweet-lucy and take off down the road. If I do the first one of these red-necked, stump-jumpin' Arkansas hillbillies I meet I'll rob him. I figure somebody oughtta pay for the beatin's and head skinnin's I've had here."

We filed from the mess hall, leaving Chief behind. As we stood in the dim light the warden told the rider he wanted one man to put in the block squad. New buildings were being constructed at Two Camp, and the concrete blocks used to construct them were made at Seven Camp.

The rider walked up and down the line twice, then I heard him give my name to the warden in a low voice.

"Woodcock," the warden bawled from behind me.

I turned to face him.

"Git over in the block squad," he said. "You ain't gonna do nothin' anyway."

The shed housing the block-making equipment was directly across the road from the barracks. As we walked into the building a hen stood in the doorway singing a cheery, half-human song. Then she stepped heavily, solemnly, aimlessly across the building and walked out the rear door.

"We eat chicken every once in a while over here," a middle-aged man grinned.

"This is the machine they built the Chinese wall with," the Mexican boy who operated the machine said to me, as I stood staring at the block-making machinery. He was branded with the inevitable name of "Poncho."

We spent the first hour carrying out blocks that had been made the previous day and stacked them in the yard at the rear of the block shed.

"This is the best job on the farm," Poncho said when we had completed carrying almost all the blocks to the yard. "But keep your eyes on that rider. He's as crazy as a 'Bessy bug.'"

The block squad rider was fifty-two years old and had spent over thirty of them in prisons. He had served three or four sentences in the Arkansas Penitentiary, which he described as his favorite prison. He was a human nearly as low in the mental scale as an animal. He spent most of his time describing the prisons he had been in, the woman he married, whom he said he had raped the first time he saw her, and the inmates he had whipped.

"When I git a headache the only thing that will cure it is to see somebody whipped," he explained each time he called for the warden to whip someone. That was the reason the Arkansas Penitentiary was his favorite prison. He was a sadist and could see and have men whipped any time he pleased.

When we completed carrying out the blocks the rider decided to make three bridge tiles to be used in constructing roads. We set up the steel molds and concrete was mixed. The rider told an elderly inmate from Indiana we had nicknamed "Pops" to get a wheelbarrow and bring the wet cement from the mixer to the molds. Pops pushed the wheelbarrow to the mixer and an inmate working there filled it full. Pops grabbed the handles and began pushing the wheelbarrow to where we stood waiting.

"Here, here, why, you ol' crazy thing," the rider barked, as he turned around, "you pick up that wheelbarrow and carry it, like you're supposed to!"

"Are you kiddin'?" Pops asked, with an incredulous frown on his face.

"About twenty-five on yore ol' rear end will show you I'm not."

"I'll carry the cement in buckets," Pops said, and pushed the wheelbarrow over on its side.

"See what I mean?" Poncho laughed. "He's a bug."

We made five tiles. The rider wrecked three of them, and we went inside the shed to begin making blocks. I stood waiting to be told where I was to work when the rider walked up beside me and asked, "Why don't you buy a pound of coffee?"

"I'll help buy it," I told him.

He called the other eight men to him and collected sixty cents from the ones who had money. I gave him sixty-five cents, and he ran to the barracks to buy a pound of coffee. He returned at a trot, built a fire under a tin can in back of the block shed, and posted two men to watch for the warden. When the coffee began boiling he carried the can inside, sat down on a concrete block, poured himself a tall glassful, sent some to the two guards outside the building, a glassful to the vegetable squad rider, then leisurely drank the remainder. He poured water over the coffee grounds and re-boiled them. This we were permitted to drink.

"That bastard will never get any more money from me to buy coffee," Poncho said, as we climbed from the pit, where we had been scraping dried, caked cement from the machine.

We began making blocks that afternoon. It was impossible to make more than two hundred blocks without the antiquated machine breaking down. Poncho would push a button bringing the machine to a clanging, thumping stop when something broke or came loose. These were the moments we dreaded, because the rider would grab a hammer or wrench and begin working on the machine. He was supposed to call the garage so that a mechanic could be sent to repair it, but he never did until he had done extensive damage.

A state engineer was in charge of the construction of the new building, and he disliked the rider because of the inferior blocks made and because he was continuously wrecking the machinery. The engineer had the rider whipped almost every week.

We had made slightly over a hundred blocks the first afternoon I worked in the block squad when the machine broke down. The rider grabbed a hammer, climbed on the machine, and tugged at an iron bar on the tamping device. He lost his temper because the bar wouldn't slide out and began hammering it. The bar bent and he threw the hammer across the building, barely missing Poncho's head.

He walked to the barracks to call the garage. Instead of coming to repair it, the mechanic called the engineer and reported that the machinery had again been damaged by the rider.

We were sitting on a board alongside one wall when the engineer drove up and parked in front of the building. The rider rose and walked to greet him, but the engineer ignored him, walked around the machine, climbed in his car, and drove away.

"To hell with him," the rider mumbled, as he returned to plop down on a sack of cement.

We were still sitting on the board when the Assistant Head Warden drove up a few minutes later. He crawled from his car and strode into the building as solemnly as Jugurtha marching to the Mamertine.[28]

"What's wrong with this outfit?" he asked the rider.

"Well, that bar –" the rider began.

"Aw, don't start no damn argument with me," the Assistant Head Warden growled. "I think I got enough arm to whip every man here. "You," he pointed to an inmate sitting beside me, "git my whip out of my car."

The inmate hurried to the car, opened the door, peered inside, turned, and said, "I don't see it."

"You ain't tryin' to see. You better git that whip, boy, or you're gonna be the first one down," the warden bellowed.

The inmate jerked the car seat out on the ground, and the car rocked as if in a heavy gale as he searched for the whip. He returned with the whip, handed it to the warden, and stepped aside.

"Git down there, ol' son-of-a-bitch," the warden growled when it became my time to be whipped. I stretched out on the hard concrete floor at his feet. He had a large, protruding abdomen, consequently he had no control over the whip. When he brought it down from over his head it might land anywhere between head and feet. The first blow landed in the small of my

---

[28]Jugurtha, king of Numidia, lived from 156-104 B.C. *The New Columbia Encyclopedia*, 1437. Mamertine was a prison in ancient Rome..

back. I braced for the next lash, hoping he would not strike me in the kidney area, which might rupture them or at least cause great pain. I had seen examples of the damage done to other inmates who had been hit in the kidneys with the whip.

The next blow landed on the back of my thighs. The edge of the whip cut into the flesh and caused a muscular spasm. I could hardly walk the following week.

When he threw the whip over his head for the sixth lash, it became entangled in the low rafters over his head. He dropped the whip and began kicking me. When he stopped kicking he stepped on my hand, lying palm down, with his heel and twisted his foot. The skin was twisted loose and a sharp piece of concrete cut deep into my wrist.

None of the rank men uttered a word when we were whipped. The rider was whipped last. He received five lashes and squealed like a hog caught in a fence.

Next morning a Negro houseboy came into the lot in back of the concrete shed where we were stacking blocks. He offered to bring us a gallon of milk each day for twenty-five cents a week, and coffee for twenty-five cents a pound. I quickly agreed to share half the bill with another inmate. The houseboy put the jug of milk under a box each evening. Next morning the milk would be ice cold.

The rider discovered the jug one morning. Because we hadn't divided the milk with him, he became enraged and chased the houseboy off the yard and told the guard to shoot him if he returned.

We failed in our quota of blocks each day. Every time the machine broke down or something went wrong, the rider placed the blame on Poncho. "It's that damn Mexican's fault," he would accuse. We always made enough blocks, but the rider would walk among the rows of blocks sitting on boards to harden and strike them with a club he usually caried. The soft, damp blocks would crumble on the floor and the rider would grab the square, metal pallet molds and throw them in all directions. When he began breaking the blocks we were forced to stop the machine to search for a hiding place as he began throwing the pallets in all directions.

The trustees were permitted radios, and the rider was deeply interested in listening to "The Adventures of Superman." Each morning before we began work he described in detail the predicament Superman was in at the conclusion of the program. On the fourth day I worked in the block squad the radio station changed the time and schedule of their programs, and "The Adventures of Superman" was aired an hour before quitting time. The rider decided to quit work an hour earlier so he wouldn't miss the program. The first evening we quit early the camp warden caught us in the building while everyone else was at work, so he whipped the entire squad.

Late on Saturday afternoon of that first week the rider sneaked up beside me and said, "I want to borrow two dollars to git in the poker game tonight. I'll pay you back Monday."

I loaned him the money and he never mentioned it again. Thereafter I resorted to subterfuge when he asked for a loan. I carried approximately 35 cents in a tobacco sack, and the remainder of my money in another sack. When the rider asked for money I would say, "Sure, if I have it." I would pull out the sack containing a few cents, dump it in my hand, and count it while he watched. This amount was never enough to satisfy him so he didn't take it.

Thanksgiving Day we were permitted to quit work at 3 o'clock. We were fed the usual peas and cornbread for dinner, but enjoyed a better supper; a pan of butter beans, sweet potatoes, white bread, coffee, and a small, thin pork chop. That was one of the five times we were served meat during the fourteen months I spent at Seven Camp.

The line straggled in from the cotton fields as we walked into the yard. "Every prison in the country knocks off for Thanksgiving," Whisky Red moaned, as we lined up in front of the mess hall door. "What do we do? Pick cotton, pick cotton. We'll probably pick cotton on Christmas Day too."

"Why do you want the day off?" Poncho asked. "There's nothing in Arkansas to be thankful for."

Black clouds had been sailing out of the west since noon and the temperature dropped to freezing by darkness. Wood was carried in and fires built in the oil-drum stoves. Only the inmates near the drums benefited from the fire. The floorwalker issued blankets and long underwear, and most of the inmates crawled into bed to keep warm. The darkness was piled against the window panes like black marble in a quarry. The wind shrieked like a banshee.

Next morning the warden decided the line and block squad should cut wood. We stood in the yard in the drizzling rain while cannonades of thunder broke against the battlements of the sky as lightning flashed with a blue glare. The horses and mules in the barn lot ran in circles, squealing and pawing at the board fence.

The drizzle continued for an hour or two, then suddenly stopped. The clouds dispersed, and through the hazy sky the wan, cadaverous light fell upon the ground as though sent from a dead sun.

I sat on the ground, pulling on a dull, warped, crosscut saw that had several teeth missing. My clothes were soaked and there was a bone-chilling wind. I could barely see the top of my saw partner's head over the top of the log.

Suddenly a strong wind came up from the west, pushing a large cloud before it. Nearer and nearer came the storm. There were short, sharp patters of raindrops upon the toilet-paper-strewn ground, like hurrying feet; the wind gusts came oftener. The cloud grew darker and ran down the sky on all sides like spilled ink. At last, out of the incessant mutter of the thunder, broke a loud, long peal, together with a flash of lightning that cleft the heavens in twain from end to end; the wind leaped down out of the dark sky like a bloodhound loosed from its leash, and the rain was as a river that had burst its bounds. Fury and chaos reigned.

"Make it up," the rider screamed.

We gathered the tools and hurriedly formed a column of twos, expecting to go to the barracks, less than a hundred yards away.

"Set down," the rider growled.

We sat on the ground in the downpour. Water poured over my face, making breathing difficult. A rivulet ran down my back. We could hardly see each other. The storm raged on with increasing fury. The lightning was one wide, white sheet of flame, the thunder one continuous roar, the wind one prolonged, demoniacal shriek.

When the rain slackened enough for the guards to see us we returned to work. We went to the mess hall at eleven-thirty, ate in the wet clothing, had a twenty-minute rest period, then returned to the wood yard in the rain.

The rain stopped about two o'clock and turned much colder. Ice formed on the logs and chips. Within a few minutes snow began to fall softly and quietly, but increased until it spread a white blindness everywhere. In the thick of the storm, and half-blinded by the force with which the wind blew the fine flakes of snow against my eyes, I walked to where the rider stood beside a bucket of fire and asked permission to change jobs. I had been chopping wood for the cookstoves in the mess hall since noon. I had forgotten my gloves that morning, and the saw handle had already rubbed blisters into the palm of my hands and on my fingers. I showed him my bloody hands.

"I lose more blood than that when I brush my teeth," he remarked. "What do you want to do?"

I asked permission to help carry wood and stack it.

"Go ahead," he drawled, "but there's gonna be blisters on your ass too when the warden gits yere." He turned and walked away, yelling, "Let's cut some wood, Bullies."

When the warden returned from the Administration Building the rider had me and seven other inmates whipped. As the first lash landed on my buttocks, I began to wish I had removed the three buttons on the seat of the underwear the yard man had issued the previous night.

When we reached the barracks I draped my overalls and jacket over one of the oil drums to dry. They steamed and smoked but dried within a few minutes.

We returned to the block shed the next day, and the rider asked to borrow two dollars before we began working. I pulled out the tobacco sack containing only a few cents and counted as he watched slowly.

"That won't help me," he said and walked over to another man.

A few minutes later I bent over to retrieve pallets from the floor the rider had thrown. The sack I kept concealed fell to the floor with a clinking sound. The rider stared at it, looked at me with a blank expression, and turned and walked away.

Next morning as we stood in the yard waiting for the yard man to complete his count the rider tapped my shoulder and said, "Catch the line, moneyed man."

I walked to the line without commenting. The line spent the morning moving a junk pile of tin cans, broken bottles, and old car bodies. I was sitting in the yard when the men working at the block shed came to dinner. All of the men in the squad went to where the yard man stood in the mess hall door.

They held a brief conversation, then Poncho ambled over to where I sat and said, "I guess you wish you had bought that rider coffee and loaned him money, eh?"

"No," I answered. "I'm not doing enough time to be forced to buy anything."

"Make it up," the yard man yelled at that moment.

After dinner the yard man counted the men in each squad, glanced at his roster sheet, and said, "Woodcock."

I turned to face him. He pointed to the block squad and ordered, "Catch in there."

"Jest a minute," the block squad rider blurted. "I put him back in the line."

"And I'm puttin' him back in the block squad," the yard man barked. "I'm runnin' Seven Camp. I want you riders and guards to understand that right now. I found out why you put him back in the line. Now, I don't want to hear any more about it."

The rider stuck out his lower jaw in defiance, his face turned livid, but he made no response.

A week before Christmas most of the trustees were given furloughs to go home or where they wished. The plow squad rider was in the first group to leave. The block squad rider replaced him, and we were returned to the line until the furloughs were over.

One trustee who had been committed for the murder of four people failed to return from his Christmas furlough. He was arrested in Utah several months later after he added two more murders to his list in that state.

The morning we began working in the line again was a bitterly cold one. There had been a heavy snowfall the night before. An icy wind blew steadily across the flat, dreary countryside. We stood in the yard shivering. The brisk wind seemed to cut like a knife, and the mud puddles in the yard were frozen solid. Some of the inmates were practically barefooted, so they had wrapped rags and sacks around their feet. We had acquired a new warden and yard man, and the new yard man refused to issue thirty pairs of new shoes that had been sent from the Administration Building. The shoes were supposed to have been issued to the inmates who needed them, but the yard man decided instead to sell them. For three dollars I got a new pair and three pairs of work socks. The inmates who had no money and were practically barefooted remained that way.

The new camp warden had recently quit his job at the Mississippi Penitentiary. He stated Mississippi had outlawed whipping so he had resigned. He believed that whipping was the only way to maintain discipline. He added his own special touch to whipping. He placed hacksaw blades near the whip handle, giving it more spring and bounce which made it hurt more.

The foggy, ruffian night had been succeeded by a bright and beautiful day. We checked axes and saws from the tool shed and headed across the top of the levee. An elderly man walked beside me. Apparently he was suffering from arthritis or some such disease, because he was forced to trot in order to keep pace with our longer strides and he whimpered with each step. I offered to carry his ax. He handed it to me, wiped his nose on the back of his hand, patted me on the back, and said, "Thanks, Slim."

"Slim" was an appropriate nickname by that date. That morning I had glanced at my reflection on the bottom of the tin can I drank coffee from. My cheeks were hollow, black circles ringed my eyes which appeared sunken. My reflection on the can belied my twenty-six years.

The area the rider chose to work in was covered with ankle-to knee-deep water which was covered with a silvered patch of thin ice.

"Hit it, Bullies," the rider ordered after he posted the guards in strategic spots.

We waded into the swamp and began cutting brush and tall trees. As wedges and axes were driven into the giants the yellow- and brown-painted leaves showered the ground. They tumbled with crisp, bumping sounds down through the limbs, glowing like Chinese lanterns in the brilliant sunlight as squirrels chattered and birds squawked in resentment of our intrusion.

The rider found a high, dry spot of ground and built a roaring fire which blazed and crackled fiercely, emanating the aromatic odor of burning resin. Near midmorning he yelled, "Come on out, Bullies. You can warm up for a few minutes."

We waded onto the high spot and gathered around the fire. There was a stamping and beating of chilled feet and hands. A few minutes later

"Mississippi Dad," as the new warden had been nicknamed, drove down the road skirting the swamp. "Why aren't these people workin'?" he asked the rider who rode out to greet him.

"Well," Poncho said, "we are now officially people instead of idiots."

The rider climbed from his horse and drawled, "They jest quit workin', Cap'n. I guess they're strikin'."

"Bring some out here," the warden replied. "I'll teach 'em to keep workin'."

The rider rode into the water and pointed at five inmates who had scampered into the water and were feverishly working. They were whipped and the warden asked for five more. The rider again rode into the water and pointed at five more inmates, including me.

The old man whose ax I had carried that morning was in the line ahead of me. After much grunting and groaning he managed to lie down on his stomach in the snow.

"Oh, Lord," he said each time the whip struck him.

As the eighteenth blow landed he screamed, "Oh, Cap'n, please don't hit me again!"

"There you are," the warden grinned, "you finally called on the right man. I'm the one who can help you, not the Lord. Git up from there."

That evening as we stood in the yard waiting to go into the mess hall the same inmate walked to where I was leaning against the building. His cheekbones and his nose were brilliant pink with the cold. His gloomy face was flushed and his eyes were watery. His thin, white hair danced on top of his head with each fresh new gust of wind.

"Doc," he said, "I've caught a cold. Could you do somethin' for me? That convict at the hospital won't do anything but give me a dose of salts."

I explained it was impossible for me to aid him. He stared at me. A disappointed look came into his face, and quickly deepened into an expression of despondency.

He went to bed as soon as we reached the barracks. He lay on his back, his chest heaving convulsively. Great drops of sweat rolled down his forehead. His face, normally bright red, was now very pale, and his feverish, watery eyes blinked helplessly at the swaying light over his bed, like a kitten's, as he lay still. Next morning he was unable to get up. The warden came into the cage, cursed, and threatened to whip him, but he was permitted to remain in bed. He lay in bed, ignored and without treatment, three days before he was carried to the hospital. Two days later the convict doctor came to the barracks and told the yard man the elderly inmate had died.

Christmas Eve we were permitted to quit work at three o'clock. A truck delivered a load of packages which were stacked on the front picket. My mother had sent a large box containing fruit, candy, canned food, cookies, my favorite magazines, and, best of all, a huge coconut cake. A large number of inmates received no packages. I divided the fruit, candy, and cookies with those around me who received nothing. I refused to share the cake, though. The prison officials presented each man with a small paper sack containing a handful of hard Christmas candy, an apple, and a handful of pecans the women inmates of Four Camp had gathered in the woods behind the levee.

"I hope you people enjoyed Christmas," the warden said after we had eaten the Christmas dinner which was the same as the one on Thanksgiving Day, "because we've been foolin' around durin' the holidays but we're gonna start farmin' tomorrow. The honeymoon is ovah. You riders heah me!"

An increase in line rider brutality did not require encouragement. In his book about time spent as a long line rider at Cummins, author K. Wymand Keith recounts chilling stories about the brutality he witnessed.[29] Not long after his arrival Keith saw a line rider use on a convict what came to be known as the Tucker Telephone. The old-fashioned phone had batteries, wires, and a crank. While three prisoners held a convict down, Keith saw a warden exhibit "strange excitement" when he tied a wire to the man's foot and a second to his genitals. As the warden turned a crank the man screamed in agony.[30]

The riders gathered around the stove on the picket laughed at his remark. Next day they kept the warden busy driving from squad to squad as they had half the rank men at the camp whipped.

---

[29] K. Wymand Keith, *Long Line Rider: The Story of Cummins Prison Farm* (New York, McGraw-Hill Book Co., 1971).
[30] A search of the assistant superintendent's residence by CID would discover the Tucker Telephone in a closet.

## CHAPTER NINE

In May we completed making enough blocks to construct the new buildings at Two Camp and we were transferred to the line. On the morning we returned to the line an inmate asked if he could go in the hospital while we were eating breakfast. The yard man told him he couldn't. The inmate remained at the table as we filed out to the yard. The yard man counted the squads, glanced at his roster sheet, then walked to the mess hall door and struck his head inside. He returned, said something inaudible to the warden, then he, the warden, line rider, and two more trustees walked into the mess hall. A few seconds later there was a deafening crash of tables and benches being overturned, and a hubbub of grunts and exclamations. A dead silence followed. Then came the swishing, cracking sound of the whip.

The inmate limped from the building holding his knee. His face was cut and covered with blood. The trustees stood in the doorway jeering, but they too were cut about the face.

The warden followed the inmate from the mess hall, and while the yard man again counted the squads the warden asked a man in the fence-building detail a question. The answer he received was merely "yes."

"Yes, what?" the warden roared. The answer he received set the caldrons of wrath to bubbling afresh. "You say 'sir' to me."

The inmate was dumbfounded, not knowing what to say or do next, so he remained silent.

"Damn you," the warden again roared, and struck the puzzled man in the face with his fist. The warden started to strike another blow with his fist, but changed his mind and used the whip instead.

When we arrived at the field the guards began shooting at the inmate who had refused to come out of the mess hall. One of the bullets ricocheted and struck the rider. As he crumpled to the ground the rank men began laughing and cheering. The warden ran into the field and rushed the rider to the hospital.

Three days later we went to the cannery where we spent the remainder of the summer. Six inmates were assigned to care for the machinery, and the rest of us were told to sit on benches on each side of a long table. We were given knives to peel and slice the beets, carrots, tomatoes, and potatoes which were to be canned and stored to feed the wardens' families.

## Part II. *Ruled by the Whip*, Dale Woodcock

While we were waiting to begin work we were entertained by "Mississippi Dad" and Eight Camp's warden who practiced breaking bricks with their whips at the front of the cannery building.

It was suffocating inside the cannery. The torrid sun beat down on the low tin roof, and steam from the huge cooking vats clouded our vision. Rivulets of water streamed down the concrete walls and formed puddles on the floor. Directly behind me sat one of the steaming vats. If I became careless and leaned backward I brushed against it. When the vat was ready to be emptied the inmate who watched over it opened the valve, permitting the hot water to scald our feet as it gushed over the floor. He never warned us, and on one occasion my feet were burned so seriously I was barely able to walk to the barracks. The steam caused a heat rash which felt like I was being stung by a thousand bees throughout each day.

We began the canning season with the peeling and slicing of beets, which was easy for me but difficult for some. I would grab the beets, twist the peeling loose, and slice the beet with the same motion. We were given five-gallon wooden buckets and permitted only ten minutes to fill each one. Anyone who failed to have his bucket filled when the rider walked around the table at the end of each ten-minute period was whipped. I had my quota each time, but we snapped beans the next day and I never had enough to satisfy the rider. We snapped the beans into gallon tin cans. I usually had mine about three-fourths full when the rider checked. Very few inmates were able to snap enough beans on the first two timed periods.

"All right," the rider snapped, "anybody that ain't got it the next time is goin' down."

I slammed the bucket against the sharp edge of the table, bending it inward. Several men sitting close saw me do it, and they, too, bent their buckets. When the rider made the next check we had a bucket full but were whipped for bending the buckets.

During the latter part of May an escape attempt took place at Two Camp. One of the inmates who was helping put a new roof on a building grabbed a knife used to cut the roofing material, jumped into the warden's car, and placed the knife at the warden's throat. He ordered the warden to drive through the main gate.

Guards riddled the car and warden, as he drove through. The car was wrecked and the warden was rushed to a hospital. One of his legs was amputated but he survived. The inmate wasn't injured, but he was tried, convicted, and given another sentence for attempting to escape. The inmate was nicknamed "Frenchy" and he told me, after I was transferred to Two Camp, that he attempted to escape because the line rider had made homosexual advances and threatened to have him whipped unless he submitted.

This escape attempt put "heat" on the other camps. That night as we watched a movie the inmate from Indiana we called "Pops" mentioned the escape attempt to the man on the cot beside him. After the movie both were whipped for discussing escaping.

Next day they were again beaten. We had barely arrived at the cannery and were waiting for the guards to take their positions, when the warden drove up, jumped from his jeep, grabbed the whip lying beside him, and walked to where we stood. He swung the whip at Pops' face as he approached within striking distance. Pops threw up his hands for protection. This enraged the warden, who knocked him down with his fist and proceeded to use the whip.

I received the most severe whipping during my two-year sentence a few minutes later. Ten inmates, including myself, were assigned to cut carrot tops. I was sitting on a wooden crate and couldn't reach the pile of carrots over the others' heads, so I asked an inmate sitting close to the carrots to throw me an armload. He scooped up both hands full and handed them to me without replying.

"All right, ol' Doc," the warden bawled from behind me. "I tol' you people about talkin' instead of workin'. Ah'm gonna tear your rump up."

I was given twenty-seven lashes as I lay on the concrete floor. The warden threw his weight behind each lash and pulled on the whip as it struck my buttocks, thus twisting and tearing the skin. Soon blood and skin together were flipped away at every blow. I was unable to regain my feet unaided, so the rider stood me on my feet. Blood was pouring from my rectum. The beating resulted in a severe case of hemorrhoids. I was so nervous and shaky I couldn't control the knife when I returned to cut carrot tops. I cut my hand severely in two places.

"You can carry carrots over to the cannery the rest of the day," the rider said with a touch of compassion in his voice and with a spasmodic effort at sympathy as he saw blood dripping from my elbow.

I was barely able to walk to the barracks that evening. A week later my buttocks were still swollen and black as a chunk of coal.

In early September I was transferred to Two Camp. We were eating supper when the yard man burst into the mess hall carrying a sheet of yellow paper in his hand. We knew immediately what it meant. A transfer occurred every time he walked into the mess hall carrying yellow paper. Everyone sat quietly, expectantly, each hoping his name would not be on the transfer list. We heard gruesome stories of brutality emanating from Two Camp almost every day.

My name was last on the list. Everyone turned to stare at me as I rose to go into the barracks.

"Hey, they got ol' Doc," I heard someone across the room say. As I walked toward the door leading to the barracks to get my possessions - a comb, toothbrush, soap, and notebook, the inmates I had lived with for fourteen months slapped my back and shoulders and wished me luck.

The yard man pushed a plaid shirt and a cheap pair of trousers through the bars to me. I quickly donned the clothing and went to the commissary to cash my check which the night yard man had given me as I left the mess hall.

"You've about got this time wrapped up, ain't you, Doc?" the warden asked, as I gave the check to the commissary trustee.

"Yes, sir," I answered, avoiding his piercing stare.

"You gonna steal another microscope? You got the name you might as well have the fame."

I clenched my fist in bitter impotence, turned without answering, and returned to my cot to gather my belongings.

The sun had withdrawn its pitiless glare, but across the sky still flamed the long rose-colored pennons of the defeated day as we marched down the dirt road, surrounded by guards walking and riding horses. The sky was turning purple and a few stars timidly appeared and took their stations in the spotless and profoundly purple expanse as we walked into the Two Camp yard. It was covered with flowers and shrubbery, and the concrete-block barracks was painted white, but the ugly, unpainted guard shacks marred its appearance.

I had feared being transferred to Two Camp since my arrival at the prison. Two Camp housed the long-termers, trouble-makers, and escapees. Until recently Two Camp's line had contained one squad known as the "Hot Spot." This squad was composed of rebellious inmates considered too dangerous to mingle with the other inmates. The "Hot Spot" had had a warden assigned exclusively to it who carried trace chains and a pick handle to maintain discipline. "A whip is too good for these sorry bastards," he stated.

We were told to remove all our clothing when we entered the barracks. We piled them on the floor and were turned into the barracks stark naked. Several men I had known at Seven Camp waved to me as the floorwalker led us down an aisle to a row of vacant cots. Anxiously I sat on the dirty mattress waiting for the yard man to search my clothing and personal belongings. He failed to look in the notebook, which would have resulted in a severe beating had the contents been discovered.

"You're sitting in a dangerous spot," the floorwalker said as he walked past me. "Bullets were flying all around here a few days ago when that boy got knocked off." He was describing an incident where a trustee had been shot in three vital areas while he was stationed at the guard post in the rear of the barracks. A few days before he was killed he had written a letter to his parents in which he listed three fellow trustees who should be investigated if anything happened to him. His death was ruled a suicide.

I took a shower, brushed my teeth, and wrote a letter to my mother telling her how well I was being treated and fed. I lied in every letter I wrote to her. I saw no reason to hint at the truth which would only cause her to worry.

After the letter had been written I sat on the cot talking to the men who walked past my cot. Most of the inmates at Two Camp were silent and morose, and stayed on their cots. A large number had closely shaved heads and wore red caps denoting they were escapees.

Two Camp's line had begun picking cotton a week before I was transferred. I was placed in the "piss leg" squad next morning, then transferred to a different squad after the first weigh-up.

"The cotton is mine and the bolls are yours," the rider said to me, as I began stuffing cotton into the long sack trailing behind me, "and you keep yore bolls out of my cotton."[31]

The line rider was a strong, merciless brute without sense of pity or compassion. He was of medium height, powerfully built, with broad, deep chest and massive shoulders. His voice was deep and full; his shock of hair was ink-black. He had a large nose which drooped toward a mouth cut in human granite. He was a notorious homosexual and had recently walked several miles in the rain and asked to be readmitted from parole. He walked up and down the rows of cotton, knocking men down with his fists. He would also challenge various men to fight. "Well, ol' thing, you got a whippin' comin'," he would say to men he disliked. "You can take it from me or the warden. Which do you want to take on?"

Most of the men the rider challenged elected to fight him. At least they would get to slug it out with the rider.

The cotton picking wasn't difficult or hard work, but each man was given an impossible quota each day. The warden whipped several men at each weigh-up.

Cold weather began in the middle of November, but snow or a freezing rain failed to stop work. We went to the fields before sunrise each morning. The cotton hanging from the bolls would be covered with frost and ice and frozen into a hard ball. Picking the cotton while it was in this condition caused our hands to swell and crack open. The frozen bolls mutilated our hands.

The day before Thanksgiving we had heard the Governor had abolished whipping. We sat on the frozen ground as the rider and wagon driver gave us the peas and cornbread we had for Thanksgiving dinner. After he had given each man a chunk of cold cornbread, the wagon driver returned to the wagon and uncovered a bucket of sweet potatoes and said, "Orville Faubus

---

[31] After blooms appear on cotton stalks the blooms turn into hard green bolls, sometimes the size of golf balls. When mature they open and expose fluffy cotton to be picked by human hands and stuffed into pick sacks. Bolls not yet matured weigh much more than lint cotton. When hidden in picking sacks, some as long as 12 feet, they significantly increase the weight of sacked cotton. Weight determines the picker's pay for that sack's contents. Green bolls are dead weight paid for by unaware owners when each sack is weighed. In this case pickers were not paid, but punished for not achieving their quota of pounds picked. The rider was warning them not to cheat.

called the warden and said he wanted the whip polished, not abolished. But he sent you all some sweet potatoes."[32]

That afternoon the warden whipped twenty-seven men.

We picked cotton until the middle of December, then went to the fields of a nearby farmer and picked cotton ribbons hanging from bolls and which had been scattered on the ground by a cotton-picking machine.

I received only six whippings during the cotton-picking season. There were approximately ninety men in the Two Camp line, and during this period the warden administered four hundred and eighty whippings.

During the remainder of my sentence we cut cotton stalks and worked in the woods clearing new ground. The rider would always assign me and three others to carry and stack the logs when we were in the woods. When we managed to get the largest logs off the ground and were staggering under the weight, the rider would run and jump on the log, daring us to drop him which would result in a whipping. During the latter part of February we managed to raise a huge log from the ground and were stumbling under the weight as the rider jumped on it. His extra weight was too much, and the strain tore the ligaments in my wrist. I dropped my end of the pole with which we carried the logs and jumped out of the way as the log rolled in my direction. The other men were forced to drop the log, and it barely missed rolling onto the rider's foot as he jumped to the ground and danced to get out of the way. We were whipped, but I was relegated to carrying brush because of the injury to my wrist.

The morning I was discharged from the prison the yard man tapped my shoulder as I sat at the breakfast table. It was still completely dark outside. "Stay where you are," he said lethargically.

---

[32]Roy Reed, *Faubus: The Life and Times of an American Prodigal* (Fayetteville: University of Arkansas Press, 1997). Born in 1910, Orval Eugene Faubus, a Democrat, served a remarkable six consecutive terms as governor. His unsuccessful effort to stop integration of Little Rock's Central High School became a memorable event in state history. Many Arkansas voters admired his stand against federal encroachment in their lives. The CID report that upended the state's prison management and practices had been completed during his governorship. But Faubus set the report aside until he handed it to Rockefeller, a Republican who became the state's next governor. So Faubus avoided the wrath of state legislators, prison authorities, and powerful business interests abusing the system. Faubus died in December 1994.

I sat sipping coffee as the line men began filing out the door to the yard. Most of them grinned, waved, and made appropriate remarks as they walked past.

After the squads had been sent to their assignments the yard man returned and led the way back to the barracks. He advised me to get dressed in a hurry as he threw me a black, frazzled shirt. I slipped into a pair of green trousers I had paid seventy-five cents for.

When I had dressed, the yard man again opened the barracks door and led the way down a long hallway. At the end of the hallway he opened a door of another hallway which led to the front office. A sleepy-eyed trustee sat behind a desk in the office. He reached under a stack of papers as I entered, pulled out my discharge papers, and handed them to me. I had a dollar disk in my pocket and he gave me a dollar bill for it.

"Where's the forty dollars in my account," I asked.

"I don't know anything about it," he answered. "You'll have to write back or wait until someone gets here."

"I'll write," I answered.

The trustee grinned, shook my hand, unlocked the door, and said, "Good luck."

As I stepped into the front yard I noticed the moon hanging low in the west, a pale crescent. The stars still glowed in undiminished radiance. There was a wealth of unutterable exultation in my heart. Far off a rooster gave a long, clear blast. The wind from the south was full of the wonderful odor of springing grass, warm, brown earth, and oozing sap. Morning it was, like the morning of life, pure, vivid, exhilarating. To breathe was to inhale nameless thrills, perfumes, dreams; to see was to entertain indescribable apparitions of beauty; to hear was to revel in a broad, tender, softly flowing tide of melody.

As a crimson glow crept into the eastern sky I stared down the dusty road leading to the highway four miles away – and freedom.

# PART III. ARKANSAS STATE POLICE CRIMINAL INVESTIGATION DIVISION REPORT

About 15 years after Woodcock's release an explosive report prepared by the state police criminal investigation division (CID) verified revelations about massive problems in the prison system. Though undertaken during Faubus' administration, he left the report to Rockefeller, who went public with its findings on January 16, 1967.[33] CID investigated Tucker from August 19 to September 7, 1966. Completed on September 7, their report ran about 67 pages, and it was ugly. Numerous interviews and photographs provided evidence of its accuracy. The extent of this investigation surprised prison authorities. Unlike previous inspections announced in advance, this one did not allow time to prepare tightly controlled, choreographed performances.

The unabridged CID report follows.[34]

---

[33] Tom Dillard, "Winthrop Rockefeller (1912-1973)," *Encyclopedia of Arkansas* (https://encyclopediaofarkansas.net: accessed 25 Apr 2023). When Rockefeller followed Faubus as governor stark differences emerged. Unlike Faubus, Rockefeller had progressive social goals. In 1953, after visiting a World War II army buddy who lived in Arkansas, Rockefeller purchased land on Petit Jean Mountain for his home. Faubus appointed him to the Arkansas Industrial Development Commission, and Rockefeller helped bring many new businesses and jobs to the state. In 1966 he ran for governor on the Republican ticket and won. Rockefeller accomplished prison reforms and other goals. He won a second term in 1968, but lost his race for a third term. He died of pancreatic cancer in 1973.

[34] The original copy of this CID Report is in Butler Center's collection. Department of Correction is sometimes referred to as Department of Corrections.

## CASE REPORT
## CRIMINAL INVESTIGATIONS DIVISION
## ARKANSAS STATE POLICE[35]

FILE NUMBER: 916-166-66

INVESTIGATORS: H. H. Atkinson, Investigator
Criminal Investigations Division
Little Rock, Arkansas

James M. Beach, Investigator
Criminal Investigations Division
Pine Bluff, Arkansas

Billy Skipper, Investigator
Criminal Investigations Division
Little Rock, Arkansas

SUBJECTS:
1. Robbery (41-3601)
2. Larceny (Over $35.00) (46-130) (43-2156) (41-3917)
3. Maiming (41-2502) (41-2504) (41-2507)
4. Extortion (12-1738)
5. Liquors into Prison (41-3109)
6. Excessive Punishment (46-158)
7. Personal use of provisions (46-129)
8. Gifts to Officers or Personnel (46-167)
9. Housing and treatment (46-108)

Investigation by board

COUNTY: Jefferson

TIME AND PLACE: As indicated in facts section of report.

NAME AND TYPE
OF ESTABLISHMENT: Tucker State Prison Farm, Tucker, Arkansas

LOSS: As indicated in facts section of report.

VICTIMS: State of Arkansas
Others as indicated in facts section of report.

---

[35] Every page throughout this report is marked Very Confidential.

FACTS:

On 8-19-66, at about 11:30 A.M., this investigator was instructed to proceed to Tucker State Prison Farm by Major W. C. STRUEBING, Commanding, Criminal Investigations Division. Further instructions were to report to the Superintendent, Mr. O. E. BISHOP, and to assist him in the investigation of an incident involving intoxication among a group of inmates or in any other matter as requested.

At about 1:30 P.M., 8-19-66, this investigator reported to Mr. BISHOP at the Administrative Building, Tucker Farm, and was advised that several inmates, on the previous night, had left the Prison and gone into town to purchase whiskey and beer. When they returned to the Prison, they were arrested by Wardens FLETCHER, MAYS, and WILSON, and a quantity of whiskey and beer was confiscated from them. Also, a number of inmates had become intoxicated during the afternoon and early evening from intoxicants obtained in an earlier visit to an off premise liquor store in Tucker, Arkansas. Mr. BISHOP requested this investigator to take charge of the investigation at hand, and, in addition, to assume full charge of the Prison Farm in an effort to correct the security situation until such a time as another person was obtained to assume the responsibility of the office of Assistant Superintendent. This request was cleared by Mr. Herman E. LINDSEY, Director, Arkansas State Police, and Major W. C. STRUEBING, Commanding, Criminal Investigations Division. All personnel employed at Tucker Prison Farm were advised of this move by Mr. BISHOP and concurred that security was in "poor" condition.

INVESTIGATORS NOTE: All persons interviewed in the course of this investigation were advised of their rights under the Fifth Amendment to remain silent and to have legal counsel present. Subject waived all rights prior to interview.

On 8-19-66, this investigator interviewed INMATE GILBERT MORRIS, WM [white male] 22, Gate guard, and was advised that on 8-18-66, he had observed INMATE FRANK BOSNICK go to the garage and motor pool located near the gate. MORRIS stated that he had noted that it was about noon when BOSNICK had come by. He stated that he later, about 2:30 P.M., observed BOSNICK drive a farm tractor back to the garage and take a large pasteboard box from it and go to the electric shop located behind the garage. MORRIS stated that he then saw BOSNICK leave the area and go toward the main prison building. MORRIS stated that at about 8:45 P.M., he observed the Night Sheriff, (INMATE WAYNE MOORE), the electrician, (INMATE CARL CORDER), and the kitchen rider (INMATE FRANK BOSNICK), cross the area behind (South) of the gate house and go to the garage. He stated that in a few minutes, the Night Sheriff, (INMATE WATNE MOORE), came

## Part III. Criminal Investigation Division Report

into the gate house and he smelled of intoxicants. MORRIS stated that at about this time, he heard a truck start and was asked by MOORE, "Did you hear that?" MORRIS stated that he told MOORE that he had heard the truck. Then he was pushed back into the gate house and told, "You'd better not say anything about this!" MORRIS stated that the Night Sheriff (INMATE WAYNE MOORE) was armed and had a "wild" look in his eyes and that he (MORRIS) was afraid to call for help. MORRIS stated that he knew if he called for help, he would have to shoot the Night Sheriff, MOORE, and he did not want to get into trouble over it. MORRIS stated that the Night Sheriff left, and in a few minutes, Captain FLETCHER, a warden, came to the gate house and asked him about the truck. MORRIS stated he lied to FLETCHER because he was afraid of what they might do to him. MORRIS stated that when the Wardens, FLETCHER, MAYS, and WILSON, came back through the gate with INMATE CARL CORDER and INMATE FRANK BOSNICK [Page #4 (Tucker Prison Farm)] in custody, he was asked by BOSNICK, "Is your insurance and burial paid up? You're going to need it!" Interview was terminated at this time. Witnesses: Wardens FLETCHER, MAYS, and WILSON, Superintendent BISHOP.

On 8-19-66, this investigator interviewed INMATE FRANK DALGLEISH, WM, 24, who stated that he had observed INMATE WINSTON TALLEY, INMATE FRANK BOSNICK, INMATE CARL CARDER, and others drink the whiskey that BOSNICK had picked up during the afternoon of 8-18-66. DALGLEISH stated that INMATE TALLEY was in charge of loans based on the two for one basis at Tucker and had been told that he (DALGLEISH) owed money to a lender at Cummins when he was transferred to Tucker and was to collect it. He continued that TALLEY decided to collect the debt of about $12.50 after he had been drinking for a while. DALGLEISH stated that TALLEY beat him four times with his fists and that he had not attempted to fight back. He stated that Talley announced to the other Inmates that they were not to let him (DALGLEISH) have any money at all. TALLEY then forced him to go around and ask each Inmate for a loan. INMATE DALGLEISH stated that MIKE BALLINTINE (Inmate Barber) had helped TALLEY whip him on one occasion and had struck him several times. INVESTIGATORS NOTE: INMATE DALGLEISH was severely bruised about the head and face at the time of the interview and was confined in the Prison Hospital. INMATE DALGLEISH stated that he did owe $12.50 to an Inmate, VERNON SLOAN, at Cummins Prison, but that he had no income and had been unable to make any money to pay the debt. INMATE DALGLEISH is a licensed veterinarian and stated that he had once been offered a job at the horse barn for $30.00 by INMATE WINSTON TALLEY and INMATE JIM REEVES. DALGLEISH stated that he had seen INMATES JOHN KILLEY, MIKE BALLINTINE, RAY THOMPSON, and LARRY KELLY take drinks from the whiskey furnished by INMATE FRANK BOSNICK and heard him (BOSNICK) say about 9:00

P.M., that more was on the way. Interview was terminated at this time. Witnesses: Wardens, FLETCHER, MAYS, and WILSON, and Superintendent BISHOP. Witnesses to beating: All inmates in Camp #1. Confirmed.

On 8-19-66, this investigator interviewed INMATE FRANK BOSNICK, WM, 38, who stated that he had taken a tractor and driven it to a liquor store in Tucker, Arkansas during the afternoon of 8-18-66, and he had purchased two (2) fifths of whiskey and brought them back to Tucker Prison Farm where he and INMATE CARL CORDER had taken some drinks from the bottles. BOSNICK stated that they had left the bottles in the storeroom at the inmates' mess hall, and upon returning, the bottles were empty. They, BOSNICK and CORDER, then decided to go out and get some more to drink. He stated that they got the Night Sheriff, (INMATE WAYNE MOORE) to go with them to the garage where they took a prison truck. He stated that when they got to Tucker, the liquor store was closed, so they went on to Pine Bluff and bought $34.85 worth of whiskey and beer. BOSNICK stated that they were arrested by the Wardens on the way back to the Prison Farm. He stated that he had been off the Prison Farm on repeated occasions to pick up whiskey, and no one seemed to care. He further stated that the owner of the liquor store in Tucker knew him and was fully aware that he (BOSNICK) was a prisoner in the Tucker Penitentiary. INMATE BOSNICK stated that INMATE CARL CORDER had driven the prison truck on the trip to Pine Bluff and had purchased some of the beverages himself. INMATE BOSNICK identified the liquor and beer as being his when it was displayed. (See Photo #30 attached to this report.) Interview was terminated at this time. Witnesses: Wardens, FLETCHER, MAYS, and WILSON, and Superintendent BISHOP.

On 8-19-66, this investigator interviewed INMATE CARL CARDER, WM, 46, who confirmed the information related in the paragraph above by INMATE FRANK BOSNICK. In addition, CORDER stated that he had been furnished vodka several times by the AP & L representative (H. P. HENDERSON) who serviced Tucker Prison Farm. CORDER stated that he had also taken whiskey from the cars of visitors and drank it rather than turn it in as related by the prison regulations. Interview was terminated at this time. Witnesses: Wardens, FLETCHER, MAYS, and WILSON, and Superintendent BISHOP.

On 8-19-66, at about 4:45 P.M., this investigator discontinued the interviews and proceeded to the Inmates kitchen to inspect the Inmates as they were eating. Upon inspecting the kitchen, this investigator observed that the entire area was filthy. The floors, tables, walls, and kitchen appliances appeared to have been wiped off rather hurriedly but were not sanitary. Flies were very thick and there was no screen on the door leading to the wash rack and

## Part III. Criminal Investigation Division Report

vegetable room. The food and meat were piled on the cook tables completely exposed to the flies, and nothing was done to protect it. Tin cans with the tops cut out were used as cups. The pitchers and trays were badly bent and damaged. All cooking utensils were in a state of disrepair or damaged beyond repair. Food had been prepared and was observed to be a very thin, watered down serving of rice. One large spoonful per Inmate. The bread was a tasteless cornbread. One medium slice per Inmate. Upon being questioned, the kitchen personnel stated that meat was served to the Inmates once a month, on visiting Sunday, and it was served in small portions at that time. This investigator ordered the kitchen cleaned up and the quality and quantity of food to be increased to a decent standard. Milk and eggs were drawn from Cummins Prison but were used only for cooking and for the trustys. Kitchen personnel stated that the Inmates received one egg per year on Christmas morning and were never given milk to drink. One kitchen helper suggested that the food supply records be examined, as the majority of the meat was being either sold by the kitchen rider (Trusty Supervisor) or carried out the "back door" by the Wardens.

At about 5:30 P.M., 8-19-66, this investigator inspected the Inmates on the long line (field workers) as they were brought to the kitchen to be fed. The entire group appeared to be forty to sixty pounds under their normal weight. Their clothing (whites) were filthy, torn up, and in bad states of repair. Several Inmates were wearing trousers torn up the inseam and out seam to the hips. Their shoes were in terrible disrepair and seemed to be several sizes too large for each of them. They were worn out, had no strings, and had holes along the soles and across the tops. Upon being questioned, the Inmates stated that they had no shoes and either were required to wear the rubber boots or go barefooted. In addition, the Inmates stated that they had never been issued underwear, and socks were issued only twice a year. Two pair of socks were in each issue. This investigator issued orders to forward requisitions to the proper authority at Cummins Prison to correct this situation.

At about 6:45 P.M., 8-19-66, this investigator proceeded to the Inmates Barracks and conducted an inspection. The mattresses were filthy and rotten and appeared to be badly discolored. The cotton was spilling out of the majority of the mattresses from worn and torn spots. The sheets were dirty and appeared to have been used for two or three weeks without change. Over half of the beds did not have any pillows on them, and the beds that had pillows were dirty and discolored. The showers were pouring water from leaks. The commodes were stopped up or would not flush. The urinals were stopped up and in general disrepair. The entire barracks area smelled from filth. The floors were filthy and littered. This investigator issued orders to clean up the area and forwarded requisitions to the proper authority at Cummins Prison to correct this situation.

At about 7:15 P.M., 8-19-66, this investigator ordered the following changes in Trusty personnel to afford better security of the main building and yard.

| Name | From | To |
|---|---|---|
| TALLEY, Winston | Floor Walker | Confinement |
| BOSNICK, Frank | Kitchen Rider | Confinement |
| REAVES, James | Day Yard Man | Confinement |
| CORDER, Carl | Electrician | Confinement |
| MOORE, Wayne | Night Sheriff | Long Line |
| EDINGTON, Vernon C. | Death Cell Guard | Quarters for Investigation |
| MALICOAT, Charles | Night Yard Man | Quarters for Investigation |
| WHITE, Hugh | Cummins Prison | Day Yard Man |
| ADKINS, J. D. | Cummins Prison | Night Yard Man |
| STANRIDGE, Odis | Line Rider | Kitchen Rider |
| HARVEY, Walter | Line Rifle | Line Sub-Rider |
| EVERETT, David | Line Sub-Rider | Line Rider |
| SPENCER, William | Tower Guard | Night Sheriff |
| FLETCHER, Carl | Death Cell Guard | First Cook |
| HILMAN, Robert | Shotgun | Line Rifle |
| COPELAND, Albert | Extra | Death Cell Guard |
| TYNER, Wayne | Ass't Electrician | Electrician |
| CRUISE, William | Long Line | Floor Walker (1 Camp) |
| BEDWELL, Carl | Long Line | Kitchen Helper |
| HOUSE, Billy | Construction | Shotgun |
| HORTON, Paul | Free Line Do-Pop | Free Line Trusty |

*[The Arkansas prison population was divided into three categories. "Rankers" were at the bottom, usually doing heavy manual labor; "Do Pops" were in the middle, although origin of the name is unclear; "trustys" or "trustees" were privileged inmates with authority over other prisoners. "Free line" referred to those with work assignments in the prison's free area, where they served prison officials and their families.]*

## Part III. Criminal Investigation Division Report

The following is a list of equipment changes and regulation changes made during the period of 8-19-66 and 8-31-66 for the improvement of security of Tucker Prison Farm.

1. Added light to front of main building to signal clearance to West Tower for personnel coming into the yard from the building.
2. Added tower guard to new South Tower at rear of main building.
3. Gateman required to stop and check all vehicles going and coming at Main Gate.
4. Added system of signals for clearance waves from yard to tower.
5. Added new Trusty and Rank head count at specific intervals.
6. Barred all personnel from the Death Cells except the two guards and authorized visitors.
7. Increased security in handling of gun cage and gun room keys.
8. All Rank Inmates required to wear white uniforms.
9. Yard Man to go on all guard personnel changes.
10. All guard personnel off duty at 4:00 A.M. and fed as a group before returning to the Main Building.
11. New filing system at Yard Man's desk for total account of prisoners.
12. Tighter and more frequent security checks on guard personnel.
13. Mounted both Day and Night Sheriffs for greater mobility in checks made on guard personnel, Do-Pop personnel, and livestock.
14. All weapons inspected and required repairs noted.
15. Ammunition ordered for main gun rooms.
16. All tower weapons test fired and cleaned.
17. All locks and bars inspected. Lock changes noted and ordered to be changed. Majority could be opened with a pocket knife.
18. Communications system requested for use between towers and yard man.
19. Improved communications system requested for Wardens house.
20. Additional shotgun and rifle guards added as required.
21. Lockers and unauthorized containers removed from Trusty, Do-Pop, and Rank Barracks to increase efficiency in weapons search and inspection.
22. New entrance and exit head count to increase efficiency.

The following is a list of weapons located in the Inmate's Barracks and seized for evidence during searches by this investigator and Trusty Hugh WHITE during the period of 8-19-66 and 9-6-66.

| | | |
|---|---|---|
| 1. | 1 | Knives of various types |
| 2. | 5 | Pair of fighting knuckles |
| 3. | 2 | Palm weights for fighting |
| 4. | 5 | Blackjacks and clubs |
| 5. | 3 | Straight razors |
| 6. | 1 | Hatchet |

(See Photo #28)

On 8-20-66, at about 7:30 A.M., this investigator interviewed INMATE CLIFFORD CASH, Laundry Rider (Supervisor), who stated that he was aware that many jobs were sold to Inmates for the laundry by INMATES JIM REAVES, Yard Man, and WINSTON TALLEY, Floor Walker. INMATE CASH stated that the jobs sold for as "much as the traffic will bear", at times as low as thirty dollars and other times for as high as one thousand dollars. He continued that almost anything could be had at Tucker Farm if you could get the money. He stated that much of the whiskey was bought by Warden WILSON and brought in to the Inmates for a price. CASH stated that he had seen Inmates buy a bottle of whiskey through Warden WILSON by buying him a bottle at the same time. CASH stated that "pills" could be had for a price and that he believed that "pills" were brought over from Cummins Prison Hospital. INMATE CASH was co-operating with this investigator until Assistant Superintendent BRUTON came into the office, and CASH seemed to "freeze up". He would not discuss anything pertaining to the operation of the Prison Farm and seemed to either avoid answers or speak in riddles. This investigator excused INMATE CASH from the interview, and when we were both outside, he said to me, "What are you trying to do? Get me killed?" Interview was terminated at this time.

On 8-20-66, at about 9:15 A.M., Mr. Jim BRUTON, Assistant Superintendent, arrived at the Administrative Office of Tucker Prison Farm and very apparently was both angry and upset that this investigator was conducting an investigation without his prior knowledge. Upon observing the mental frame of mind of Mr. BRUTON, this investigator explained that the investigation had to do only with the traffic of intoxicants by inmates and was not intended to bring discredit upon Mr. BRUTON. After considering this for several minutes, Mr. BRUTON asked this investigator if he would like to have the job of Assistant Superintendent. When this investigator answered in the affirmative, Mr. BRUTON stated that he thought that he could arrange it and would like to see this investigator get the job. Mr. BRUTON continued that the job paid $8,000.00 per year, a new car each year, a fourteen room house, a complete expense account, and all food furnished. He assured this investigator that the smallest part of the job would be the $8,000.00 salary. He stated that a lot of gifts would be offered from business people in the farm supply trade, people in the clothing business, and other "interested persons". Mr. BRUTON stated that it was only "smart" to accept the gifts and for this investigator to be sure to do so. He stated that he did not have to worry about the "rules" and would do anything he wanted to do without fear. He stated that if this investigator accepted the position to "run the God Damned place" and let the prisoners and Wardens know who was boss, that if a prisoner got out of line to "hit him with anything you can get your hands on" because that's the only thing that they respect. Mr. BRUTON advised this investigator to be smart enough to "keep your mouth shut" and not let anyone know your business. He stated that if anything came up that was not understood, to sit back and act like "you knew all about it". He stated, "Make everybody think you're the smartest son-of-a-bitch in the world, and you'll get by". Mr. BRUTON then terminated the interview, stating that he needed to run down to the house and take a bath, and for this investigator to come along and look over the house.

During the trip to the house, Mr. BRUTON stated that if this investigator took the job to watch out for the Wardens. He stated that WILSON "is a drunken whore chaser" and had to be under constant observation, or he would spoil the entire works. He continued that FLETCHER "is a good man but was a thief and too open with it". He concluded that MAYS is a short hair (new on the prison farm) and did not know a "damn" thing. Mr. BRUTON stated to "let them know right away who was the boss, and don't get friendly with them".

After arriving at the house, Mr. BRUTON insisted that this investigator "look over the place". He pointed out a rug on the large living room floor and stated that it had cost $1,250.00 and had just recently been installed. He stated that the "board" would buy anything for the house that he wanted and that very little furniture had to be furnished by the Assistant Superintendent. Also, he indicated the dishes and stated that "they even furnish the dishes in the place". Mr. BRUTON asked this investigator if he knew anything about horses and stated that his hobby was horses, and he had made a "pile of money" fooling with them while at the prison farm. He explained that he would buy them, the prisoners would break them, and he managed to "sell them at a good profit". He again told this investigator to take anything anyone offered him and not to be foolish. Mr. BRUTON then left this investigator to look over the house while he took a bath and changed his clothing. Upon completing his bath, Mr. BRUTON again advised this investigator that he would see that the "job" would be offered and to be sure to take it. Mr. BRUTON explained that he was leaving the farm to get him retirement under the "Henslee Act" as it was a much better deal than the new legislation. Mr. BRUTON insisted that this investigator move into the house and act like it "belongs to you". He concluded by stating that if the food or anything wasn't to the liking of this investigator, to send the boy (house boy) out to get it at the store and to sign his name. Mr. BRUTON then left the Prison Farm, stating that he was going to the home of his in-laws in Morrilton, Arkansas.

The remainder of this date was utilized in inspection of living and working conditions of the Inmates in the fields and quarters. Several recommendations were made and complied with on a local level.

On 8-21-66, at about 8:30 A.M., this investigator received information from Inmate Informer FL-17 that the "Tucker Telephone" had been hidden in the residence of former Assistant Superintendent BRUTON. This investigator had been told of "long distance calls" and the "Tucker Telephone" by several Inmates since arrival at Tucker Prison Farm but was not familiar with the workings of this instrument. FL-17 stated that this instrument was designed by Dr. ROLLINS (Former Prison Doctor) and consisted of an electric generator taken from a ring type telephone, placed in sequence with two dry cell batteries, and attached to an undressed Inmate strapped to the treatment table at the Tucker Hospital, by means of one electrode to a big toe and the second electrode to the penis, at which time, a crank was turned sending an electric charge into the body of the Inmate. FL-17 stated that several charges were introduced into the Inmates of a duration designed to stop just short of the Inmate "passing out". Informer FL-17 stated that Mr. BRUTON utilized this device to both punish the inmates and to extract information from them. FL-17 stated that an Inmate Doctor (DOC MORGAN) had used this device extensively at the order of Mr. BRUTON and the other Wardens. Mr. FLETCHER was mentioned as having ordered and observed a great number of these torture periods. FL-17 stated that while he had never been subjected to the "Tucker Telephone," he could and did furnish a list of Inmates who had been "rung up" at the order of Mr. BRUTON. Upon being questioned, FL-17 stated that he had observed several Inmates receive whiskey from Mr. WILSON by buying him a bottle in payment. FL-17 also suggested that this investigator might look into the "hay deals" conducted at the farm of a Mr. VENABLE in Coy, Arkansas. FL-17 stated that he had been told by other Inmates that the hay was out on a half portion deal by the Inmates of Tucker Prison Farm, but that the Tucker Prison share had been transferred to the barns of Mr. BRUTON'S son, RONNIE BRUTON, whose property was near Tucker Prison. In addition, that RONNIE BRUTON had come into the Black Angus cattle business rather suddenly when Tucker Prison Farm changed their cattle from Black Angus to the Charlois breed. FL-17 stated that many new born Angus calves were never put on the Prison count, and the mortality rate on the livestock was adjusted to a greater loss of cattle than were actually lost by death and disease. FL-17 stated that the Pine Bluff stockyards might be checked regarding the sale of a number of goats that were the property of Tucker Prison Farm in the name of Jesse WILSON of England. Further, he stated that he had observed Mr. BALL, of the Board, go to Cold Storage and take large amounts of meats from there through the front gate and that this could be confirmed with other prisoners who had also observed the transaction. FL-17 stated that while he was afraid, he would testify to everything that he had said in the event this case comes to trial. This interview was terminated with the understanding that his investigator could return for further information.

On 8-21-66, at about 10:15 A.M., this investigator interviewed Inmate Informer FL-14, who, while reluctant and apparently in great fear, furnished the following information. FL-14 confirmed the information regarding the

"Tucker Telephone" and furnished additional names of Inmates who had been "rung up" on the telephone. FL-14 furnished this investigator with the name of an inmate who was "rung up" by Mr. BRUTON so severely that the Inmate Doctor (DOC MORGAN) had to drag Mr. BRUTON away from the crank of the generator. INVESTIGATORS NOTE: This information confirmed several times during the course of this investigation. FL-14 stated that he and several other Inmates had personal knowledge of the "hay deal" between Mr. VENABLE and Mr. RONNIE BRUTON, and Mr. JIM BRUTON, Assistant Superintendent. FL-14 stated that he had observed Wardens WILSON and FLETCHER take large quantities of food issued to the Inmates kitchen from the kitchen and carry off this food to their homes for their own consumption. He further stated that large quantities of food were furnished to Mr. WILSON'S son in England and Mr. FLETCHER'S sons who are employed by the Arkansas State Police. In addition, FL-14 furnished names of Inmates who had participated in the hauling of livestock in the form of goats, to the auction sale in Pine Bluff. These goats were the property of Tucker Prison Farm and were sold by Mr. BRUTON and Mr. WILSON in the name of Jesse WILSON, England, Arkansas. FL-14 furnished this investigator with the name of Inmate John TOLLIVER and stated that his mother had paid Jim REAVES and Mr. BRUTON $1,000.00 for his job in the laundry. FL-14 further stated that he had heard that Mr. Jimmy ROMAN had paid $600.00 for a $50.00 horse from Mr. BRUTON in order to secure a better job for his step-son, Inmate Eddie STEVENS. INVESTIGATORS NOTE: The information of both related job sales were checked and confirmed with other Inmates and principals of the transactions. FL-14 stated that the information related was true, and that he would testify in a court of law if necessary. This interview was terminated at this time.

On 8-21-66, during the afternoon visiting hours in the death cells, Inmate Jim REAVES called this investigator to the bars and asked if he was to be punished for activities that were authorized by Mr. BRUTON. He continued that he was acting as Mr. BRUTON'S representative in job selling and loaning money to the other Inmates. He stated that in order to conduct this business, it had been necessary to carry a large amount of "green". (Prison term for paper money. REAVES had $507.00 in paper money at the time of his arrest which was confiscated by Superintendent BISHOP.) REAVES stated that this was with the "full knowledge" of the "man" (Mr. BRUTON). This investigator declined to discuss this matter at this time and advised REAVES that an interview would be set up at a later date, when other information had been confirmed. REAVES, at this time, advised this investigator that he might be in possession of some very interesting tape recordings of whippings and conversations of Mr. BRUTON during money transactions. INVESTIGATORS NOTE: This information was confirmed when a tape recorder and several tapes were located and confiscated by this investigator and Inmate Hugh White, Day Yard Man. One of the tapes was not completely erased and was of a whipping that this investigator and Major W. C. STRUEBING, C.I.D., had witnessed of two prisoners who were returned to Tucker from "escape" status. Mr. BRUTON conducted this whipping on the [bare] buttocks of both prisoners, in the presence of the mentioned arresting officers. This interview was terminated at this time.

On 8-21-66, during the evening hours, this investigator conducted an extensive search of the Assistant Superintendent's house, including all closets and storage areas. In the upstairs, south bathroom, this investigator found the "Tucker Telephone" in a hat box on the top shelf of a linen closet. This instrument was photographed in its resting place and also in a more detailed manner on the bathroom floor. (See attached photos #32, #33, #34, #35, and #36). This search was conducted on the basis of state property and the "invited guest" rule of search and seizure. Following the photographing of the instrument, it was returned to its original hiding place. During this search, a great number of clothing belonging to Mr. RONNIE BRUTON was located and matched with laundry slips to the Inmate laundry, indicating that said RONNIE BRUTON sent his and his family's laundry to the Prison laundry. INVESTIGATORS NOTE: This information was confirmed by Prison laundry personnel, who stated that RONNIE BRUTON had sent so much laundry, that he had been assigned marker number 6. (See attached photos #37 and #38). The search was discontinued at this time.

On 8-22-66, at about 8:00 A.M., this investigator interviewed Inmate informer FL-1, who stated that he had observed Mr. BRUTON commit many brutal beatings upon inmates in the past two years. FL-1 stated that no hearings were ever conducted prior to whippings in accord with the Prison regulations. FL-1 stated that Mr. BRUTON would hit inmates for anything he suspected they might have done and with anything he could get his hands on, mostly his cane, since after the accident, it was always handy. FL-1 stated that RONNIE BRUTON was constantly having his personal trucks overhauled and repaired at the Prison Garage and with State purchased parts. He continued that in 1965, RONNIE BRUTON had his combine completely overhauled and painted at the garage with Prison labor and parts. FL-1 stated that he had known of some of the job selling deals of JIM REAVES and Mr. BRUTON, and he mentioned that John TOLLIVER and Jimmy ROMAN case in particular. He stated that anyone could get anything on Tucker Farm if he had the right amount of money. FL-1 stated that since his arrival at Tucker Prison Farm, he and his parents had paid Lawyer Q. BYRUM HURST of Hot Springs over $10,000.00 to arrange for an early release from the penitentiary either by a deal with the "board" or with a higher official of the State government. FL-1 stated that he could and would prove these allegations by cancelled checks, sold and mortgaged property, his parents' testimony, and witnesses. INVESTIGATORS NOTE: This matter was referred to the Internal Revenue Service. Several other inmates names were mentioned in this same type of

## Part III. Criminal Investigation Division Report

violation with Lawyer HURST. FL-1 stated that the Prison Garage had built a horse trailer, using State materials, for Mr. BRUTON, which he had in turn sold for $750.00. Also, they had built a horse trailer for Mr. FLETCHER, using state materials, which was parked in front of the Prison Garage at that time. INVESTIGATORS NOTE: This information was confirmed by personal inspection of a blue, two-horse trailer parked in front of the garage on this date. This information was also confirmed by conversation with Mr. Mike FLETCHER, presently employed as a Radio Operator with the Arkansas State Police. Mike FLETCHER stated that he and his father had purchased part of the materials, and the trailer had been built by convict labor. FL-1 further stated that Mr. HOWARD, Prison bookkeeper, had a house trailer built by convict labor. The house trailer was later sold for an unknown amount. FL-1 continued that Mr. HOWARD also had built a cabin in the mountains near Russellville, Arkansas, using prison labor and a great amount of Prison materials, particularly plumbing materials. INVESTIGATORS NOTE: Information regarding the cabin was later confirmed by Mr. and Mrs. HOWARD who both admitted utilizing Prison labor on weekends while building the cabin. FL-1 further confirmed that whiskey could be purchased through Mr. WILSON by buying him a bottle to deliver a bottle. This interview was terminated at this time.

On 8-22-66, in the morning hours, this investigator inspected the horse barns at Tucker Prison Farm and obtained the following information from Inmate Informer FL-21, who stated that Mr. FLETCHER presently owned two horses that were being kept at Tucker Prison Farm and fed State hay and grain. FL-21 pointed out the two horses. INVESTIGATORS NOTE: This information was later confirmed by Mike FLETCHER while out horseback riding with this investigator. FL-21 stated that these horses were not utilized for any detail work on the farm and were for the owner's pleasure only. FL-21 stated that any of the Wardens who wanted to could bring horses to the Prison Farm for boarding and training, utilizing State feed and Prison labor. FL-21 stated that Mr. BRUTON constantly bought untrained horses and brought them to the Prison horse barn to be broken to ride and work cattle. FL-21 indicated a new, red barn which was utilized to house Mr. BRUTON'S personal stallion. INVESTIGATORS NOTE: No other horses were observed in this barn during the entire stay of this investigator on Tucker Prison Farm. FL-21 pointed out a horse, stating that it had been purchased by Mr. MAYS from Mr. BRUTON and was presently in the process of being trained as a riding horse. INVESTIGATORS NOTE: This information was confirmed by Mr. MAYS during a conversation later in the day. Also, this particular horse was sold back to Mr. BRUTON by Mr. MAYS prior to the inventory count of the livestock by the State Audit Department and carried on the count. In addition, following the resale of this horse to Mr. BRUTON, the horse jumped into a stream with Inmate Vernon EDINTON riding and severely injured his chin and neck. FL-21 stated that Mr. BRUTON also kept several cows at the

Prison to be fattened for sale, utilizing Prison feed. FL-21 confirmed that Prison labor had been utilized to cut hay at the farm of Mr. VENABLE near Coy on a half and half deal, but he refused to implicate Mr. BRUTON, stating that he was afraid of what might happen. FL-21 furnished the names of several inmates who had participated in the "hay deal". FL-21 admitted that many "free world" horses were trained and fed at the Tucker Prison Farm horse barn, utilizing prison labor and feed, and that he had participated in this matter for money received. Further, he stated that horses were shod for "free world people" by inmate labor and with State equipment and horseshoes. At the time of this inspection, this investigator observed one mare which was identified by FL-21 as belonging to a "free world owner" that was in process of being trained and was shown several times by the Horse Barn Rider at "Free World" horse shows. This information was confirmed when the "owner" requested permission to take the "Horse Barn Rider" (Trusty-in-charge) to a horse show to exhibit his mare. The request was denied by this investigator. This interview was terminated at this time.

The balance of this date, 8-22-66, was utilized in the inspection of facilities, working conditions, and security matters at Tucker Prison Farm. During the course of this date, this investigator was informed that trucks were to be brought to Tucker Prison Farm the next day to move Mr. BRUTON'S personal effects to his home. All recommendations were at a local level.

During the early evening hours of 8-22-66, this investigator was contacted by Mr. B. C. HOWARD, bookkeeper, and requested to take a ride off Tucker to talk about some "matters of importance". This investigator picked up Mr. HOWARD at his residence and drove out the front gate of Tucker Prison Farm, across the highway, and west toward the new dam site. During this ride, Mr. HOWARD stated that he had been sent to Tucker Prison Farm by Governor Faubus to "keep an eye on things" and keep extensive notes on the operation of the Prison. Mr. HOWARD stated that he had done just this and had the notes locked up in his safe. He continued that he was "clean" and his books could be copied and examined by anyone of proper authority. He stated that there had been a lot of "graft by those in authority", and that he would help me get on the right track. Mr. HOWARD mentioned the "hay deal" with Mr. VENABLE and stated that, in his opinion, several cattle deals should be investigated. He concurred in the belief that RONNIE BRUTON is in possession of a great number of Tucker cattle. Also, he mentioned that some attention should be given to the horses and some horse trades made in the past. Mr. HOWARD mentioned that some of the Board members were as guilty in some things as anyone else. He also mentioned that some electric fans and air conditioners had been stolen from the State Hospital and were presently on Tucker Prison Farm. Mr. HOWARD stated that Mr. BRUTON and Mr. WILSON had almost been caught in the theft of these items by someone in authority at the State Hospital.

Mr. HOWARD indicated that the items were stolen during the time that inmates were helping on some construction at the Hospital. Mr. HOWARD stated that Mr. WILSON might still have some of the air conditioners in his possession at his home in England, Arkansas. Mr. HOWARD further indicated that Mr. BRUTON, Mr. WILSON, and Mr. FLETCHER, had been guilty of furnishing meat and food products to relatives and friends. These products had been drawn from Cold Storage and the Commissary. Mr. HOWARD stated that Tucker Prison Farm had been instrumental in making at least three wealthy men in the past, and unless something was done, it would make some others wealthy. Mr. HOWARD indicated that a lot of the Prison Farm equipment was "out on loan" to persons outside the Prison system by authority of the Wardens and Mr. BRUTON. Mr. HOWARD stated that the reason that the crops on Tucker were so poor was that the Wardens spent all their time on the front porch of the Administrative Building rather than in the fields with the inmates. Mr. HOWARD appeared to be very upset during this conversation, and specific information was hard to extract. In addition, Mr. HOWARD insisted that everything he said to me be held in strict confidence and not related in this report. He stated that if anything were related in my report, he would not verify it. Under more favorable circumstances, this investigator feels that a great deal of information could be obtained from Mr. HOWARD. The interview was terminated upon return to Tucker Prison Farm and Mr. HOWARD'S residence.

On 8-24-66, this investigator proceeded to Little Rock headquarters for a C.I.D. Troop Meeting. During this meeting, information obtained to this point was related to Major W. C. STRUEBING and Director Herman E. LINDSEY, and a request for additional personnel was made. Investigator James BEACH was assigned to this case to assist this investigator. Both investigators arrived at Tucker Prison Farm at about 4:00 P.M. Upon arrival, investigators were informed that Mr. BRUTON had sent trucks and moved his property from the Assistant Superintendent's house. Investigators proceeded to that location and conducted another search of the property. The "Tucker Telephone" was found in a box on the floor in an upstairs bedroom, apparently forgotten during the loading of Mr. BRUTON'S property. Inspection of this investigator's belongings were made; apparently all bags and brief cases had been searched. This information was confirmed by both house boys, who stated that RONNIE BURTON had gone through all luggage of this investigator after having been told that the luggage was not the property of Mr. BRUTON. Nothing of value was determined to be missing, and all evidence had been removed to a place of safekeeping at C.I.D. Headquarters, Little Rock. The "Tucker Telephone" was examined by both investigators and marked in evidence. Balance of this date was utilized in briefing of investigator BEACH.

On 8-24-66, this investigator, accompanied by investigator James BEACH, received in evidence a letter addressed to Inmate Clifford CASH, Laundry Rider, (Trusty supervisor), indicating a payoff to be made in the case of Dallas Ray MAYS for an assignment to the Laundry detail. The letter is dated "August 21, 1966" and is signed "Gladys". The return address is that of Mrs. Gladys MAYS, Route #4, Pocahontas, Arkansas. The entire body of the letter is punctuated with dollar signs ($). This letter was marked in evidence and made an addition to this report.

On 8-25-66, this investigator, accompanied by investigator James BEACH, interviewed Inmate Informer FL-22, who stated that he had observed Inmate Frank BOSNICK repeatedly bring whiskey into Tucker Prison Farm for the past several months. FL-22 stated that Inmate BOSNICK would use a Prison tractor to get back and forth to the liquor store in Tucker, Arkansas, while he was out checking the skunk traps. He stated that the money to purchase the whiskey was furnished by Inmate Winston TALLEY. In addition, FL-22 stated that Inmate TALLEY furnished the money for all money loans to Inmates at Tucker Prison. He continued that Inmate Jim REAVES got a cut of all money loaning deals, and Inmate TALLEY did the loaning and the collecting in Camp #1, while Inmate "Buddy" NICHOLS did the loaning and collecting in Camp #2. FL-22 stated that it was common knowledge that Mr. BRUTON got a good portion of the money, and that he had seen him sit down at the desk located in the hallway and call Inmates out that owed money to TALLEY, and collect the money himself. INVESTIGATORS NOTE: The information repeatedly confirmed from other inmates. FL-22 stated that Jim REAVES often bought clothings from Mr. BRUTON, such as $100.00 pairs of alligator shoes, $25.00 shirts, and other used clothing. He stated that the clothing and shoes were all used and not worth very much money, but this was the way that Inmate Jim REAVES paid off his obligations to Mr. BRUTON. FL-22 stated that he had heard a rumor that Inmate John TOLLIVER had paid a thousand dollars ($1,000.00) to Mr. BRUTON through Inmate Jim REAVES for a job in the Prison Laundry. FL-22 stated that Inmate Jim REAVES was Mr. BRUTON'S front man, and before Inmate REAVES, it had been the Inmate Doctor "Doc" MORGAN. FL-22 stated that he had been in the truck with Inmate REAVES and Mr. WILSON one morning in April when Inmate REAVES bought Mr. WILSON a bottle of whiskey at the liquor store in Tucker, Arkansas. FL-22 stated that they were on a trip to England, Arkansas, to buy some "free world" clothing. FL-22 stated that he had also been present when Inmates Bill "Doc" MORGAN, Inmate DAVIS, and Inmate Bobby WILKERSON, had bought whiskey for Mr. WILSON. He also stated that Inmate Jim REAVES did not drink whiskey, but would take "pills" and had them furnished at one time by Jerry BLANKENSHIP, an Inmate Doctor. FL-22 stated that Inmate REAVES now gets delivery of "pills" from a Bobby FERGUSON, used car salesman in North Little Rock, and offered to "set up" FERGUSON for an arrest. He

## Part III. Criminal Investigation Division Report

continued that Inmate Carl CORDER always brought in whiskey when he went to town for electric supplies. FL-22 stated that Inmate CORDER had brought in a bottle of "VODKA" while on a trip about two weeks before, and he had hidden the bottle in the ceiling over the barber shop in the new building. INVESTIGATORS NOTE: This empty bottle found in the ceiling over the new barber shop and marked in evidence. See photo #30. FL-22 stated that he was on his bed on 8-18-66 with Larry MCFEE, Inmate, and Carl BIGGS, Inmate, at about 8:00 P.M., when Inmate Carl CORDER came in looking for Inmate BIGGS. FL-22 stated that he could smell whiskey on the breath of Inmate CORDER and that he appeared to be intoxicated. He stated that Inmate Winston TALLEY gave inmate CORDER $55.00 to purchase additional whiskey, and Inmate CORDER left. He continued that Inmate MALICOAT came into the building and said that Inmate CORDER and BOSNICK were drunk and had stolen a truck to go after more whiskey. FL-22 stated that Inmate REAVES told Inmate MALICOAT to call the Wardens and tell them about it, which he did. FL-22 stated that he heard later that Inmates CORDER and BOSNICK had been arrested when they came back to the Prison Farm. FL-22 stated that he had been on the work crew that had been sent to Mr. VENABLES to cut and bale hay, and that they had stacked half the hay in a barn to be used by Mr. VENABLE and the other half in a barn to be used by Tucker Prison Farm. He stated that he had later been on a work crew that went back to Mr. VENABLES and loaded hay on a truck and hauled it to the barn of RONNIE BURTON. FL-22 stated that they had gone on back roads to haul this hay from VENABLES barn to RONNIE BURTONS barn. FL-22 stated that he has helped work on RONNIE BURTON'S personal trucks at the Prison garage five or six times in the past year. FL-22 also stated that he had watched Inmate labor overhaul and paint a combine that was the property of RONNIE BURTON. FL-22 stated that Mr. WILSON and Mr. HOWARD had both taken Inmate labor to their homes in the "free world" and had them work on their homes. Also, that Inmate labor was taken to the farm of Pat HENDERSON, a U.S. Marshal, near England to cut hay. FL-22 stated that none of this hay has ever been been brought to Tucker Farm. FL-22 stated that he had heard several tapes from a tape recorder that were in the possession of Inmates Jim REAVES and Winston TALLEY. FL-22 stated that one tape was of a money transaction concerning John TOLLIVER, Inmate, between Inmate REAVES and Mr. BRUTON, and the other tapes were of beatings administered by Mr. BRUTON. FL-22 stated that Inmate REAVES had keys to Mr. BRUTON'S office and had already "bugged" it for recordings. INVESTIGATORS NOTE: This information was confirmed after location of the ceiling tile that had been altered to accommodate a mike over the desk of Mr. BRUTON in the new section. Also, the keys were located to the office and to the barred doors. See Photos #1, #2, #3, and #29. FL-22 stated that the important tapes had been sent out of the Prison. The interview was terminated at this time.

On 8-25-66, at about 3:00 P.M., this investigator, accompanied by investigator BEACH, was called to come to the office of Mr. BRUTON at the Administration Building. Upon arrival there, investigators found Mr. BRUTON in a highly agitated state of mind, due to his vehicle being stopped and checked each time he went in and out of the gate. He stated that the "God Damned" prisoners knew who he was, and there was no reason for him to be checked. He then threatened to call "Herman LINDSEY" or Mr. BISHOP and find out about this. This investigator explained that the gate inspections were all a part of the new security system and not designed to embarrass him personally. Following this explanation, he seemed to get much more calm and began telling the investigators how he ran the penitentiary here at Tucker. He stated that he had always let the Wardens and convicts both know who the boss was. Further, he stated he had hit the convicts with anything he could get his hands on, because that was the only thing they respected. Mr. BRUTON stated that gambling, selling jobs, drinking, and so forth was as "old as the penitentiary", and while it might be slowed down, it will continue regardless of what is done to stop it. He stated that a person must learn to turn his back on some things, such as wives, and girl friends visiting Inmates and going off places together. Mr. BRUTON stated that while this is a violation of regulation, it seemed to keep the Inmates in a better frame of mind. Mr. BRUTON then went into his receiving of gifts from unknown persons. He stated that a new suit of clothes might come from the "Chamber of Commerce" or a new hat from a "Deer Club". This conversation lasted for about 45 minutes, and this investigator noticed that Mr. BRUTON seemed to stare almost constantly at investigator BEACH, possibly because he had called for this investigator, and both of us had arrived. The interview was terminated at this time.

On 8-26-66, this investigator interviewed Inmate Informer FL-7, who stated that he had personal knowledge of the "hay deal" and could show investigators where the "hay" is presently stored on the property of RONNIE BRUTON. He further stated that he had been present or in the area when the $1,000.00 payoff had been made to Mr. BRUTON, and he could substantiate the testimony of the other witnesses. FL-7 confirmed that RONNIE BRUTON had his personal vehicles worked on in the Prison garage by convict labor and with State parts. Also, he confirmed that RONNIE BRUTON had his combine overhauled and painted in the Prison garage by convict labor. FL-7 stated that he had observed Mr. WILSON bring liquor to Inmates from outside the Prison. He stated that he had seen Mr. WILSON and Mr. FLETCHER haul food away from the kitchen and carry it to their homes. He continued that he had "heard" that Mr. FLETCHER was getting a payoff from his Rice Squad Ride (Inmate Slick ANSCHULTZ) out of what the Rider was extorting from the Inmates on the rice squad. FL-7 stated that he knew of five (5) cases of tile that had been stolen from the Carpenter Shop by Mr. WILSON and had heard WILSON say that it was going to [be] used in his bathroom in a house in England Arkansas. INVESTIGATORS NOTE: This

## Part III. Criminal Investigation Division Report

information was confirmed when the five (5) cases of tile were found in the residence of WILSON immediately after he moved his personal property off the Prison Farm. FL-7 stated that he had observed Mr. HOWARD take plumbing supplies and Prison materials off the Prison Farm to use in his cabin near Russellville, Arkansas, and he had seen him take convict labor out to work on this same cabin. FL-7 stated that he knew of many "deals" that had been made by Mr. BRUTON through Inmate Jim REAVES for payoff on job assignments. FL-7 further showed this investigator a bed over the office of Mr. BRUTON that he stated had been rented out for $50.00 each time it was used for sexual purposes by the Inmates. He stated that Mr. BRUTON had received over $200.00 for the use of this bed from Inmate "Maverick" EDINGTON. (See photos #41, #42, #43, and #49. Sheets and covers seized in evidence for analysis by laboratory for semen and other stains.) FL-7 stated that almost anything could be "bought" on Tucker Farm for the right amount of money. FL-7 stated that he was aware, but he could not prove how the cattle and hogs were taken off Tucker Farm to be sold and to "stock" the farm of RONNIE BRUTON. FL-7 further had "heard" of some of the "horse" deals made by Mr. BRUTON, but he was unable to produce positive proof. FL-7 stated that he had seen Mr. BRUTON beat the Inmates with anything he had in his hands on many occasions, and this was done with little or no provocation. He stated that the Inmates could tell the investigators many things if they were not afraid of the abuse when the investigators left the Prison Farm. The information received during this interview was substantiated by Inmate Informers FL-1, FL-2, FL-3, FL-9, FL-10, FL-16, FL-18, and FL-19 in interviews conducted later on this same date.

During the evening hours of 8-26-66, this investigator, accompanied by Investigator BEACH, requested and received additional personnel to assist in this case. Investigator SKIPPER and Trooper Photographer Paul SCHALCHLIN responded. Investigator SKIPPER and Investigator BEACH spent the entire night in the Main Prison Building interviewing inmates and taking statements. Trooper Photographer SCHALCHLIN took photographs of the physical evidence and scars on the bodies of the Inmates which were pertinent to the statements made. (See photos #4, #5, #6, #7, #8, #9, #10, #11, #12, #13, #14, #15, #16, #17, #18, #19, #20, #21, #22, #23, #24, #25, and #26). This investigator, accompanied by Inmates Hugh WHITE, and J. D. ADKINS, conducted an extensive search of the Main Prison Building. This search produced instruments of torture (See photo #27), whiskey bottles (See photo #29), keys to open all cell doors (See photo #29), gambling equipment in the form of playing cards and "crooked dice" (See photo #29), illegal drugs and narcotics (See photo #30), recording equipment, outlets, and places of concealment (See photo #1, #2, #3, and #28). All evidence was photographed and seized.

The following paragraphs are synopsis of statements taken from Inmates of Tucker Prison Farm by State Police Investigators on the night of 8-26-66.

LL-1 states that in June of 1963, a long line rider and he got into a fight, and he was hit on the foot with a hoe. He stated that Mr. FLETCHER brought him to the hospital where he stayed for three days. He stated that Mr. BRUTON came to the hospital where he was and asked him what happened, and when he told him, Mr. BRUTON had Bill MORGAN, Inmate Doctor, wire him up on the telephone, one wire to his penis and one to his big toe. He states that MORGAN cranked the telephone five or six times. He stated that he was put on a table in the Prison Hospital and belted down with one strap across his chest and one across his legs.

LL-2 states that he came to Tucker in March of 1965 and was assigned to the long line. He stated that the long line was cleaning ditches and two of the long line riders were beating the Inmates with rubber hoses and blackjacks. He continues that one day at lunchtime, the two riders called Walter PERRY to the end of the line and made him stand there while they shot at his feet and near his head. The riders were named as Butch HARPER and Douglas BURKE. He stated that during strawberry season last year, he was beaten four or five times by riders and his ear began to bleed one night in the building. He stated that his hearing had been affected from these beatings. He stated that he witnessed the shooting of LL-31, who was shot in the arm by a rider (Dale JOHNSON). He continued that he saw the condition of LL-46 after he had been beaten by the yardman (Richard DAVIS). He stated that the yardman or floorwalker charged from $1.00 to $5.00 to give the Inmates a good bed. He stated that the food in the mess hall was very bad, consisting mostly of greens that had bugs in them, but if an Inmate would pay the Kitchen rider, he could have better food. He concluded, stating that on visiting Sunday, when some of the family would bring food or clothing to Inmates, the Trustys would take it for themselves as soon as the family left. LL-2 stated that he would testify in court to any of the happenings.

LL-8 stated that the rice squad rider ("Slick" ANGELO) beat him because he would not give him $6.00. He stated that the yardman took green money from him to exchange it for brozene, but he never did get the brozene. He stated that he only had sixty-five days left to do and is afraid that the rice squad rider would cause him some trouble. He concluded that he had witnesses to his beating, but he did not name them.

LL-11 stated that he came in 1964 to Tucker, and that Mr. FLETCHER was the long line Captain. He stated that Bennie EAVES, Elbert KEATHLY, and himself were beaten by the long line riders, Jack

SPURLOCK and David SIMMONS with a knotted rope. He stated that he was unable to see, due to the swelling in his face following the beating.

    LL-13 stated that he is in poor health and was assigned to work in the garden squad, but was put in the field hauling hay, picking strawberries, [etc], which he could not do. He stated that David EVERETT, long line rider, tried to get some money from him, and when he refused, had him whipped. He stated that he was examined by a Doctor and told to lift nothing heavier than three pounds and to do as little walking as possible. He stated that a few days after this, he was made to haul hay and feed upstairs at the [?]. He stated that he had an operation three weeks ago, and was subsequently put in the garden squad, and the rider (J. D. COCHRAN) was told that he was to do nothing but peel potatoes, shell peas, ect. for 30 days. He states that he is now picking beans, tomatoes, and carrying dirt for sixty-five yards with a shovel. He stated that on 8-26-66, he had to walk four miles to the potato field. He concluded, stating that he is to go to Little Rock for an operation for a "slipped disc" two weeks from 8-26-66.

    LL-16 stated that he came to Tucker on July 16, 1966, and shortly following that time, Mr. BRUTON wrote him a note, advising him to write to his mother. He stated that then he wrote her the following: "Dear Mom, I am at Tucker. Please help me." and signed it. He stated that the following night, Mr. BRUTON and Mr. FLETCHER came into the building and asked him to read the letter, which he did. He stated that Mr. BRUTON ordered Mr. FLETCHER to five him five licks with the strap, which he did, and because he did not say "Oh!", "Captain" with each lick, he was given six more lashes. After the whipping, Mr. BRUTON told him that if he did not write a two page letter to his mother, he would "whip his head".

    LL-19. Witness to above circumstances.

    LL-20. Witness to above circumstances.

    LL-21. Witness to above circumstances.

    LL-22 stated that when he arrived at Tucker, he was placed in the long line, and the rider (David EVERETT) asked him for $2.00 a week or he would have him whipped. He stated that he told EVERETT that he did not have the money, and EVERETT took a $69.00 Lord Elgin watch from him in place of the money. He stated that for a few weeks he had it pretty easy. He stated that a little later, the long line was picking pickles [cucumbers] and were told not to eat any, but EVERETT told him that it was all right to eat them. He stated that when he got one to eat, the rider (EVERETT) told the line Captain, and he was given five lashes with the strap and returned to the line. He stated that upon his return, EVERETT asked him if it had hurt and he said "No". He stated that he was then taken back and given seven more lashes on the bare buttocks. LL-22 stated that he is sixteen years old, and that EVERETT tried to talk him into being his "punk" which he refused.

LL-26 stated that since he has been at Tucker Farm, he has been beaten by the following riders: "Butch" HARPER, Robert BARNES, Nelson HENDERSON, and Douglas BURKE. He stated that on August 5, 1965, the floorwalker (Jimmy GOSSETT) tried to force him to give him the money that he received from his family. He stated that he refused, and was taken into the shower, beaten, and "stomped" on the head with a pair of cowboy boots. He stated that, as a result of this beating, his head required twelve stitches, and he was unable to eat because he could not open his mouth.

LL-28 stated that he was brought in from the fields (cotton) and was given fourteen lashes for being behind. He stated that while picking pickles, he left some on the vine and was brought into the building and given ten lashes by Mr. MAYS, made to stand on the "teeter board" for two hours, then given ten more lashes on the same charge. He stated that Inmate Dick WILLIAMS beat him in the barracks one night because he got off his bed.

LL-30. Witness to preceding circumstances.

LL-31 stated that in 1965 while picking pickles, he was shot in the left arm by Dale JOHNSON, long line rider. He stated that he was brought to the Prison hospital, where the Inmate Doctor treated him without giving him a shot causing him to pass out. He stated that he was in the hospital for two days, then went back to work. He also stated that Mr. BRUTON had told him that JOHNSON should have killed him, and if he ever shot a gun again, he had better have a dead convict to show for shooting a state shell. He continued that he had been given forty-seven lashes for an offense that called for no more than ten lashes. He further stated that in the winter of 59/60, the Inmates were forced to stand in twelve degree water to change the flow of water while they were building a bridge across a creek. He stated that he will testify to any or all of the above statements.

LL-34 stated that he was with LL-31 when Inmates were forced to work in the water. He stated that in June of 1966, long line rider (David EVERETT) severely beat him for not getting into a ditch they were cleaning out. Also, he stated that in April of 1966, EVERETT brought him into the building to have him whipped for not picking enough pickles. He stated that Mr. BRUTON, Mr. MAYS, and Mr. FLETCHER were at the building, and Mr. BRUTON ordered his head peeled, then Mr. FLETCHER administered ten lashes to his bare buttocks. He stated that he did not say anything while Mr. FLETCHER was whipping him, so he was locked up for an hour, and Mr. WILSON administered ten lashes on the bare buttocks. He stated that he still did not say anything, so he was locked up for another hour, and Mr. BRUTON administered twenty lashes. He stated that the ex-yardman, Richard DAVIS whipped him with a "blackjack" for missing his number in a yard count. He further states that long line riders (David SIMMONS and Jack SPURLOCK) had whipped him with "blackjacks" and clubs on many occasions. He states that he will testify in a court of law.

LL-38 stated that inmates in the laundry have stolen clothes from him, and that one must pay $2.00 a week to a laundry worker to have his clothes cleaned. He stated that the inmates, yardmen, or building tenders steal personal items from the barracks while the Inmates are gone. He stated that the most common items stolen are stamps, toothpaste, and toilet items. He stated that he has seen Inmate Winston TALLEY beat Inmates on occasions. He stated that he will testify in a court of law.

LL-41 stated that in November of 1964, Inmate Richard WILSON beat him with a "blackjack" and kicked him hard enough to dislocate his shoulder. He stated that these beatings were repeated several times.

LL-43 stated that he has been in Tucker for three years, and he has seen Mr. WILSON deliver whiskey to Inmate Jim REAVES on several occasions. He states that he has smelled liquor on Mr. MAY'S breath on several occasions. He stated that he had witnessed the shooting of LL-31 by Inmate JOHNSON. He further states that he can show investigators where liquor was hidden in the building.

LL-44 states that he came to Tucker in June of 1964, and that within a month, he was beaten by a long rider until he was unable to stand. He stated that this beating was administered under the direction of Mr. FLETCHER, and the long line rider was Burl ASHWORTH. He stated that in October of 1964, he and Inmate Douglas KEMP were involved in an assault and that Mr. FLETCHER brought them to the building where they were locked up in the Death Cells overnight. He stated that the next morning, Inmate Doctor Bill MORGAN and Yardman Frank MILLER took them from the cell and to the hospital where they were met by Mr. BRUTON. He stated that they were strapped to the operating table, one at a time, and a wire was then attached to a big toe and another wire to the penis. Mr. BRUTON ordered MORGAN to turn the telephone crank, which was done three times. He stated that in April of 1965, he was planning to escape. He stated that Inmate Douglas BURKE was long line rider about that time, and he had told Inmate KENNEDY that if he didn't pay him $20.00, he would kill him. He stated that KENNEDY and

Wayne GARRISON cut another Inmate's throat with a piece of glass in the tool shed one morning, and they were brought to the building and beaten until they implicated LL-46. He stated that LL-46 was brought in and beaten until he told them about his (LL-44's) planned escape. He stated the following day, Mr. BRUTON and Richard DAVIS, Inmate, came to the long line and called him, Carl MOSLEY, and James CROFT, out of the line and brought them to the building where they were questioned about their planned escape and a riot in the mess hall. He stated that he told Mr. BRUTON about the escape, but that he did not know anything about a riot. He stated that, at this time, Mr. BRUTON started to beat him on the head and told DAVIS to get a statement from him any way he could. He stated that Carl MOSLEY and himself were tortured for several hours by means of wirepliers on their fingers, toes, ears, noses, and private parts. He stated that needles were stuck under their fingernails at least an inch deep. He continued that their fingers were beaten with wirepliers while they were lying on something solid. He stated that he was beaten so badly that he was unable to work for about three weeks. He stated that when he first came to Tucker, the food in the mess hall was very poor. He stated that a full meal consisted of green beans and sweet potatoes. He stated that he has loaned money, sold coffee, ect. to make money. He stated that the yardman, Richard DAVIS, gave him $15.00 and told him if he wanted to stay out of trouble, to make some more money. He stated that he later got some more money and loaned it out $1.00 for $2.00. He stated that his last whipping was by Mr. MAYS for protecting himself from a beating by a line rider. He stated that he has seen Mr. FLETCHER take items from the Inmates mess hall.

LL-51 stated that the long line rider ("Butch" HARPER) beat him with a "blackjack" for not working enough. He further witnessed the beating of LL-45.

LL-53 stated that he came to Tucker in October of 1964 and was placed in the long line. He stated that Douglas BURKE was the rider and told him that unless he was his "punk", he would whip him and have the line Captain whip him too. He stated that he refused, and two days later, BURKE ran his horse over him, knocking him to the ground, then got off the horse and beat him with a rubber hose, then kicked him until one tooth was knocked out. He stated that he received this type of treatment for two or three weeks, and when he went to the hospital, Inmate Doctor Bill MORGAN told him that unless he gave him $20.00, he could not stay in the hospital. He stated that he had only $10.00 which he gave to him, and was allowed to stay one day. He stated that a kitchen rider whipped him with a "blackjack" for dropping a spoon on the floor. He has a scar on his left ear that he stated was obtained at this time. He stated that Mr. FLETCHER had whipped him with his trousers and underwear down for not picking ten quarts of strawberries in one hour. He stated that he would testify in court.

## Part III. Criminal Investigation Division Report

LL-56 stated that in March of 1965, he had a large boil on his leg and was denied medical treatment for several days. He stated that when he was given medical treatment, the Inmate Doctor (Bill MORGAN) strapped him to treatment table and lanced the boil. Then he beat him about the head, stomach, and legs, until he signed a paper admitting self abuse. He stated that he had been beaten by a long rider (Douglas BURKE) several times.

LL-59 stated that Mr. BRUTON and Mr. WILSON came to a field where he was plowing, picked him up, and brought him to the building where they whipped him for escape. He stated that he was not even trying to escape, and that Mr. BRUTON cursed him and called him names.

LL-61 stated that he escaped from Tucker and was picked up in Louisiana four days later. He stated that he was returned to Tucker, had his head shaved, made to stay on his bed, was allowed to go to the rest room once a night, was allowed no coffee or cigarettes, and not allowed to talk. He stated that Mr. BRUTON broke his nose and refused him medical attention. He stated that he was kept in the Death Cells during Christmas, and after Christmas, he was put back in the line, where he was hit with a rifle for using the rest room. He stated that the long line rider was told to whip him, and he did so using hoe handles or sticks or anything else he could find.

LL-63 stated that he arrived at Tucker in December of 1964 and was beaten by the Convict Barber with a razor strap. He stated that he was assigned to the long line, and a rider called INDIAN would whip the Inmates with a rubber hose on Mr. FLETCHER'S orders. He stated that after Mr. FLETCHER left the line, Mr. HUGHES took over, and he also would have the riders beat them. He stated that he was whipped by an Inmate for forgetting his number in the count. He stated that after INDIAN left the line, Inmate Dale JOHNSON and Inmate Butch HARPER were the riders and they also beat the Inmates. He stated that after Mr. HUGHES left the line, Mr. YOUNG took over and that he would whip the Inmates with a "blackjack" and with the "hide" in the field. He stated that he witnessed the shooting of LL-31. He stated that he paid Inmate Doctor Bill MORGAN for a job in the garden squad. He further stated that when the rules and regulations came out, Mr. WILSON addressed the garden squad and told them that they did not mean anything there. He stated that Mr. MAYS whipped Inmate Walter PERRY on several occasions, and that PERRY is now in the State Mental Hospital. He stated that Mr. BRUTON came out to the line frequently and whipped the Inmates for leaving a pickle on the vine or leaving some grass. He stated that he has seen Mr. BRUTON double the hide and beat inmates on the head with it.

LL-65 stated that he was beaten by the garden squad rider about the first of March with a rubber hose. He further was beaten by the yardman, Jim REAVES, because he would not volunteer to clean up the hall.

LL-66 stated that he escaped from Tucker Farm in May of 1965 with Doyle RICH. He stated that they were gone for about twenty-five hours when they were arrested by three trustys [trustees] and the dog boy. He stated that they were beaten by the trustys, returned to the farm, had their heads shaved, and put to work without any medical attention. He stated that the yard man hit him in the eye with the prison keys when they returned to the building.

LL-70 stated that on a visit on 6-5-66, Inmate David EVERETT made dirty remarks to his mother and his bride-to-be.

LL-72 stated that there were seventy head of hogs sold and forty head of cattle sold from the Farm. He stated that he did not know what had happened to the money. He further stated that Mr. WILSON took two hogs to the farm of C. C. VENABLE at Keo, Arkansas. He continued that twelve head of mules were also sold.

LL-73, LL-74, LL-75, and LL-76 witnesses to the above circumstances.

LL-77 stated that he was transferred to Tucker in January of 1966, and Inmate Bill MORGAN took $9.60 from him to be exchanged for brozene which he never received. He stated that in June, his wife and another woman came to see him on visiting day, and they had a flat in front of the office. Mr. Jesse WILSON got as near to his wife as possible and suggested that if she would "act right", he might be able to influence the Parole Board.

LL-79 stated that the "telephone" was used on him and this happened on two occasions by Inmate Doctor Bill MORGAN with Mr. BRUTON present. He stated that after the "telephone" was used on him, he was beaten and then stomped by both Mr. BRUTON and Inmate MORGAN. He stated that the long line rider (SPURLOCK) beat him with a rubber hose. He stated that he once received twenty-eight lashes with the strap. He further stated that he gave "Buddy" NICHOLS $60.00 to buy a job off the line. He stated that once while picking strawberries, Inmate David SIMMONS placed a box of strawberries on his face and stomped them at Mr. BRUTON'S orders.

LL-81 stated that in March of 1964, Mr. BRUTON told him that if he could get $200.00, he would be a free man. He stated that Mr. BRUTON let him call Mr. Henry PRYOR, his uncle, who brought a check for $200.00.

## Part III. Criminal Investigation Division Report

He stated that Mr. BRUTON told him to get the check cashed, take the money to his house, and a lawyer would come by to get it. He stated that Glen WALTERS came by after it, but he would not let him have the check until a receipt was signed. He stated that the lawyer told him, Mr. PRYOR, that he would be a free man the next Saturday. He stated that Mr. BRUTON had left for the Worlds Fair the next day, and he is still in the penitentiary. He stated that Inmate Frank HARRIS, on Death Row, heard some of the conversation between him and Mr. BRUTON. He concluded, stating that Mr. BRUTON had let James Dean WALKER[36] use a cell on Death Row to visit a girl for at least an hour.

LL-85 stated that he will testify to any of the following and that he personally witnessed what he said. He stated that LL-83 paid $1,000.00 for a transfer to the laundry and to have two years good time added to his record, therefore making him eligible for a new number to start, serving an escape charge. He stated that this money was paid to Mr. BRUTON through Inmate Jim REAVES. He stated that LL-79 paid him $50.00 to give to Inmate Jim REAVES for a laundry job, and that LL-79 made another payment to Inmate Winston TALLEY. He stated that Dallas Ray MAYS paid $100.00 for a job in the laundry, $40.00 of it on the books by his mother, and he does not know about the other $60.00. He stated that he was present during the time that

---

[36] The conviction of James Dean Walker became a controversial matter in Arkansas and beyond for many years. He died in Idaho on January 24, 2023, and "Legacy Remembers" published an obituary running from Feb. 8 to Feb. 12 that year. These details about his life came from that obituary. Born in in 1940, Walker was abandoned during his childhood and raised in foster homes part of the time. He grew up in Boise, Idaho, and traveled with his father, a heavy equipment operator, when jobs became available. Walker joined the army on his 19$^{th}$ birthday and served in France. After discharge he returned to Boise and became a bootblack. Unfortunately, while traveling through Little Rock in 1963 with other men, he became involved in a bar fight. After a policeman stopped the car Walker was riding in a violent confrontation ensued, and the officer died from a fatal gunshot. He managed to shoot Walker five times. Though Walker held a loaded pistol, it had not been fired. However, at two trials with a prejudiced judge, Walker was convicted. A few days before his execution date the Arkansas Supreme Court reversed this decision based on the judge's improper conduct. Life became his new sentence, and Walker went to Cummins. There he became a trustee, but feared for his life in 1975 when a warden reportedly said he would bury Walker in the prison yard. He escaped and relocated to Lake Tahoe. Authorities found him there in 1979 and returned Walker to jail in Arkansas. Walker's plight caught the attention of lawyers who believed him innocent and the victim of an unfair trial. They represented him pro bono throughout the 1980s. In May 1985 his lawyers prevailed when a United States Court of Appeals ruled that Walker be retried or released. Previously suppressed evidence by authorities indicated that the car's driver, not Walker, fired the fatal shot. In 1993 Walker returned to Boise and became a bootblack again. He retired in 2017 and lived his final six years of his life there.

vodka was being consumed by Inmates Winston TALLEY, Jim REAVES, Vernon EDINGTON, Carl CORDER, and Larry MCFEE, which was brought into Tucker Farm by an employee of the Arkansas Power and Light Company. He stated that the AP & L employee was paid in green money by Carl CORDER for the deliveries. He stated that CORDER would call the AP & L employees by telephone and order the liquor. He stated that he has seen Dristan Nasal Inhalers turned into liquid and injected into the veins of Inmates Winston TALLEY, Jim REAVES, Vernon EDINGTON, Larry MCFEE, Carl CORDER, Lincoln MCGLOTHINE, and John BARR. He stated that Inmate REAVES would buy the necessary items in England when Mr WILSON or Mr FLETCHER would take him and he would buy them a shirt or something. He stated that he personally was given a medicine vial half full of 50 mg of thoroyine tablets by Inmate Terry DABBS, Cummins, and was told to give them to Inmate Jim REAVES, telling him that Inmate John TEBEE, Cummins Hospital, sent them. He stated that he has witnessed injections of morphine by the same Inmates. He stated that this came from Inmate Leroy CALLAHAN, ex-inmate Doctor, and Ollis PATRICK, Inmate Doctor. He stated that PATRICK did not know what it was being used for, and when he found out, he put a stop to it. He stated that he has personally witnessed Mr BRUTON beat, threaten, and verbally abuse Inmates.

LL-89 stated that he is nineteen years old, and when he was transferred to Tucker, he was placed in the long line in the strawberry field. He stated that he had never been in a strawberry field before and did not know how to pick them, and the long line rider ("Butch" HARPER) beat him with a rubber hose. He stated that Indian BURKE also whipped him in the field, then he was brought to the building by Mr HUGHES. He continued that after they arrived at the building, Mr. HUGHES was told by HARPER to go back to the field, that he'd take care of this. He stated that after the line Warden left, they had what is called a "house party". He stated that there were five trustys: Butch HARPER, Richard DAVIS, Tommy DESACOZO, and others that he did not know, and a building tender, Jimmy GOSSET. He stated that these men beat him with blackjacks, rubber hoses, and brass knuckles for about an hour, then rested and drank a cold drink, then beat him again for about thirty minutes and locked him up in the barracks. He stated that later, Mr. BRUTON came to him and told him that he would personally beat him to death if he ever tried to fight a line rider again. He stated he was forced to return to work the next day, without any medical attention. He stated that Inmate Bill MORGAN, Inmate Doctor, offered to sell him a job for a price. He stated that on the next visiting day, MORGAN met with his mother and set a price of $150. He continued that his mother paid MORGAN $20.00 at that time, and the next day, Mr. BRUTON called him and LL-92 over to the laundry detail. He then stated that MORGAN told him he could stay there as long as his mother or he made the payments. He stated that he worked there about four months, and during this time, his mother had paid the entire $150.00. He stated that the trustys named above have all since made parole or a time out on recommendation of Mr. BRUTON.

LL-90 stated that in June of 1966, his mother and step-father paid Mr. BRUTON $450.00 to give him a job in the Prison hospital. He stated that during a visit at the Farm, he told his mother and step-father about some ill treatment he was receiving there, and Vernon EDINGTON, Inmate, told Mr. BRUTON what he had said. He stated that Mr. BRUTON ordered for Mr. FLETCHER to whip him on his bare buttocks, and he was whipped until blood was running down his legs. He stated that on one occasion, he was whipped by Mr. FLETCHER at 3:00 A.M. for not issuing a pair of shoe strings the night before. He stated that long line rider, David EVERETT, whipped him with an axe handle in the field during May of 1966. He continued that Carolyn EDWARDS, girl friend of Inmate Vernon EDINGTON, brought "dope" into the Farm, and that it is kept in the medicine cabinet. He stated that Inmate Jim REAVES has a key to the medicine cabinet, and that he has seen REAVES and Inmate Jerry BLANKENSHIP cook the "dope" in a big spoon and shoot it into their arms. He concluded, stating that Bobby FERGUSON, ex-inmate, has also brought morphine to the farm for them.

LL-91. Witness to above circumstances.

LL-92 stated that when he first arrived at Tucker Farm, Jimmy GOSSET was the floorwalker and whipped him for no reason. He stated that he was also beaten by the longline rider. He stated that about the middle of April, Mr. BRUTON called him out of the line and told him that he was going to make him a "Do-Pop" in the 720 squad (tractor squad). He stated that he went to the building to get Do-Pop clothing, and Inmates Richard DAVIS and Frank MILLER beat him with a "blackjack" and accused him of trying to escape. He stated that he was forced to lay in for two days as one eye was swollen shut, and his face was swollen. He stated that in about two days, he was put back into the line, and Mr. BRUTON stopped in the yard and told him that if he would keep his mouth shut, he would get a "job" when his face cleared up. He stated that about two weeks later, Mr. BRUTON called him into his office and told him that if he could get his wife to spend some time with him, he would get him a good "job". He told Mr. BRUTON that he would, and the next day, he was put on the "Little Rock" crew. He stated that the last day of July, Inmate Bill MORGAN told him that unless he paid him $50.00, he would be ranked[37] within two days. He stated that he did not have the money, so he was ranked. He stated that he was caught attempting to smuggle a letter out, and Mr. BRUTON told him to go into the building. He stated that as he started up the steps, Mr. BRUTON knocked him down and continued to do so until he was

---

[37] See page 196.

knocked down five times. He stated that when he did get up the stairs and inside the building, Mr. BRUTON gave him twenty-seven lashes and put him into the line. He stated that in September, 1965, Inmate Bill MORGAN told him that for $100.00, he would get him a laundry job. He stated that on the next visit, his mother gave MORGAN $60.00 and put $40.00 on the books, and on the next Tuesday, Mr. BRUTON put him into the laundry.

LL-93 stated that he was beaten by long line riders in the winter of 1966. Inmates Bobby DENTON, Douglas BURKE, and Ray VARNER were named as the riders involved. He stated that he tried to fight back, but was beaten with a "blackjack" and "rubber hose". He stated that Mr. BRUTON told him that if he ever fought back again, he would kill him, and that he would flatten his time[38] on the long line.

LL-94 stated that in July of 1965, he had about $20.00 on the books when the long line rider, (Dale JOHNSON), approached him and told him for $30.00, he would let him make it; if not, he would beat his head with a "blackjack". He stated that he was told to pay Inmate Bill MORGAN and what he lacked having the $30.00, MORGAN would loan to him, and he could pay MORGAN when he got his next money. He stated that the loan would be $2.00 for each $1.00 loaned. He stated that he refused and was beaten by the rider. He stated that on the next visit, his father paid MORGAN $150.00, for which he stayed in the building for two weeks, then went to work in the laundry. He stated that after a new yard man came, he was ranked, and Mr. FLETCHER approached him and asked for money to get him a better job. He stated that he refused, and after that, he could do nothing right and was abused and beaten repeatedly.

LL-95 stated that he is in Death Row and Mr. BRUTON on occasions has cursed them and stated to them that if they told anything, they would be killed. He stated that Mr. BRUTON and eight trustys came into his call on Death Row, and he received a beating with the strap. He concluded by stating that he received fifteen lashes.

LL-96 stated that he was fifteen years old when he came to Tucker, and the long line rider (David SIMMONS) beat him with a shovel.

LL-97 stated that he was beaten with a rubber hose by the long line rider (Douglas BURKE) and that two more long line riders (Bobby DENTON and

---

[38] Flat time refers to a sentence that must be served without reduction of time for good behavior or other credits. Such prisoners are not eligible for parole, pardon, work furlough, or any other benefits.

## Part III. Criminal Investigation Division Report

David EVERETT) also beat him. He stated that he was whipped on his bare buttocks for not picking enough strawberries.

LL-98 stated that he was beaten on several occasions by the long line rider (Douglas BURKE). Also, he was beaten by Inmates Butch HARPER, Danny GORDON, and Dale JOHNSON. He stated that Mr. BRUTON knocked him down in the field because he did not know how to plant seed tomatoes. He stated that since he has been at Tucker Farm, he has been beaten with the following: a baseball bat, a trace chain, a rope with knots tied in it, a hoe handle, a shovel, a rubber hose with lead in one end, and a tractor fan belt.

LL-99 stated that when he arrived at Tucker Farm, the trustys stole several items from him and the bed assigned to him was in very bad condition. He stated that the "short hair" Inmates were not allowed to get off their beds without permission. He stated that he was beaten by a rider (Douglas BURKE) for not picking enough cotton. Also, he stated that BURKE would not let him eat lunch on one occasion and made him continue to pick cotton while the other Inmates ate.

LL-100 stated that he passed out in the field while working in the long line, and Mr. FLETCHER beat him in the field, then brought him into the hospital. He stated that after three days, Mr. BRUTON came to the hospital and gave orders for him to be rung up on the telephone. He stated that one wire was attached to his big toe and one wire to his penis and a crank type telephone was turned causing an electrical shock to go through his body. He stated that Mr. BRUTON, Inmate Bill MORGAN, and Inmate Troy HARRIS were present. He stated that longline rider (Earl WYNN) beat him with a "blackjack" in the field. He further stated that he was forced to have oral and anal intercourse with Inmates or be beaten. He named the Inmates as Edward OWENS, Earl WYNN, Floyd MARTON, and Richard DAVIS. He stated that he was beaten by Inmate Douglas BURKE, long line rider. He stated that Mr. BRUTON would not let him answer sick call when he was sick, and that he once placed a tomato on his head and stomped it into his eyes.

LL-3 stated that in September of 1964, Danny GORDAN, building attendant, kicked him out of bed and kicked him in the face for mopping the wet bathroom floor with a dust mop, which he did not do. LL-4 and LL-5 are two witnesses to this. In 1965, Larry SMITH, building attendant, beat him in the face for missing some paper on the floor when he was sweeping. He received no medical attention for this beating. LL-6 and LL-7 witnessed this. He stated that he was beaten unconscious for not fighting Frank WYNN, building attendant, by Inmate Jimmy GASSETT, Bobby WILKERSON, and Frank WYNN. LL-9 and LL-10 are witnesses to this.

LL-12 stated that he was beaten by the long line rider (Douglas BURKE) for not being able to keep up with the rest of the line. This left a 3" scar over the eye, for which no medical attention was received. He stated he was told to give money to the garden shack rider, (J. D. COCHRAN) to keep from getting whipped.

LL-14 stated he has been doing work that he is not physically capable of doing because of bad legs and knees. He stated he was threatened by the garden shack rider (J. D. COCHRAN) and Prison doctor (Bill MORGAN) if he kept complaining.

LL-15 stated that he was whipped by the long line rider for not picking enough cotton, and has had money taken away from him. He stated that he has done without food.

LL-17 stated he has used hoes and shovels with rough tree limbs for handles that cut his hands. He stated that he was whipped, with his pants down, by Mr. FLETCHER until he bled. He stated he has been whipped by the line riders with "blackjacks", trace chains, axe handles, hoe handles, and rubber horses for things that they did not like.

LL-18 stated he was whipped with a rubber hose and the "hide" for not picking enough cotton. He stated that he was whipped by the line rider, (Douglas BURKE), on Mr. BRUTON'S orders and in front of Mr. BRUTON.

LL-23 stated that he paid the Prison Doctor (Bill MORGAN) $20.00 to be turned into a trusty. He stated that he has seen Inmates brutally beaten and tortured by Inmates Richard DAVIS, Ray VARNER, and Tony DeSHAZO, all line riders. He stated that he has seen needles run under Inmates fingers, penis pulled and squeezed with pliers, and has seen Inmates set on coke bottles, and if they fell off, they would get whipped.

LL-24 stated that he is not capable of doing heavy work, but has been made to do so and was threatened by the line rider (Charles MANN).

LL-25 stated that he has been whipped many times for not doing enough and being fast in his work. He stated that he was whipped by line riders, Douglas BURKE, Nelson HENDERSON, Sam BEAN, and Richard WILSON. He stated he had seen Mr. BRUTON kick and rupture an Inmate.

LL-27 stated that the long line rider tried to force him to do unnatural sexual acts.

## Part III. Criminal Investigation Division Report

LL-29 stated that he was whipped with the "hide" by Mr. WILSON and was put in the hospital. He stated that he was kicked out of the hospital for not paying any money to stay, by the Inmate Doctor, (Bill MORGAN).

LL-32 stated that he was whipped several times with the "hide" by Mr. BRUTON and Mr. FLETCHER for not picking enough cotton. He stated that the whippings were administered with his pants off.

LL-33 stated that in January of 1965, he, LL-35, LL-36, and LL-37 were planning to escape because of the treatment and not enough food. He stated they were all "slapped" around by Inmates Richard DAVIS, Dale JOHNSON, and Jimmy GORDON, yardmen, because they would not give them money. He stated that a line rider (Richard DAVIS) found out about the escape and brought them to Mr. BRUTON who whipped them with the "hide" on the buttocks with their pants down, and on the back and head. He further hit them with his fists and kicked them. Mr. BRUTON then left the building and told the riders to work them over real good. Rider Richard DAVIS got Tony DeSHAZO, Ray VARNER, George THORN, and Danny GORDON to help him beat them up. He stated that they came into the building with "blackjacks", wire pliers, nut crackers, and knives. He stated that they stripped all the clothes off LL-33, and Richard DAVIS stuck needles under his fingernails and toenails. DeSHAZO and VARNER pulled his penis and testicles with wire pliers and kicked him in the groin. VARNER and THORN ground out cigarettes on his stomach and legs. VARNER stuck him in the ribs with a knife and left a scar. THORN squeezed his knuckles with a pair of nut crackers. He stated that they worked on him all afternoon, and the next day, he was put out in the field and made to go to work. He stated he was unable to work, and they put him in the hospital and would not let anyone see him until he healed up.

LL-39. Witness to the above circumstances.

LL-40. Witness to the above circumstances.

LL-42 stated that he is a floorwalker in barracks, and has seen Mr. BRUTON punish Inmates for nothing more than he wanted to whip someone. He stated that he has cleared new land in the free world for people who were not associated with the Prison. He stated that he saw Mr. BRUTON make an Inmate with a bad heart run five miles, and when the man got into the Prison yard, he fell dead. He stated that he saw a colored Inmate beaten real bad and put in the hospital where he died. He stated that he has seen Inmates commit sexual acts for food.

LL-45 stated that he had been beaten many times for the way he talks. He stated that he has given Mr. FLETCHER bread, milk, and syrup, on his demand, so he could take them to the free line. He stated that Mr. FLETCHER has taken food that belonged to the Inmate's kitchen.

LL-46 stated that he was beaten and tortured for five hours because he was supposed to know something about a riot which was to take place. He stated that he knew nothing about any riot. He stated that he had pins stuck in him. LL-3, LL-6, LL-37, and LL-25 are witnesses to this.

LL-47. Witness to above circumstances.

LL-48 stated that he was denied medical attention after a severe beating.

LL-49 stated that he was beaten because he was unable to do enough work to satisfy riders and was refused medical attention after each beating.

LL-50 stated that he was beaten because he could not pick strawberries fast enough, and he was refused medical attention after each beating.

LL-52 stated that he was beaten because he could not meet the quota on cotton along with the others. LL-3 and LL-4 are witnesses to this.

LL-54 stated that he was beaten by the line rider (David EVERETT) when he failed to see some cucumbers.

LL-57 stated that Mr. HOWARD, bookkeeper, confiscated postage stamps from him that were sent by his family.

LL-58 stated that he was shot and beaten by the line rider (Jack SPURLOCK). He stated that upon his release from the hospital, Mr. BRUTON gave him twenty-seven lashes with the "hide". He stated that he was kicked for reading the Bible. He also stated that he had some teeth kicked out by the line rider (Richard DAVIS). LL-31, LL-60, are witnesses to this incident.

LL-19 stated that he was to have received a transistor radio through the mail from his sister, but that he was made to sign a receipt and did not get the radio.

LL-62 stated that he was whipped with the "hide", with his pants down, by Mr. BRUTON and Mr. MAYS for talking to another Inmate.

## Part III. Criminal Investigation Division Report

LL-64 stated that he was whipped the first day he arrived at Tucker Farm for being a "new" man. He stated that his shoes were taken away from him, and he was made to walk barefoot in mud and gravel. He further stated that he has some teeth knocked out, and Mr. BRUTON refused to let him get some more. He stated that after two years, he was put on as a floorwalker due to a bad heart, and his family Doctor explained to Mr. BRUTON. The yardman (Frank MILLER) told him that he would have to make Mr. BRUTON at least a $75.00 payment per week to get to keep his job as floorwalker. He stated that Mr. BRUTON gave him "blackjacks" and a night stick and told him to get the money if he had to beat it out of the Inmates. He stated that he refused to hit anyone or collect any money, so Mr. BRUTON tried to make him pay $35.00 for a pair of worn out shoes. He stated that he again refused, and was put out on the long line the next day. He stated that Mr. BRUTON told his family that he would help him get out of Prison for $350.00, and he was beaten because his family would not pay. He then stated that Mr. BRUTON offered his wife a deal to help him get out of Prison, if she would have intercourse with him on her visits. He stated that he was refused medical attention when he broke out in blisters, so he paid a yardman to get him some medicine and was whipped by the Inmate Doctor (Bill MORGAN) for not paying him. He stated that he is a witness to one of the Inmates getting the "telephone" used on him in the presence of Mr. BRUTON.

LL-67 stated that he received a severe beating while being questioned about an attempted murder that he knew nothing about. He stated that he was beaten by Inmates Richard DAVIS, Ray VARNER, Tony DeSHAZO, and he had needles stuck under his fingernails. LL-3, LL-63, LL-68, and LL-69 are witnesses to this incident.

LL-78 stated he was whipped and had more work put on him by the line rider (Ralph SHARPE) because he would not give him any money. He stated that he tried to kill SHARPE after abusive treatment.

LL-71 stated that he was beaten by Inmate Douglas BURKE, line rider for not picking enough cotton and was refused medical attention after the beating. Mr. MAYS whipped him, and several others, with the "hide", with their pants down, for not being able to keep up with the other Inmates. He stated that the line rider (David EVERETT) threatened to kill anyone who complained about the way he ran the line.

LL-80 stated that he was whipped by Inmate Butch HARPER, line rider, the first day in the pickle patch for missing some cucumbers that were small. He stated that he was given fourteen lashes a day for two days in a row by Mr. BRUTON for not picking enough cotton. He stated that he was whipped by

Inmate Jim GOSSETT, floorwalker, for not giving him any money. He stated that he paid Inmate Jim REAVES, yardman, $40.00 for a "job".

LL-82 stated that he was whipped because he could not pay back some money that he borrowed at the two for one rate. He stated that he has seen Mr. BRUTON drunk in the fields. LL-58 is a witness to this incident.

LL-83 stated that he and LL-84 were taken to the hospital. He stated that LL-84 was taken into the hospital first, and in a few minutes, he heard some screaming. He stated that after a few more minutes, he was taken in and strapped to the operating table by Inmate Doctor Bill MORGAN, and a wire was attached to his penis and another wire was attached to his big toe, and the telephone was cranked three times. Mr. BRUTON and Mr. FLETCHER were both witnesses to this. He stated that he overheard Mr. FLETCHER say that this is good for the Inmates. On June 1, 1966, he stated that he asked his mother for $1,000.00 to get a soft job and to keep from being beaten. On June 14, 1966, his mother and step-father arrived with a cashiers check for the $1,000.00. Mr. BRUTON refused the check, and Jim REAVES told him to tell his folks to bring cash. Around June 31 or July 1, 1966, they brought ten $100.00 bills and gave them to Jim REAVES, the yardman, and he took them into Mr. BRUTON'S office. Mr. BRUTON then came out and told his parents that he was going to help the boy get out of Prison, and he told Jim REAVES to put me on the construction crew. He stated that REAVES later put him into the Prison laundry as this assignment would help out on good time.

LL-84 stated that he had the "telephone" used on him;

LL-87 stated that he was whipped for not working fast enough, hard enough, and not picking enough cotton.

LL-86 stated that he had the "telephone" used on him for being sick.

LL-31 was a witness to this.

LL-88 stated that he was whipped by Inmate Jimmy PIKE, line rider, for falling behind the rest of the line. He stated that this whipping resulted in a back and hip injury, and he was refused medical attention. He stated that later, PIKE whipped him for stopping work because he was too sick to stand up.

On 8-27-66, this investigator, accompanied by investigator BEACH, investigator SKIPPER, and Trooper Photographer SCHALCHLIN, advised Inmate James REAVES of his Constitutional Right to counsel and to remain silent. Inmate REAVES waived all his rights and was interviewed at the residence of the Assistant Superintendent. Inmate REAVES produced a tape recording that he stated was of fourteen whippings administered by Mr. BRUTON to Inmates of Tucker Prison Farm for not picking enough strawberries during the past season. Upon listening to the tape recording, it was determined by voice to be of Mr. BRUTON administering whippings to Inmates on the bare buttocks and without benefit of a Board hearing, as prescribed in the Prison Regulations. One of said whippings was for a count of thirteen lashes, also in excess of that prescribed in Prison Regulations. Mr. BRUTON'S voice and demeanor during the course of said whippings seemed to be that of a very excited person bordering insanity. He swore and screamed throughout the whippings and repeatedly asked the Inmate in question, "What's your sorry old name?". INVESTIGATORS NOTE: This in itself is a direct indication that no hearing by any Board was conducted for the alleged offenses committed. Mr. BRUTON'S voice was hysterical, and his language was very profane during the entire time of the whippings. His excitement and profanity seemed to increase by degrees to a certain point, then diminish and begin all over again. Inmate REAVES allowed this investigator to make a copy of this tape recording and gave him permission for the entire interview to be tape recorded. INVESTIGATORS NOTE: Mr. BRUTON repeatedly told the Inmates and Wardens present that if the Inmates did not pick up their work quota, to bring them back in an hour for another whippings. This also is in direct conflict with the Prison Regulations.

During the interview, Inmate James REAVES stated that he had never heard of a Board Meeting being held to determine the punishment of an Inmate for any offense whatsoever since he had been at the penitentiary, nor had he ever heard of one. REAVES stated that he had been the day yardman for three months, and that one of his duties was to hand the "man" (BRUTON) the strap when he wanted to whip one of the Inmates. He stated that there was no set time for BRUTON to whip the Inmates, just when he was "available" or "felt like it". REAVES stated that BRUTON "acted like a man out of his mind" when he was whipping the Inmates. REAVES stated that he had seen BRUTON strike the Inmates with his crutch and cane, and that BRUTON would hit them with anything he could "get his hands on" at anytime. REAVES admitted that he had been the "front man" for BRUTON and had set up "many" deals for "payoffs" for jobs and assignments. He stated that he paid Mr. BRUTON $200.00 per month for his "job", and that Inmate Winston TALLEY also paid BRUTON $200.00 per month for his "job". Inmate REAVES stated that in the incident of John TOLLIVER, he collected $1,000.00 from John TOLLIVER'S mother in ten one hundred dollar bills and paid them directly to BRUTON. REAVES stated that he had the office "bugged" and took a tape recording of the entire transaction, including his counting the one hundred "loans" at this time. Inmate REAVES stated that he had possession of the "green" with the full knowledge of Mr. BRUTON and had been told to confiscate any "green" that he found, and that they (he and Mr. BRUTON) would "dispose" of it. He stated that he had never taken any "green" from the Inmates. He further stated that he "knew" about the bed for rent by Mr. BRUTON for the use of the Inmates and their girl friends or wives. REAVES stated that Mr. BRUTON got $50.00 per visit for the use of the bed. INVESTIGATORS NOTE: Inmate REAVES had been in solitary confinement since the beginning of this investigation and could not have been aware that the investigators had discovered information confirming his statements. Inmate REAVES stated he had placed twenty-five to thirty-five Inmates on "jobs" for "payoff" since he had been made day yardman, and that all of these jobs were with the knowledge of Mr. BRUTON. Inmate REAVES cited two females that were visiting Inmates that Mr. BRUTON "fondled" and named them as: Patsy HOLLOWAY, visiting Winston TALLEY, and Carolyn EDWARDS, visiting Vernon EDINGTON. Inmate REAVES stated that both females would probably make written statements to this effect. He stated that he had been told by many Inmates that Mr. BRUTON had approached their wives and girl friends and stated that if they would have "sexual intercourse" with him, that he would make it "easier" on their loved ones. See attached transcript of interview.

The details in the interview related above were confirmed later on the same date in an interview with Inmate Winston TALLEY conducted by this investigator in his cell in Death Row. Inmate TALLEY admitted that he, in company with Inmate James REAVES, conducted the "job" selling and the "loan" racket as a front for Mr. BRUTON, and that the majority of the proceeds went to Mr. BRUTON. During the course of this interview, Inmate TALLEY asked for paper and a pencil to prepare a Writ to the Federal Judge at Pine Bluff, Arkansas. No new information was related during this interview.

On 8-28-66, these investigators spent the day checking security at the Main Building and the Yard Tower. No security weakness was observed, and all weapons appeared to be in firing order.

On 8-29-66, these investigators were relieved at Tucker Prison Farm and returned to Headquarters in Little Rock, where Major W. C. STRUEBING, Commanding, C.I.D., was briefed.

On 8-30-66, this investigator was ordered by the Governor to return to Tucker Prison Farm and assume full authority at that installation. This investigator, accompanied by investigator BEACH, investigator SKIPPER, trooper ROSE, and trooper SMITH, arrived at Tucker Prison Farm at approximately 4:00 P.M., this date, and assumed control of all the security and work details. All Wardens were relieved from their positions, pending further action by the Office of the Governor on the next date.

## Part III. Criminal Investigation Division Report

On 8-31-66, all Warden personnel received official notification of termination of employment from Mr. BISHOP, Superintendent, Cummins Prison Farm, and prisoners were detailed under supervision to assist in the removal of household property. All wardens, with exception of Mr. FLETCHER, cleared the Main Gate and were off the installation before 5:00 P.M., this date. Mr. MAYS was cleared and inspected first without incident. Mr.WILSON upon attempting to clear the Main Gate, was found to have a pickup truck load of canned coffee, toilet paper, wax paper, soap, and other canned goods in his possession. (See Photo #A3). Mr. WILSON was reluctant to leave Tucker Prison Farm following seizure of this property and returned to the Administrative Building, claiming that when he was employed, he was promised any and all food stuffs that he desired. Mr. WILSON had been allowed to retain one-half of all the Prison food stuffs found in his possession, but he was very insistent that he should keep it all. Upon being informed that he would not be given any of the property back, he (Mr. WILSON) stated that he felt that he was in need of medical attention as he felt that he was about to have a "heart attack". Medical aid, in form of the Inmate Doctor, was called from the Prison hospital and stated that he could find no indication of an impending "heart attack". Mr. WILSON was, at that time, requested by this investigator to leave the Prison, and he complied.

On 9-1-66, Mr. FLETCHER completed clearing and packing and checked out through the Main Gate without incident. He stated that he would return for his horses and his horse trailer. INVESTIGATORS NOTE: Said trailer was indicated earlier in this report as having been built with Prison labor and material.

On 9-1-66, at about 8:00 A.M., this investigator was informed by several prisoners that a search of the garage office would reveal the "field straps" used by the Wardens to whip prisoners in the field without benefit of the hearing required by Prison Regulations. A search of said office produced three (3) leather whipping straps. All personnel working in the garage stated that the "straps" had been hidden in the office by the Wardens when this investigation was initiated. "Straps" were seized in evidence and photographed with the "strap" seized earlier at the Main Building. (See Photo #A2).

On 9-1-66, this investigator interviewed Inmate Informer FL-3, who stated that he had personal knowledge of the "hay deal" at Mr. VENABLE'S farm. FL-3 stated that said hay was cut by prison labor, and one-half was placed in Mr. VENABLE'S barn and the other half was placed in a barn to be used by the Prison. He continued that Ronnie BRUTON hauled 2,500 to 3,000 bales to his farm, utilizing a back route to avoid discovery. FL-3 stated that prisoners David ALLEN, James EARCHART, Donald POE, Claude WOODS, and Dixie JONES were used in the exchange of hay and would testify. FL-3 stated that on one occasion last year, the State Purchasing Agent had been present at a hog sale and remained until a semi-truck had been loaded, then had left. He continued that immediately after he left, a small trailer pulled up and ten big sows were loaded and carried away. He further stated that in the early spring of 1966, ten of the fattest goats were selected and sold at the Pine Bluff Stockyards by Mr. BRUTON and Mr. WILSON. FL-3 stated that the check was made out to "Jesse WILSON, England, Arkansas" and that David ALLEN had helped haul the goats to the Stockyards. FL-3 stated that Mr. "Pat" HENDERSON, U.S. Deputy Marshal, had made "many" horse deals with MR. BRUTON, and he may still have some of the Prison horses on his farm near England. FL-3 stated that in 1964, in February or March, the prisoners were used to clear about thirty acres of land belonging to Ronnie BRUTON, and that MR. BRUTON told the prisoners that RONNIE BRUTON bought the Prions a load of goose-necked hoes in return for the labor. He stated that this land is near the Judy Hole. he also stated that in 1962/63, the prisoners cleared "free world" land at a location known as "Garrison and Main" without compensation. FL-3 stated that the prisoners were used every year to hoe Mr. RICHARDSON'S cotton until this year, and that no compensation was received by the prisoners for the labor. FL-3 stated that three or four lift cylinders are missing from the Prison Farm, and that Mr. BALL has two of them at this time. He concluded, stating that RONNIE BRUTON had a prison ground plow for four months, and that it was returned to the Prison on the day before the inventory of property was conducted.

On 9-2-66, Governor Faubus was present at Tucker Prison Farm and conferred with several Prisoners and with personnel assigned to this investigation for a progress report. Reporters were present with the Governor, and all questions asked were referred to his office.

On 9-6-66, this investigator was relieved from assignment at Tucker Prison Farm and returned to Little Rock Headquarters for purposes of reports.

On 9-7-66, Inmate Informer FL-10 was interviewed by investigator BEACH, and he stated that Mr. Charlie ADAMS, who is on the Parole Board, is running a "Little Tucker" near Hughes, Arkansas, on a farm he owns. He stated that Mr. ADAMS will parole convicts out and work them on this farm. He continued that the convicts are beaten, and if they contest, he sends them back to Prison. He stated that if an Inmate does not go to work for him, he (Mr. ADAMS) will prevent him from getting a parole. FL-10 gave the names of two Inmates who have been there, as Bill RICHARDSON and Donald ARMSTRONG and stated that they probably would testify. He stated that the garage at Tucker has built several land levelers and that only one is still on the Prison Farm. He also stated that the garage has built a house trailer for Mr. HOWARD, the bookkeeper. He further stated that the garage has built horse trailers for RONNIE BRUTON and Mr. FLETCHER, with State material

## Part III. Criminal Investigation Division Report

and Prison labor. He stated that while he was on the Prison Farm in 1958, there were several horse trailers built, and upon his return in 1964, none of these trailers are there now. He also stated that when Jimmy RABY was the garage rider, he built a house trailer and a horse trailer for Mr. BRUTON. FL-10 stated that the Mr. HOWARD has an axel and plans for a house trailer to be built now, and that the items are being kept at the garage at this time. He stated that the garage has built a dog trailer and two (2) campers for Mr. HOWARD. One camper is presently at the home of Mr. HOWARD on the Farm, but the whereabouts of the other is unknown. FL-10 stated that Mr. HOWARD has used convict labor and materials to build his house near Russellville. He stated that Mr. HOWARD has taken plumbing supplies and wiring from the Prison and used Inmates to install it. FL-10 stated that one of the Inmates used is Carl GOINS.

FL-10 stated that MR. BALL, of Star City, borrows equipment from the Farm and presently has Farm Equipment that belongs to the State. He stated that he was present last year when a lift cylinder was placed in the car of MR. BALL, and it has not been returned. FL-10 stated that Ronnie BRUTON would come to the Farm, pull off equipment, use it for several weeks, then return it to the Farm. He stated that Ronnie BRUTON kept a cotton trailer all fall of last year. He stated that two combines froze up on the Farm, apparently ruining the engines, and Mr. BRUTON let Ronnie BRUTON and several "free world" farmers strip them for parts. He continued that Ronnie BRUTON had a combine overhauled and painted in the Prison Garage last year, utilizing prison materials and labor.

FL-10 stated that both Mr. FLETCHER and Mr. WILSON have had repairs made to their personal vehicles at the Prison garage, and both have taken several items that were the property of the State. He continued that the gas book at the garage and the book used to charge items out of the garage do not match the books kept by Mr. HOWARD and that one of the books kept by Mr. HOWARD, and that one of the books kept at the garage has turned up missing since the investigators arrived on this case. FL-10 stated that the rice crop last year was fathered with a prisoner in charge, because Mr. BRUTON was in the hospital, Mr. FLETCHER stayed at home or in the office, and Mr. WILSON stayed drunk. He stated that on several occasions, Mr. WILSON had gotten drunk in the garage and made the statement that he could "stand on the unmarked grave in the Warren Field". He stated that "Doright" JONES, an inmate now on parole, might give more information of the reported killing and of the above mentioned grave. FL-10 stated that last Christmas, he, accompanied by Mr. WILSON and Inmate Bobby WILKERSON, went to England, and Mr. WILSON bought whiskey. He further states that in 1958, Mr. WILSON told him not to tag two bales of State cotton, and they later disappeared.

FL-10 stated that Willie KING, now on parole, worked at the dairy barn and also took care of Ronnie BRUTON'S cows that were on the Prison Farm. He stated that KING might be able to supply information as to how the calves were taken from the Prison Farm to Ronnie BRUTON'S farm. FL-10 confirmed information related earlier in this report of the "hay deal" at Mr. VENABLE'S farm and stated that Mr. WILSON had given Mr. VENABLE two (2) state owned hogs about the time the "hay deal" was going on.

FL-10 stated that he had witnessed Richard DAVIS, ex-inmate yardman, abuse and beat several Inmates in the storeroom in the Main Building in an effort to "shake" them down. He further stated that Bobby WILKERSON, an ex-yardman, was [?] because of his beating the inmates and his drinking.

FL-10 concluded, stating that Mr. WILSON had approached his wife and asked her to take a "trip" with him, and he would help out FL-10. He stated that she refused and would testify.

## CID Report Photos

SUBJECT: Photographs taken at Tucker Prison Farm.

DATE: August 27, 1966.

PHOTOGRAPHER: Paul M. Schalchlin, Trooper

The following photographs were taken by this photographer on the morning of August 27, 1966. Photo #1 was taken at 3:10 A.M. Photos #2 and #3 were taken at 3:55 A.M., and photo #4 was taken at 6:50 A.M.

#1. Wire from conduit showing where tape recorder was hooked by inmates.

#2. Front side of acoustical ceiling section where microphone was placed by inmates.

#3. Back side of acoustical ceiling section showing how the microphone was placed in ceiling section.

#4. Scar on heel of W. W. HENDERSON, Inmate. Struck with a hoe by Inmate Early WYNN, line rider, after he refused to let him hit him with a blackjack. Cut sewed up by Inmate Doctor.

## Part III. Criminal Investigation Division Report

The following photographs were taken on the morning of August 27, 1966, between 9:00 and 9:30 A.M., of scars and marks on the following Inmates:

#5. James Edward STEPHENS-Teeth knocked out, scar across nose, and over left eye. Struck by rider.

#6. James Edward STEPHENS-Bruises on hip from whipping which was administered by Mr. FLETCHER on bare buttocks.

#7. Cleatus ECHOLS-Bruises on feet from working without shoes after escape-Mr. BRUTON'S orders.

#8. Jerry D. IVENS-Bruises on hip from 11 lashes administered by Mr. FLETCHER on bare buttocks on 7-15-66.

#9. James SHERRY-Scar on head from being hit with a stick by rider.

#10. Dallas Ray MAYS-Scar under left eye where yardman hit him with blackjack.

#11. J. W. STUDDARD-Scar on upper lip where he was struck by rider.

#12. Revious HAMILTON-Scar over right eye where floorwalker stomped him.

#13. Jimmy SMITH-Operation scar on stomach where Inmate had to be operated on after being stomped by a yardman.

#14. Bobby KEY-Front teeth knocked out by rider.

#15. Bobby KEY-Shot in back by rider.

#16. Cecil McWILLIAMS-Scars on left eye and lips where Inmate was hit by riders with blackjacks and hoe handles.

#17. Clyde SOFLEY-Scars on left wrist and right hand.

#18. Raymond HICKS-Scar on head from bullet fired by trusty.

#19. Raymond HICKS-Scar under left eye from being hit with prison keys by yardman.

#20. William Ponderly CASEY-Scars from 10 lashes on the bare buttocks administered by Mr. MAYS.

#21. Williams E. CRUISE, Jr.-Scars on left upper arm from being shot with shotgun by rider.

#22. William E. CRUISE, Jr.-Scars on buttocks from being shot with shotgun by rider.

#23. Eugene BIDDLE-Struck with a lead pipe by long line rider.

#24. Carl MOSLEY-Scars from needles under fingernails.

#25. Carl MOSLEY-Scar under left arm from stomping.

#26. Floyd SULLIVAN-Scar on head from beating with a blackjack.

#27-#31. Photographs made at Arkansas State Police Headquarters on Monday, August 29, 1966, of articles and evidence collected by Investigator Atkinson at Tucker Prison Farm.

#32-#36. Tucker Telephone. Photos taken by Investigator Atkinson on 8-25-66.

#37-#38. Clothing, property of Ronnie BRUTON, shown hanging in closet after being returned from the Prison laundry.

#39. Strap used at Tucker Prison Farm, showing width and reinforcements.

#40. Strap used at Tucker Prison Farm, showing the length.

#41-#43. Bed located in loft over Mr. BRUTON'S office, alleged to have been rented for immoral purposes.

#44-#46. Photos showing the boiler corridor in the Main Building at Tucker. Taken by Investigator Beach.

#47-#50. Photos showing outside and inside of Administrative Building at Tucker Prison Farm.

#A1. Hypodermic needles seized in the Main Building, alleged to have been used in torture of Inmates.

#A2. Strap from Main Building and Field Straps seized from Office at Prison garage.

#A3. Photographs of food stuffs, property of Arkansas Prison System, taken from the household goods of Mr. WILSON, former Warden at Tucker Prison Farm, as he attempted to leave the Prison grounds following his discharge from employment.

PART III. CRIMINAL INVESTIGATION DIVISION REPORT

## CRIES FROM THE WALLS

#3

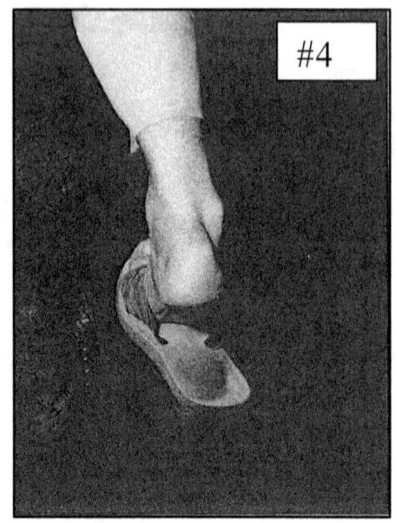
#4

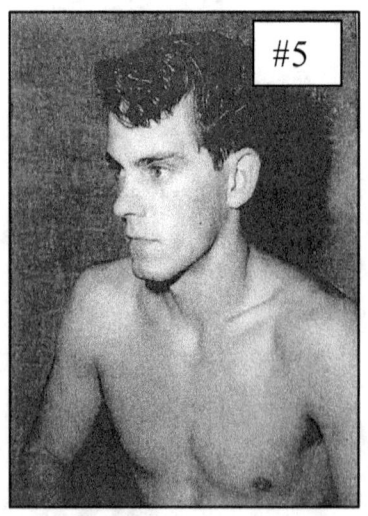
#5

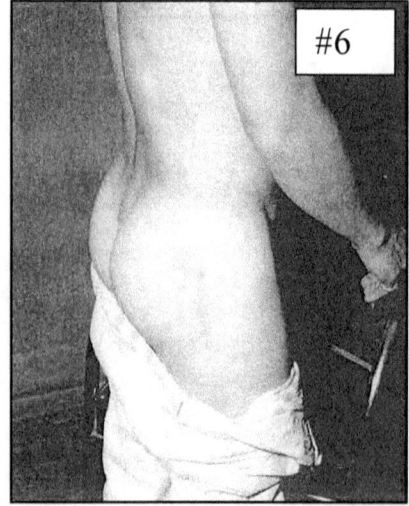
#6

# Part III. Criminal Investigation Division Report

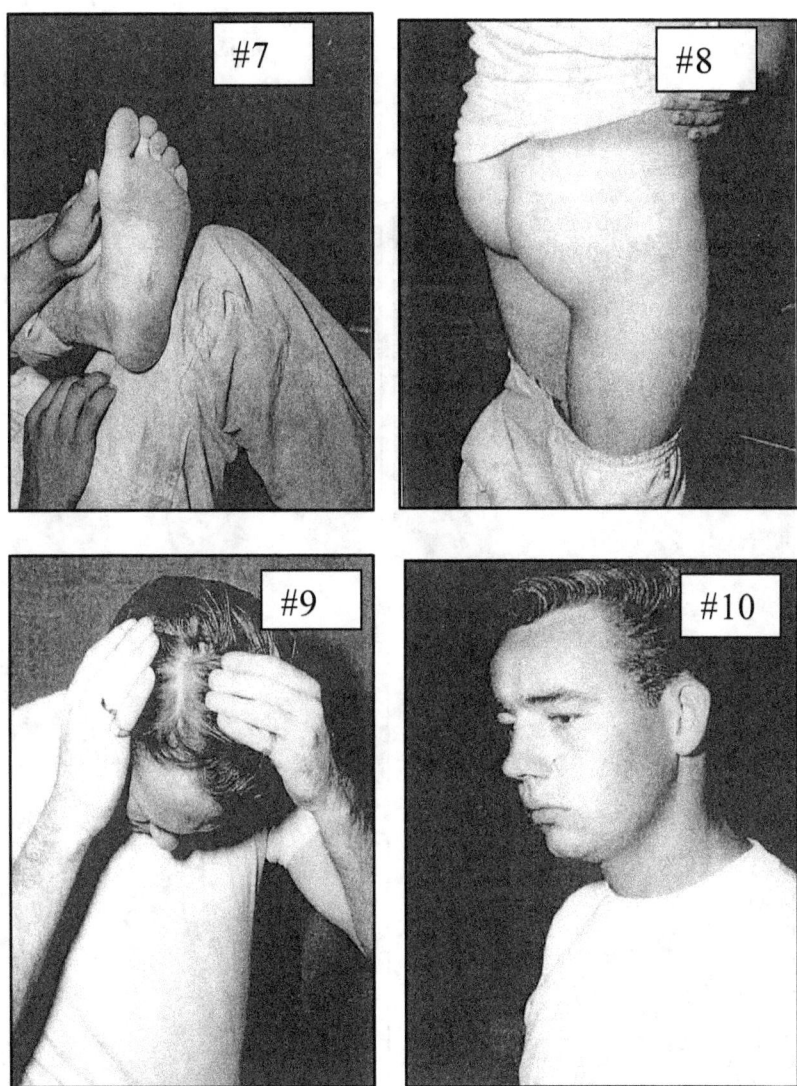

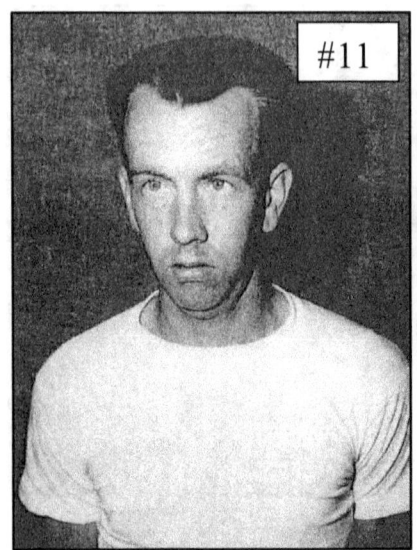
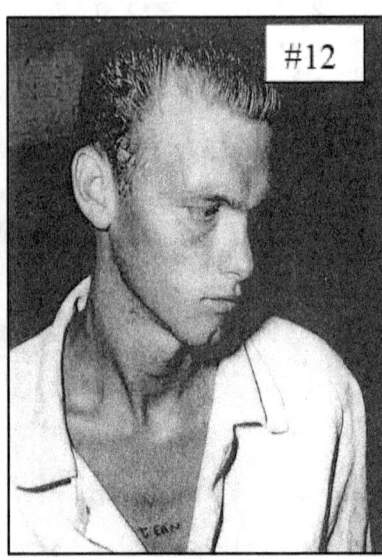
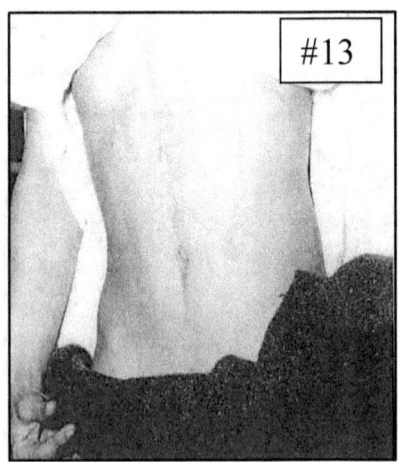
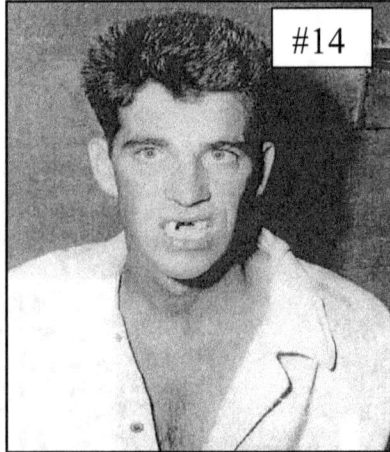

## Part III. Criminal Investigation Division Report

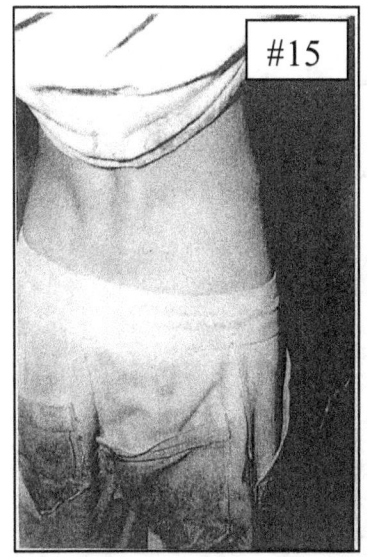

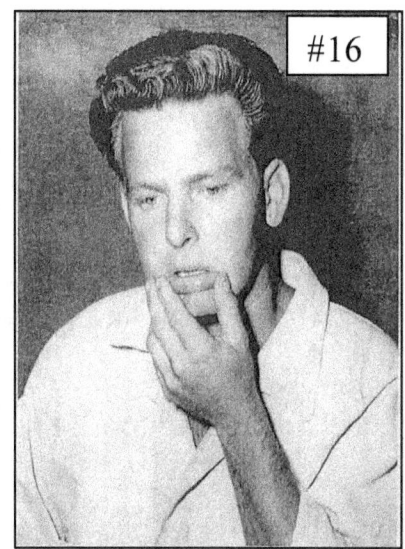

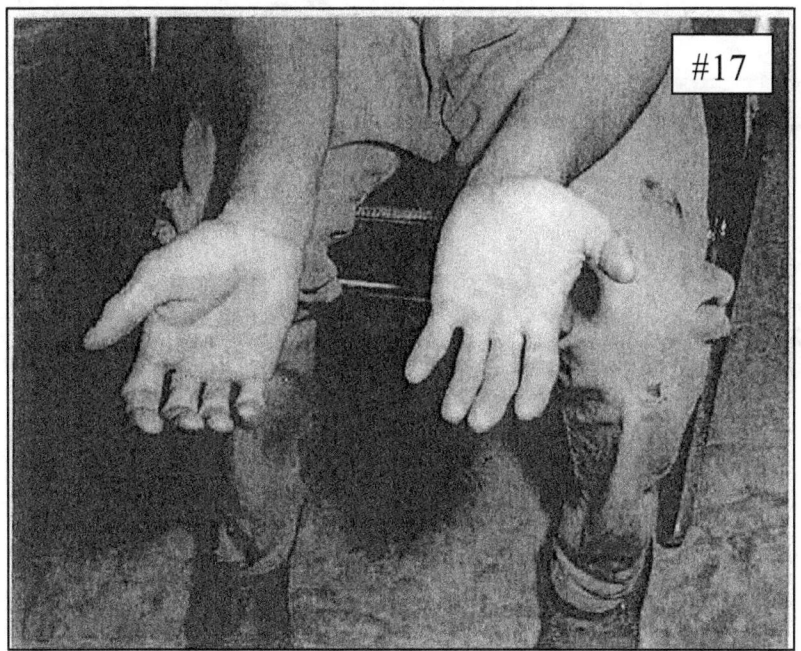

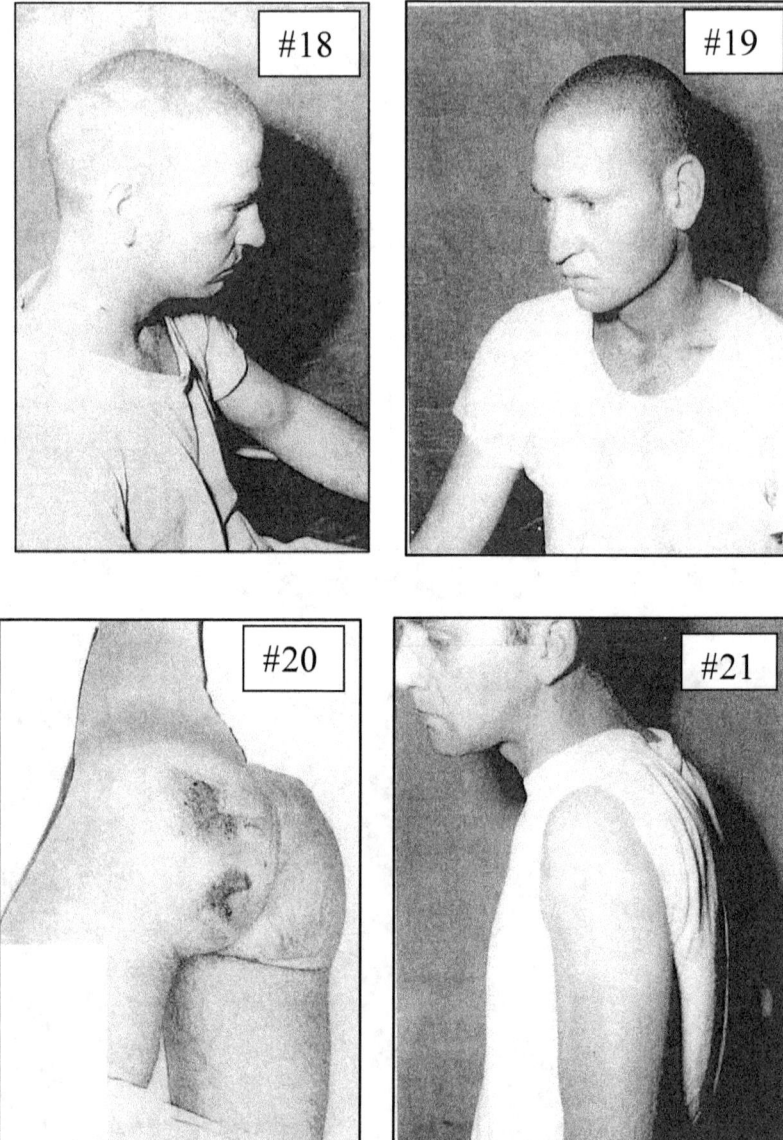

PART III. CRIMINAL INVESTIGATION DIVISION REPORT

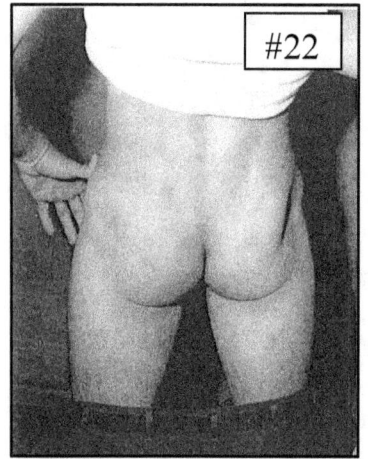

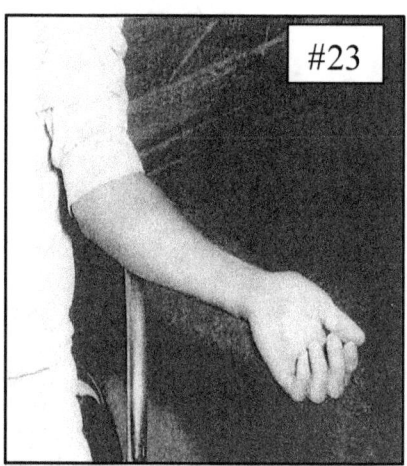

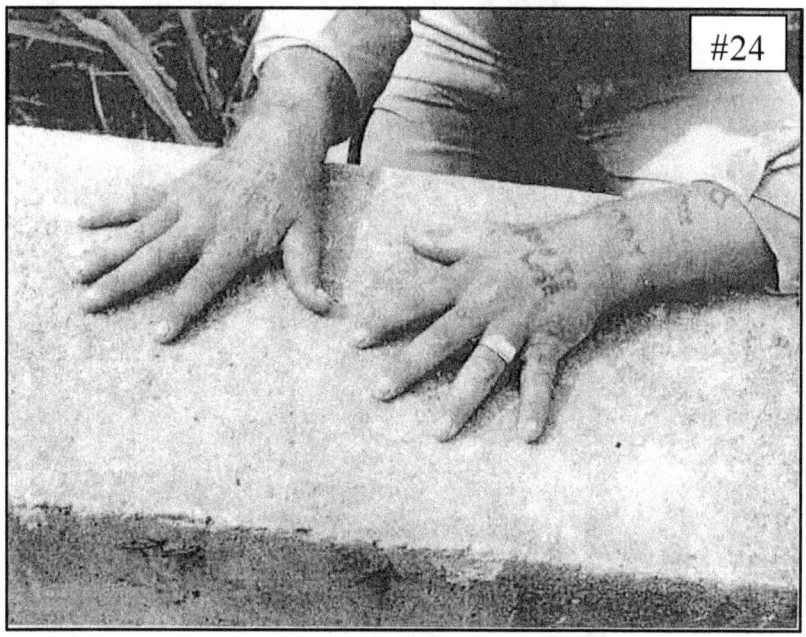

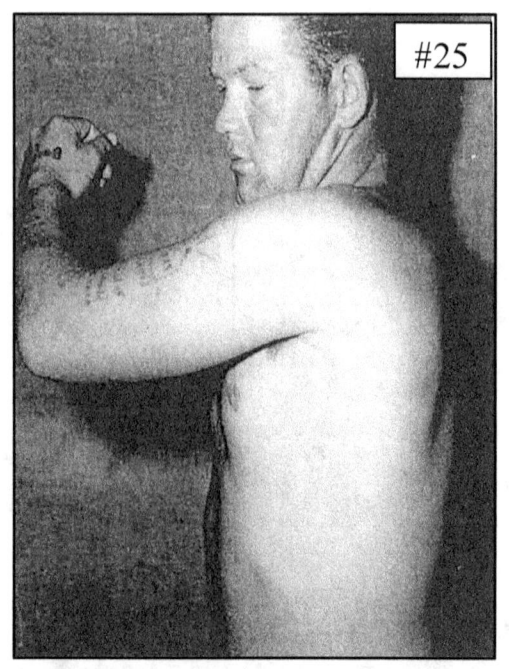

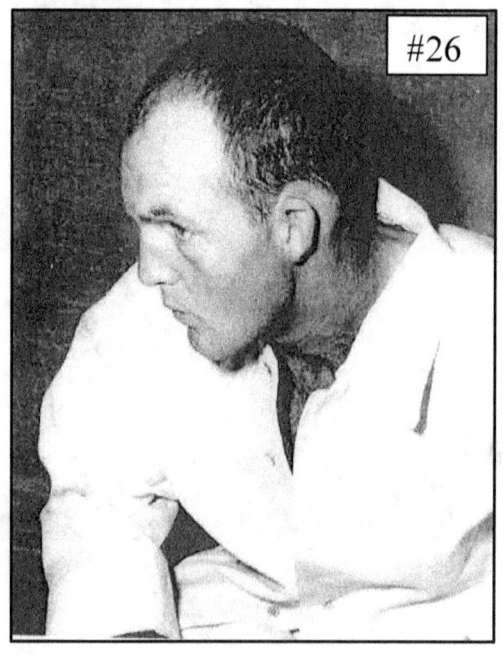

## Part III. Criminal Investigation Division Report

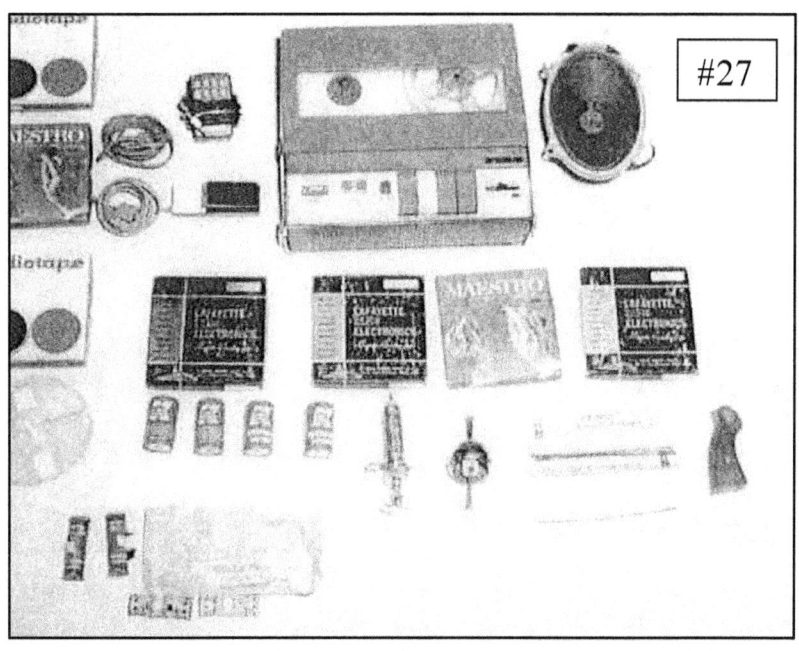

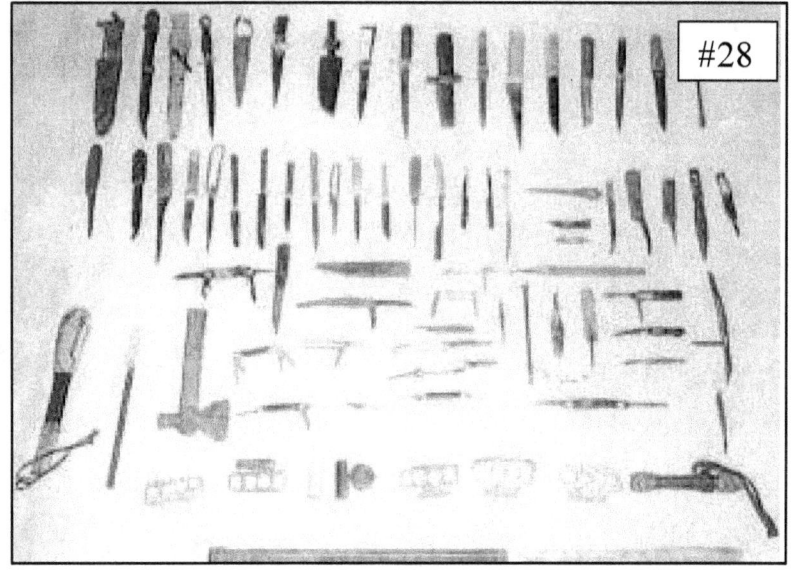

CRIES FROM THE WALLS

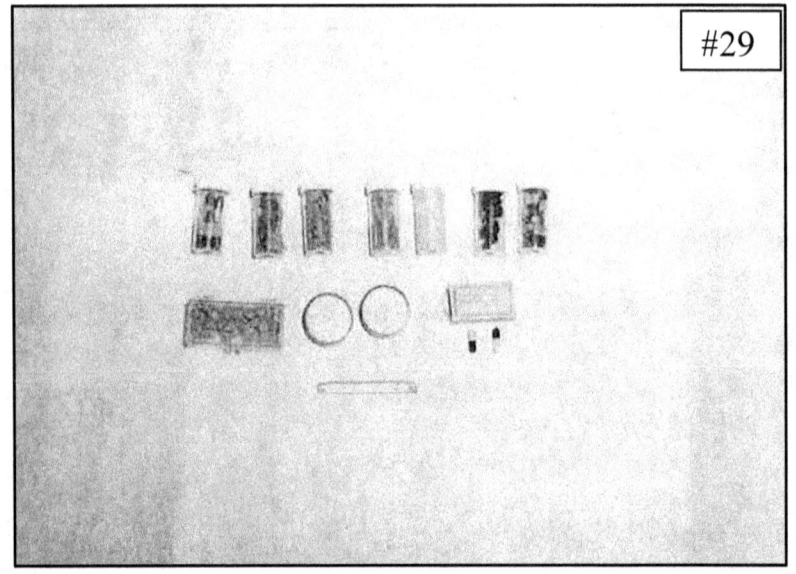

## Part III. Criminal Investigation Division Report

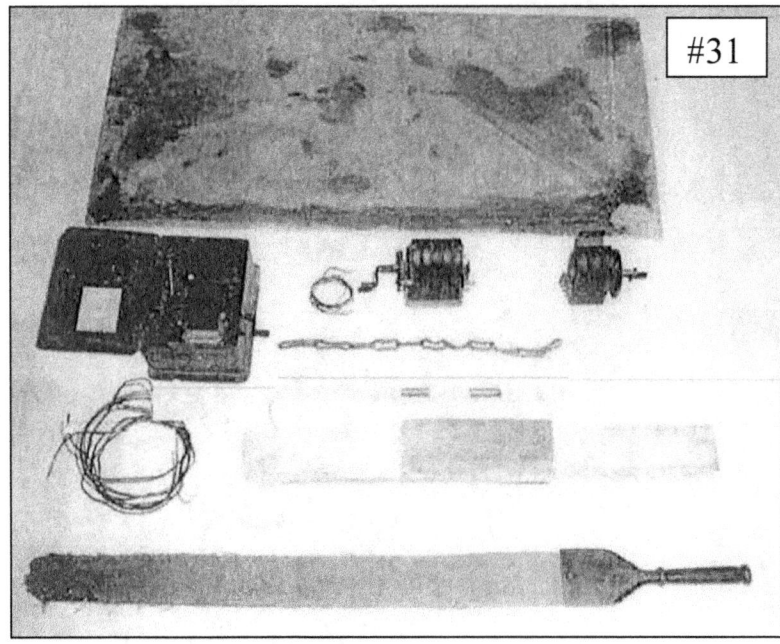

PART III. CRIMINAL INVESTIGATION DIVISION REPORT

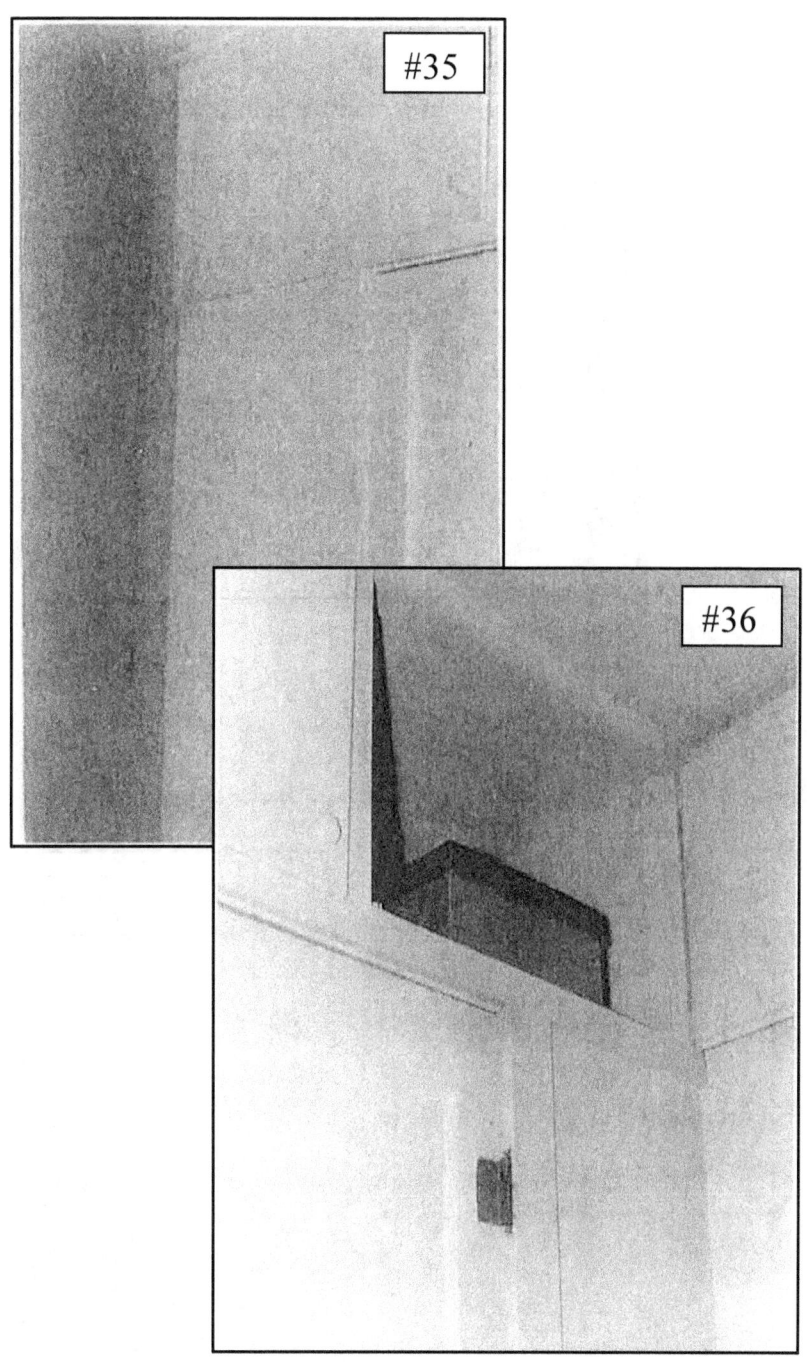

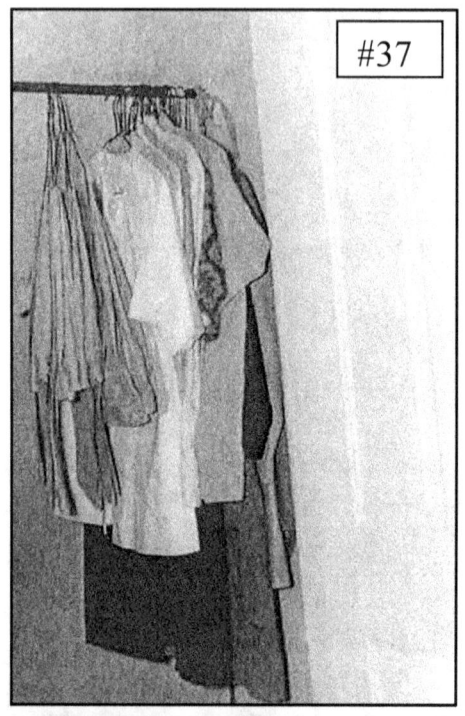

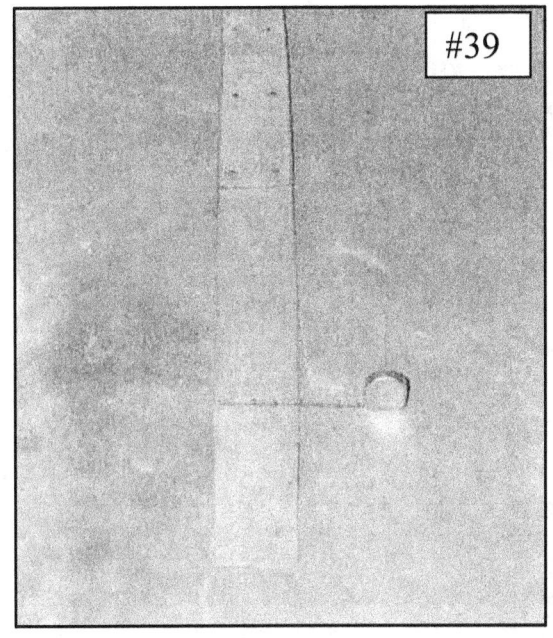

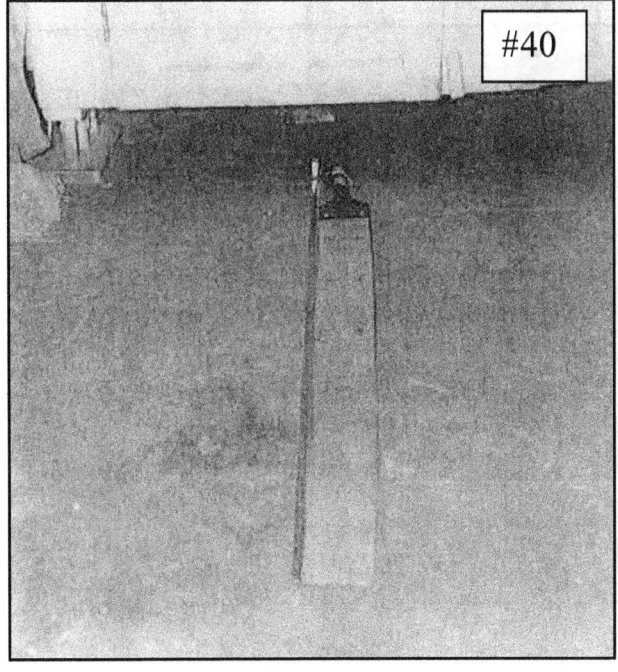

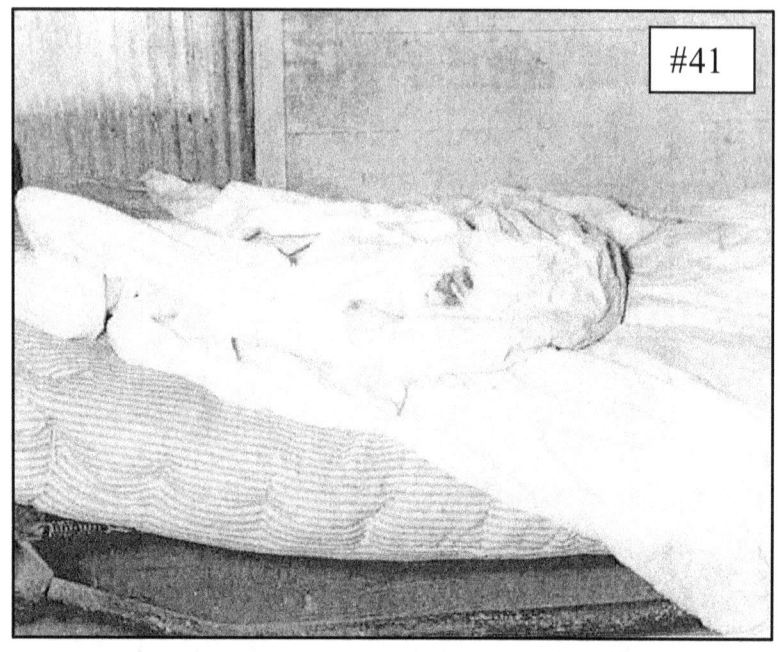

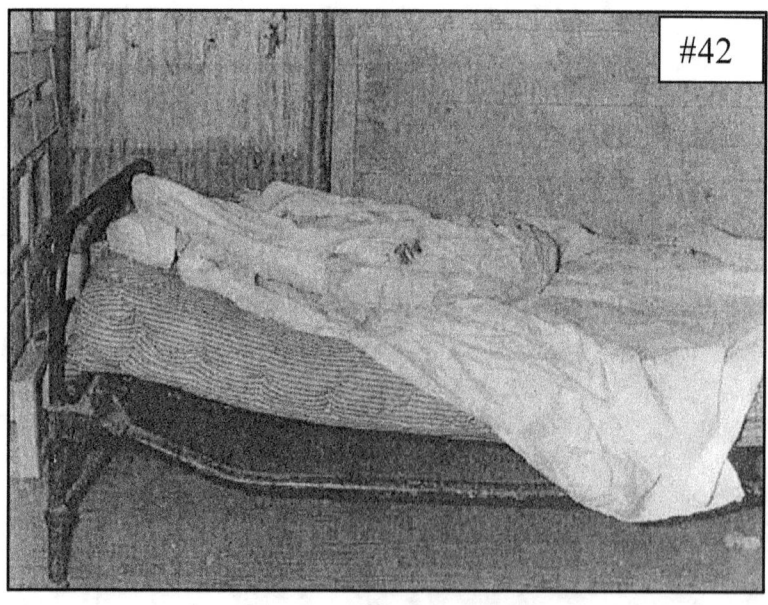

## Part III. Criminal Investigation Division Report

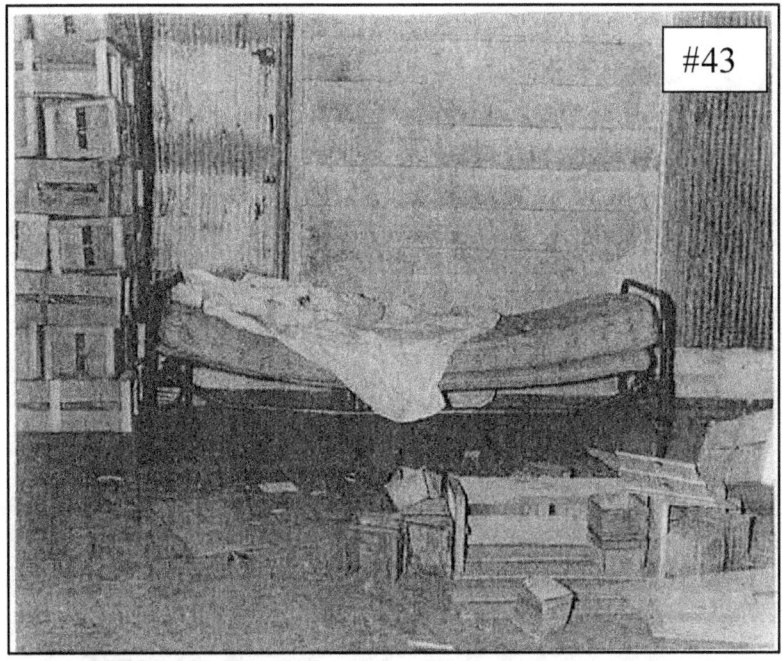

## PART III. CRIMINAL INVESTIGATION DIVISION REPORT

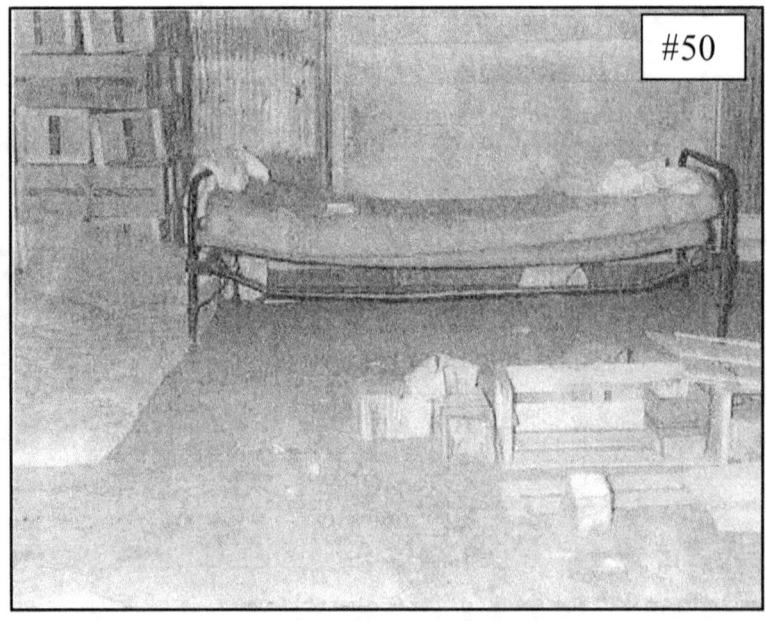

## Part III. Criminal Investigation Division Report

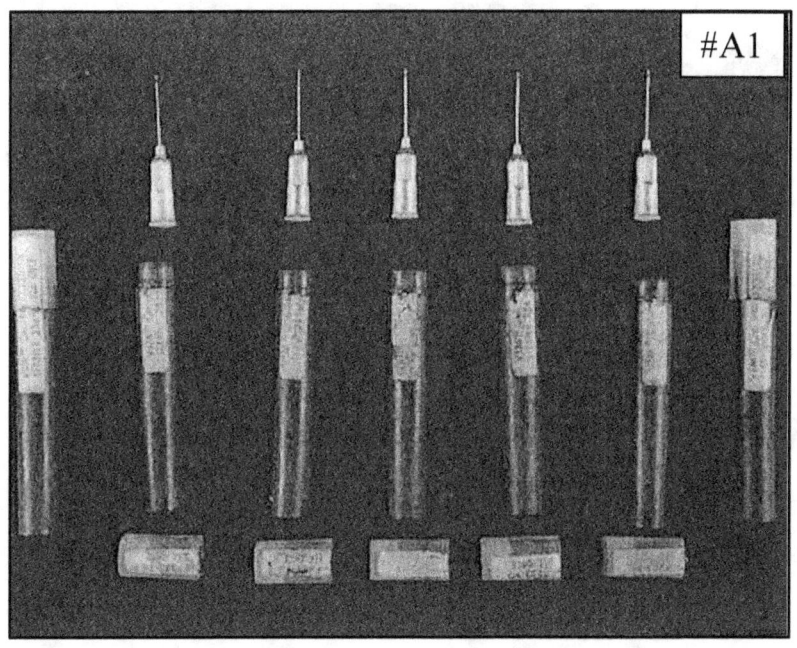

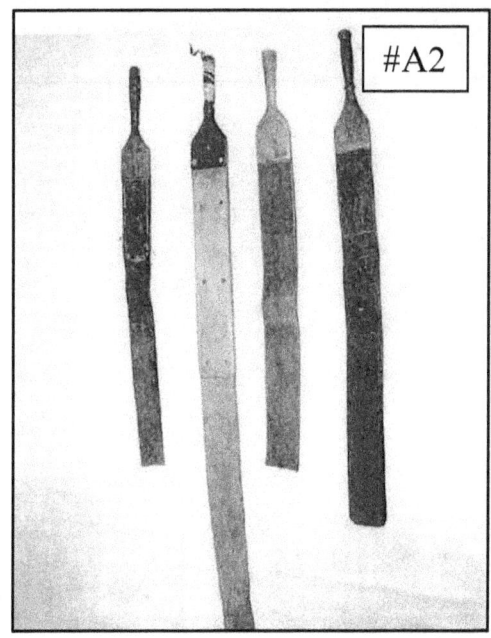

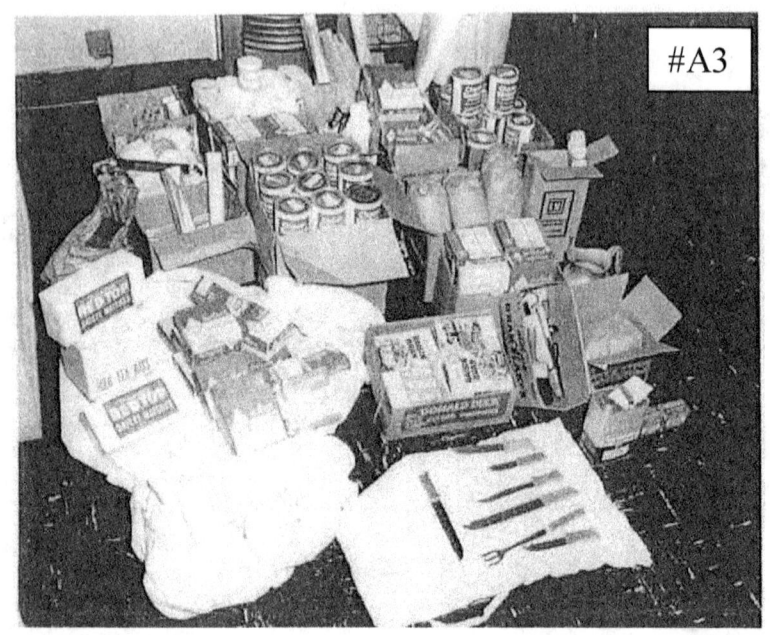

PART III. CRIMINAL INVESTIGATION DIVISION REPORT

# CID REPORT AFTERMATH

Despite this report's carefully documented conclusions, many authorities and politicians denied its accuracy. An indignant state representative, Lloyd Sadler, claimed that 95 percent of convict complaints were lies. He added, "I don't believe none of that stuff," according to the January 17, 1967, *Gazette*. Sadler's remark may be evaluated in the context of his having been for 14 years chairman of the penitentiary board. Additionally, his nephew, assistant prison superintendent Jim Bruton, became the target of numerous brutality and corruption complaints.[39]

Job-seeker Tom Murton read this CID report and met with Rockefeller to apply for a position as superintendent of Tucker. The governor hired him, and it turned into a troubled relationship that ended with acrimony.[40] Murton planned to run facilities by competent, "free world" outsiders and convicts he trained and trusted, instead of corrupt, sadistic trustees. When Murton arrived at Tucker more than a dozen unarmed state troopers served there to maintain order. His first steps included arming troopers. Murton soon formed a depressing opinion about state-wide toleration of this appalling prison system. He believed that no one wanted to know about inhumanity at Tucker. According to him, they were like Germans living near Dachau who chose not to ask what caused the constant greasy smoke from concentration camp chimneys. People living near Tucker, he said, would not believe that men they knew would participate in torture and murder, "and that's the whole problem in Arkansas. With a few rare exceptions, people refuse to acknowledge that their prisons are evil places."[41]

Murton introduced "reforms" without consulting the governor or the prison board and created enemies of virtually everyone associated with state prisons.

---

[39] Federal authorities charged Bruton with 19 counts of violating inmates' rights and torture. However, the government dropped ten charges, and a jury acquitted him on eight others. Found guilty on the last count, he received a $1,000 fine and suspended one year sentence. Laura Choate, "Prison Reform," *Encyclopedia of Arkansas* (https://encyclopediaofarkansas.net\entries/prison-reform-4159: accessed 18 Jun 2023).

[40] Tom Murton and Joe Hyams, *Accomplices to the Crime.* (New York: Grove Press, 1969). Murton served with the state prison system from January 1967 to March 1968. He arrived in Arkansas with diverse experiences in criminology, law enforcement, and management of correctional facilities. This book became a key resource for Robert Redford's film "Brubaker."

[41] *Accomplices,* 98-99. Dachau became an infamous Nazi concentration camp in southwest Germany.

He criticized Rockefeller's lack of support, and this put in motion controversies that led to Murton's termination. Events that culminated in his professional downfall began with exhumations of three bodies from unmarked graves near a prison farm. He claimed their deaths resulted from prison mistreatment. This generated extensive press coverage and made Murton a celebrity, a status he appeared to enjoy. Neither prison officials nor the governor shared his enjoyment. An irritated Rockefeller sent aides to take charge of an investigation about the three bodies. When Murton told a reporter that he planned to dig up more human remains the press turned it into major news. As negative press coverage continued, Rockefeller expressed impatience with persons taking "controversial measures" without the governor's approval. Murton's courtship with the press and resulting bad publicity ended their trust in each other.[42]

Murton asked the prison board for additional authority and threatened to resign without it. Board members refused, and his request indicated that Murton did not fully anticipate the disastrous personal consequences from this political firestorm he ignited. Politicians, prison authorities, and businessmen produced testimony that refuted Murton's claims of atrocities. A deputy state medical examiner testified to a grand jury that the three unearthed men probably died of natural causes, not physical abuse. Though Murton wanted to dig up more bodies the governor stopped exhumations and declared Murton unsuitable to lead the Department of Correction. The prison board took charge of system management, and Murton's permanent dismissal came in the form of two letters in March 1968.[43] John Haley, Rockefeller's aide who fired Murton, described what he believed had been Murton's problem. He said, "Your difficulties stem from lack of communication. And your problems ought to be kept within the family. Word of discord gets out and it's bad for the image of Arkansas. It might reflect negatively on the governor and his chances of re-election."[44]

One thing Murton and Governor Rockefeller did agree on was atrocious treatment of prisoners. In a June 1967 speech Rockefeller said, "We have probably the most barbaric prison system in the United States. Some of the tortures that are inflicted on prisoners are beyond belief. Since I have taken office, we have started a variety of things moving. . . . We have a Study

---

[42] *Accomplices*, 186.
[43] In a "History Minute" piece in the *El Dorado News-Times* on November 16, 2022, Dr. Ken Bridges described personal wreckage in the aftermath of Murton's collision with Arkansas politics. "Unable to find work, the family descended into poverty. The pressures radiating from the Arkansas prison scandals eventually caused his marriage to collapse. He and his wife divorced, and the relationship with his children was reportedly strained. He lived his final years in Oklahoma, operating a small farm and teaching sporadically. Murton died of cancer in 1990 at age 62."
[44] *Accomplices*, 139.

## Part III. Criminal Investigation Division Report

Commission working on the long-range problem of what kind of a prison system we want."[45] Despite the governor's prison reform efforts, author John L. Ward accuses Murton of issuing a "continuing stream of highly quotable criticism," not always well aimed. Murton's "almost psychopathic disregard for channels of authority and for the need to get along with those with whom he must work [plunged] Murton and the administration [into] hot water with nearly everyone but members of the press, who loved the whole thing." The governor suggested that "Murton's ego equals only his ability as a penologist."[46] Murton stirred up a caldron of trouble for a governor who ran on a reform ticket. It became a public relations debacle for the state and affected the governor's agenda.

Since the governor lacked authority to fire Murton he asked board members to do it for him, and they did. In a letter to the board Rockefeller pointed to Murton's inability to work in harmony with a governmental structure. Haley, while board of corrections chairman, on March 8, 1968, advanced reasons for Murton's removal, including managerial incompetence. It became a bitter divorce with both sides accusing each other of betrayal. However, Ward quotes Murton of having said that a true reformer must "accept each challenge with the knowledge that ultimately he would be consumed in the process."[47] Though the prison system and its allies defeated Murton's efforts to diminish their power, Judge J. Smith Henley could not be stopped.

---

[45] John L. Ward. *The Arkansas Rockefeller* (Baton Rouge: Louisiana State University Press, 1978), 103, citing WR speech in Sun Valley, Idaho, June 19, 1967, in Winthrop Rockefeller Archives.
[46] *Arkansas Rockefeller*, 104. One should keep in mind that Ward worked as director of public relations for Rockefeller from May 1964 until 1971.
[47] *Arkansas Rockefeller*, 14.

# PART IV. JUDGE J. SMITH HENLEY RULES ARKANSAS PRISONS UNCONSTITUTIONAL

The February 19, 1970, issue of the *Arkansas Democrat* reported that Federal Judge J. Smith Henley ruled conditions at Cummins and Tucker unconstitutionally cruel and unusual punishment. He issued this opinion 19 days after prisoners and free world employees testified in a hearing about practices at the facilities. The case commenced when 23 inmates complained about conditions. It became a class action on behalf of all prisoners at Tucker and Cummins. Henley gave the state Board of Correction and Correction Commissioner C. Robert Sarver until April 1 to report about their plans to achieve constitutional conditions.

The following is Henley's unabridged decision.[48]

---

[48] Born in 1917, Henley came from a Republican family in Searcy County and was not considered a reformer. He had a colorful past. He never graduated from high school, and apparently a college expelled him. However, Henley managed to graduate from the University of Arkansas law school. He went into private practice then accepted federal appointments. In 1959 Henley became a federal district judge in the Eastern and Western districts. His legal decisions put him in the vanguard of institutional litigation that placed federal judges in oversight of some troubled public facilities. Henley combined several prisoner petitions into a class action lawsuit. Litigation led to a consent decree in 1978, and in 1982 Judge G. Thomas Eisele ruled that the system had completed many improvements and planned to achieve others in order to be in compliance. Henley died in 1997. *Encyclopedia of Arkansas History & Culture.*

# *Holt v. Sarver II*, 309 F. Supp. 362, (E.D. Ark. 1970)

Lawrence J. HOLT et al., Petitioners,
v.
Robert SARVER, Commissioner of Corrections, State of Arkansas; John Haley, Payton Kolb, Marshall Rush, W. L. Currie, and William Lytle, Individually and in their capacities as Members of the Board of Corrections of the State of Arkansas, Respondents.

Travis Eugene FIELDS, Petitioner,
v.
Robert SARVER, Commissioner of Corrections, et al., Respondents.

George W. OVERTON, Petitioner,
v.
Robert SARVER, Commissioner of Corrections, et al., Respondents.

Stanley W. BROOKS et al., Petitioners,
v.
Robert SARVER, Commissioner of Corrections, et al., Respondents.

Jack Allen BARBER, Petitioner,
v.
Robert SARVER, Commissioner of Corrections, et al., Respondents.

Jerry DENHAM, Petitioner,
v.
Robert SARVER, Commissioner of Corrections, et al., Respondents.

Carlton J. CARNEY et al., Petitioners,
v.
Robert SARVER, Commissioner of Corrections, et al., Respondents.

Thomas Mitchell HILDERBRANDT, Petitioner,
v.
Robert SARVER, Commissioner of Corrections, et al., Respondents.
Nos. PB-69-C-24, 25, 29, 71, 75, 76, 80 and 91.

United States District Court, E. D. Arkansas, Pine Bluff Division.
February 18, 1970.

Jack Holt, Jr., Philip Kaplan, Little Rock, Ark., for petitioners.
Don Langston and Mike Wilson, Asst. Attys. Gen., State of Arkansas, for respondents.
**Memorandum Opinion**

HENLEY, Chief Judge.

These eight class actions have been brought by inmates of the Cummins Farm Unit of the Arkansas State Penitentiary System and the Tucker Intermediate Reformatory which is a part of that System against the members of the Arkansas State Board of Corrections and the State Commissioner of Corrections who administer the system. Plaintiffs contend on behalf of themselves and on behalf of other inmates and on behalf of other persons who may in the future be confined at Cummins or at Tucker that the forced, uncompensated farm labor exacted from Arkansas convicts for the benefit of the State is violative of the Thirteenth Amendment to the Constitution of the United States. They contend further that conditions and practices within the System are such that confinement there amounts to a cruel and unusual punishment proscribed by the Eighth Amendment to the Constitution of the United States, as carried forward into the Fourteenth Amendment. And they contend still further that unconstitutional racial segregation is being practiced within the System in violation of the Fourteenth Amendment. Federal jurisdiction is invoked under the provisions of 28 U.S.C. A. § 1343(3) and 42 U.S.C.A. § 1983.

It appearing to the Court that constitutional questions raised by the petitions submitted by the complaining inmates per sese [among themselves] were substantial, the Court appointed Messrs. Jack Holt, Jr. and Philip Kaplan of the Little Rock Bar to represent Petitioners without charge. Messrs. Holt and Kaplan accepted the appointments and have done yeoman service on behalf of their clients. The Court wishes to thank them for their efforts.

Petitioners' complaints are well summarized in Paragraph 20 of the Consolidated Amended and Substituted Complaint which is as follows:

"The actions of defendants have deprived members of the plaintiff class of rights, privileges and immunities secured to them by the due process and equal protection clauses of the Fourteenth Amendment to the Constitution of the United States, including (a) the right not to be imprisoned without meaningful rehabilitative opportunities, (b) the right to be free from cruel and unusual punishment, (c) the right to be free from arbitrary and capricious denial of rehabilitation opportunities, (d) the right to minimal due process safeguards in decisions determining fundamental liberties, (e) the right to be fed, housed, and clothed so as not to be subjected to loss of health or life, (f) the right to unhampered access to counsel and the courts, (g) the right to be free from the abuses of fellow prisoners in all aspects of daily life, (h) the right to be free from racial segregation, (i) the right to be free from forced labor, and (j) the right to be free from the brutality of being guarded by fellow inmates."

## PART IV. *HOLT V. SARVER II* (E. D. ARK. 1970)

The prayer is for a declaratory judgment to the effect that Respondents' acts, policies, and practices violate Thirteenth and Fourteenth Amendment rights and for appropriate permanent injunctive relief.

Shortly before the cases, hereinafter called collectively at times simply "the case" or "this case," were tried, Respondents, represented by Messrs. Don Langston and Mike Wilson of the Office of the Arkansas Attorney General, moved to dismiss the petitions on the ground that the case was nothing more than an effort to coerce the Arkansas Legislature into appropriating more money for the System, and that the Court was without jurisdiction to entertain such an action. The Court did not and does not so characterize the case, and the motion was denied. The Court is satisfied that it has jurisdiction under the federal statutes heretofore cited, and so finds.

On the merits, Respondents do not contend that they are operating a "good" prison or a "modern" prison. With commendable candor they concede that many of the conditions existing at the Penitentiary are bad. However, they deny that they are operating an unconstitutional prison or are engaging in unconstitutional practices. They say that they are doing the best they can with extremely limited funds and personnel. They point, justly, to the fact that over the past several years a number of significant improvements have been made within the System and they say that more are in the offing.

This case, unlike earlier cases to be mentioned which have involved specific practices and abuses alleged to have been practiced upon Arkansas convicts, amounts to an attack on the System itself. As far as the Court is aware, this is the first time that convicts have attacked an entire penitentiary system in any court, either State or federal.

The cases were consolidated for purposes of trial and were tried [in] the Court without a jury for almost an entire week. Much testimony was taken and a substantial body of documentary evidence was introduced. The Court had the benefit of the expert testimony of a recognized authority on prisons and their administration, Mr. James V. Bennett who for many years was Director of the Federal Bureau of Prisons. The Court had indirectly the benefit of the views of Mr. Austin McCormick of New York City, another recognized penologist, who is Executive Director of the Osborne Association, Inc., and who served as Chief Consultant to the Penitentiary Study Commission created by the Arkansas Legislature in 1967. (Act 22 of 1967, approved January 31, 1967.) The views of Mr. McCormick are set forth in the formal report of the Commission submitted on January 1, 1968, a copy of which report was introduced in evidence. There has also been made available to the Court a copy of a report in letter form from Dr. Charles M. Friel, Director of Research, Institute of Contemporary Corrections and the Behavioral Sciences, Sam

Houston State University, Huntsville, Texas, to the Arkansas Commission on Crime and Law Enforcement. That report is dated January 29, 1970, which date was the third day of the trial of this case. While the report was not formally introduced in evidence, it will be made part of the record, and the Court feels at liberty to consider it.

Apart from the foregoing, the Court heard the testimony of inmates and free world employees of the Penitentiary System; the Court also saw a motion picture film depicting certain prison conditions and has examined a number of photographs and other documentary material.

This Memorandum incorporates the Court's findings of fact and conclusions of law. In view of the serious nature of the case, in view of the fact that in a sense the real Respondents are not limited to those formally before the Court but include the Governor of Arkansas, the Arkansas Legislature, and ultimately the people of the State as a whole, the issues presented have been given the most careful consideration of which the Court has felt itself capable. The questions presented are grave and will be discussed fully. The Court deems it well, however, to state in advance of discussion its ultimate findings and conclusions on the constitutional issues presented.

1. The Court rejects the contention of the Petitioners that the forced, uncompensated labor of Arkansas convicts violates the Thirteenth Amendment.
2. The Court sustains the claim that conditions and practices in the Penitentiary System are such that confinement of persons therein amounts to a cruel and unusual punishment prohibited by the Eighth and Fourteenth Amendments.
3. The Court sustains the claim that to the extent that unconstitutional racial discrimination is being practiced in the System it must be eliminated.

Having so stated its findings and conclusions, the Court will proceed to discuss them and thereafter will pass to a consideration of the relief to be awarded.

## I. *Introduction*

The Arkansas Penitentiary System consists of the 16,000 acre Cummins Farm located in Lincoln County, the Tucker Intermediate Reformatory located on a 4,500 acre farm in Jefferson County; and the small Women's Reformatory located on the Cummins Farm.[1] The inmate population at Cummins now consists of somewhat less than 1,000 persons; about 325 persons most of whom are under 21 years of age are confined at Tucker. Prior to the passage of Act 377 of 1969 the Tucker Intermediate Reformatory was known simply as the Tucker Farm Unit of the Arkansas State Penitentiary. It is a much smaller institution than Cummins and its problems and those of its inmates are not nearly as severe as those existing at Cummins. For that reason discussion will be directed chiefly at Cummins, and references to the "Penitentiary" will in general be references to Cummins. Specific mention of Tucker will be made where such mention appears necessary or desirable.

The report of the Penitentiary Study Commission to which reference has been made contains as its second section a historical account of the Arkansas penal system prepared originally at some unspecified time by John L. Ferguson, State Historian, and covering the period from 1838 to 1933.

Arkansas was admitted to the Union in 1836. In 1838 the Legislature authorized the construction of a "Jail and Penitentiary," and in 1840 such an institution was constructed in the City of Little Rock. It was a jail type structure located on the present site of the Arkansas State Capitol. When it was decided to build the Capitol on its present site, the Penitentiary was moved to another location in the southwestern part of the City and became known as the Penitentiary Walls.

In 1902 the State purchased the Lincoln County lands that became Cummins Farm; some years later the smaller Tucker Farm was acquired. In 1933, due at least in part to financial stringencies imposed by the Depression, the Walls were abandoned as far as prison use was concerned, and the entire penitentiary operation was transferred to the farms. While Cummins has customarily been the headquarters of the Penitentiary System, the electric chair for executions was installed at Tucker and the cells for condemned men were located at Tucker.

Tucker was designed primarily for the confinement of young white convicts and for the confinement of both whites and Negroes awaiting execution. Negro convicts, other than those condemned to die, were confined at Cummins, and Cummins was also used as a place of confinement for more hardened white convicts.

Prior to the Civil War Arkansas convicts were leased to private employers and were frequently mistreated seriously by the lessees. There was strong public opposition to the system for both humanitarian and economic reasons and it was abolished in 1913. Since that time Arkansas convicts have been required to work for the State, and their work has consisted largely of agricultural and other manual labor for which they are paid nothing either actually or constructively.

At both Cummins and Tucker the inmate population is divided into three categories. At the bottom of the list are ordinary laboring convicts known as "rankers." At the top of the list are privileged inmates known as "trusties." Between those two categories is a third class of convicts known as "do pops;" how they came to be so called is not clear.

As indicated, most of the inmates at Tucker are young men who are not, in general, a particularly vicious lot, although there are exceptions. The Cummins population is extremely varied. Some are run-of-the-mill non-violent criminals; others are extremely violent and dangerous; many are incorrigibles; some are properly classified as either sociopathic or psychopathic, if not psychotic. A few of them have to be kept in isolation cells for 24 hours a day to protect them from other inmates or to protect other inmates from them.

Certain characteristics of the Arkansas prison system serve to distinguish it from most other penal institutions in this country. First, it has very few paid employees; armed trusties guard rank and file inmates and trusties perform other tasks usually and more properly performed by civilian or "free world" personnel. Second, convicts not in isolation are confined when not working, and are required to sleep at night in open dormitory type barracks in which rows of beds are arranged side by side; there are large numbers of men in each barracks. Third, there is no meaningful program of rehabilitation whatever at Cummins; while there is a promising and helpful program at Tucker, it is still minimal.

Prior to about 1965 the people of Arkansas as a whole knew little or nothing about their penal system although there were sporadic and sensational "exposes" from time to time about alleged conditions at the farms.

Those "exposes" created little, if any, lasting impressions on the Arkansas public. As of that time it is probably fair to say that many otherwise well informed Arkansas people viewed the Penitentiary as a self-sustaining even profit-making institution, operated by a few strong willed men who were able to make the convicts behave themselves and work; while it was recognized that the life of the convicts was probably hard, that was as it should be; they had been sent to the Penitentiary to be punished and were not entitled to lead a "country club" existence. Reports of whippings might cause passing concern which was easily allayed by the thought that the convicts who were whipped deserved to be whipped, and that a man who went down to the Penitentiary and behaved himself and did his work would be treated fairly and would get along fairly well.

That popular impression of the Penitentiary was not accurate in former years, and to the extent that it is still present it is not accurate today, as will be seen presently. However, the myth tends to be preserved by glowing reports of members of conducted tours of the farms who are shown in daylight hours what their conductors want them to see, who talk to selected convicts, and who are fed a good meal accompanied by the assurance that they are eating "just what the inmates eat."

In 1961 the Supreme Court of the United States handed down its landmark decision in the case of Monroe v. Pape, 365 U.S. 167, 81 S.Ct. 473, 5 L.Ed.2d 492, holding that old section 1979 of the Revised Statutes, derived from section 1 of the "Ku Klux Act" of 1871, and which became 42 U.S.C.A. § 1983, gave to individual citizens a viable remedy in the federal courts for deprivations of federally protected rights by persons acting under color of law.[2]

By 1965 Arkansas convicts were becoming more articulate about the conditions under which they lived than in years past and were having more success in bringing their complaints to the attention of free world authorities, including the federal courts sitting in this State.

In that year litigation about Penitentiary conditions began in this Court and has continued here and in the Court of Appeals ever since. The litigation has up to this time produced three published opinions of the District Court and two opinions of the Court of Appeals. Arranged chronologically, those opinions are: Talley v. Stephens, E.D.Ark., 247 F.Supp. 683, opinion by this writer; Jackson v. Bishop, E.D.Ark., 268 F. Supp. 804, joint opinion of Judges Gordon E. Young and Oren Harris, reversed in part, 8 Cir., 404 F.2d 571; Courtney v. Bishop, 8 Cir., 409 F.2d 1185; Holt v. Sarver, E.D.Ark., 300 F.Supp. 825, opinion by this writer and hereinafter called *Holt I*.[3]

In all of those cases, except *Courtney,* it was found that unconstitutional practices were being carried on at the Penitentiary, and injunctive relief was granted. The final result of the Talley and Jackson cases was that corporal punishment of inmates, practiced for years at the farms, was outlawed along with the use of such devices of torture as the "Tucker Telephone" and the "teeter board" [A board placed close to the ground on a pivot, with the prisoner required to stand on it and keep it balanced. Lashes landed each time it touched the ground.] In *Holt I* this Court held that the State owed a constitutional duty to inmates at Cummins to use ordinary care for their safety, and that the State had failed and was failing to discharge that duty; the Court also found that due to overcrowding confinement in the Cummins isolation cells was unconstitutional.

The decree entered in *Holt I* in the summer of 1969 brought about some improvements in conditions at Cummins, notably what appears to be an elimination of gross overcrowding in the isolation cells. However, continuing complaints from inmates of both Cummins and Tucker and disturbing information that financial difficulties might have caused a retrogression to former conditions to set in prompted the Court not to approve the report of the Commissioner filed in *Holt I* and to give further consideration to overall conditions at both institutions.

Aside from the litigation just outlined, there have been significant recent developments at the farms. In the late summer of 1966 serious trouble with inmates broke out that led to a full investigation of conditions at both farms by the Arkansas State Police and by the Federal Bureau of Investigation. That investigation plus an additional investigation brought about by another violent episode at Cummins in October 1968 produced certain prosecutions in the Circuit Court of Jefferson County, Arkansas, and in this Court.[4]

When the Legislature convened in January 1967 it promptly created the Penitentiary Study Commission. The Emergency Clause included in Act 22 of 1967 creating the Commission and directing it to make a detailed study of the farms recited that widespread publicity about the Penitentiary had "raised serious questions in the minds of public officials and the general public regarding the facilities, practices, and disciplinary procedures at the State Penitentiary and that it is necessary that a thorough study and evaluation of the penal system in Arkansas be made as soon as possible."

The Commission's study was detailed, and its report was sharply critical of many aspects of the prison system; numerous reforms were recommended. Responding to the report, the Legislature in special session in early 1968 adopted Act 50 of that year, a sweeping statute dealing with the prison system and which recognized that training and rehabilitation should be essential objectives of the farms. That Act, among other things, created the Department of Corrections which took the place of the old Penitentiary Board.

The legislation adopted in 1967 and 1968 and Act 377 of 1969 establishing the Tucker Intermediate Reformatory are forward looking; but at least as yet they have not had any significant impact on the distinctive characteristics of the Arkansas penal system mentioned heretofore.

Returning now to this case, the testimony of Director Bennett, the report of the Study Commission, and the 1969 report of Dr. Friel to the Commission on Crime and Law Enforcement, are all to the effect that the Arkansas Penitentiary System is substandard and outmoded when measured by accepted penological standards, and that improvements are needed in many areas. Commissioner Sarver himself has come forward with sweeping recommendations for radical improvements to be made over a period of about ten years.

The Court, however, is limited in its inquiry to the question of whether or not the constitutional rights of inmates are being invaded and with whether the Penitentiary itself is unconstitutional. The Court is not judicially concerned with questions which in the last analysis are addressed to legislative and administrative judgment. A practice that may be bad from the standpoint of penology may not necessarily be forbidden by the Constitution. And a prison system that would be excellent from the point of view of a modern prison administrator may not be required by the provisions of the Constitution with which the Court is concerned.

## II. *The Thirteenth Amendment Claim*

The Court takes up first the Thirteenth Amendment contention of Petitioners. Some facts relevant to that claim have been stated already; other facts to be stated are relevant not only to the Thirteenth Amendment claim but also to Petitioners' claims based on the Fourteenth Amendment.

The Thirteenth Amendment, adopted immediately after the Civil War, provides explicitly that:

"Neither slavery nor involuntary servitude, except as a punishment for crime whereof the party shall have been duly convicted, shall exist within the United States, or any place subject to their jurisdiction."

The purpose of the Amendment was, of course, to abolish African slavery and practices related or analogous thereto. It will be observed that the Thirteenth Amendment, unlike the Fourteenth and certain other Amendments, is more than a prohibition upon the States. The Thirteenth Amendment abolishes slavery and involuntary servitude, except as punishment for crime, everywhere in the United States, its Territories, and possessions.

The Thirteenth Amendment claim with which the Court is concerned relates primarily to the requirement that Arkansas convicts work for long hours without pay in the fields on the farms for the financial benefit of the State. Not all rank and file Arkansas convicts are required to perform labor of that type, but substantial numbers of them are. As in other contexts, the principal problem is at Cummins. That is true because the farming operation now being conducted at Tucker is limited to the production of food for inmate consumption. Tucker farmlands not used for that purpose have been leased to private operators.

Cummins Farm is located on fertile land well adapted to producing just about any kind of crop that can be grown in Arkansas. The principal crops produced on the farm are cotton, soybeans, rice, vegetables, fruits, and berries. Other substantial farm operations include livestock, dairying, and poultry production.

According to the report of the Study Commission, there were 9,070 acres of land in cultivation at Cummins as of December 15, 1967. As of the same date the Farm had 2,070 cattle, 800 hogs, 40 horses, 160 mules, and 1,600 poultry.

Again according to the Commission, during 1967, 60 percent of the cultivated acreage at Cummins was devoted to crops raised for sale on the market; 30 percent to crops that supported the livestock and poultry; and 10 percent to garden vegetables and other crops for the feeding of civilian personnel and inmates.

The Commission's report reflects that with respect to the fiscal year ending June 30, 1966, the Penitentiary, both farms apparently, derived an income of $1,415,419.43 from the sale of crops, including field crops, vegetables, fruit, and pecans; the corresponding figure for the year ending June 30, 1967, was $1,242,191.38. Sales of farm products other than crops amounted to $213,561.22 for fiscal '66 and to $131,806.13 for fiscal '67.

Total receipts of the Penitentiary from all sources for fiscal '66 was $1,763,487.09 and total expenditures came to $1,473,497.70. Corresponding figures for fiscal '67 were $1,566,712.76 and $1,785,570.33.

The December 15, 1967, inventory of equipment at Cummins, appearing at page 6.09 of the Commission's report, indicates that there has been substantial mechanization of the Farm's operation. However, the evidence reflects that much of the work is still done by hand, and the fact that in 1967 the Farm owned 160 mules indicates that a good deal of power utilized at the Farm is "mule power."

In 1967 the Farm had a cotton allotment of 962 acres worked largely by hand, and the production of fruits and vegetables involves a great deal of what is commonly called "stooped labor."

Men assigned to the fields are required to work long hours six days a week, except for a few holidays, if weather permits. They are worked regardless of heat, and summers can be very hot at Cummins; in the winter they are not required to work when the temperature is below freezing, but they are required to work in merely bad or wet weather regardless of the season of the year. The men are not supplied by the State with particularly warm clothing for winter work, nor are they furnished any bad weather gear. There is evidence that at times men have been sent to the fields without shoes or with inadequate shoes.

## Part IV. Holt v. Sarver II (E. D. Ark. 1970)

The field work is arduous and is particularly onerous in the case of men who have had no previous experience in chopping and picking cotton or in harvesting vegetables, fruits, and berries. What skills they may acquire in connection with their field work are of very little, if any, value to them when they return to the free world.

Naturally, the inmates do not like to work in the fields. Prior to the decision of the Court of Appeals in *Jackson,* supra, most of them could be forced to do so by applications of the strap. Now there is no sanction, except confinement in isolation, to compel the men to work, and many of them are willing to undergo solitary confinement in order to avoid field work.

Rankers assigned to work in the fields do so in groups known as "long lines." The numbers of men in long lines may vary considerably. Theoretically, each long line is under the supervision of a free world employee known as a field warden. Actually, the rankers are under the immediate and direct supervision of trusties known as "long line riders" and inmate "pushers." As his name implies, the long line rider is a mounted man who rides back and forth among the working men. Since he is in very close proximity to the rankers and is somewhat vulnerable to attack from them, he ordinarily does not carry a firearm, although he may do so on occasions. The real guarding of the rankers in the field is done by other trusties armed either with high powered rifles and known as "high powers," or with shotguns and known, logically, as "shotguns."

According to the Study Commission's report, a long line at Cummins on a typical date might be made up of, say, 56 rankers, nine trusty guards, and a long line rider. The perimeter of the plot in which the rankers are working is occupied by guards armed with rifles; guards armed with shotguns work in closer proximity to the rankers.

If a ranker tries to escape, the trusties are instructed to fire one warning shot into the air; if the ranker persists in his effort to get away, the trusties fire at him to "stop" him; it makes no difference whether he is killed or not. Whether a ranker is trying to escape is at times subject to question, and the question is answered summarily by the guards. Thus, a ranker who unwittingly strays across an imaginary deadline may be fired upon. In addition to running the risk of being shot by an overzealous guard or by one with merely poor judgment there is always the possibility that a guard will deliberately murder an inmate on the pretense that he was trying to escape.

As stated, the men are paid nothing for their work. If an inmate wants to earn money legitimately in his spare time while in the Penitentiary, there are only two ways in which he can do it. The inmates as a class are permitted to have an Inmate Welfare Fund which operates a commissary type store and which also operates a blood bank. Profits from the store and the blood bank inure to the Fund which, parenthetically, appears as of this moment to have more money available to it than Respondents have available to them to run the Penitentiary. A very limited number of inmates are employed in the store and are paid small monthly salaries. Other inmates can sell their blood once a week at the blood bank and receive $5 per visit. The inmates refer to selling their blood as "bleeding at the blood bank." However, not all inmates are permitted to "bleed" and, hence, cannot earn the $5; for example, the bank will not accept blood from an inmate with a morbid condition of the liver.

What small comforts and luxuries the inmates have legitimately are not furnished by the State but by the Welfare Fund, and it is the Fund, not the State, that gives a departing inmate the nominal sum of $25 to see him on his way.

Director Bennett testified that inmates of federal prisons and of many State prisons can earn legitimate although usually very low wages while confined. He thinks that such wage payments are desirable for several reasons: they give a man an incentive to work; they improve his morale; they enable him to be of some assistance to his dependents; and they perhaps enable him to build up a small stake for himself against the day on which he is to be released from prison. Mr. Bennett conceded, however, that there are still some States, like Arkansas, that pay their convicts nothing.

The picture of working conditions at Cummins that has been painted is not attractive, and the system would not be called humane by modern standards. But, the question for decision at this moment is whether the system is prohibited by the Thirteenth Amendment.

The Arkansas system of working convicts is not "slavery" in the constitutional sense of the term. The State does not claim to own the bodies of its prisoners. The situation does involve "servitude," and there is no doubt whatever that the "servitude" is "involuntary."

But, it is equally clear that this servitude has been imposed as punishment for crimes whereof the inmates have been duly convicted. Conceding that the work required is hard and tedious, that it is performed under harsh conditions, that the State requires it to produce income for the State, and that the system serves little other purpose, if any, the Court is not persuaded that the system violates the Thirteenth Amendment.

According to Director Bennett, the idea that prisons and prisoners ought to support themselves is as old as American penology. He referred to the fact that the convict-leasing system came into existence at a very early stage as the States found that it was more profitable to lease their convicts than to work them themselves. And he pointed out that one of the best descriptions of the leasing system is to be found in Margaret Mitchell's Civil War novel, "Gone With The Wind."

When Congress submitted the Thirteenth Amendment to the States, it must have been aware of generally accepted convict labor policies and practices, and the Court is persuaded that the Amendment's exception manifested a Congressional intent not to reach such policies and practices.

Heflin v. Sanford, 5 Cir., 142 F.2d 798, is instructive on this phase of the case although it did not involve convict labor. Heflin, a conscientious objector, was ordered to report for work of national importance during World War II; his compensation would have been but nominal. He refused to report and was sent to the penitentiary for violating the Selective Service Act. On habeas corpus he contended that to require him to do work of national importance with little or no pay amounted to prohibited slavery and involuntary servitude. His contention was rejected. The Court pointed out that there is a difference between "involuntary servitude" and "uncompensated service," and that the Thirteenth Amendment prohibits the one, except as punishment for crime, but does not prohibit the other.

### III. *Fourteenth Amendment Claim — Cruel and Unusual Punishment.*

The Eighth Amendment to the Constitution of the United States prohibits the infliction of "cruel and unusual punishments." Originally a restriction on the federal government, it has been held that the Eighth Amendment has been carried forward into the Fourteenth Amendment, Robinson v. California, 370 U.S. 660, 82 S.Ct. 1417, 8 L.Ed.2d 758, and it was on the basis of the Eighth Amendment that relief was granted in *Talley, Jackson,* and *Holt I,* all supra.

An individual convict may, of course, be subjected to a cruel and unusual punishment actually inflicted on him personally, as by his being beaten with the Penitentiary strap, or by being shocked electrically by the Tucker Telephone, or by being compelled to stand upon the "teeter board" for long periods of time, or by other means of punishment or torture.

It appears to the Court, however, that the concept of "cruel and unusual punishment" is not limited to instances in which a particular inmate is subjected to a punishment directed at him as an individual. In the Court's estimation confinement itself within a given institution may amount to a cruel and unusual punishment prohibited by the Constitution where the confinement is characterized by conditions and practices so bad as to be shocking to the conscience of reasonably civilized people even though a particular inmate may never personally be subject to any disciplinary action. To put it another way, while confinement, even at hard labor and without compensation, is not considered to be necessarily a cruel and unusual punishment it may be so in certain circumstances and by reason of the conditions of the confinement. That is certainly the law in the case of prisoners confined in isolation, Courtney v. Bishop, supra, *Holt I,* supra, and cases there cited; and the Court sees no reason why it is not the law in cases of prisoners confined "in population," as it is called.

In the instant case Petitioners contend that overall conditions in the Arkansas penal system, including but not limited to those relating to inmate safety, may be so bad that it amounts to an unconstitutional cruel and unusual punishment to expose men to those conditions, regardless of how those conditions may operate fortuitously on particular individuals. Is that contention sustained by the evidence?

The distinguishing aspects of Arkansas penitentiary life must be considered together. One cannot consider separately a trusty system, a system in which men are confined together in large numbers in open barracks, bad conditions in the isolation cells, or an absence of a meaningful program of rehabilitation. All of those things exist in combination; each affects the other; and taken together they have a cumulative impact on the inmates regardless of their status. That should be borne in mind as one reads the following descriptions of the trusty system, the barracks system, the isolation cells, and other aspects of prison life.

Again, these descriptions are based primarily on conditions at Cummins. They are based on a large volume of testimony much of which was really a repetition of what the Court heard when it tried *Holt I.*

### The Trusty System.

No one questions the propriety or desirability of according trusty status to deserving convicts, and perhaps all prisons do. But the trusty system as it exists in Arkansas is *sui generis.* The trusties run the prison. They not only guard other inmates; they also perform many administrative tasks normally performed by free world people, and their authority over other convicts of lesser rank is great. Commissioner Sarver testified without contradiction that more than 90 percent of prison functions relating to inmates are performed by trusties. The few free world people are only nominally in command of the situation at Cummins, and the trusties could take it over in a moment. Perhaps the reason they do not do so is that they do not want to spoil a good thing.

## Part IV. *Holt v. Sarver II* (E. D. Ark. 1970)

The extent of Arkansas' reliance on trusties is apparent when it is realized that there are only 35 free world employees at Cummins in ostensible charge of slightly less than 1,000 men. Of those 35 only eight are available for guard duty, and only two of them are on duty at night.

The use of trusty guards is universally condemned by penologists, and the system is now in use only in Arkansas, Louisiana, and Mississippi. According to Director Bennett, the reliance that Louisiana places upon trusty guards is much less than that which exists in Arkansas. He did not testify with respect to Mississippi. The reasons for penological disapproval of the use of trusty guards are that it creates an unhealthy prison climate and atmosphere; it breeds fear and hatred between the guards, on the one hand, and those guarded, on the other hand; it tends to be brutal and to endanger the lives of inmates who live and work "under the guns" of other convicts; and it leads to other abuses.

In this connection it may be observed that some inmates of the Penitentiary have refused to accept trusty guard status due to their feeling that it is "wrong" for one convict to guard another and to their fear of what might happen to them should they ever be demoted to the ranks. And Mr. Bennett testified that when he was head of the Bureau of Prisons, it was frequently necessary to take strong protective measures with respect to inmates of federal prisons who had formerly been trusty guards in Arkansas.

Apart from the use of trusties as guards, they can be given too much authority in other areas of prison life. When that is done, various abuses come into existence. When all is said and done, the fact remains that a trusty is a convict, and many trusties will on occasions act like felons and thieves. They will take bribes, they will engage in extortion, they will smuggle contraband, and they will connive at violations of prison rules. Opportunity for abuse is particularly present where, as in Arkansas, trusties have access to prison records pertaining to themselves and to other inmates. A trusty with such access can remove damaging material, such as a detainer, from an inmate's file; he can insert improper material; or he can impart to other inmates confidential information that ought not to be imparted. The undesirability of having prison telephone communications with the outside world in the control of trusties, as it is in Arkansas, is too obvious to require description.

This does not mean that trusties should never be given responsible jobs. One of the chief functions of rehabilitation is to teach convicts to assume and discharge responsibilities. But, it does mean that the areas of trusty responsibility should be limited, and that the trusties, both individually and as a body, should be under the full control and adequate supervision of free world people.

The danger of excessive reliance on trusties was discussed fully in the report of the Study Commission, and one of the recommendations of the Commission was that the system be retained "insofar as it conforms to the type found in the better American state and federal prisons," but that "trusties no longer be given duties, responsibilities or authority that should be given only to civilian employees who can be held legally responsible."

As the Court's description of the trusty system in Arkansas proceeds, it will be seen, to the extent that it has not become apparent already, that just about every abuse which the system is capable of producing has been produced and is being practiced in this State.

An inmate gets to be a trusty in Arkansas by promotion from the ranks or from "do pop" status. While promotions and demotions are formally made by committees of free world personnel, as a practical matter such actions are usually based uncritically on initial recommendations of trusties. In the case of a field worker, the recommendation is usually made by a long line rider.

Actually, few, if any, objective criteria are used in selecting trusties; that a man is a bad man, or a dangerous man, or that he has a bad criminal record is by no means a disqualification; on the contrary, it may be a recommendation. In the case of a trusty guard probably the principal criterion of promotion is his willingness to prevent escapes and support the free world people vis a vis the general inmate population, shooting to kill if necessary to achieve those objectives. A trusty is not expected to take any steps to protect an inmate from violence at the hands of another inmate, and the trusties do not do so.

In a very real sense trusty guards have the power of life and death over other inmates. Some guards are doubtless men of some judgment and humanity; others are not. It is within the power of a trusty guard to murder another inmate with practical impunity, and the danger that such will be done is always clear and present. Very recently a gate guard killed another inmate "carelessly." One wonders. And there is evidence that recently a guard on night duty fired a shotgun into a crowded barracks because the inmates would not turn off their television set. In any event, the rankers live in deadly fear of the guards and entertain deadly hatred for them, and their feelings are reciprocated fully.

The Study Commission recommended that the guard system be phased out as soon as possible, starting with the trusties guarding field workers. The Court thinks that that is a good recommendation, but the trusty guard system itself, bad as it is, does not give the Court as much trouble as do other facets of the overall trusty system.

## Part IV. *Holt v. Sarver II* (E. D. Ark. 1970)

By virtue of their positions of authority and the functions they perform trusties can make or break rankers and "do pops." They can make prison life tolerable or they can make it unbearably hard. They can and do sell favors, easy jobs, and coveted positions; they can and do extort money from inmates on any and all pretexts. They operate rackets within the prison, involving among other things the forcing of inmates to buy from them things like coffee at exorbitant prices. They lend money to rankers and then use force or threats of force to collect the debts.

Controlling the slaughter house, the kitchen, and the prison stores, trusties steal food and other commodities from the institution and then sell them to other inmates. An inmate can eat well at the Penitentiary if he can pay for what he gets; if he cannot pay, he eats as regular issue what the trusties have seen fit to leave.

Trusties have rather broad privileges about leaving the farms. Coming back they bring with them weapons, liquor, and drugs which they sell to less privileged inmates. As might be expected liquor is much in demand, and its price is high. A pint of taxpaid whiskey sells for $10, much more than twice its free world price.

When a new inmate arrives at the Penitentiary, about the first person to interview him is a trusty who frequently starts out to relieve him by threats or promises of what money and property he may possess.

An enterprising trusty who makes the most of his opportunities can do quite well for himself. Some do so well that they do not want to leave the institution. While it can hardly be said that the trusty system in Arkansas is a "free" enterprise system, it is certainly a capitalistic system with some of the worst features commonly attributed to "Mafia" techniques in organized crime.

One of the worst features of the system is that the trusties form a living barrier between ordinary inmates and institutional facilities and services that are available and to which an inmate ought to be able to have access as a matter of course. If a ranker can pay or is on good terms with the trusties, he can get what he needs when he needs it; he can get to the infirmary when the doctor is there; he can get prescribed medications. If he cannot pay or does not get along with the trusties, the case is far otherwise.

Additionally, inmate access to free world personnel too often depends on trusty good will, whim, or caprice. This Court has long been convinced that many of the complaints that it receives from inmates stem from a simple lack of communication between the complainants and civilian personnel, the lack being due to trusty interference or indifference.

Not only can the trusties prevent a ranker from getting into contact with a civilian employee; they can and frequently do bring unmerited discipline down on the head of a ranker by "writing him up" for unsatisfactory work or for refusal to work; their reports are frequently, if not usually, taken at face value by the employees to whom they are made.

In fairness to the trusties it should perhaps be said that their roses are not without thorns. Just as a trusty can make or break a ranker, so can he be broken or demoted by a superior trusty or by free world personnel. And if he is demoted to the ranks, he is at the tender mercy of those whom he may have persecuted or exploited, and it may become necessary to put him in isolation for his own protection.

Before leaving its description of the trusty system, the Court will say that it has not overlooked the fact that many of the abuses practiced by trusties could also be practiced by free world personnel, but the Court thinks that free world people, carefully selected and properly paid, would be far less likely to commit such abuses than are the felons now holding positions of authority.

### *Life In The Barracks.*

The report of the Study Commission reflects that there are eight barracks at Cummins and three at Tucker. Only five of the barracks at Cummins appear to be in use at the present time perhaps due to the fact that the population of Cummins is lower now than it has been in years past. White trusties occupy one barracks; Negro trusties occupy another barracks; white rankers have a barracks of their own; and Negro rankers have a barracks of their own. At the present time "do pops" at Cummins have their own barracks; the record does not disclose whether there are any Negro "do pops." The Commission's report indicates that when "do pops" are not sleeping in their own barracks, they are housed with rankers.

A barracks is nothing more than a large dormitory surrounded by bars; the barracks are separated from each other by wide hallways, and the complex of hallways is referred to as the "yard." At the present time the barracks house more than 100 men each assigned without regard to anything but rank and race. The inhabitants of a given barracks have free access to each other at all times. Only two free world people are on duty in the yard at night. Inmate "floor walkers" are stationed inside the barracks proper for the purpose of keeping order and reporting disturbances. In their barracks the trusties are not armed except with their own knives which they continually keep at hand;

however, there are probably one or more armed trusties in picket posts within the barracks building.

In *Holt I* the Court discussed life in the Cummins barracks in some detail; it was said (pp. 830-831 of 300 F.Supp.):

"Prisoners who are not confined in the isolation unit sleep in open barracks. There are two barracks for trusties and two for `dopops' and rankers. Those barracks amount to enclosed dormitories in which the inmates sleep on cots arranged in rows. At night there are one or more free world guards on duty outside the barracks proper, but they are not actually inside the sleeping area. Those areas are supposedly patrolled by inmate `floorwalkers' whose duty it is to report disturbances to the guards.

"Since the inmates sleep together in the barracks, an inmate has ready access to any other inmate sleeping in the same barracks. Many of the inmates have weapons of one sort or another, and the evidence indicates that in spite of efforts to do so it is impossible from a practical standpoint to prevent inmates from having small weapons such as knives or scissors in their possession.

"At times deadly feuds arise between particular inmates, and if one of them can catch his enemy asleep it is easy to crawl over and stab him. Inmates who commit such assaults are known as `crawlers' and `creepers,' and other inmates live in fear of them. The Court finds that the `floorwalkers' are ineffective in preventing such assaults; they are either afraid to call the guards or, in instances, may be in league with the assailants.

"The undisputed evidence is to the effect that within the last 18 months there have been 17 stabbings at Cummins, all but one of them taking place in the barracks, and four of them producing fatal results. At least two of the petitioners now in isolation have been assailants in stabbing incidents and others have been the victims of such incidents.

"Respondent and his subordinates deplore the situation just described but insist that until the maximum security unit can be put into use there is nothing that they can do about it. Respondent testified that when he was the head of a penitentiary in another State convicts there slept in individual cells and there were 170 paid guards; he also testified that the incidence of stabbings at Cummins was no higher than that at the other institution he had headed. He conceded, however, that more free world guards at Cummins might ameliorate the situation somewhat.

"The Court recognizes, of course, that assaults, fights, stabbings, and killings may and do occur in penal institutions that are unquestionably well equipped, well staffed, and well managed. It occurs to the Court, however, that such incidents in such institutions take place in spite of all reasonable precautions taken by prison authorities. At Cummins there are no precautions worthy of the name, and the `creepers' and `crawlers' take deadly advantage of that fact.

"The Court is of the view that if the State of Arkansas chooses to confine penitentiary inmates in barracks with other inmates, they ought at least to be able to fall asleep at night without fear of having their throats cut before morning, and that the State has failed to discharge a constitutional duty in failing to take steps to enable them to do so."

Conditions in those barracks have not changed significantly since *Holt I* was decided, except that there has been a decline in the rate of stabbings. There is, however, something more to be said about the barracks in the light of the evidence produced in this case.

The Court heard much testimony about homosexuality in the barracks and elsewhere at Cummins. Homosexuality probably is practiced in all prisons in the United States, and there is a great deal of it practiced at Cummins, some consensual, a great deal nonconsensual. An inmate who is physically attractive to other men may be, and frequently is, raped in the barracks by other inmates. No one comes to his assistance; the floor walkers do not interfere; the trusties look on with indifference or satisfaction; the two free world people on duty appear to be helpless.

Inmates who are passively homosexual are called "punks." There are varieties of "punks," including the "pressure punks" who will engage in homosexual acts if more or less pressure is put upon them to induce or compel them to do so.

In an effort to protect young men from sexual assaults, they are generally assigned to the two rows of cots nearest the front bars of the barracks, which portion of the barracks is called "punk row." It appears, however, that if would-be assailants really want a young man, his being assigned to the "row" is no real protection to him.

To the extent that consensual homosexual acts take place in the barracks, they are not carried out in any kind of privacy but in the full sight and hearing of all of the other inmates.

Sexual assaults, fights, and stabbings in the barracks put some inmates in such fear that it is not unusual for them to come to the front of the barracks and cling to the bars all night. That practice, which is of doubtful value is called "coming to the bars" or "grabbing the bars." Clearly, a man who has clung to the bars all night is in poor condition to work the next day.

Conditions in the barracks are worsened by the prevalent consumption of liquor and beer and by the use of drugs. It is not uncommon for many, if not all, of the inmates of a particular barracks to become intoxicated by drugs and alcohol all at the same time. The resulting commotion, violence, and confusion are quite imaginable. The free world people cannot control the situation; the trusties will not and are not supposed to; and the floor walkers frequently participate in the orgies.

All of this is not to say that a barracks system of confinement properly regulated and limited may not have a place in a well run penal institution. If barracks assignments are confined to small groups of men, properly classified and selected and subject to adequate control, the barracks system is not objectionable and in certain respects may be preferable to confinement in individual cells. It is obvious, however, that the Cummins barracks do not satisfy those conditions.

### *The Isolation Cells.*

The isolation cells at Cummins, located in a building set apart to itself and surrounded by a fence, were considered by the Court in *Holt I*. They were found to be overcrowded, filthy, and unsanitary. Pursuant to the Court's order in that case, the overcrowding seems to have been ameliorated; the other conditions still exist.

The Study Commission's report refers to the existence of 12 isolation cells and the construction of 28 more. After the Commission's report was filed, the Legislature authorized the construction of a maximum security unit at Cummins which will be in operation, hopefully, in 1971. After that authorization was given, construction of the additional isolation cells was halted. While there are 12 cells in the isolation unit, one of them has been fitted up as a shower room so that actually there are only 11 cells for the confinement of prisoners.

The isolation unit is guarded by trusties, and free world people seldom come around it. That situation is a source of constant trouble. The trusties threaten and harass the prisoners, and the prisoners probably reciprocate in kind. The isolation diet is carelessly served to the inmates of the cells and at times is permitted to become cold and wet.

The cells are occupied by prisoners who have been confined there for disciplinary reasons or for "protective custody." The isolation inmates who are in "protective custody" are some of the most incorrigible and dangerous prisoners in the Penitentiary. They are sociopathics [sic] with no constructive motivation whatever. They damage and destroy fixtures in the cells to the extent of their ability to do so; they set fire to their bedding and to their clothing. They take no interest in the conditions of the cells except to complain about them. They refuse to obey at times the lawful orders of free world people, and obedience has to be compelled by force exerted by free world people and trusty guards; the inmates resist violently and then complain about their "ill treatment."

As the Court understands it, the isolation cells at Tucker are located in the main building of the institution. Some of them are, or at least have been from time to time, occupied by Cummins inmates sent to Tucker for protective custody. The condition of the Tucker isolation cells is about the same as that of the Cummins cells, except that the Tucker cells are inexcusably infested by rats, a problem that does not seem to be particularly troublesome at Cummins.

In view of the fact that the isolation cells are no longer grossly overcrowded, and in view of the fact that most of the conditions existing therein are due to the conduct of the inmates themselves, the cells do not give the Court as serious a constitutional problem as do other aspects of Penitentiary life.

### *Lack of a Rehabilitation Program.*

In Act 50 of 1968 the Legislature recognized the important place of training and rehabilitation in the Arkansas penal program and directed the Department of Corrections to initiate and prosecute such a program. A program has been initiated at Tucker and is doing much good. Nothing has been done at Cummins.

While inmates newly arriving at the Penitentiary are given intelligence and aptitude tests disseminated by the Vocational Rehabilitation Service, the results of the tests are of little official interest. No regard is paid to the tests and their results in assigning prisoners to barracks or to work. As far as the inmates are concerned, the tests are of no benefit whatever.

A large proportion, perhaps a majority, of the inmates of the Penitentiary are ignorant and unskilled. Many are illiterate. The contribution of ignorance and lack of skills and specialization to crime today is well known. If a man who is ignorant and unskilled when he goes into prison can come out with some education and some usable skill, he has an improved chance of staying out of prison in the future. If he comes out as ignorant and unskilled as he goes in, recidivism on his part is almost inevitable.

Since it costs money to confine convicts, more than many taxpayers realize, it would seem to be in the enlightened self-interest of all States to try to rehabilitate their convicts, as the Arkansas Legislature and Respondents have recognized. But, does the Constitution require a program of rehabilitation, or forbid the operation of a prison without such a program?

Many penologists hold today that the primary purpose of prisons is rehabilitation of convicts and their restoration to society as useful citizens; those penologists hold that other aims of penal confinement, while perhaps legitimate, are of secondary importance. That has not always been the prevailing view of what penitentiaries are for, if, indeed, it is today. In years past many people have felt, and many still feel, that a criminal is sent to the penitentiary to be punished for his crimes and to protect the public from his further depredations. Under that view, while there is no objection to rehabilitation, it is not given any priority.

This Court knows that a sociological theory or idea may ripen into constitutional law; many such theories and ideas have done so. But, this Court is not prepared to say that such a ripening has occurred as yet as far as rehabilitation of convicts is concerned. Given an otherwise unexceptional penal institution, the Court is not willing to hold that confinement in it is unconstitutional simply because the institution does not operate a school, or provide vocational training, or other rehabilitative facilities and services which many institutions now offer.

That, however, is not quite the end of the matter. The absence of an affirmative program of training and rehabilitation may have constitutional significance where in the absence of such a program conditions and practices exist which actually militate against reform and rehabilitation. That is the situation that exists in Arkansas today, completely at Cummins and to a lesser degree at Tucker.

It can be said safely that except in a very, very few and unusual cases confinement in the Arkansas State Penitentiary today is the opposite of beneficial. As a generality it may be stated that few individuals come out of it better men for their experience; most come out as bad as they went in, or worse.

Living as he must under the conditions that have been described, with no legitimate rewards or incentives, in fear and apprehension, in degrading surroundings, and with no help from the State, an Arkansas convict will hardly be able to reform himself, and his experience in the Penitentiary is apt to do nothing but instill in him a deep or deeper hatred for and alienation from the society that put him there. And the failure of the State to help him become a good citizen will be compounded by the ever present willingness of his fellow inmates to train him to be a worse criminal.

Thus, the absence of rehabilitation services and facilities of which Petitioners complain remains a factor in the overall constitutional equation before the Court.

### *Other Prison Conditions.*

Like the absence of a meaningful rehabilitation program, there are other aspects of prison life which in and of themselves do not rise to constitutional dignity but which aggravate the more serious prison defects and deficiencies. The Court will mention some of those aspects briefly.

Medical and dental facilities leave much to be desired. It is not so much that the facilities and services themselves are particularly inadequate for institutions like Cummins and Tucker; rather, it is their unavailability to an inmate when needed that creates the problem. That is largely the fault of the trusty system. If an inmate needs to see the doctor or the dentist, that need is not filled if he is not permitted to go to the infirmary; and it does him no good to go to the infirmary if the doctor is not there when he arrives. Nor does prescribed medication do him any good if it is withheld by a trusty. Making due allowance for malingering, and the Court is sure that there is much of it, there is a great deal of room for improvement in this area of prison life.

Sanitary conditions in the kitchen at Cummins are deplorable according to the testimony of Respondents' own medical witness. Again, that is due largely to the fact that trusties are in charge of the kitchen and do not care whether it is kept clean or not.

The evidence is to the effect that the State supplies its convicts with nothing but the bare necessities of life; no niceties are supplied. Granted, that the State may not be required constitutionally to make it possible for a convict to live comfortably, its failure to do so certainly operates to lower inmate morale. A man who gets only one toothbrush and one tube of toothpaste, who is supplied with no towels, and with insufficient socks and underclothing, and who is required to sleep night after night on filthy bedding is certainly not stimulated to take any pride in himself or to try to be a good inmate of the Penitentiary to say nothing of being a good citizen in the free world when he is released.

It now becomes necessary for the Court to consider in combination the aspects of the Penitentiary System which it has endeavored to describe separately, and to determine whether the situation as a whole is such that confinement in the Arkansas Penitentiary constitutes a cruel and unusual punishment within the prohibition of the Constitution.

In Jackson v. Bishop, supra, 404 F.2d 571, the Court discussed the concept of "cruel and unusual punishment" in some detail; and in the recent criminal cases that have been mentioned this Court undertook to define the term to trial juries.

The term cannot be defined with specificity. It is flexible and tends to broaden as society tends to pay more regard to human decency and dignity and becomes, or likes to think that it becomes, more humane. Generally speaking, a punishment that amounts to torture, or that is grossly excessive in proportion to the offense for which it is imposed, or that is inherently unfair, or that is unnecessarily degrading, or that is shocking or disgusting to people of reasonable sensitivity is a "cruel and unusual" punishment. And a punishment that is not inherently cruel and unusual may become so by reason of the manner in which it is inflicted.

Assume that a person accused of an ordinary felony in Arkansas, say grand larceny, pleads not guilty and stands trial before a jury. The jury finds him guilty, and under Arkansas law may fix his punishment at imprisonment in the Penitentiary for any number of years not less than one nor more than 21. The Circuit Judge accepts the verdict and acting more or less ministerially imposes sentence in accordance with the verdict of the jury.

The convicted person receives his sentence of course; but, he receives much more than that. By his sentence he is subjected to the conditions that have been described; conditions about which the trial jury probably knew little, if anything, and about which the sentencing judge may have been equally ignorant.

For the ordinary convict a sentence to the Arkansas Penitentiary today amounts to a banishment from civilized society to a dark and evil world completely alien to the free world, a world that is administered by criminals under unwritten rules and customs completely foreign to free world culture.

After long and careful consideration the Court has come to the conclusion that the Fourteenth Amendment prohibits confinement under the conditions that have been described and that the Arkansas Penitentiary System as it exists today, particularly at Cummins, is unconstitutional.

Such confinement is inherently dangerous. A convict, however cooperative and inoffensive he may be, has no assurance whatever that he will not be killed, seriously injured, or sexually abused. Under the present system the State cannot protect him.

Apart from physical danger, confinement in the Penitentiary involves living under degrading and disgusting conditions. This Court has no patience with those who still say, even when they ought to know better, that to change those conditions will convert the prison into a country club; the Court has not heard any of those people volunteer to spend a few days and nights at either Tucker or Cummins incognito.

The peril and the degradation to which Arkansas convicts are subjected daily are aggravated by the fact that the treatment which a convict may expect to receive depends not at all upon the gravity of his offense or the length of his term. In point of fact, a man sentenced to life imprisonment for first degree murder and who has a long criminal record may expect to fare better than a country boy with no serious record who is sentenced to a term of two years for stealing a pig.

It is one thing for the State to send a man to the Penitentiary as a punishment for crime. It is another thing for the State to delegate the governance of him to other convicts, and to do nothing meaningful for his safety, well being, and possible rehabilitation. It is one thing for the State not to pay a convict for his labor; it is something else to subject him to a situation in which he has to sell his blood to obtain money to pay for his own safety, or for adequate food, or for access to needed medical attention.

However constitutionally tolerable the Arkansas system may have been in former years, it simply will not do today as the Twentieth Century goes into [its] eighth decade.

### IV. *The Fourteenth Amendment — Racial Segregation.*

The Fourteenth Amendment prohibits racial discrimination within prisons, and the prohibition extends to the racial segregation of inmates. Board of Managers of the Arkansas Training School for Boys at Wrightsville v. George, 8 Cir., 377 F.2d 228, 232; cf. Cooper v. Pate, 378 U.S. 546, 84 S.Ct. 1733, 12 L.Ed.2d 1030, and Lee v. Tahash, 8 Cir., 352 F.2d 970.

As to Tucker the Court finds that that facility is essentially integrated, and that no substantial desegregation problem exists there. With respect to Cummins, certain aspects of prison life have been integrated, and Respondents recognize their duty to eliminate all vestiges of racial segregation, including separate barracks for white and Negro inmates, both rankers and trusties.

Respondents contend, however, and the Court agrees, that to order immediate desegregation of the barracks would create disciplinary problems that Respondents are not able to solve at the moment and would tend to make the already bad situation at the Penitentiary substantially worse than it is.

It must be remembered that we are not dealing here with school children. We are not dealing with free world housing; we are not dealing with [theaters], restaurants, or hotels. We are dealing with criminals, many of whom are violent, and we are dealing with a situation in which the civilian personnel at the Penitentiary are not in control of the institution.

In such circumstances, while the inmates at Cummins are going to have to be integrated, the Court thinks that the process should be part of the overall transition of the Penitentiary from an unconstitutional to a constitutional institution, which transition will be discussed in the following and final section of this opinion.

## V. *The Relief To Be Granted.*

As has been seen, Petitioners seek both declaratory and injunctive relief. They also seek relief for themselves as individuals and for other convicts similarly situated. Two aspects of those prayers give the Court little or no trouble.

As far as the individual claims of the individual Petitioners are concerned, including the individual complaints of inmates now in isolation, the Court does not consider that any of the Petitioners has made a case for specific individual relief.[18] However, all of the Petitioners are subject to the overall situation which renders the Penitentiary unconstitutional and all are entitled to class relief with respect to that situation.

As to the claim for declaratory relief, the Court will declare that to the extent indicated heretofore confinement in the Arkansas Penitentiary System under existing conditions amounts to a cruel and unusual punishment constitutionally prohibited. While the situation at Tucker is much better than that which exists at Cummins, the fact remains that Tucker inmates, like those at Cummins, are subject to the trusty system, including the trusty guard system, and are also confined in large numbers in open barracks. That the situation at Tucker is less severe than that at Cummins seems to the Court to be more significant from the standpoint of the injunctive relief to be ordered than from the standpoint of declaratory relief.

The Court will also declare that racial discrimination in the Penitentiary System, including racial segregation of inmates, is a violation of the Equal Protection Clause of the Fourteenth Amendment and must be eliminated.

That brings the Court to the question of injunctive relief, and it will take occasion to repeat here what was said in *Holt I* when the Court reached the point in that opinion which it has now reached in this opinion (p. 833 of 300 F.Supp.):

"The task of the Court in devising a remedy in this case is both difficult and delicate.

"Subject to constitutional limitations, Arkansas is a sovereign State. It has a right to make and enforce criminal laws, to imprison persons convicted of serious crimes, and to maintain order and discipline in its prisons. This Court has no intention of entering a decree herein that will disrupt the Penitentiary or leave Respondent and his subordinates helpless to deal with dangerous and unruly convicts.

"The Court has recognized heretofore the financial handicaps under which the Penitentiary system is laboring, and the Court knows that Respondent cannot make bricks without straw."

Respondents will be ordered to make a prompt and reasonable start toward eliminating the conditions that have caused the Court to condemn the System and to prosecute their efforts with all reasonable diligence to completion as soon as possible. The lives, safety, and health of human beings, to say nothing of their dignity, are at stake. The start must be prompt, and the prosecution must be vigorous. The handwriting is on the wall, and it ought not to require a Daniel to read it. Unless conditions at the Penitentiary farms are brought up to a level of constitutional tolerability, the farms can no longer be used for the confinement of convicts.

The questions that trouble the Court at this juncture are: What must be done within the immediate future, and how long should Respondents be allowed to achieve their ultimate objective? In approaching those questions certain things should be kept in mind.

First, over the past several years conditions at the Penitentiary have ameliorated somewhat, due in part, but by no means entirely, to the decrees of this Court in the earlier stages of the overall litigation. The alleviation began in the mid-sixties when Dan D. Stephens became Superintendent of the Penitentiary, and it has continued under his successors. While the Penitentiary is still a bad place,

PART IV. *HOLT V. SARVER II* (E. D. ARK. 1970)

an unconstitutional place in the Court's eyes, it is in some respects a better place than it was several years ago.

Second, the legislation adopted in 1967, 1968, and 1969, the report of the Study Commission, and the report to the Commission on Crime and Law Enforcement, indicate that the Arkansas State government is more interested than ever before in the prison system and is aware of the fact that the system is deficient. That increasing awareness of the problem is evidenced not only by the items just mentioned but also by increased appropriations for the Penitentiary over the past several years.

Third, notice may be taken of the fact that the Governor of Arkansas has issued his call for the Legislature to meet in special session on March 2 of the current year. Legislation for the benefit of the Penitentiary is included among the numerous items on the agenda, although the specific nature of the legislation to be sought has not yet been spelled out, and the scope of it may depend to some extent on the provisions of the Court's decree in this case.

It is obvious that money will be required to meet the constitutional deficiencies of the institution, and there is no reason to believe that, subject to the overall financial needs and requirements of the State, the Legislature will be unwilling to appropriate necessary funds.

Finally, if Respondents had unlimited funds at their disposal tomorrow, they could not solve their constitutional problem overnight. Obviously, free world people are going to have to be recruited and employed, and that is going to take some time. In this connection it should be emphasized that to replace trusties with venal, corrupt, sadistic, and underpaid civilian employees would be but to substitute another form of tyranny for that which now exists. Thus, Respondents are going to have to be allowed some reasonable period of transition within which to achieve their objective, but that period is going to have to be measured in months, not years.

The Court thinks in this context, as it has thought in other contexts, that Respondents should be given an opportunity to come forward with a plan to eliminate existing unconstitutionalities, to state what they plan to do, and how long they plan to take to do it. The Court also thinks, however, that it should now proceed to lay down some guidelines for Respondents and should mention what it now considers will probably be minimum requirements if persons are going to continue to be confined in the Penitentiary.

This Court rejects out of hand any approach that would phase out the trusty guard system as such while leaving intact other aspects of the overall trusty system even more objectionable than the guard system itself. All of the trusties are going to have to be brought under control; and trusties, whether guards or not, are going to have to be stripped of their authority over the lives and living conditions of other convicts. Responsibilities that ought to be discharged by free world people may no longer be delegated to trusties whether in the office, in the infirmary, the kitchen, or the fields. Trusties must not have it in their power to bring about promotions or demotions of other inmates and must not be allowed to stand as obstacles to reasonable access of ordinary inmates to civilian employees. The right of a man to talk to the Superintendent or the Assistant Superintendent, or to go to the infirmary when necessary, or receive necessary treatment or medication, must not be permitted to depend on the whim of one or more trusties. It should be taken out of the power of trusties to steal prison food for resale, and it should go without saying that trusties ought not to have access to addictive or stimulating drugs in the prison pharmacy.

The Court thinks that when the trusties as a class are deprived of their authority over inmates, they will largely lose the power of extortion and other undesirable powers which they now possess. This does not mean that trusties may not be assigned responsible jobs, but they must be "jobs," not "offices of profit," and they must be performed under adequate supervision.

While the Court is not prepared at this juncture affirmatively to order the elimination of the trusty guard system or a commencement of a general phase out of the system, the system is going to have to be overhauled. The tower guards and picket guards give the Court no particular problem; the gate guards and the field guards do.

As to the gate guards, it seems evident to the Court that without the connivance of such guards the widespread smuggling of contraband into the prison which is now practiced would be impossible or at least would be made much more difficult. Additionally, gate guards have opportunities for extortion and corruption that other guards do not possess. The gate guards should be replaced by free world personnel as soon as possible.

The system of field guards and the system of using trusty long line riders and inmate pushers go hand in hand, and the combination of the two is one of the things that makes the field guard system so dangerous to rankers. Field guards are much less likely to fire on a ranker or on a group of rankers in the immediate presence of a civilian long line supervisor than they are in a situation where the rankers are actually being worked by other inmates. It appears to the Court that the answer, however unpalatable it may be, is to eliminate the positions of long line rider and inmate pusher and to put each long line under the immediate charge of one or more free world people.

The barracks system of confinement has got to be changed, and the change cannot wait on the completion of the maximum security unit that has been mentioned. The barracks are going to have to be made smaller by subdividing existing barracks or otherwise, and more discrimination, other than racial, is going to have to be practiced in assigning men to barracks. It may be necessary to proceed with the construction of more isolation cells at Cummins to take care of men who simply should not be assigned to barracks.

Apart from the foregoing Respondents are going to have to do more than they have done in the past about keeping order in the barracks at night and about protecting inmates from violent assaults of whatever kind.

As to the isolation cells, while the plight of the inmates is largely of their own doing, they are suffering seriously from neglect. Free world people may no longer leave those inmates to the mercies of trusty guards; additionally, the Court thinks that the method of serving them their food must be changed so as to make sure that it gets to them in more sanitary and palatable condition. In that connection the report to the Commission on Crime and Law Enforcement points out, among other things, that the people in isolation have "no decent or Christian" way in which to eat their food. The report suggests that prisoners in isolation be taken from the cells to the main dining hall to eat either before or after other inmates have been served. That recommendation should be within the power of Respondents to follow without substantial expense and without danger to any inmates.

If Respondents will move in good faith and with diligence in the areas of prison life just discussed, namely, the trusty system, the barracks system, inmate safety, and the isolation cells, the Court thinks that subsidiary problems will tend to take care of themselves. It would be a mistake to order too much at this time; but, in the areas just mentioned Respondents will be required to move. And, of course, the remaining vestiges of racial segregation must be eliminated.

The Court will not be dogmatic about time just now. If there are things that Respondents can do now with available funds and personnel, they will be expected to do them now. If necessary steps cost money, and they will, Respondents must move as rapidly as funds become available. The opening of the new maximum security unit in 1971 should be set as at least a tentative target date for the completion of the removal of unconstitutional conditions and practices. The schedule on which Respondents will be required to move may be shortened or lengthened as circumstances and developments may dictate.

At the moment Respondents will be ordered to submit to the Court and to counsel for Petitioners not later than April 1 of this year a report and plan showing what, if anything, they have done up to that time to meet the requirements of the Court, what they plan to do, and when they plan to do it.

If the initial report is approved, the Court may require additional reports from time to time and may require specific information in certain areas. If the initial report is not approved, it will then become necessary for the Court to consider what specific steps it will take to implement its declarations of the unconstitutionality of the existing system.

Let there be no mistake in the matter; the obligation of the Respondents to eliminate existing unconstitutionalities does not depend upon what the Legislature may do, or upon what the Governor may do, or, indeed, upon what Respondents may actually be able to accomplish. If Arkansas is going to operate a Penitentiary System, it is going to have to be a system that is countenanced by the Constitution of the United States.

A decree in accordance with the foregoing will be entered.

[1] All of the Petitioners in this case are men. However, the Court heard some evidence about the Women's Reformatory. That institution houses about 35 inmates; not all of them are felons; some are simply chronic alcoholics.

[2] While *Monroe v. Pape* involved police officers who had unlawfully searched a private dwelling, its applicability to convicts and their keepers was obvious.

[3] *Holt I* was actually three cases which were consolidated for purposes of trial and were tried in 1969. Those cases were never actually terminated, and they are presently before the Court along with five additional cases which the Court permitted to be commenced and prosecuted.

[4] Following the 1966 investigation certain former employees at the Tucker Farm were charged in the Circuit Court of Jefferson County, Arkansas, with having violated Ark.Stats. § 46-158 which made it a felony for any Penitentiary employee to inflict a punishment on a convict in excess of the punishment prescribed by the then Penitentiary Board. The Circuit Court held that the Arkansas statute was violative of the Arkansas Constitution in that it involved an invalid delegation of legislative power to the Board. The informations [sic] were dismissed by the Circuit Court, and the Supreme Court of Arkansas affirmed. State v. Bruton, 246 Ark. 288, 437 S.W.2d 795.

In 1968 a number of prisoners at Cummins went on a sit down strike and refused to disperse. They were fired upon with shotguns loaded with birdshot by a number of free world people and trusty guards. Some inmates were wounded, one seriously. Fortunately, no one was killed.

The abortion of the State court prosecutions and the 1968 episode just described caused the United States Department of Justice to ask the Court to call the federal Grand Jury for the Eastern District of Arkansas into special session in the summer of 1969. That was done, and a number of indictments were returned against Penitentiary employees and former employees and against a number of former inmates charging violations of 18 U.S.C.A. § 242. The Court conducted a number of jury trials which with one exception resulted in verdicts of not guilty, although the evidence in all of the cases was ample to convict. In one case the jury was not able to agree. As to that case the defendant ultimately pleaded nolo contendere, and another plea of nolo contendere was entered by another defendant.

[5] One of the Petitioners, James E. Jackson, a Negro inmate of the isolation unit at Cummins wrote the Court in advance of trial expressing the view that the Court was biased, prejudiced and corrupt, and that the Court is a racist. Jackson repeated his statements when called to the witness stand. While the Court is not sensible of any feelings of bias or prejudice in the case and is not aware of anything that would justify a charge of racism or corruption, the Court nevertheless disqualified itself in open court as far as Jackson's individual claim is concerned. He is free to litigate that claim further before some other Judge if he cares to do so.

# PART V. JUDGE THOMAS EISELE CURTAILS PRISON INTERVENTION

The February 22, 1982, issue of the *Arkansas Democrat* ran this headline: "Judge Rules Prison Complies with Law." The story announced that a federal judge ruled the state prison system had achieved substantial compliance with the U.S. Constitution, and he would not appoint a monitor to oversee Department of Correction operations. The article disclosed that "U. S. District Judge G. Thomas Eisele filed a copy of his opinion with U. S. District Clerk Carl R. Brents.

"Eisele had strongly hinted after five weeks of hearings last September that he might rule the Arkansas Prison system was at last constitutional if the system lived up to its promises of improvements." The system was found unconstitutional in 1970 by U.S. District Judge J. Smith Henley, and has been under a federal court order to improve conditions since then."

Eisele's unabridged legal opinion follows.[49]

---

[49] Garnett Thomas Eisele, born in 1923, served 41 years as a federal judge for the Eastern District of Arkansas. After service in the army during World War II he earned a law degree at Harvard University's law school. Eisele became an advisor to Rockefeller and helped recruit Murton, not a wise choice, as it turned out. Still, Eisele worked with the controversial penologist to achieve prison reforms. In 1970 President Richard Nixon appointed Eisele judge of U. S. District Court, Eastern District of Arkansas. His oversight of prison improvements helped achieve a remarkable transformation of the state's system. Eisele died in 2017.

# *Finney v. Mabry*, 534 F. Supp. 1026 (E. D. Ark., 1982)

Robert FINNEY, et al., Petitioners,
v.
James MABRY, et al., Respondents.

No. PB-69-C-24.

United States District Court, E. D. Arkansas, Pine Bluff Division.

February 19, 1982.

Philip E. Kaplan, Jack Holt, Jr., Phillip McMath, Little Rock, Ark., for petitioners.

Steve Clark, Atty. Gen., A. Carter Hardage, Asst. Atty. Gen., State of Ark., Little Rock, Ark., for respondents.

## MEMORANDUM OPINION

EISELE, Chief Judge.

This case, which was originally filed in April 1969, is a class action on behalf of all inmates confined in the Arkansas Department of Correction. The plaintiff class challenges the constitutionality of the conditions of confinement at the various institutions administered by the Arkansas Department of Correction. During the long history of the case numerous hearings have been held, and the Court has entered many orders determining the rights of the parties. In addition, the parties entered a Consent Decree in October 1978, which was made an order of this Court, setting forth certain minimum requirements that the respondents agreed to meet in the administration of the Arkansas Department of Correction. The Consent Decree set up a mechanism to monitor the degree of compliance by the respondents with the terms of the Decree, and allowed either party to petition the Court for dismissal of the case upon compliance with the terms of the Decree or upon the expiration of eighteen months from the date of the Decree, whichever occurred first. The Arkansas Department of Correction operated under the Consent Decree until March 1981, when it became apparent that the cooperation of the parties, necessary for continued progress within the framework of the Decree, was no longer forthcoming. Upon the request of the plaintiff class, a hearing was scheduled for August 1981 to determine the extent of compliance by the Arkansas Department of Correction with the Constitution, the Consent Decree, and other prior orders of the Court in this case.

The plaintiff filed an amended petition setting forth approximately forty particular practices or conditions of the Arkansas Department of Correction which it alleged to be unlawful. The respondents denied that any conditions or practices of the Arkansas Department of Correction were unlawful, and requested that the case be dismissed. In addition, the respondents submitted at trial a list identifying approximately fifty additional issues which they contended were raised by the Consent Decree or prior orders of the Court, and therefore were in dispute at the hearing, although not included in the plaintiffs' petition. The plaintiffs agreed that the issues listed should be considered in dispute, so that the record could be made complete on the extent of compliance of the respondents. There were therefore pending approximately ninety matters upon which a determination was to be made concerning the extent of compliance of the Arkansas Department of Correction with the Constitution, the Consent Decree, and prior orders of the Court.

As would be expected, the degree of compliance demonstrated by respondents differed for the various issues in dispute. For many of the identified issues, the Court found that the respondents were in compliance, and in many cases had been in compliance for some time. In other areas, the Arkansas Department of Correction had changed practices or policies shortly before or during the trial, or had adopted plans to do so, and the Court found that, with the implementation of those changes, the respondents would be in compliance. There were a few matters which were identified by the Court as still-existing problems in the Arkansas Department of Correction, and the respondents were held, with respect thereto, not to be in compliance with either the Constitution, prior orders of the Court, or the Consent Decree.

The conclusions of the Court concerning the degree of compliance of the respondents on the various identified issues, and the factual findings in support thereof, were stated on the record during the course of the trial and during the oral arguments following the trial on September 28, 1981, and October 5, 1981. The purpose of this Memorandum and Order is to summarize and supplement some of the findings and conclusions of the Court previously made from the bench during the trial, at the end of the trial, and during oral argument. The findings and conclusions so made from the bench are hereby ratified and readopted. If, however, there are any conflicts or inconsistencies between those findings and conclusions and the ones stated in this written Memorandum, the latter shall supersede and control.

PART V. *FINNEY V. MABRY* (E. D. ARK. 1982)

# I

Although this case was originally filed on behalf of all inmates of the Arkansas Department of Correction, housed in all institutions of the Department, it has become apparent that the problems remaining involve primarily the Cummins Unit and, to a lesser extent, the Tucker Unit. The remaining institutions operated by the Department are essentially in compliance with respect to their "local" conditions of incarceration. The evidence presented at trial centered upon conditions at the Cummins Unit and the Tucker Unit, as did the arguments of counsel after the trial. The attorney for the plaintiff class conceded in a letter to the Court dated October 13, 1981, that "[s]ince the entry of the Consent Decree in this matter on October 15, 1978, the Department has achieved constitutional status at some of its institutions," but he did not specify any certain institutions. There is no question but that the conditions at the Women's Unit, which has been highly acclaimed by experts in the field, are sufficient to meet all the requirements of the Constitution and the prior orders of this Court. The Court also finds that the conditions at the Benton, Wrightsville, and the Diagnostic Units, and all of the separate work release units satisfy such requirements. It is therefore the opinion of the Court that these institutions will not require continuing supervision. Furthermore, the Cummins and Tucker Units will need only limited court controlled supervision during the "windup" period discussed below.

It should be noted that the Court is finding only that the conditions specific to the named institutions are being approved. As will be discussed in this opinion, there are several matters which apply to the entire Department, such as the provision of medical and mental health care, the grievance procedure and the affirmative action program, as to which a finding of total compliance cannot be made at this time. As to those services which are provided to all inmates of the Department on a systemwide basis, rather than on an institution by institution basis, the "release" of the specified institutions has no effect. The Department remains, of course, under an obligation to provide those services in a suitable manner to all inmates in all units, not just to those inmates at the Cummins and Tucker Units. As to all matters that are provided on a "local" rather than a "system-wide" basis, all units except Cummins and Tucker are in compliance.

It should also be noted that the release of these institutions does not mean that the Arkansas Department of Correction will necessarily be free of all future scrutiny concerning the conditions at them. The attorney for the plaintiff class opposed the release of any particular institutions or the dismissal of the suit as to any specific issues until the entire case was dismissed, apparently because of his concern that unless the entire department and all issues remained under the direct or indirect supervision of the Court until the Department is in compliance on all particulars, that the Department would "backslide" in those areas released from control in order to more easily bring those areas still under direct scrutiny into compliance. Although such a possibility does exist, the Court concludes that all deference should be given to the intentions of the respondents not to allow such "backsliding" to occur. The respondents are aware of their responsibilities to maintain the entire Department in a constitutional manner and have, indeed, made exceptional progress toward that goal. It is very doubtful that the success that they have worked so hard to achieve over the years would be forfeited easily through neglect or a lack of perseverance. Furthermore, the ruling of the Court is only that the institutions in question are in compliance with the requirements of the Constitution and the prior orders of the Court at this particular time. This decision would not preclude the inmates from raising the issue again in the future if conditions fall below the constitutional minimums. At some point, hopefully soon, jurisdiction over the Department must be relinquished completely by this Court and the respondents must be trusted with the responsibility to maintain conditions at the level that allowed dismissal of the case, without continual monitoring by the Court or a Court-approved third person. To relinquish active oversight in stages, and thereby to transfer greater responsibility back to the respondents in a somewhat gradual way, will increase the independence of the Department and will make this litigation more manageable for all concerned.

The remainder of this opinion will therefore deal with and resolve the disputes between the parties concerning the degree of compliance by the respondents within the requirements of the Constitution, the Consent Decree, and the prior orders of the Court in the various substantive areas, or issues, identified.

## II

With respect to the largest group of issues identified, the Arkansas Department of Correction is in compliance, and had been in compliance for some time before the hearing. For many of these issues, which include such matters as the adequacy of and access to the law library, mail regulations and the opening of legal mail, and provision for religious requirements for Muslim inmates, the reports prepared by the Compliance Coordinator indicate that the Arkansas Department of Correction was in compliance at the time the report as to those matters was prepared. Although reluctant to concede any issue, the attorney for the plaintiff class did agree that further evidence beyond the reports of the Compliance Coordinator would not be required in order for the respondents to carry the burden of showing compliance. The Court accepts as true the uncontested findings of the Compliance Coordinator, and concludes that the Arkansas Department of Correction is in compliance with the Constitution, the Consent Decree, and other prior orders of this Court on all matters identified by the respondents in the list submitted which were not actively contested by the attorney for the plaintiff on the record during the trial of this case. These matters have been identified to the Court by the following abbreviated references which are known to the parties.

Use of force *policy* (emphasis supplied)

Running to and from work

Any punishment not authorized

Dental care

Two inmates in two-bunk punitive cell

Reporting requirement for exceptions

Privileges

Personal appearance

Discrimination against Muslims

Muslim diet

Muslim religious practices

Proper diet on punitive

Exercise on punitive

Legal advisor to inmates

Law libraries

Access to law libraries

Opening of legal mail

Mail regulations

Visiting regulations

Charging officer not on committee

No adjudication solely on informant

Informant's name and written statement must be before committee

Contraband must be presented to committee

Witness statement must be read into tape

Entire hearing must be tape recorded and kept three years

Hearing to be conducted weekdays between 6:00 a. m. and 6:00 p. m.

Written charges given to inmate 24 hours prior to hearing

> Composition of committee: chairperson plus one security plus one treatment
>
> Review of chief security officer prior to hearing
>
> Charges/consequences fully explained
>
> Charging officer excluded from hearing room
>
> No supervision of inmate by charging officer during time of hearing
>
> Written reason to inmate within 24 hours after hearing
>
> Statement if no black on committee
>
> No racial discrimination allowed in disciplinary proceedings
>
> Minor discipline

It should also be noted that a few issues which were raised in the petition and amended petition by the plaintiff class were not actually disputed at trial. Specifically, the plaintiffs had alleged subversion by the respondents of the procedure for the investigation of complaints of excessive force, staff shortages resulting in curtailed time for recreation and inadequate supervision during recreation periods, and termination of the Compliance Coordinator as particular matters for which the respondents should be held to be not in compliance with the Constitution, the Consent Decree and prior orders of the Court. However, at times before and during the hearing these particular allegations were either abandoned by the plaintiffs or resolved after rulings by the Court. Except for the allegation of staff shortages for recreation, these allegations had raised new issues not addressed in the Consent Decree or court orders prior to the Consent Decree; therefore, the record is clear that they are not pending and no new or specific findings are required at this time. The problem of adequate supervision during recreation is part of the larger problem of inadequate staffing of the institutions at all times, and will be met through the plan for increased staffing as discussed herein below.

## III

A second group of issues may be identified as to which the Arkansas Department of Correction was in compliance at the conclusion of the hearing and as to which it is not necessary to determine if the prior practices of the respondents would have been sufficient if still in effect. This group includes such matters as cleanliness in the East Building at Cummins, the grievance procedure, and provision of medical care for inmates. As to these matters the Court is satisfied that the recently adopted changes in practice meet the applicable standards, but does not, thereby, intend to sanction or condemn the prior practices of the respondents. It would be a waste of judicial resources to analyze carefully and technically each allegation about prior practices that have

## PART V. *FINNEY V. MABRY* (E. D. ARK. 1982)

now been discarded in order to determine if they would be acceptable if still in effect. With respect to such issues the state of compliance of those policies or practices which were in place at the conclusion of the hearing will be examined without regard to the fact that the hearing itself may have been the catalyst for the changes in one or more of such areas.

As to most matters pertaining to conditions in the maximum security facility of the Cummins Unit, the Court found that the respondents are now in compliance, but will require that record-keeping procedures be established and that the newly adopted practices and procedures be monitored for a period of time to assure continuing compliance. The plan established by the respondents to rotate officers through the East Building on a regular basis, as required by the Consent Decree, is adequate if followed in practice. Similarly, the problem of maintaining minimum sanitation standards in the East Building has been accomplished recently through the efforts of Mr. Howard Smith, the maintenance director. As to both officer rotation and sanitation standards in the East Building of the Cummins Unit, the Court has concluded that the respondents are now in compliance with the Constitution, the Consent Decree and prior orders of the Court, but that continued compliance should be monitored before the Department is actually released on these issues.

The Court also concluded that the respondents are in compliance as to the repair of damaged facilities in the East Building and the periodic reevaluation of residents of the maximum security facility, except that further documentation will be required. The Arkansas Department of Correction has recently adopted a procedure to effectuate prompt repair of damage in the East Building, and has begun to keep an inventory of necessary supplies so that the time lapse before a repair or replacement can actually be made will be shortened. A new lighting system has also been installed in the maximum security facility and was reported by the attorney for the respondent to have become operational. Assuming that the procedures function as planned by Mr. Smith, the maintenance director, the Court is satisfied that repairs will be carried out in a satisfactory manner. However, because this, too, involves very recent changes in the procedures of the Department, some period of actual practice will be required before the Court may relinquish oversight. Furthermore, because incidents such as that involving Mr. Sherrod, which the Court believes to be the exception rather than the rule, are likely to occur if needed repairs are not reported and documented in a systematic fashion, an appropriate chain of paperwork must be established. The Court will require that a record report be made promptly of any needed repairs in the East Building by the person responsible for administration of that facility. The report must show the day that the fixture was damaged. After the report is sent to the maintenance department, the schedule for correction of the deficiency should be noted. Finally, after the repair has been completed, the date should be noted. Such a "paper-chase" will aid the Department in accomplishing the repairs promptly, and will enable later review of the problem by the Court if necessary.

As stated above, the Court also found that the respondents are now in compliance on the evaluation of residents of the East Building of the Cummins Unit and periodic reevaluation of those persons, but concluded that more complete records should be maintained. A record must be made of what the evaluation consisted of and should indicate the reasons that purportedly justify keeping the person in maximum. Any psychological counseling or testing, or other reference and the results thereof, should be noted. If no such reference is felt to be required, the reason should be noted. The maintenance of such records will cause the persons making these decisions to have to consider the problem thoroughly in all cases, and will document information for later reference within the institution, and by the Court if necessary.

The Court concluded that the respondents are now in compliance on the maintenance of constitutional conditions for those housed in punitive isolation. Very recent improvements have been made in programs for exercise and recreation, and in lighting and sanitation as discussed above, which are applicable to persons housed in punitive isolation. The major contested issue regarding punitive isolation was the policy of the Department of removing mattresses during daytime hours from the cells of those persons being held in punitive isolation. Without approving or disapproving the policy, the Court concludes that the removal of mattresses, and the denial of other privileges by the respondents as punishment, are matters fully within the discretion of the administrators of the prison. These are matters which reflect attitudes toward the use of punishment as a method of managing inmates within the context of a prison and do not rise to constitutional magnitude as presently enforced. The Court concludes that the conditions imposed on those persons being held in punitive isolation, as enforced at the conclusion of the hearing, are in compliance with the Constitution, the Consent Decree, and all prior orders of this Court.

The Court also concluded that with procedural changes recently adopted by the Department of Correction, and with the addition of a recording requirement now imposed by the Court, the disciplinary procedures followed by the respondents meet standards required by the Constitution, the Consent Decree, and prior orders of the Court. During the time the trial was being held, personnel of the Department finalized a new form to be completed by the disciplinary committee during the course of every disciplinary proceeding. A copy of the new form was made an exhibit during the closing arguments on this issue, and counsel for the respondents represented that the forms would actually be in use at the institution within a short time from that date (after they had been received from the printer). In addition, a new policy has been formulated concerning disciplinary procedures, and Mr. Battles and Mr. Dorsey testified on behalf of the Department of Correction that training sessions had been conducted to aid personnel in implementation of the new policy and forms. Counsel for the plaintiff class conceded, and the Court agrees, that if the new form is effectively used, many past problems that have been noted regarding the disciplinary procedures will be resolved. However, because the forms are so new, the forms and policy were not actually in effect in the Department at the time the hearing was recessed, some period of monitoring the new disciplinary procedures will be required. Furthermore, one problem with past disciplinaries that was not adequately dealt with by the new form is the requirement that medical personnel be consulted before a disciplinary is imposed for malingering when the inmate alleges a medical justification for refusing to work.[11] The forms do state that such consultation is required. However, it is the opinion of the Court, as expressed at the oral argument, that some record must be made of those who have checked the medical records and determined that the inmate has not been given an excusal from work for medical reasons. There must be a record made which identifies the person in the infirmary who is giving the information to the Disciplinary Committee. The notation may be written in the medical records, in the disciplinary records, or both, at the preference of the Department. Although the petitioners charged in the amended petition that the respondents' provision for counsel substitutes during disciplinary proceedings was inadequate, counsel for the petitioners agreed during the oral argument that recently implemented practices of the Department will satisfy constitutional requirements. Finally, the Court has concluded that the continuing use of multiple overlapping charges by the Department for a single incident does not create a problem as long as the practice of punishing for only a single infraction is continued. For example, the evidence showed that an inmate will often be charged with refusal to work, staying in living quarters, and refusal to follow the order of an officer for one incident in which he stayed in the barracks and refused to go to work. The evidence also demonstrated, however, that the same inmate would be given the same penalty as if he had been found to have violated only one rule. As long as multiple punishments are not imposed, charging the inmate with multiple infractions does not implicate constitutional standards. The conclusion of the Court was that the respondents would be in compliance if the new practices and procedures were implemented, as represented to the Court, and if records were made on the medical authority contacted on malingering charges, as required by the Court.

A new grievance procedure was also adopted during the course of the trial and modified following a discussion on the record concerning it. The Court approves the new procedure as modified, and finds that with the implementation of it the respondents will be in compliance on that issue. The implementation of the procedure is, however, an important and fairly complicated task that will require the training of numerous personnel at the institutions. Therefore, as with other recently adopted procedures and practices, the progress on the implementation and use of the grievance procedure must be monitored for a time. In this regard, the Court will require the Department to submit periodic self-evaluations for a short time on the progress that is made.

The Court has concluded also that the new classification system adopted by the Department, if implemented as described during the hearing, complies with the Constitution, the Consent Decree, and prior orders of the Court. It was planned that the new work classification system would be in effect at the institutions by the end of 1981 and that all manuals would be written and training completed concerning it by July 1982. Implementation of the new classification system is closely related to the medical contract and the intake unit procedures, both of which are also new. Therefore, progress toward implementation of the new medical classification system will be monitored. If it is put into effect in the way and according to the timetable planned, the respondents will be held to be in compliance.

An allegation by the petitioners, related to the classification system, was that the requirement that some inmates work in jobs that required long hours seven days a week, particularly jobs in the kitchen at Cummins, was unconstitutional. The evidence indicated that some jobs to which inmates were assigned did require significantly greater hours of work than did other jobs and that assignments to those jobs were often perceived as punishment by the prisoners, even if that were not the intention of those making the assignments. The Court concluded that, although it might be more equitable not to have such disparity in working hours among the inmates, and that it might be a good practice to rotate all or most inmates through those jobs, nevertheless these were matters within the administrative discretion of the management personnel of the prison and did not violate constitutional standards or any prior order of the Court.

The structure for the provision of medical services within the Department of Correction has been dramatically changed within the last several months. The Department had maintained a staff of medical personnel as its employees and had operated the medical facility directly. A contract for the provision of medical services has now been entered with a private company. Virtually all physicians in the Pine Bluff, Arkansas, area are to be involved on a limited basis in supplying medical care at the various institutions. The company will maintain a pharmacy service and emergency medical capability. All personnel of the medical facility will be employees of the independent company rather than personnel of the Department of Correction. Also, the use of inmate aids in the infirmary facility will be greatly reduced, and access by inmates to the medical files of other inmates will be more closely restricted and regulated. There are plans also, with the addition of new security personnel, to change the place of sick call to a more private area, and possibly to change the time of

## PART V. *FINNEY V. MABRY* (E. D. ARK. 1982)

sick call.[2] Although the Court does not feel it is necessary to evaluate the medical services offered by the respondents prior to the contract, it does clearly appear that the services provided will be greatly improved as a result of the contract if implemented in accordance with the testimony. A trial period will be required to allow the contract system to become fully operational before its success may be adequately measured. The provision of medical services is, therefore, another area that must be monitored for a time before it may finally be said that the respondents are in full compliance. The Court will require periodic reports on the progress of the new medical services system and its capability to adequately meet the needs of the inmate population.

The Court has concluded that the respondents have supplied adequate amounts of clothing and sanitation supplies at the Cummins and Tucker Units. There was evidence that there were problems with such supplies during periods in the past. However, the Court is satisfied that those problems have been resolved and that, with the increase in maintenance staff, there is a more systematic approach that is expected to insure that such problems will not arise in the future. The respondents are, therefore, in compliance with the standards of the Constitution, the Consent Decree and prior orders of the Court on the provision of minimum supplies of clothing and sanitation items.

With recent improvements in the kitchen and planned improvements in the shower areas, it is also true that the respondents will have adequately met applicable sanitation standards at the Cummins Unit.[3] Most evidence presented on the question of sanitation concerned conditions in the kitchen. Warden Sargent has now placed the kitchen under his direct supervision and impressed the Court that he recognizes the importance of the issue, and that he intends to use his best efforts to insure that the kitchen produces nutritionally adequate foods in a sanitary manner. A new boiler and a new scullery have been installed and will soon be operational, if they are not at this time. Examination reports by the state Health Department show that, although there have been some problems, for example with hot water, the kitchen has passed inspection. Mr. Smith, the maintenance director, explained the improvements that are being made in the shower areas at the institution and outlined the schedule for completion of those improvements. The Court concludes that the prior problems with sanitation that have existed have been largely resolved and that there are definite plans for improvements and a commitment to carry through with those plans. The completion of the planned improvements will be monitored, and the Court will require periodic status reports on the operation of the kitchen, particularly the availability and use of the new boiler and scullery. Therefore, considering those improvements, the Court will not find that the respondents are not in compliance in the maintenance of minimum sanitation standards.

The availability of notary service to inmates is another matter concerning which the Department of Correction recently implemented a new policy, and the Court may find that the new policy is adequate without the necessity of examining past practices of the Department. A new schedule for notary service was put into effect by the Department on May 21, 1981, and was introduced at trial as petitioners' exhibit 81-111. Counsel for the petitioners stated at the arguments that complaints about the lack of notary service had sharply decreased since the new schedule was adopted, and that it appeared to be adequate. The new schedule is so new, however, that it would not be proper for this Court to dismiss the issue without allowing some time to monitor the availability of notary service to determine if the new schedule is retained and if it will indeed be adequate to allow access by inmates to notary service as needed.

Similarly the Department has recently adopted a "System Six" as a method of evaluating youthful inmates that are transferred from the Tucker Unit to the Cummins Unit. Although little evidence was presented to the Court regarding how the process works, or how effective it is to accomplish the purpose, counsel for the petitioners indicated at the closing argument that it is adequate, if maintained at the present level. The Court will accept this evaluation and finds that the recently adopted process for the evaluation of youthful inmates transferred to the Cummins Unit complies with the requirements of the Constitution, the Consent Decree, and prior orders of the Court. Again, the operation of the system will be monitored until it has been actually in operation for a reasonable time before a final determination of compliance is made.

As to the matters just discussed, the Court concludes that if the respondents maintain conditions as they were at the time the hearing was concluded, or in some cases (as indicated above) complete planned improvements which were scheduled at the time the hearing ended, a final finding of compliance will be made. The Court will require that a final report be filed covering all outstanding issues sometime during the week of May 3, 1982, such report to reflect the factual developments concerning compliance and implementation that have occurred since the August 1981 hearings. The Court anticipates that the plaintiffs, with appropriate assistance as discussed below, will then have until June 14, 1982, to file any objections or exceptions to the report or to otherwise show cause why the respondents should not be found to be in compliance with the Constitution, the Consent Decree, this Opinion and Order, and all other prior orders of the Court, and why this proceeding should not be dismissed. If objections and exceptions are filed, the Court will give respondents until July 6, 1982, to respond. If a hearing is necessary, it will be scheduled for August 9, 1982.

PART V. *FINNEY V. MABRY* (E. D. ARK. 1982)

## IV

There are two issues, the provision of mental health care and the use of inmate security, as to which the respondents made significant changes shortly before and during the hearing, which the Court finds will, if implemented, cure the defects in compliance, but as to which, nevertheless, the Court feels compelled to make a specific finding that the prior practices of the respondents were unconstitutional. The prior inmate mental health arrangements of the Department and the use of inmates in positions of power and control over other inmates, as reflected in the evidence, were unconstitutional, and continuation of those practices could not have been further tolerated. The respondents must understand that they may not revert to the old practices, regardless of lack of funds, or any other circumstance that might prompt a desire to do so. However, the new mental health facility and the new practices of the respondents bring them within compliance with the standards of the Constitution, the Consent Decree, and prior orders of the Court.

The Department of Correction has made drastic improvements during the history of the case in the mental health services available for inmates. The evidence indicates that personnel of the Department, who appear to have first been skeptical about the need for such services, now recognize the need and the assistance that can be provided by the mental health staff. When the case was originally filed, the Department had no mental health personnel. During the course of the most recent hearing, a separate facility with space for 44 inmates with the most severe needs became operational at the Diagnostic Unit as an interim facility to be used until the planned new permanent facility for mental health is completed. This progress shows the dedication of the Department to the long-term resolution of this serious problem. The Court was impressed with the testimony of Drs. Mobley and Powitzky concerning the needs for mental health programs and their efforts to meet those needs. These efforts are laudable and have brought the Department into a situation now where the Court can and does find, with the opening of the interim facility, that the respondents are in compliance.

The Court is equally convinced, however, that prior to the opening of the interim unit at the Diagnostic Center the situation of the Department in supplying mental health services was intolerable. As the evidence shows, the need is such an important one and the prior situation was so clearly inadequate that the Court is compelled to specifically state its conclusion that provision of a separate facility and treatment for the most severely mentally disturbed is constitutionally required. Persons who are severely sick simply cannot be held in custody unless they are provided with necessary medical services. Mental health treatment is clearly a necessary medical service in certain cases. Many inmates who have mental and emotional problems, and need temporary or "outpatient" type of treatment or counseling by psychiatrists or other mental health personnel, may, of course, remain in the general population; but there must be some manner of dealing with them while in the population. A facility such as had been provided in Barracks 16 may serve this purpose. However, in addition, there must be a permanent, separate facility so that those people who are most severely mentally disturbed may be removed, for their own protection and for the safety of others, from the correctional environment of the general population and provided with the treatment and services they need. Such a separate facility that is adequate for the present needs of the Department is now operational, and the respondents plan for a permanent facility to be built within the near future.

The Court also concludes that, if the institutions are staffed as planned, the respondents will be in compliance in providing for adequate security personnel to protect the lives of inmates. Nevertheless the Court feels it imperative to state specifically that the practice of using inmates as security personnel, with power over other inmates, is unconstitutional and may not be reverted to by the Department. The records of staffing introduced at trial demonstrate that the institutions, particularly the Cummins Unit, have been severely understaffed. The respondents have historically made up for the deficiency in free-world security personnel at the institutions by using trusted inmates in security positions. As the Court has discussed in prior opinions in this case, at one time the Cummins Unit was operated almost entirely by inmates with only a skeleton staff of free-world persons. The number of inmates in security positions has been reduced drastically over the years, as ordered by the Court. The transition from inmate to free-world control has been gradual, as it had to be. At the August 1981 hearing it was established that inmates were still being used as "turnkeys" and "floor walkers"[14] at the Cummins Unit. However, the respondents also introduced evidence at the hearing concerning a plan that has been adopted which calls for the Department to hire 128 new correctional officers over approximately a seven month period beginning in June 1981 and completed by February 1, 1982. Of the 128 new correctional officers, 116 are to be assigned to the Cummins Unit and eight to the Tucker Unit. *See* petitioners' exhibit 81-114. With the addition of these free-world security personnel and the staffing plan that has been adopted, it will be possible for adequate security to be provided without the use of inmates as security personnel. Accordingly, the respondents represented a firm and fixed intention to phase out the use of inmates in positions of control entirely, including the positions of floor walkers and turnkeys as those jobs existed at the time of the hearing. Inmates will still be used as turnkeys on the riot gates, but only to mechanically open and close the gate under the direct supervision of a free-world guard. The turnkeys will exercise no inmate control discretion whatsoever. Under this plan, as represented to the Court during the hearing and arguments, the respondents will be in compliance on the issue of adequate inmate security staffing.

## PART V. *FINNEY V. MABRY* (E. D. ARK. 1982)

As stated on the record during the trial and the arguments, the respondents will not be allowed to return to the use of inmates in security positions at any of the institutions of the Arkansas Department of Correction. Inmates may not be placed in positions of authority over other inmates and may not be given power to exercise discretion in the control of other inmates in any way. The use of inmates in such control positions is unconstitutional. The respondents are to have phased out the use of all inmates in such positions on or before Monday, April 12, 1982. An injunction will be entered permanently prohibiting the respondents from placing inmates in positions of authority or discretion and control over other inmates after that date except in the most serious emergencies when absolutely no alternative for control is available and, even then, only for the minimum period necessary to bring the situation under the complete control of free-world authorities.

The respondents understand that the increases in staffing that are planned must be carried out. The number of free-world personnel working at the institutions has not been adequate to protect the safety of the inmates on a 24 hours basis as, indeed, respondents fully recognize. The Court is hesitant to require that a specific, rigid staffing pattern be maintained. Such matters are better left to the reasonable discretion of those whose job it is to manage the Department so that needed flexibility is available to adapt to changing circumstances. The Court is concerned, however, that minimum constitutional standards be met. The Court is satisfied that if the staffing plan is implemented as described during the hearing and the arguments those standards will be met. The Court is equally convinced that the past staffing of free-world personnel at the institutions has been inadequate. This deficiency in staffing has, in turn, contributed to most of the problems of the system. The respondents have the responsibility to staff the institutions with free-world personnel in such numbers, of such professional quality, and in such manner as will adequately protect the safety of the persons incarcerated in those facilities. The new staffing plan will meet this responsibility if the correctional officers are hired, trained, motivated, and scheduled to work at the institutions as it was represented to the Court that they would be. No return to the *status quo ante* is constitutionally permissible.

## V

There are several issues as to which the Court has concluded that the policies or practices of the respondents have not complied with the requirements of the Constitution, the Consent Decree or the prior orders of the Court, and as to which the respondents have not as yet adopted proposed changes that would comply. One such issue, involving the procedural requirements that must be followed before a person may be placed in administrative segregation and the conditions that may be imposed in administration segregation, has been discussed in a separate order of this Court entered on December 15, 1981. Other matters as to which the respondents are not in compliance, specifically open barracks, overcrowding, affirmative action in the hiring of minorities, integration of the East Building and Barracks 14 and 16, and the use of racial slurs by officers in the presence of inmates, are discussed herein.

As previously noted by the Court, the problems of overcrowding and inadequate security are closely related in the context of this litigation. Although actual lack of space could be a constitutional deprivation resulting from overcrowded conditions in some circumstances, that is not the principal problem faced at this time by the Arkansas Department of Correction.[5] The evidence indicated that, by the time of the hearing, the respondents had sufficiently reduced the number of inmates housed in the Cummins Unit so that overall population limitations had been met. As a result, in most parts of that institution the sheer number of inmates confined was not a major problem. The crowded conditions in certain barracks of the Cummins Unit, however, make it impossible for the inmates living therein to be adequately protected or supervised. For example, although a large number of inmates are housed in Barracks 19, the multiple use building, the barracks is arranged in such a way that adequate supervision is possible despite the large numbers, and security has not been a problem there. This is not true, however, in Barracks 5 through 12 at the Cummins Unit, the "100-man" or "open" barracks. In those eight barracks, the placement of double bunks along the walls and in the rear areas in the close proximity that is required makes it virtually impossible for a security guard to have an unobstructed view through the barracks from any angle. This inability to effectively monitor the barracks is made even worse by the practice of permitting[6] some inmates to drape blankets over the bunks to create some sense of privacy in the large and crowded room. The abilities of the guards to supervise the barracks is hampered also after lights have been turned out because the area of the barracks farthest from the hall (of which vision is greatly blocked by the bunks) is also the darkest area. The inadequate staffing of the Cummins Unit, as discussed earlier, has further complicated the problem. However, the increase in security personnel that is planned may not be enough to completely cure the problem.

The Court has attempted to interfere as little as possible with the daily administration of the Department of Correction throughout this litigation. It has been the practice of the Court to allow the respondents as much flexibility as possible in devising solutions to the various problems faced at the institutions, as long as minimum standards are established. It is the intention of the Court to maintain this practice for the resolution of this problem, if possible. With this objective in mind, the Court, by an order filed December 1, 1981, required the respondents to report to the Court in the following way:

The respondents shall report ... how they would implement an Order by the Court that the population in the eight barracks in question be reduced to 90 inmates within a period of four months and further reduced to 80 inmates within the following four months. The respondents should indicate how they would respond to such an order, what problems would be created by such an order, and how they would deal with the increased population problems that would result from that type of order. The respondents should also suggest alternatives which might make such an order unnecessary, such as internal patrols, or an adequate surveillance or communication system. The respondents should only suggest such alternatives that they consider feasible and which could be actually implemented within the institution by August, 1982.

The report of the respondents recounted briefly the history of the large open barracks and the reductions in population and improved conditions therein brought about by prior orders in this case. The respondents also provided statistical data concerning the number of inmates to be housed at Cummins, and the available bed space under existing arrangements in the barracks. In conclusion, the respondents stated that "[t]he bottom line of all of this is that the Department does not have available beds to absorb 80 or 160 inmates currently being housed in the open barracks at Cummins."

The respondents did not, however, state any specific new alternatives for solving the inmate safety problem without reducing the population in the open barracks. The respondents did point out the increases in security staff at the Cummins Unit that have occurred during and since the August 1981 hearing, and indicated their belief that the additional personnel should solve the safety problems in the open barracks cited by the Court. It was argued that the staffing patterns at the institution are now in place, as it was testified they would be during the hearing. "There is an officer present in the hall between each of the facing open barracks at all times. In addition to other officers periodically present in the barracks, there is a patrol officer whose only duty is to patrol the barracks." Response filed December 28, 1981, at p. 5. According to the testimony at the hearing and the description of the respondents, there are also other security personnel on duty in the institution performing certain tasks, such as the "shake-down detail," which should make the institution more secure throughout. The respondents also pointed out, as had been testified at the hearing, that the Department plans to place telephones in the hallways between each of the two facing open barracks for use by officers to obtain security assistance. Although the respondents were the ones, during the hearing, who originally suggested the use of cameras or sound equipment within the open barracks to allow limited numbers of security personnel to more effectively monitor each of the open barracks, they rejected such as an option in the Response because such fixed devices would be amenable to tampering or destruction by inmates. The respondents did suggest that the Department "has made a decision to purchase" a "Body Alert System" for use by security personnel throughout the Cummins Unit. As described by the respondents, in that "System" each officer would carry a small transmitter with which he could communicate with a person monitoring a receiver located at the telephone switchboard, a secure area. The respondents conceded, however, that this equipment is very expensive, the Department at this time does not have the funds to purchase the equipment, and it is not known when such funds might become available.

The position of the respondents was, basically, that improvements that have been made, or which are planned, in security at the Cummins Unit, as described at the August 1981 hearing, are sufficient to solve any security problems created by the overcrowding the Court found in the 100-man barracks, and therefore further measures should not be required. This position, however, reflects a misunderstanding of the Court's statements concerning the problem during the hearing and the intentions of the Court in the December 1, 1981 Order requiring a report from the respondents.

The Court has concluded that some additional measures are required to make the 100-man barracks reasonably safe. It is true that the problems of the number of security personnel on duty and the kind of equipment they have at their disposal, the use of inmate security personnel, the number of inmates housed at the institution, and many other factors are all related in determining the level of security and protection provided at the institution. Although the Court has ordered that the respondents will no longer be allowed to use inmates as security personnel with discretion over the actions of other inmates, it has attempted to provide the respondents with flexibility in how they will "juggle" the other factors to achieve the required result of a prison that is both secure and safe. The increases in security staff that the respondents have planned, and are implementing, were necessary and should be sufficient. However, the finding that the staffing patterns proposed for security personnel would be adequate did not mean that no other factors affecting security would have to be adjusted. Even with the increased personnel, the respondents are not able to adequately supervise the 100-man barracks as they are presently arranged. As discussed above, with bunk beds and blankets blocking the view, an officer in the hallway between the open barracks cannot monitor what is happening in all parts of the barracks. The situation is made worse at night when the lights are off. The fact of having so many persons in such close proximity only makes it more likely that incidents will occur, making adequate supervision that much more essential while it also makes it more difficult. Although having a security officer in the hall between the barracks is a great improvement over the situation as same existed before the hearing (with no free-world security even in the area for long periods of time), it is not sufficient.

Additional measures, above those already planned by the respondents as testified at the August 1981 hearing, are required.

It should be noted also that the respondents' assertions that they cannot reduce the population in the barracks because they do not have enough additional beds elsewhere in the institution to accommodate the inmates that would be displaced are not a sufficient response to the problem. The Court is not unaware of the limited resources of the respondents; however, limited resources cannot be considered an excuse for not maintaining the institution according to at least minimum constitutional standards. If the State requires that certain persons be institutionalized, as it may, it has the corresponding obligation to meet their basic human needs, which includes some degree of protection, where necessary, from other persons that the State also requires to live in the institution. The goal of the Court in allowing flexibility to the respondents in how they meet these needs is to permit them to use the resources they have in the way they deem the most efficient and most desirable. But the obligation to meet those minimum standards in some way is unchanging.

The Court has concluded that resolution of this issue should remain open to allow the respondents another opportunity to devise a solution to the problems of security and safety in the open barracks. In the response filed on December 28, 1981, the respondents mentioned that as an experiment in Barracks 8 all double bunks had been removed. The respondents reported that the same number of inmates are housed in the barracks as were housed there before, but no details concerning the actual arrangement of the bunks was given. The results of the experiment were described as follows:

[T]he elimination of double bunks has been well received by both inmates and officers. The technique has, quite frankly, been more helpful than was anticipated. A number of problems have decreased, most notably the hanging of sheets from the top bunk to hide activity of whatever nature from view. As problems decrease, so do tensions.

However, despite this promising report on a potential solution to the problem, the respondents did not provide the details to the Court of exactly what the "experiment" required, suggest it as an alternative for use in other barracks, or explain why the bunks in other barracks should not be similarly eliminated. In fact, it is not known to the Court if the "experiment" in Barracks 8 was temporary and the beds have again been stacked, or if the respondents considered it suitable to leave the beds at one level in that barracks. The potential of such a solution to the problem, however, restores the hesitancy of the Court to simply require that the population in the various barracks in question be reduced by a specific number. It is the desire of the Court to allow the respondents to develop a solution to the problem that is most acceptable to them, if that is possible.

Therefore, the Court will again direct that within 30 days of the date of this Order the respondents provide to the Court proposals that it would favor as methods of resolving the inmate safety problem in the open barracks at the Cummins Unit. The Court's Order of December 1, 1981, together with the discussion of that order herein, should serve as a guide to the respondents. This problem must be dealt with despite the additional security arrangements that have been placed in effect by respondents. The petitioners will then have an opportunity to respond to the report by the respondents. A hearing will be scheduled promptly thereafter, if necessary, to determine a final solution to the problem.

Another issue as to which a final solution cannot be ordered at this time is the provision for the full integration of the East Building and Barracks 14 and 16 at the Cummins Unit. As was discussed at the oral arguments following the August 1981 hearing, the level of racial integration of the institutions of the Department has been greatly increased since this litigation was commenced, and has been the subject of many prior discussions and orders by the Court. At present the Court finds that the institutions are satisfactorily integrated, except for the above named areas at the Cummins Unit.

The segregation in the East Building and Barracks 14 and 16 has been allowed by the respondents on the basis that such segregation was required to minimize the possibilities of violence at the institution. However, the allowance of segregation has been much broader than would, in the Court's opinion, be necessary to protect the safety of the inmates. Previous orders of the Court have recognized that there could be potential danger in individual situations in integrating two-person cells. The inmates at the Cummins Unit are convicted felons, and the possibility of violence cannot be dismissed lightly. It has been because of this possibility of violence that the Department of Correction has avoided integrating two-person cells in the maximum security units. However, as early as 1973 the Court made the following observations and order:

The Court finds that as of now the populations of both institutions are fully desegregated, except that inmates of the maximum security unit at Cummins are still assigned to racially segregated cells. Desegregation of the barracks has been accomplished without the creation of any problems in the areas of security and discipline, and the Court cannot accept the argument put forward by respondents that members of both races cannot dwell peaceably together in the cells in the maximum security unit. And it should be pointed out in this connection that not all of the inmates of the unit have been put there for disciplinary reasons.

## Part V. *Finney v. Mabry* (E. D. Ark. 1982)

This is not to say, of course, that there may not be some inmates, whether white or black, who cannot safely be confined in a cell with a member or members of the other race. In such cases the Constitution does not require assignment to integrated cells ... But the existing general policy of racial segregation in the maximum security cells cannot be approved and must be brought to an end.

Respondents will be directed forthwith to consider the situations of all inmates now in the unit and determine on an individual basis which of those inmates, if any, cannot safely be put in a cell with a member of the other race. The rest of the inmates presently confined in the unit are to be assigned to cells on a non-racial basis.

No present or future inmate of the unit is to be assigned to a cell on the basis of race unless the Superintendent of the institution personally finds in writing and with a statement of supporting reasons that the inmate in question should not be confined in an integrated cell; such finding is to be made a part of the inmate's prison record.

*Holt v. Hutto,* 363 F.Supp. 194, 203-204 (1973) (footnote and citations omitted). Thereafter, the respondents were permanently enjoined from assigning inmates of the maximum security unit to racially segregated cells, except under the narrow limits authorized by the above quoted language. Order of August 13, 1973, at p. 1.

However, the respondents have not yet actually integrated the cells of the maximum security unit. The respondents did develop a questionnaire that is answered by all inmates upon entering the East Building. Respondents' exhibit 81-37. The integration questionnaire simply asks the inmate to indicate if he does or does not "have objections to being integrated in the East Building." Space is then provided to allow the inmate to indicate what his objections, if any, are. On the basis of responses on this questionnaire, the respondents have said that integration is not possible. However, the questionnaire seeks what amounts to a statement of preference. The focus is not on the real issue of when an inmate's safety might be involved. The form definitely creates the situation where, if the inmate says the right thing, he can avoid having a person of a different race in the cell with him. This does not meet the limited criteria set forth in the Court's earlier opinion, as quoted above.

The policy has been clearly stated and is still correct. Racial segregation cannot be allowed to continue. The attitude of the Department in general, and of the superior officers, seems to be consistent with that policy. However, the procedures employed have not accomplished that result in the East Building and Barracks 14 and 16. A better approach for identifying the few cases where safety is actually involved must be found. For those individuals as to which violence is a real threat, if celled with an individual of a different race, segregation for that reason is acceptable. The method devised for identifying such persons must be no broader than is necessary to accomplish that goal.

The respondents shall suggest to the Court within 30 days of this date proposals for accomplishing integration of the East Building and Barracks 14 and 16 of the Cummins Unit. A reasonable transition period to accomplish this integration shall be allowed. If the respondents contend that there are real hazards posed by integrating some individuals, the proposal should suggest as precise a method as possible for identifying those individuals. The petitioners will then be given an opportunity to respond to the proposal by the respondents, and a hearing will be scheduled promptly if necessary.

As to the final two matters of which the Court has found the respondents not to be in compliance, the use of racial slurs and the affirmative action program, the problem does not lie with the policy of the Department, but rather with the success of the Department in accomplishing the goals they have set. The Court does not doubt that the respondents have made efforts to attract black persons into upper level position and to stop the use of racial remarks by officers in speaking to and about inmates. However, the evidence was clear that the efforts have not been wholly successful in accomplishing those results.

The issue of the use of abusive language toward inmates has been the subject of several prior orders of the Court. See, e.g., Holt v. Hutto, 363 F.Supp. 194, 214 (1973); Finney v. Hutto, 410 F.Supp. 251, 272 (1976). The Consent Decree provides that no Department of Correction employee is to "verbally abuse, curse, or use racial slurs when addressing or talking with inmates." The Court is not now concerned with cursing in general by officers. The Court also is not concerned with language used by inmates. Although higher level officers should continue to discourage cursing, in efforts to promote the professionalism of the Department and the officers, it would not be realistic to hope to "sanitize" the language used in such an environment. However, the use of racial slurs toward inmates cannot be tolerated to any degree. The prior orders of the Court have been very explicit in this regard.

The problem has not been resolved, in the opinion of the Court, because the upper echelon personnel have not taken a sufficiently forceful position on the issue. It does not appear that the very high ranking officers actually use such language themselves. Also the written policies of the Department prohibit the use of racial slurs in addressing inmates, and this prohibition is most probably pointed out to newly hired officers during training. However, this warning accomplishes little when, as apparently has frequently been the case, the new officer goes to work and the low and mid-level officers then provide the example of the use of such language. Although there was some evidence that persons using racial epithets toward inmates have on occasion been reprimanded, there was also evidence from high level employees, including the Warden, that they knew such language was being used but passed it off as local custom. It is not a local custom, or a local problem; it is a national problem. The use of racial slurs in speaking to inmates is a direct violation of the orders of this Court, and such a violation of the law cannot be tolerated by supervisory personnel for any reason. The respondents must see that the use of racial slurs in addressing inmates is no longer allowed to continue at any level. It must be understood down the line of all supervisory personnel and correctional officers that not using such language in speaking to or about inmates is a condition of employment.

The implementation of the affirmative action program is a more complex issue with which to deal.[7] This is not an employment discrimination case where the court is interested in testing, and remedying if necessary, possible discrimination against blacks by the respondents in their hiring practices. The reason the affirmative action program is so important is not to benefit potential employees of the Department, although they are indirectly benefited. Rather, the importance is in obtaining a racial mix of the security personnel in order to alleviate feelings by black inmates, which are approximately half of the inmate population, that they are being discriminated against. The primary effort must be to hire qualified blacks and place them in positions of authority in all aspects of prison life.

The evidence demonstrated that the respondents have increased their efforts to recruit qualified black persons to work within the Department. Those efforts have been successful to the extent that blacks are well represented among the highest and the lowest ranking officers. In fact, it was shown that at the time of the hearing 53 percent of the correctional officers, the lowest level officers, were black. However, there have not been, and still are not, blacks in the middle management positions in significant numbers. This situation must be carefully monitored by respondents.

As discussed on the record during the oral arguments, the Court credits the testimony of Mr. Housewright that sincere efforts have been made to recruit blacks into middle positions, but such efforts have not been very successful. Several factors may be cited as contributing to that failure, the principal ones being an inability to pay competitive salaries and the rural location of the prisons. However, this failure cannot be used as an excuse for not continuing diligent efforts to recruit blacks who are already experienced in corrections work, and who could join the department at a middle or high level position. Recent improvements in the administration of the institutions and the working conditions for the officers, as discussed herein, should help to make the

Department a more attractive place to work, and thereby aid in recruiting experienced personnel.

Furthermore, the respondents must intensify efforts to identify black correctional officers who are employed by the Department without prior correctional experience, but demonstrate potential that would qualify them for promotion within the Department. Efforts must be made to train such persons and promote them at a rate commensurate with their abilities, so that blacks will be better represented in the middle officer positions. The testimony was that the respondents have made efforts to train and promote from within, but have not achieved the success desired for various reasons. However, the Court finds it difficult to understand, with a pool of black persons for potential advancement as high as 50 percent of the relevant work force, why greater efforts at selection and training would not result in promotion and retention of a greater number of blacks.

A certain rigid percentage of black officers will not be established as a requirement for compliance. However, the respondents must know that blacks, as previously ordered, must be employed in reasonable numbers at *all* levels of free-world personnel.

## VI

It is the conclusion of the Court that a third party should not be appointed as a "monitor" to oversee the operations of the Arkansas Department of Correction as had been requested by the plaintiff class. The parties are well aware of the efforts by this Court to avoid court appointment of a monitor throughout the history of this litigation.[8] Such court involvement in the daily administration of the institutions should be undertaken only if absolutely necessary. The progress made by the respondents through their own efforts without a court-appointed monitor leads to the conclusion that no person need be now appointed to oversee the operation of the Department through the time of the final report by the respondents that is contemplated by the Court, as discussed herein.

The respondents will be required to file periodic reports on the progress being made in various areas in the next several months and a final report on all outstanding issues during the week of May 3, 1982, as discussed above. These reports shall be comprehensive, specific, and factual. Copies of the reports shall be served upon counsel for the plaintiff class at the time they are filed.

It is expected that counsel for the plaintiff class will require both financial assistance and additional personnel during the time period allowed for review of the respondents' final report. As discussed above, the attorney for the plaintiffs is to file any objections or exceptions he might have to the final report of the respondents on or before June 14, 1982. Some investigation and review of the facts presented by the respondents will be necessary in order to make such objections.

The parties shall jointly determine how the investigation and review by the plaintiffs contemplated by the schedule established by the Court shall be conducted. The primary financial obligation shall necessarily fall upon the respondents. After consultation with the respondents, counsel for the plaintiff class shall propose, on or before March 29, 1982, a plan for who shall conduct the investigation and review and what resources will be necessary. The respondents shall then notify the Court in writing on or before April 9, 1982, whether they agree with the proposal by the plaintiffs. If the respondents do not agree with the proposal by the plaintiffs, they shall state with specificity their objections thereto, and suggest to the Court an alternative proposal. The Court will thereafter enter an order resolving the issue, if necessary.

## CONCLUSION

The findings of the Court during the August 1981 hearing, as reflected on the record and discussed herein, demonstrate that the respondents have made great progress in improving conditions for inmates of the Arkansas Department of Correction. However, more progress must be made before this case can be dismissed. Vigilance by the respondents is required to assure, in areas in which the policies of the Department were found to be in compliance with the applicable standards, such as on the issue of excessive force, that those policies are actually practiced and followed by personnel at all levels. If a policy or regulation of the Department is constantly ignored, the effect is the same as if there were no such policy. Equal diligence will be required to put into effect various practices and policies, approved by the Court, in the way and according to the timetable that was presented to the Court. The findings of compliance are conditional upon the proper effectuation of the various programs. Therefore, the respondents must continue directly on the path they have charted to achieve success.

[1] A related problem has been the alleged failure of the respondents to employ an adequate medical classification system that would define the capacity of the inmate to perform certain jobs in a meaningful way. The Department of Correction has developed and is implementing a new classification system that will be adequate if put into operation as planned. *See* discussion, *infra,* at 1034.

[2] The Court has concluded, contrary to the allegations of the petitioners, that the time and place of sick call are administrative decisions within the

discretion of prison management. The Court therefore finds no violation of a constitutional standard or of a prior order of this Court in the fact that the respondents have held sick call at 4:30 a. m.

[3] The evidence presented by the plaintiffs concerned sanitation standards at the Cummins Unit of the Arkansas Department of Correction. The parties appear to be in agreement that sanitation has not, in recent times, been a problem at other units of the Department.

[4] These terms are commonly used by the parties and were defined on the record at the hearing. Briefly, a "turnkey" is the person in charge of opening and closing the various barracks and corridor gates that control movement in the corridors and between the barracks. A "floor walker" is a person housed in a barracks who is responsible for maintaining peace and order within the barracks, reporting problems or infractions, and summoning help if necessary. There was much evidence of the abuses of the inmate control system and of its lack of effectiveness in protecting the safety of other inmates.

[5] The provision of a minimum amount of space for the number of inmates confined at the institution has been an issue during earlier stages of this litigation, and has been the subject of prior orders of the Court. *See, e.g., Finney v. Hutto,* 410 F.Supp. 251, 254-58 (E.D.Ark.1976).

[6] Although the draping of blankets over the bunks in that way is against regulations, the respondents have not stopped the practice by the inmates, and therefore its effects must be considered as if the practice were officially permitted.

[7] The plaintiffs attempted to raise as part of this issue possible discrimination by the respondents against blacks, both inmates and free-world personnel, in job assignment and benefits of employment. The particular questions raised concerned the allegations that black officers rarely live on the "free line" and that "houseboys" for persons living on the free line are almost always black inmates. As noted on the record during the oral arguments following the August 1981 hearing, the Court does not perceive these as major issues in the case, and was not provided with sufficient evidence upon which to decide if the allegations of racial discrimination on these points are well taken. The Department was admonished only to avoid actual discrimination, of course, and also to avoid appearances of discrimination through stereotypes if possible.

[8] The parties agreed in the Consent Decree entered on October 5, 1978, that a person should be employed as Compliance Coordinator for the Arkansas Department of Correction, and Mr. Stephen LaPlante was so hired. The position of Compliance Coordinator was not created upon the order or

suggestion of the Court, and the Court did not designate or appoint the person to serve in that position. Mr. LaPlante was selected jointly by the Commissioner of Correction, the Attorney General, and counsel for the plaintiffs, and his salary was paid by the respondents, as agreed upon in the Consent Decree. The powers and duties of the Compliance Coordinator were those agreed upon by the parties and set forth in the Consent Decree and were not established by the Court.

[9] It merits repeating that this Memorandum Opinion is not intended to be a comprehensive statement of the Court's findings concerning the various issues raised during the August 1981 hearing. Most of the Court's findings were made on the record during the course of that hearing, principally during the oral arguments held at the conclusion of the hearing. This Memorandum Opinion was intended to restate and discuss, perhaps adding greater elaboration, the findings of the Court stated on the record. Although in the case of conflict this written memorandum should be considered controlling, the findings and orders made orally from the bench are equally binding as those contained in this Memorandum Opinion in those instances where there is no conflict.

# EPILOGUE

Judge Eisele's decision marks an end to the story told in this book. Though some improvements came about thanks to Henley and Eisele, the system remained a bad place, as Henley once described it. In this bad place powerful men allowed or did horrible and illegal things to imprisoned people. Though difficult to admit, this is true, and it should never be denied or forgotten. One expects that following the CID's damning report, scores of abusers were arrested, tried, and convicted. But that did not happen. Dr. Martin Luther King Jr. believed that "The arc of the moral universe . . . bends toward justice." Maybe so, but not this time.

# BIBLIOGRAPHY

## Books

Crosley, Clyde. *Unfolding Misconceptions. The Arkansas State Penitentiary 1836-1986.* Arlington, TX: Liberal Arts Press, 1986.

Crosley, Clyde. *Men Or Mules.* Jonesboro, AR: Clyde Crosley, 1978.

Donaghey, George W. *Autobiography of George W. Donaghey. Governor of Arkansas 1909-1913.* Benton, AR: L. B. White Printing Company, 1939.

Dougan, Michael B. *Arkansas Odyssey: The Saga of Arkansas From Prehistoric Times to Present.* Little Rock, AR: Rose Publishing Company, 1993.

Hill, William N. *Story of the Arkansas Penitentiary.* Little Rock, AR: Democrat Printing & Lithographing Co., 1912.

Keith, K. Wymand. *Long Line Rider. The Story of Cummins Farm.* New York: McGraw Hill Book Company, 1971.

Lichtenstein, Alex. *Twice the Work of Free Labor: The Political Economy of Convict Labor in the New South.* New York: Verso, 1996.

Miller., Vivien M. L. "Murder, 'Convict Flogging Affairs,' and Debt Peonage. The Roaring Twenties in the American South," *Reading Southern Poverty Between the Wars, 1918-1939.* Athens: University of Georgia Press, 2006.

Mosley, Walter. *Workin' On the Chain Gang. Shaking off the Dead Hand of History.* New York: Ballantine Publishing Group, 2000.

Murton, Tom and Joe Hyams. *Accomplices to the Crime.* New York: Grove Press, Inc., 1969.

Niedeman, Donald G., ed. *Black Southerners and the Law, 1865-1900.* New York: Garland Publishing, Inc., 1994.

Pierce, Michael, and Calvin White Jr., eds. *Race, Labor, and Violence in the Delta.* Fayetteville: University of Arkansas Press, 2022.

Ward, John L. *The Arkansas Rockefeller.* Baton Rouge: Louisiana State University Press, 1978.

Woodcock, Dale. *Ruled by the Whip. Hell Behind Bars in America's Devil's Island---The Arkansas State Penitentiary.* New York: Exposition Press, 1958.

## Journals, Reports, Court Cases, and Theses

Arkansas Penitentiary Study Commission, "Report of the Arkansas Penitentiary Study Commission." January 1, 1968. Arkansas Documents, Arkansas State Library, Little Rock, AR.

Barnard, Lewis. "Old Arkansas State Penitentiary," *Arkansas Historical Quarterly* 13:3 (Autumn 1954), 321-323.

Baxley, Thomas L. "Prison Reforms During the Donaghey Administration." *Arkansas Historical Quarterly* 22:1 (Spring 1963), 76-84.

Bayliss, Garland E. "The Arkansas State Penitentiary Under Democratic Control, 1874-1896." *Arkansas Historical Quarterly* 34:3 (Autumn 1975), 195-213.

Choate, Laura, "Prison Reform." *Encyclopedia of Arkansas* (https://encyclopediaofarkansas.net/entries/prison-reform-4159; accessed May 20, 2023.

"Convict Labor: 1923." *Monthly Labor Review* 18:4 (April 1924), 1-33.

Criminal Investigation Division, Arkansas State Police. "Case Report: Tucker State Prison Farm, Tucker, Arkansas," January 16, 1967.

Donaghey, George W. "Why I Could Not Pardon the Contract System." *The Annals of the American Academy of Political and Social Science* 46, *Prison Labor* (March 1913), 22-30.

*Finney v. Mabry,* 534 F. Supp. 1026, 8th Circuit, Eastern District of Arkansas, 1982.

*Holt v. Sarver II,* 309 F. Supp. 362, 8th Circuit, Eastern District of Arkansas, 1970.

Leopold Classic Library. "Report of the Penitentiary Joint Committee of Arkansas; Penitentiary Committee Report 1901."

McKelvey, Blake. "A Half Century of Southern Penal Exploitation." *Social Forces* 13:1, (Oct 1934-May 1935), 112-123.

Smith, Ryan Anthony. "Laura Conner and the Limits of Prison Reform in 1920s Arkansas." *Arkansas Historical Quarterly* 77:1 (Spring 2018), 52-63.

Smith, Ryan Anthony. "Gender Confines: Women's Prison Reform in 1920s and 1930s Arkansas," Master's Thesis, Arkansas State University, 2017.

Zimmerman, Jane. "The Convict Lease System in Arkansas and the Fight for Abolition." *Arkansas Historical Quarterly* 8:3 (Autumn 1949), 171-188.

# Acknowledgments

I believe it is accurate to say that a book with good editors has more than one author.

First, my wife Ruth. As she has done with all my books, Ruth made this one possible and better, much better.

Tom Dillard helped me sharpen my focus and provided astute copy editing. His knowledge of Arkansas history is wide and deep. I can't thank him enough.

Dr. Kenneth Bridges suggested improvements to my citations of sources and offered other valuable advice.

Dr. Rodney Harris recommended important structural changes.

Ryan Smith pointed out ways to improve my narrative.

Cassidy Clayton assisted with manuscript preparation.

Worthy parts of this book in many ways belong to all of us. I own any mistakes.

www.ingramcontent.com/pod-product-compliance
Lightning Source LLC
Chambersburg PA
CBHW051934290426
44110CB00015B/1980